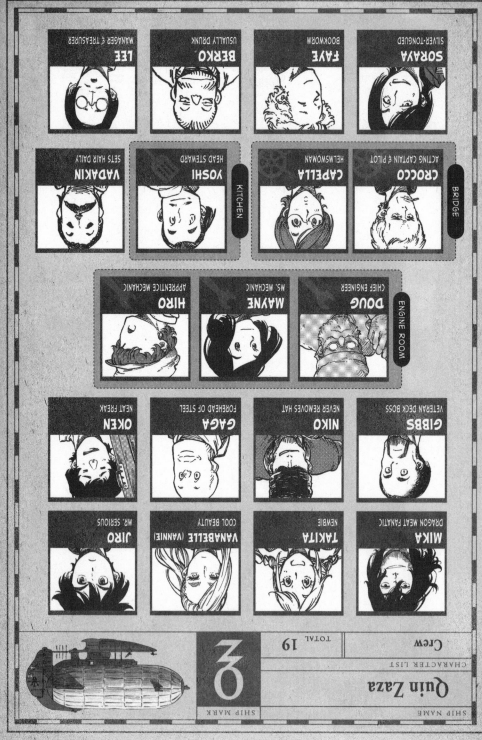

SHIP NAME

Quin Zaza

SHIP MARK

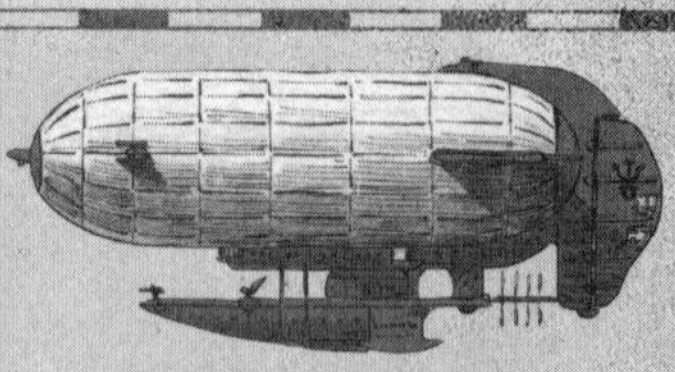

CHARACTER LIST

Crew

TOTAL 19

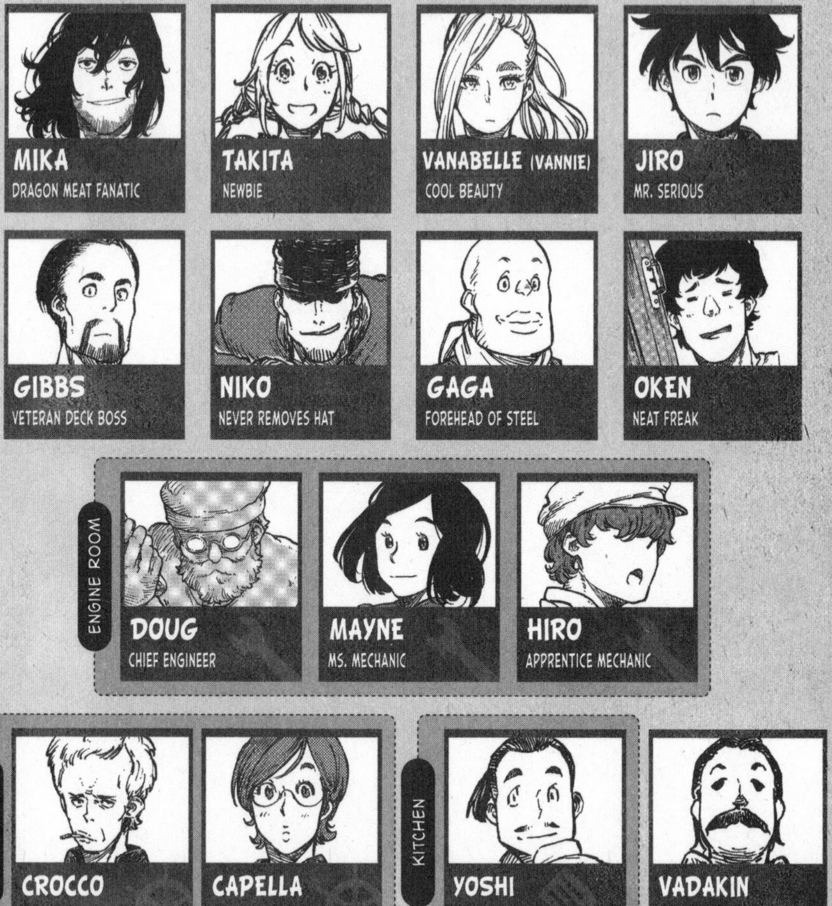
MIKA
DRAGON MEAT FANATIC
TAKITA
NEWBIE
VANABELLE (VANNIE)
COOL BEAUTY
JIRO
MR. SERIOUS
GIBBS
VETERAN DECK BOSS
NIKO
NEVER REMOVES HAT
GAGA
FOREHEAD OF STEEL
OKEN
NEAT FREAK
ENGINE ROOM
DOUG
CHIEF ENGINEER
MAYNE
MS. MECHANIC
HIRO
APPRENTICE MECHANIC
BRIDGE
CROCCO
ACTING CAPTAIN & PILOT
CAPELLA
HELMSWOMAN
KITCHEN
YOSHI
HEAD STEWARD
VADAKIN
SETS HAIR DAILY
SORAYA
SILVER-TONGUED
FAYE
BOOKWORM
BERKO
USUALLY DRUNK
LEE
MANAGER & TREASURER

*This is a work of fiction. Any resemblances to real people, groups, and events are purely coincidental.

DRIFTING DRAGONS

Taku Kuwabara

11

DRIFTING DRAGONS

Table of Contents

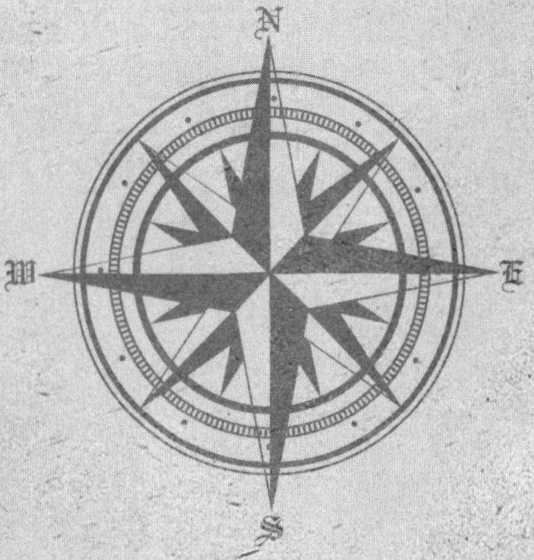
N
W
E
S

Flight 57 Lurkers in the Mist

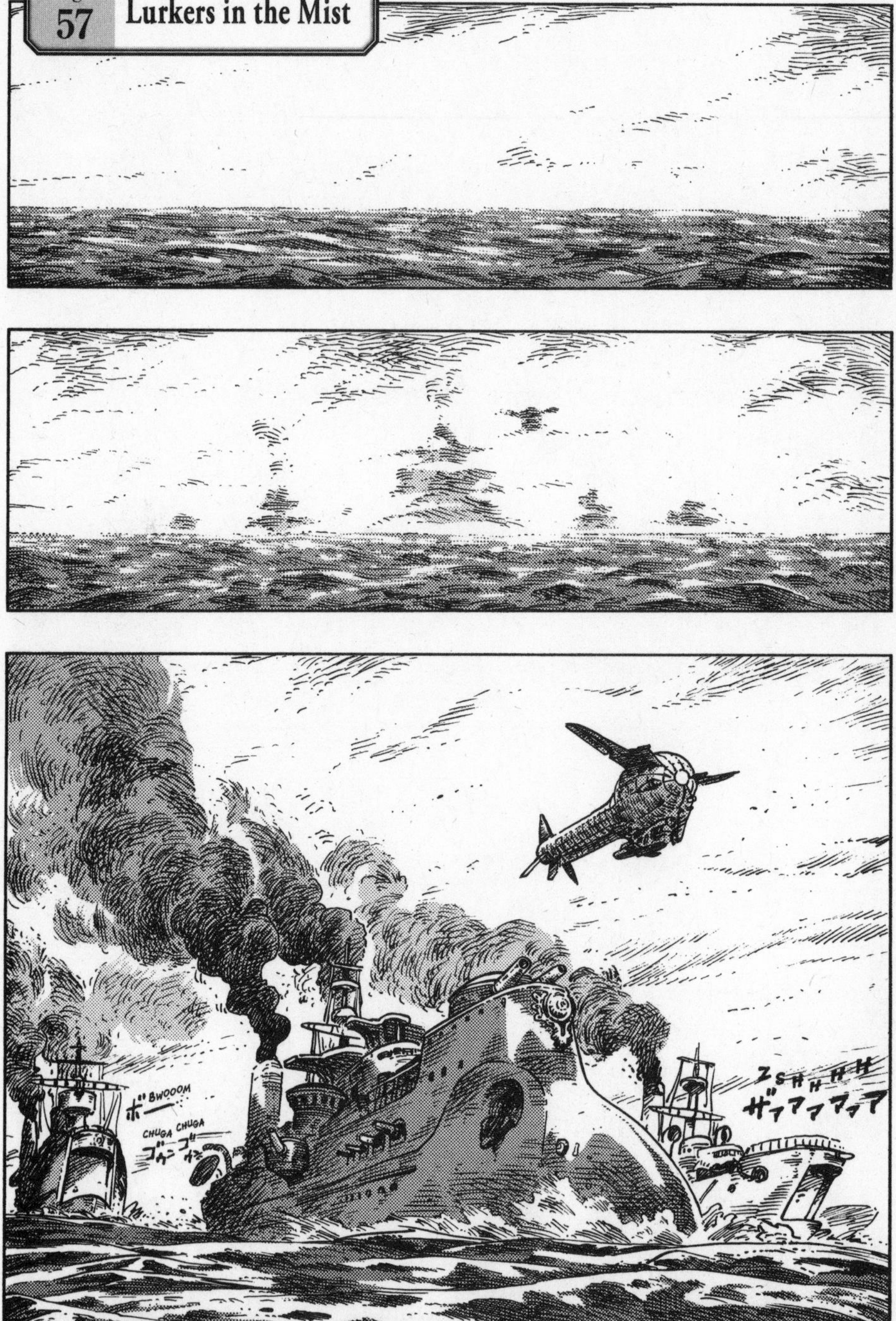
ZSHHHH
BWOOOM
CHUGA CHUGA

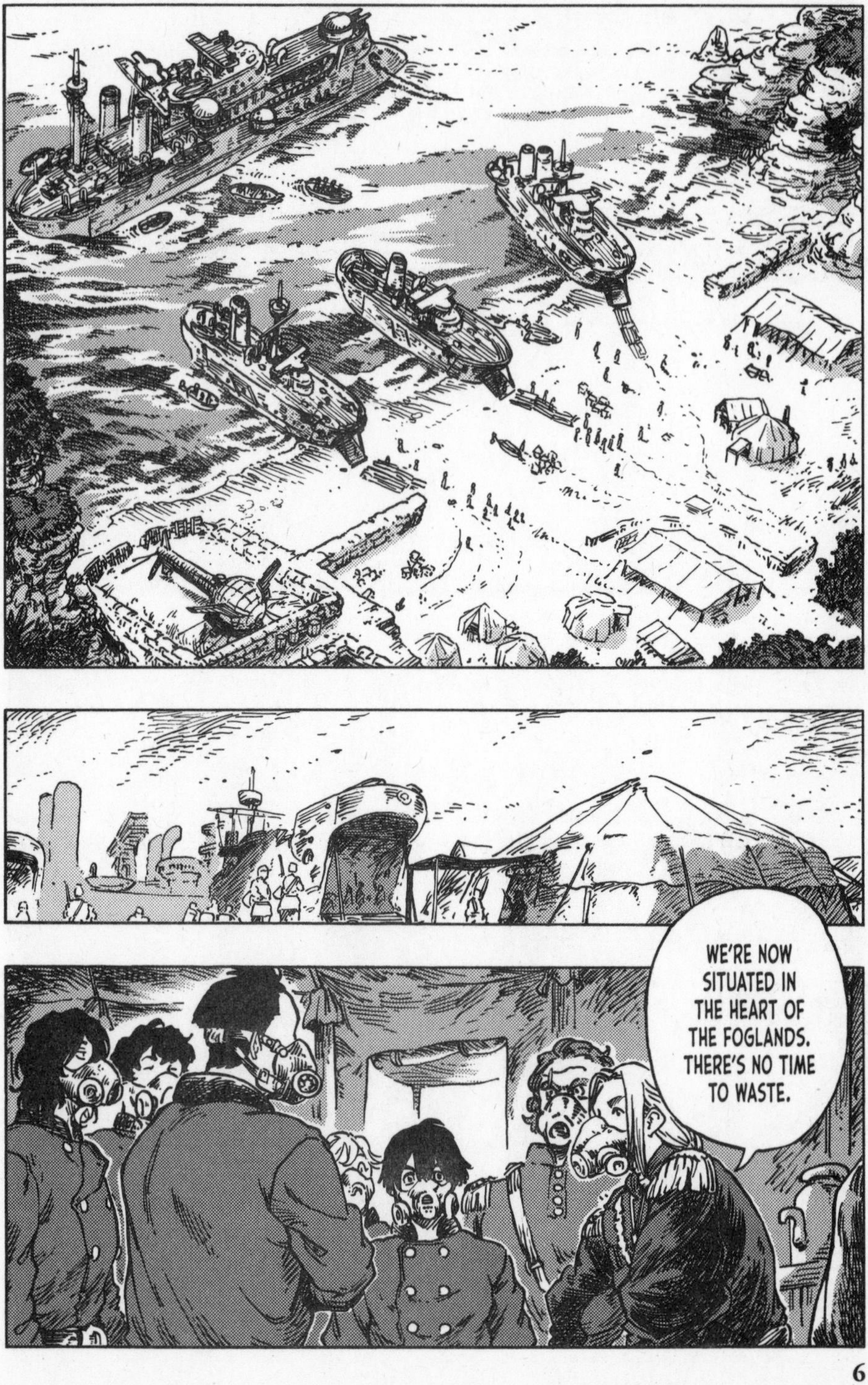
WE'RE NOW SITUATED IN THE HEART OF THE FOGLANDS. THERE'S NO TIME TO WASTE.

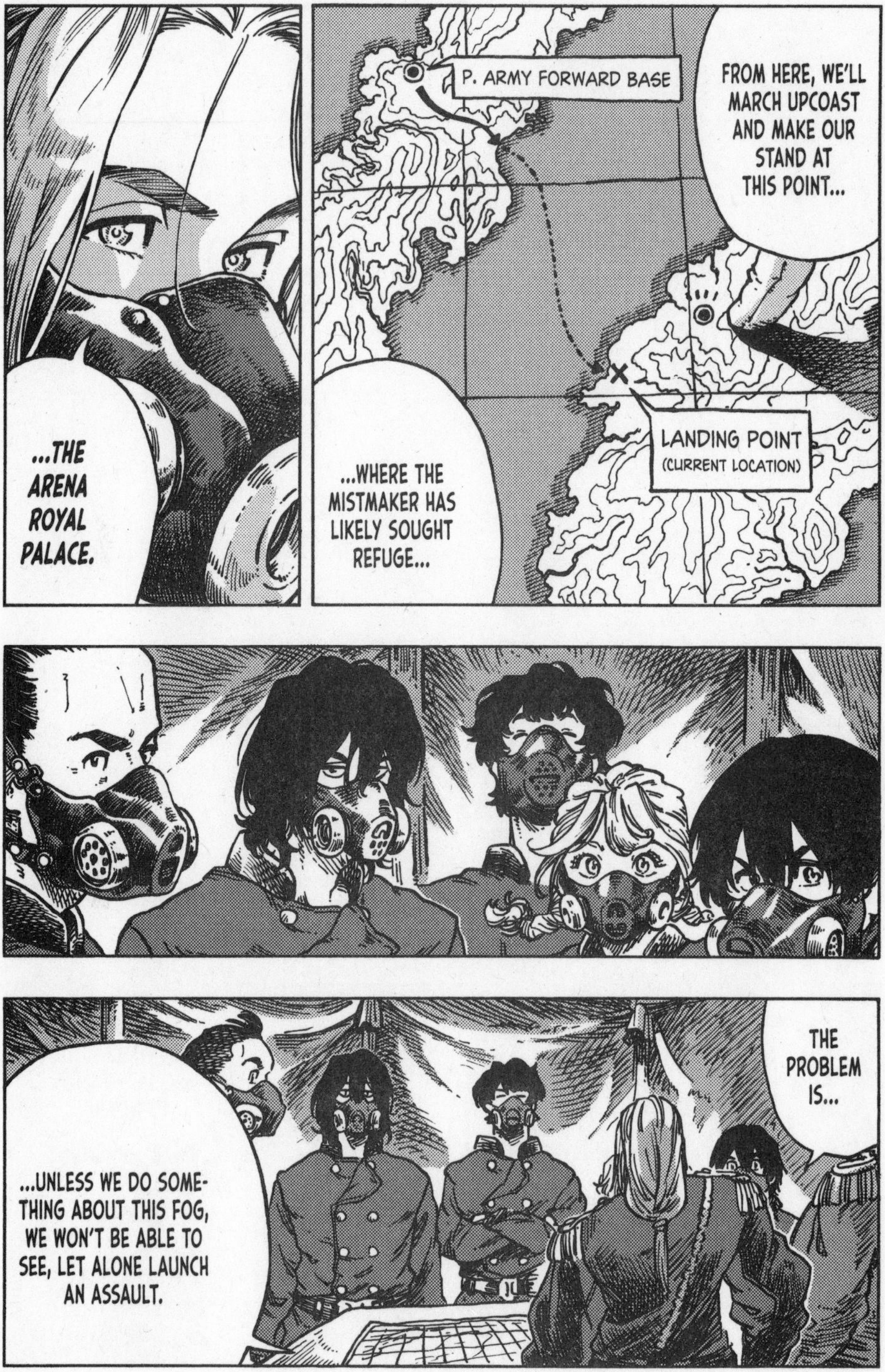
FROM HERE, WE'LL MARCH UPCOAST AND MAKE OUR STAND AT THIS POINT...
P. ARMY FORWARD BASE
LANDING POINT (CURRENT LOCATION)
...WHERE THE MISTMAKER HAS LIKELY SOUGHT REFUGE...
...THE ARENA ROYAL PALACE.
THE PROBLEM IS...
...UNLESS WE DO SOME-THING ABOUT THIS FOG, WE WON'T BE ABLE TO SEE, LET ALONE LAUNCH AN ASSAULT.

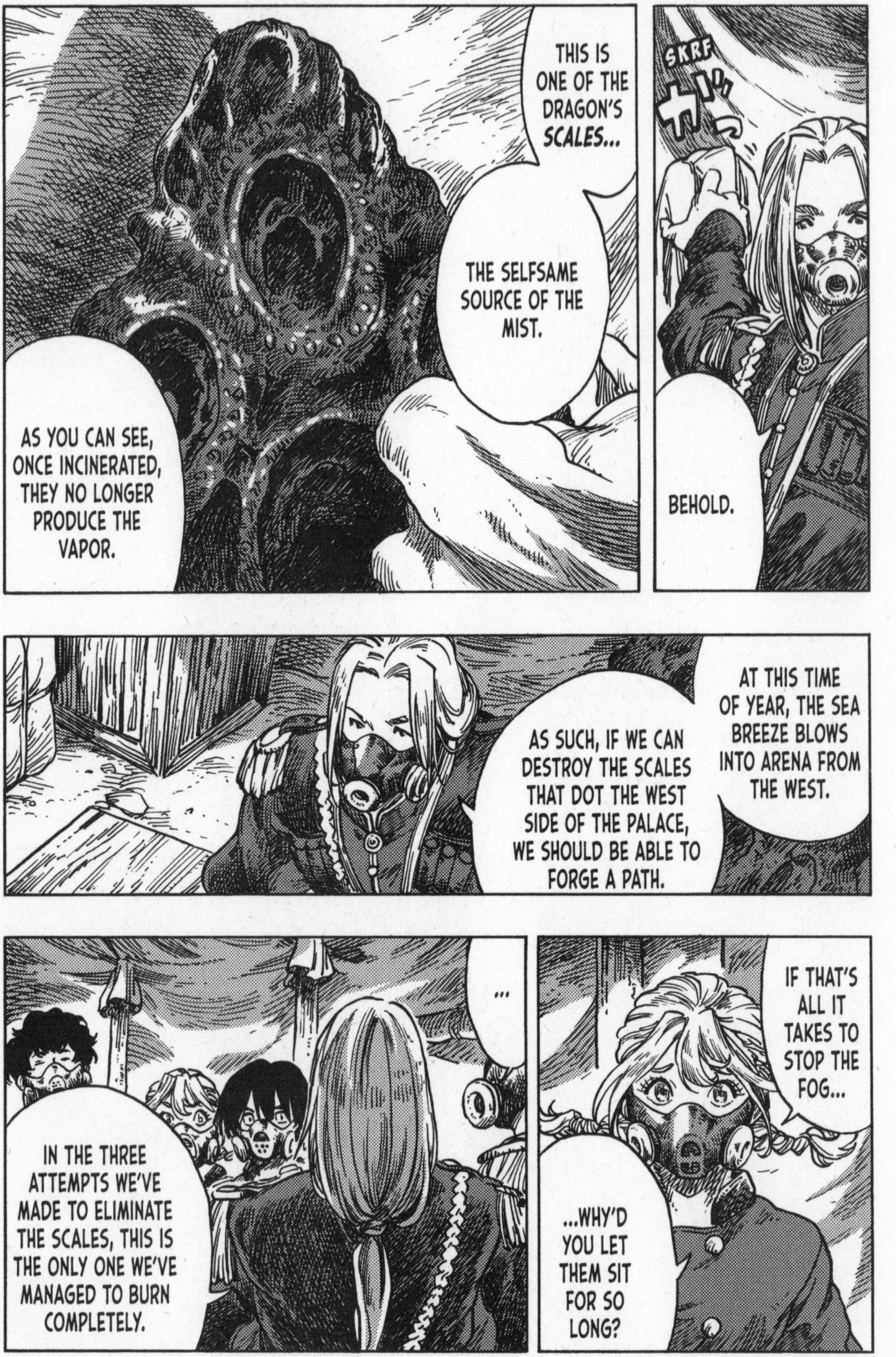
SKRF
BEHOLD.
THIS IS ONE OF THE DRAGON'S *SCALES*...
THE SELFSAME SOURCE OF THE MIST.
AS YOU CAN SEE, ONCE INCINERATED, THEY NO LONGER PRODUCE THE VAPOR.
AT THIS TIME OF YEAR, THE SEA BREEZE BLOWS INTO ARENA FROM THE WEST.
AS SUCH, IF WE CAN DESTROY THE SCALES THAT DOT THE WEST SIDE OF THE PALACE, WE SHOULD BE ABLE TO FORGE A PATH.
IF THAT'S ALL IT TAKES TO STOP THE FOG...
...WHY'D YOU LET THEM SIT FOR SO LONG?
...
IN THE THREE ATTEMPTS WE'VE MADE TO ELIMINATE THE SCALES, THIS IS THE ONLY ONE WE'VE MANAGED TO BURN COMPLETELY.

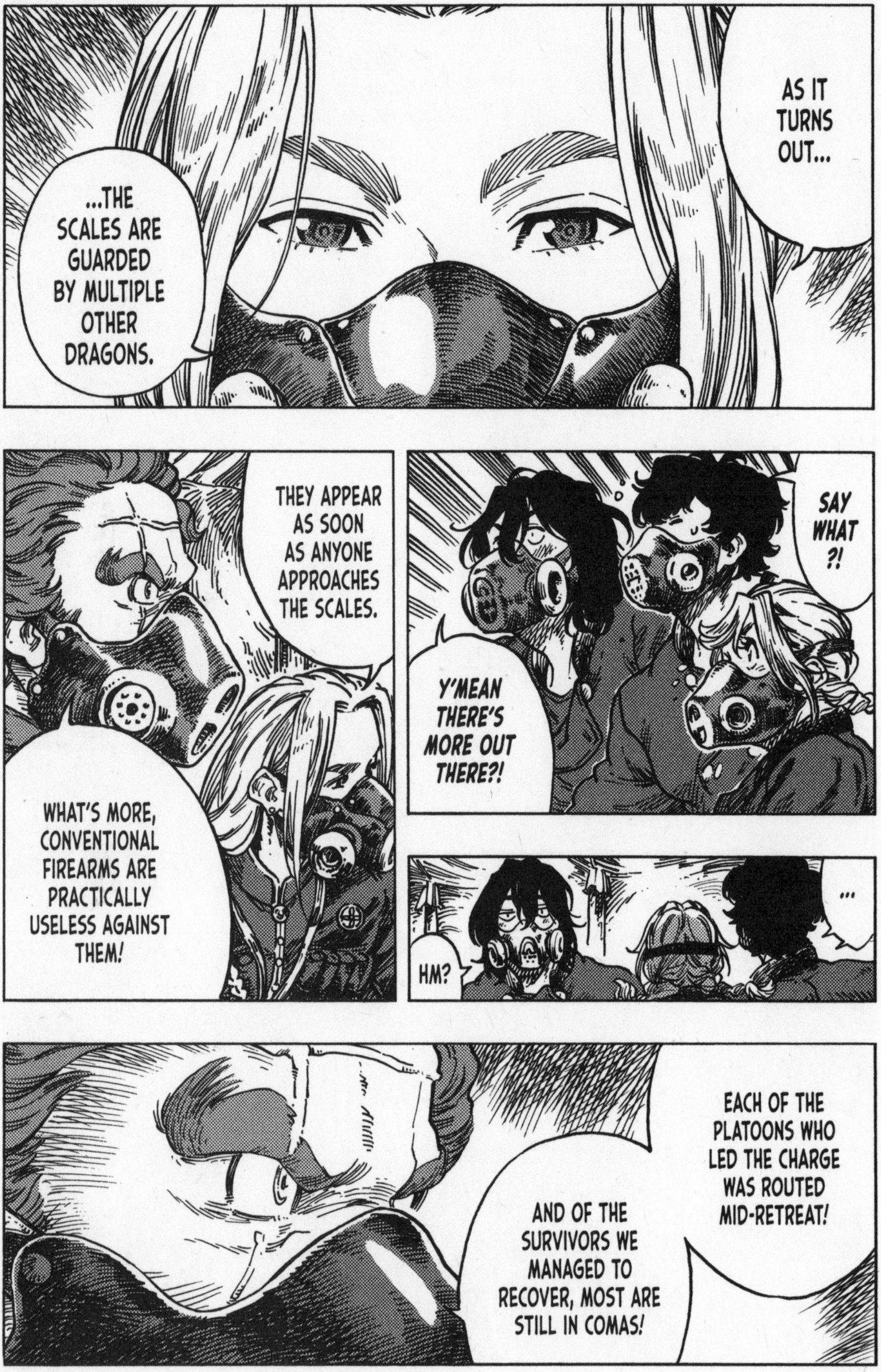
AS IT TURNS OUT...
...THE SCALES ARE GUARDED BY MULTIPLE OTHER DRAGONS.
SAY WHAT ?!
Y'MEAN THERE'S MORE OUT THERE?!
...
HM?
THEY APPEAR AS SOON AS ANYONE APPROACHES THE SCALES.
WHAT'S MORE, CONVENTIONAL FIREARMS ARE PRACTICALLY USELESS AGAINST THEM!
EACH OF THE PLATOONS WHO LED THE CHARGE WAS ROUTED MID-RETREAT!
AND OF THE SURVIVORS WE MANAGED TO RECOVER, MOST ARE STILL IN COMAS!

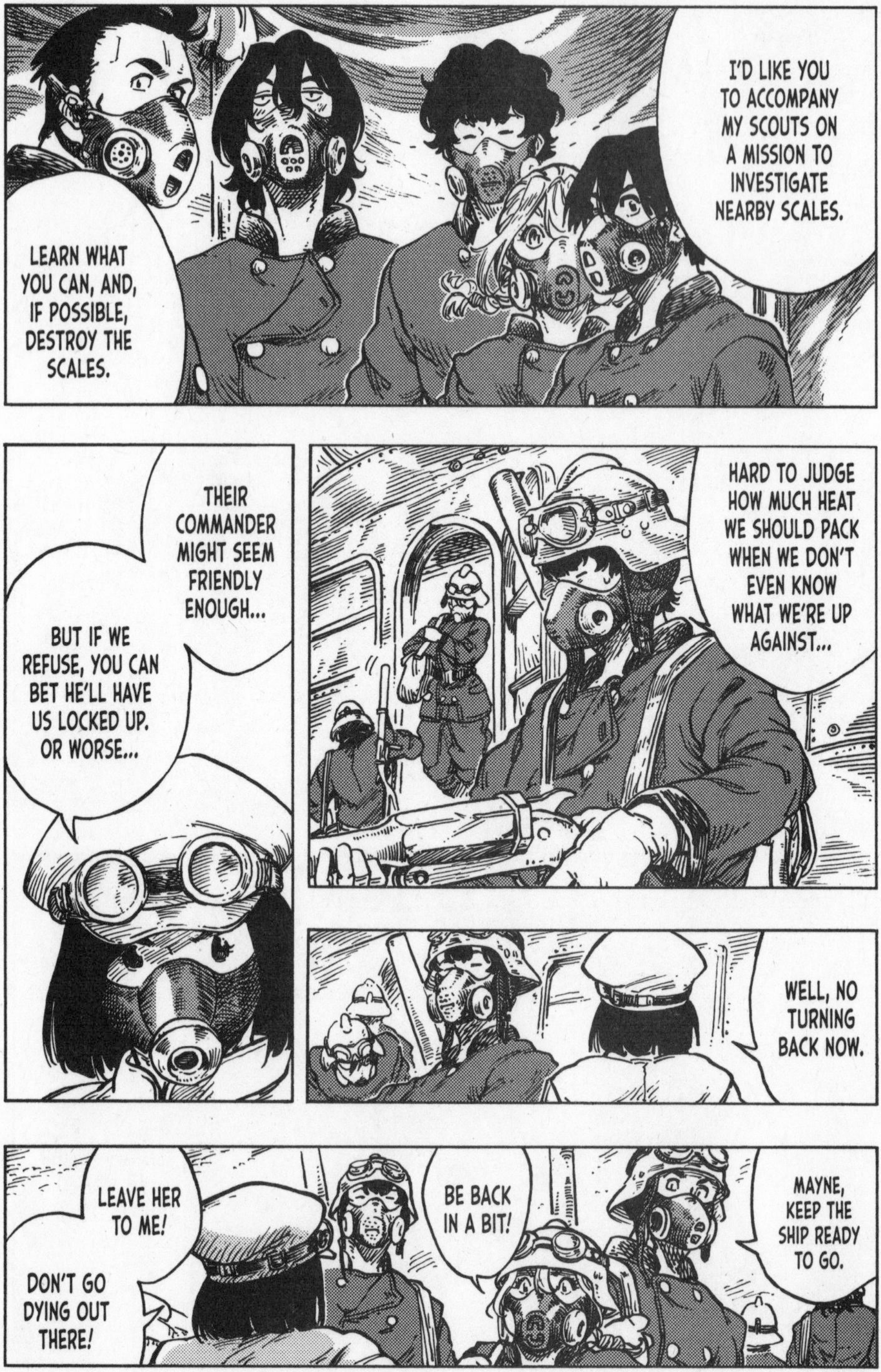
I'D LIKE YOU TO ACCOMPANY MY SCOUTS ON A MISSION TO INVESTIGATE NEARBY SCALES.
LEARN WHAT YOU CAN, AND, IF POSSIBLE, DESTROY THE SCALES.
HARD TO JUDGE HOW MUCH HEAT WE SHOULD PACK WHEN WE DON'T EVEN KNOW WHAT WE'RE UP AGAINST...
WELL, NO TURNING BACK NOW.
THEIR COMMANDER MIGHT SEEM FRIENDLY ENOUGH...
BUT IF WE REFUSE, YOU CAN BET HE'LL HAVE US LOCKED UP. OR WORSE...
MAYNE, KEEP THE SHIP READY TO GO.
BE BACK IN A BIT!
LEAVE HER TO ME!
DON'T GO DYING OUT THERE!

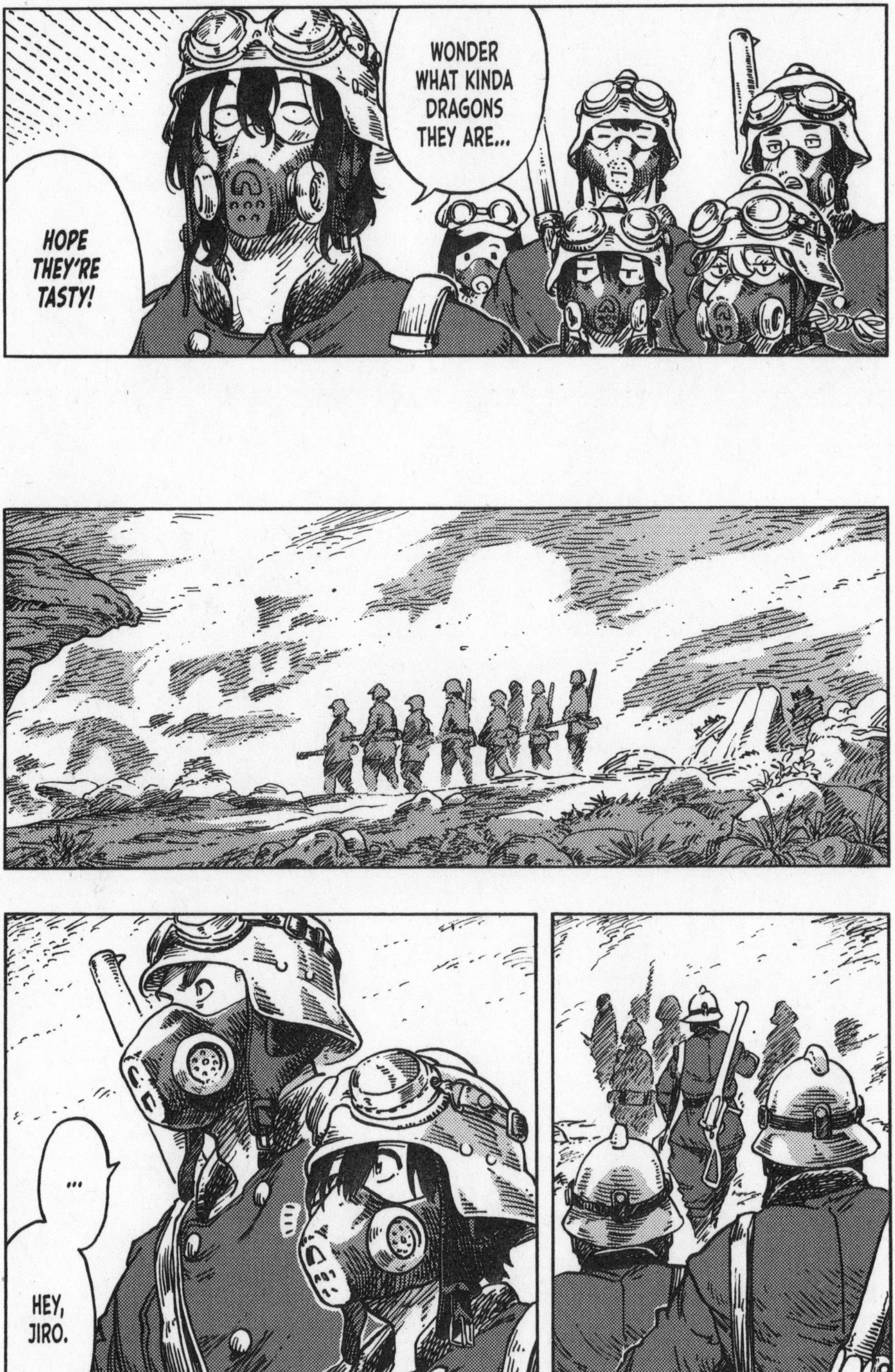
WONDER WHAT KINDA DRAGONS THEY ARE...
HOPE THEY'RE TASTY!
...
HEY, JIRO.

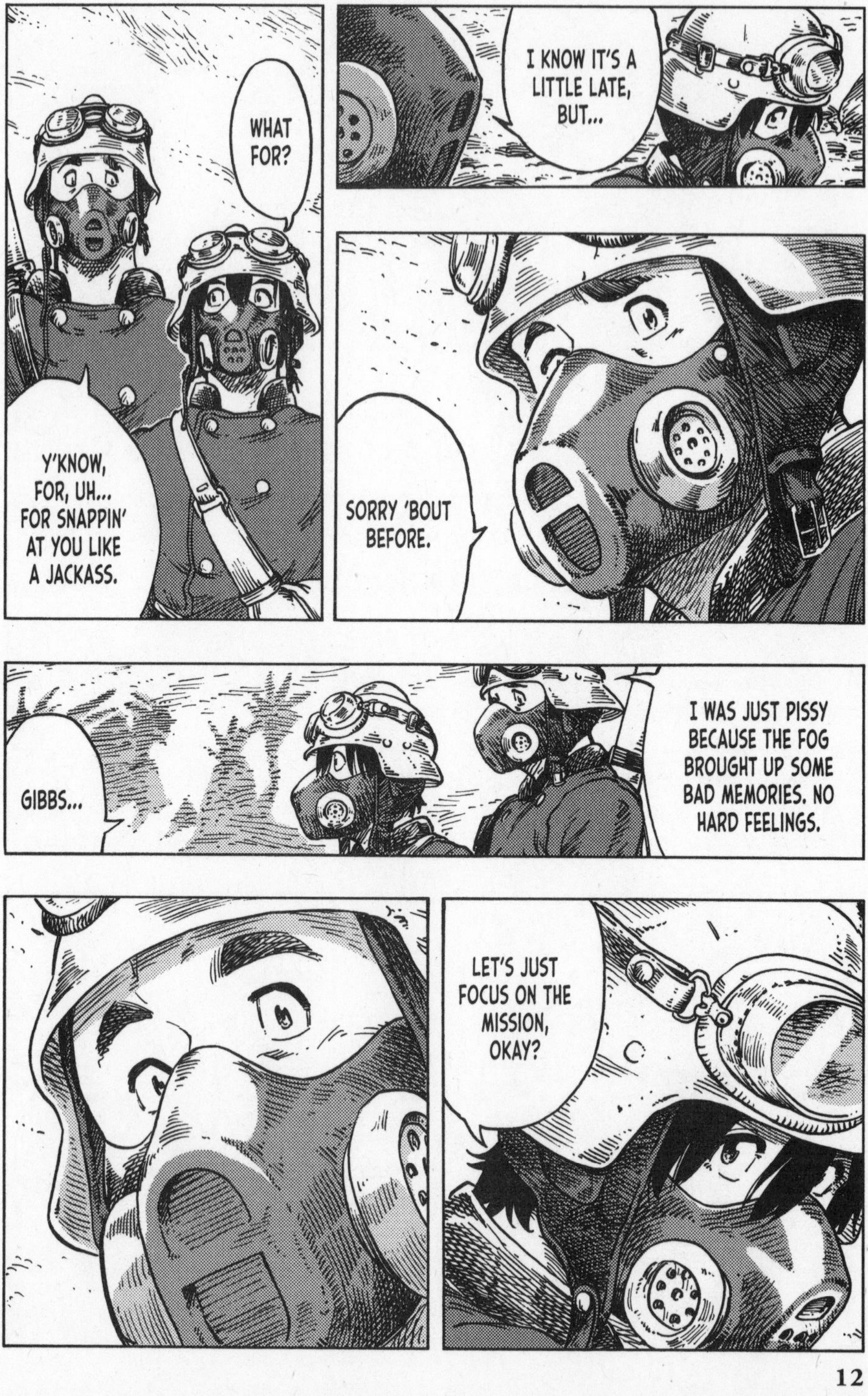
I KNOW IT'S A LITTLE LATE, BUT...
SORRY 'BOUT BEFORE.
WHAT FOR?
Y'KNOW, FOR, UH... FOR SNAPPIN' AT YOU LIKE A JACKASS.
I WAS JUST PISSY BECAUSE THE FOG BROUGHT UP SOME BAD MEMORIES. NO HARD FEELINGS.
GIBBS...
LET'S JUST FOCUS ON THE MISSION, OKAY?

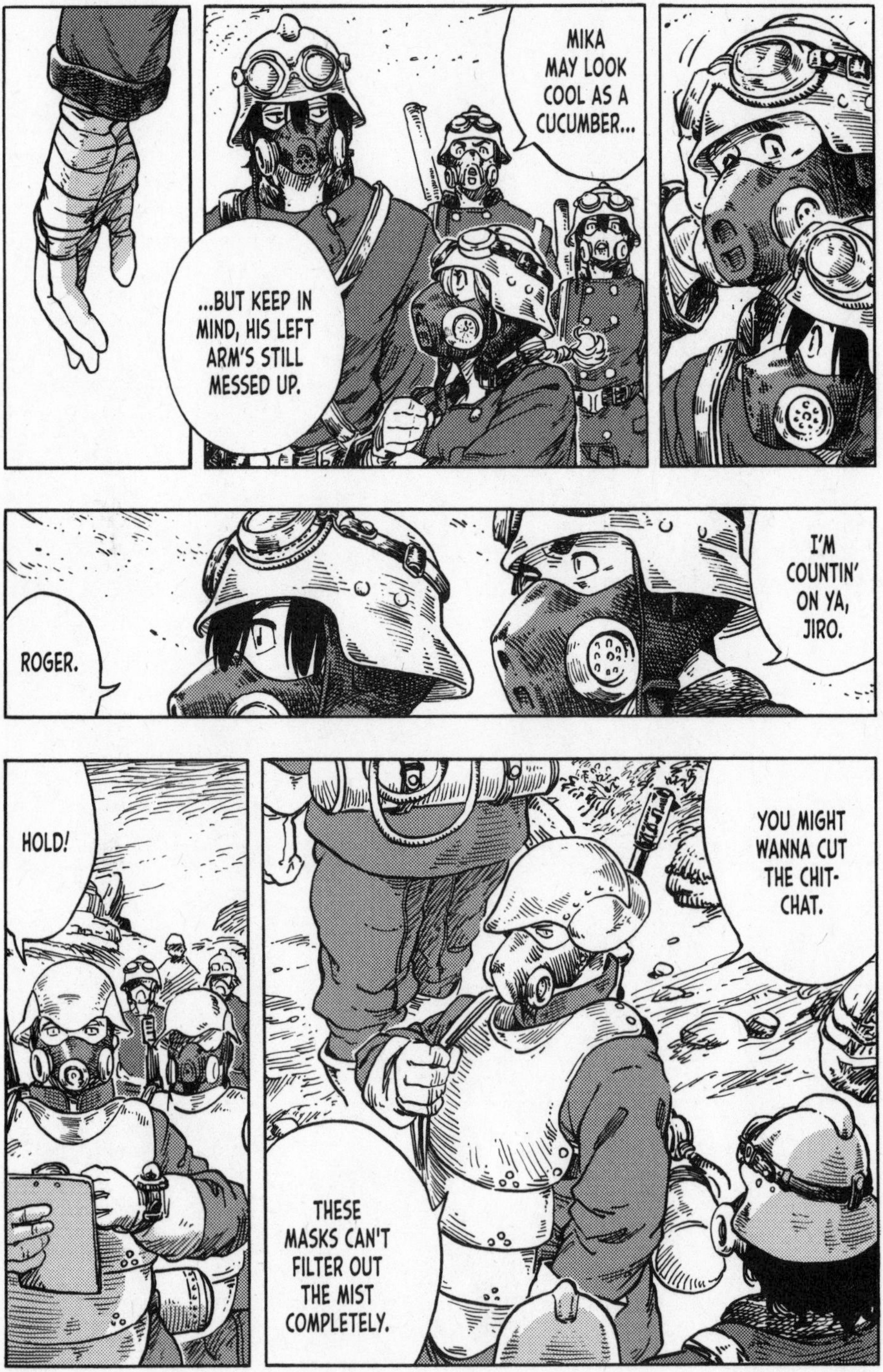
MIKA MAY LOOK COOL AS A CUCUMBER...
...BUT KEEP IN MIND, HIS LEFT ARM'S STILL MESSED UP.
I'M COUNTIN' ON YA, JIRO.
ROGER.
YOU MIGHT WANNA CUT THE CHIT-CHAT.
THESE MASKS CAN'T FILTER OUT THE MIST COMPLETELY.
HOLD!

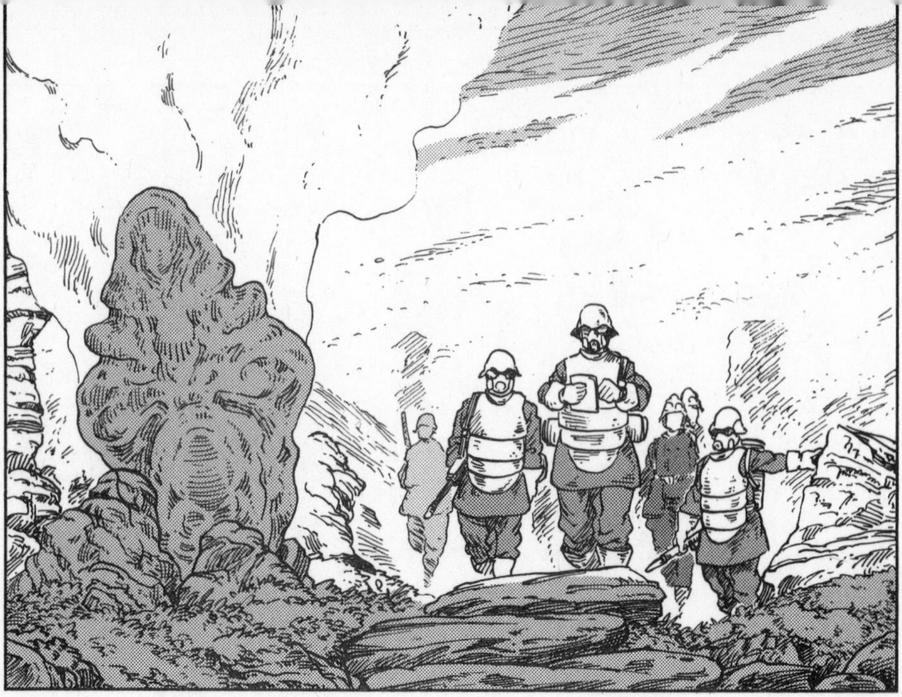
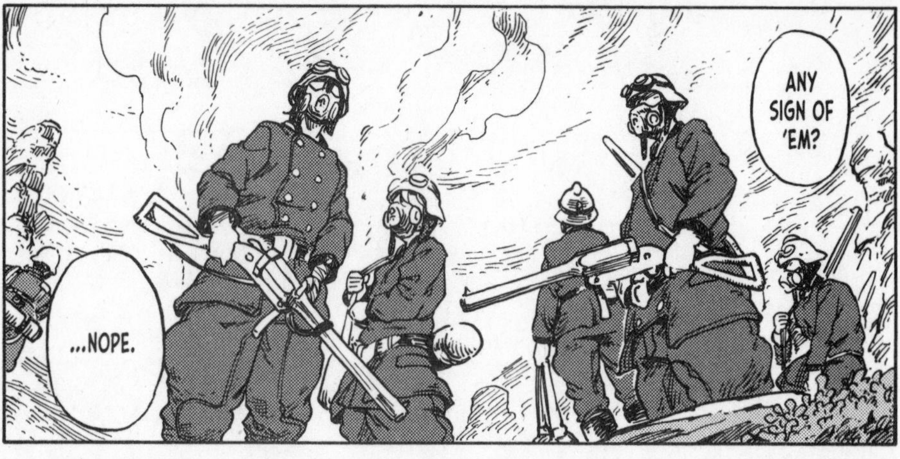
ANY SIGN OF 'EM?
...NOPE.
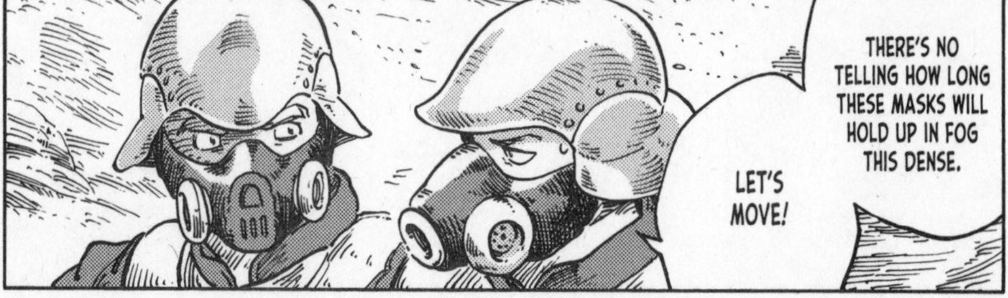
THERE'S NO TELLING HOW LONG THESE MASKS WILL HOLD UP IN FOG THIS DENSE.
LET'S MOVE!

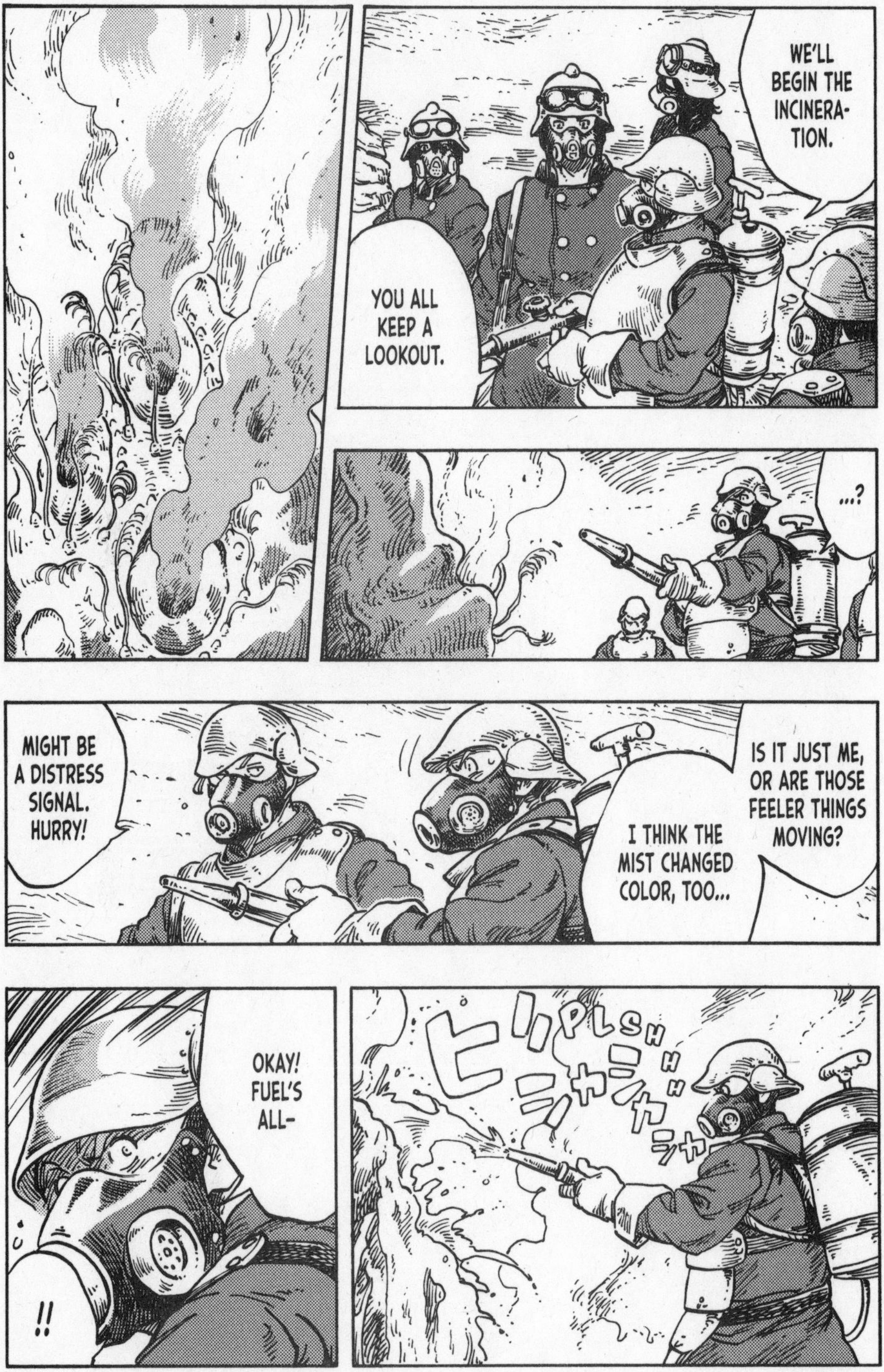
WE'LL BEGIN THE INCINERA-TION.
YOU ALL KEEP A LOOKOUT.
...?
IS IT JUST ME, OR ARE THOSE FEELER THINGS MOVING?
I THINK THE MIST CHANGED COLOR, TOO...
MIGHT BE A DISTRESS SIGNAL. HURRY!
PLSHHHH
OKAY! FUEL'S ALL-
!!

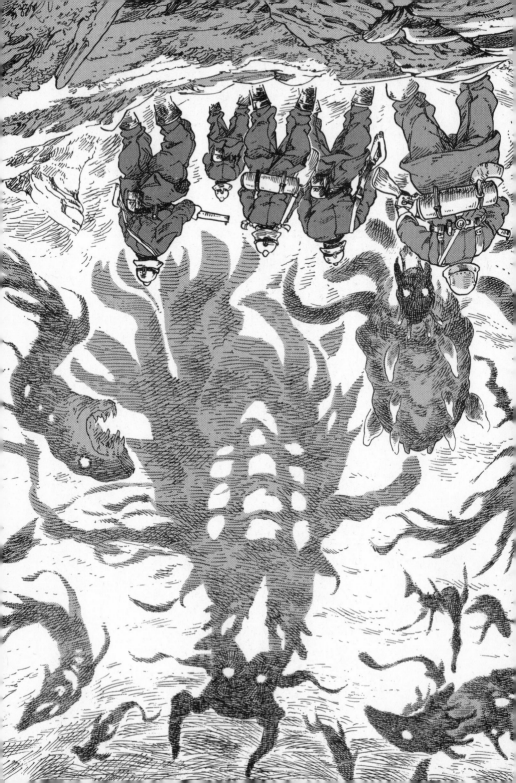

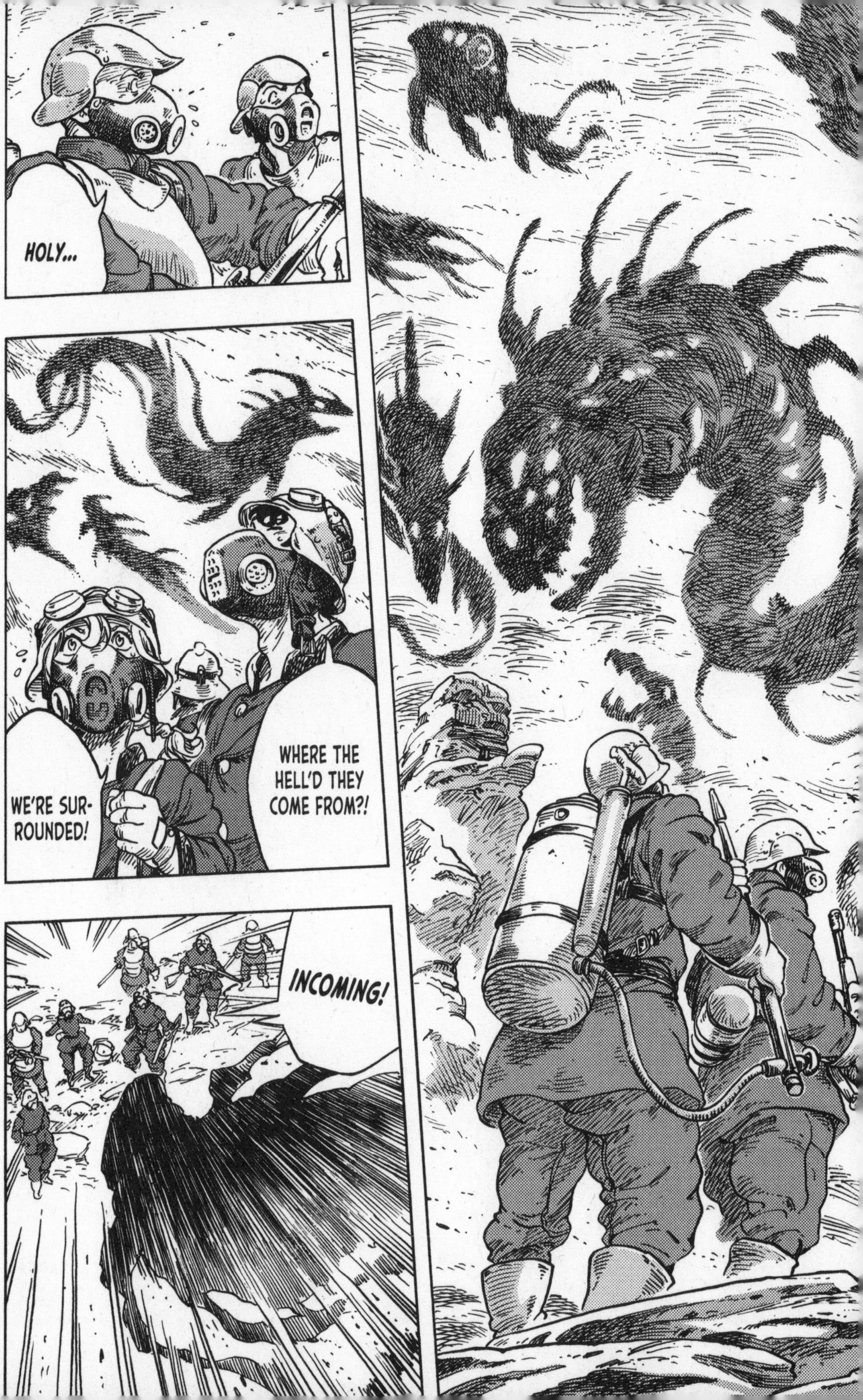
HOLY...
WHERE THE HELL'D THEY COME FROM?!
WE'RE SUR-ROUNDED!
INCOMING!

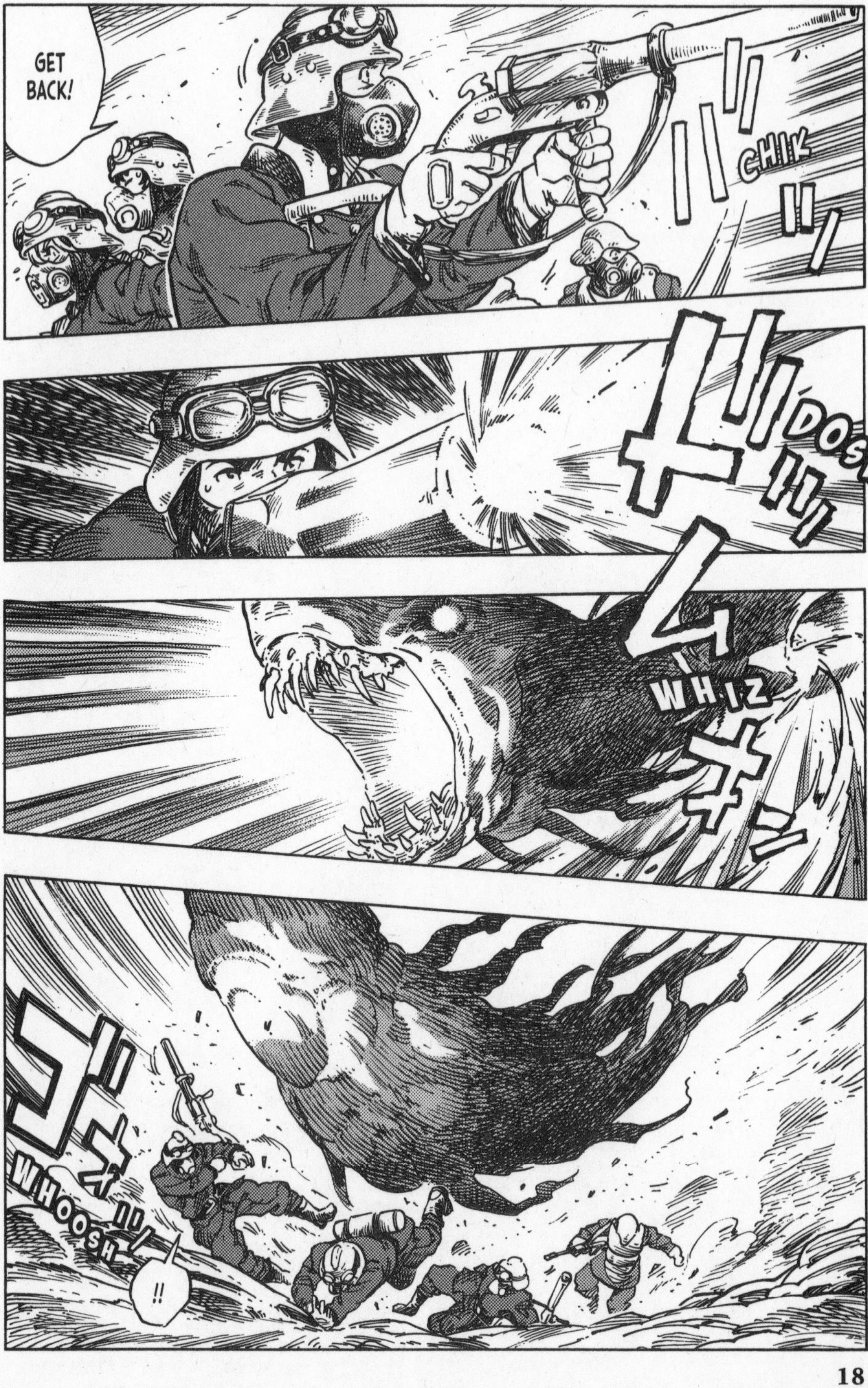
GET BACK!
CHIK
DOSH
WHIZ
!!
WHOOSH

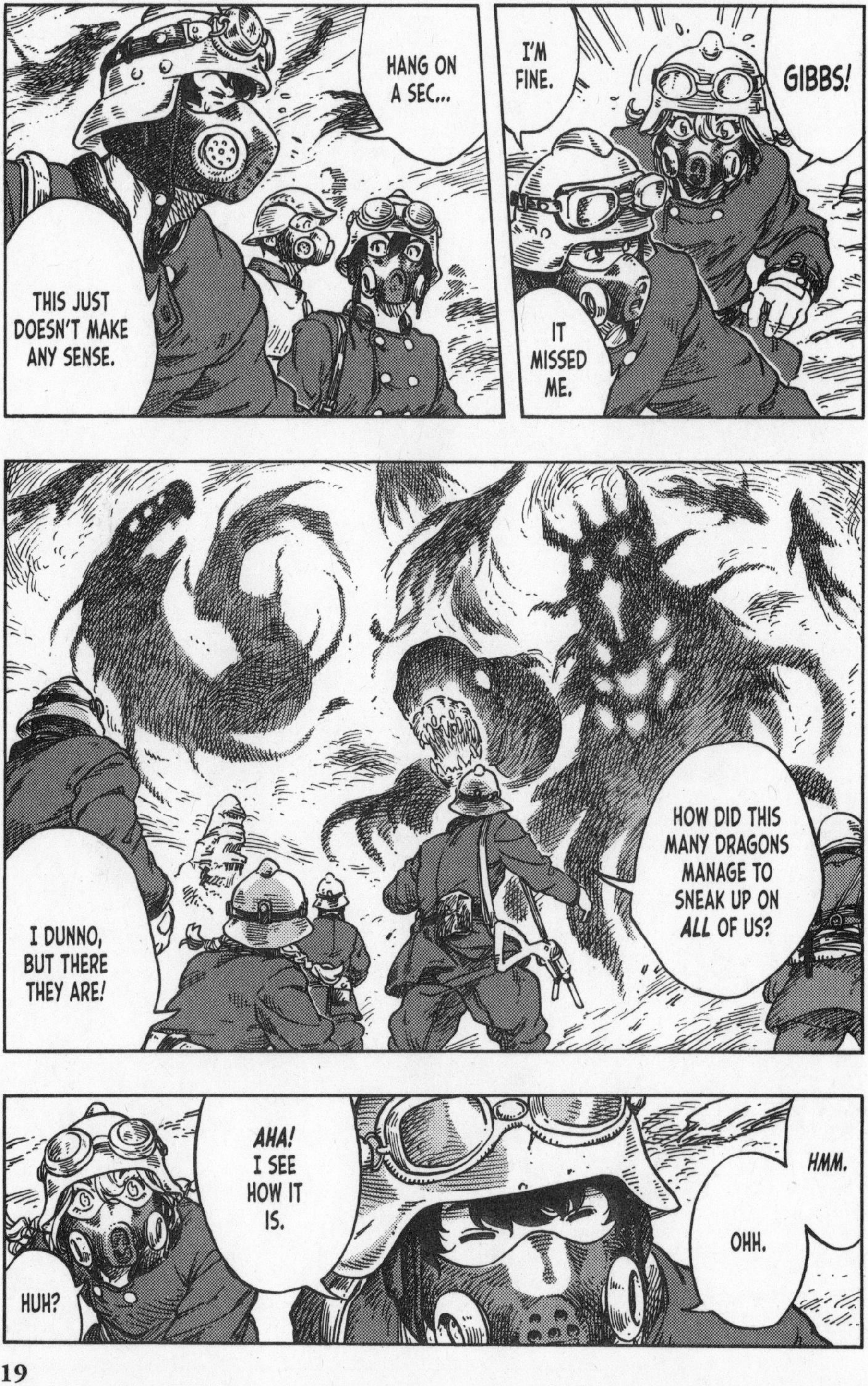
GIBBS!
I'M FINE.
IT MISSED ME.
HANG ON A SEC...
THIS JUST DOESN'T MAKE ANY SENSE.
HOW DID THIS MANY DRAGONS MANAGE TO SNEAK UP ON *ALL* OF US?
I DUNNO, BUT THERE THEY ARE!
HMM.
OHH.
AHA! I SEE HOW IT IS.
HUH?

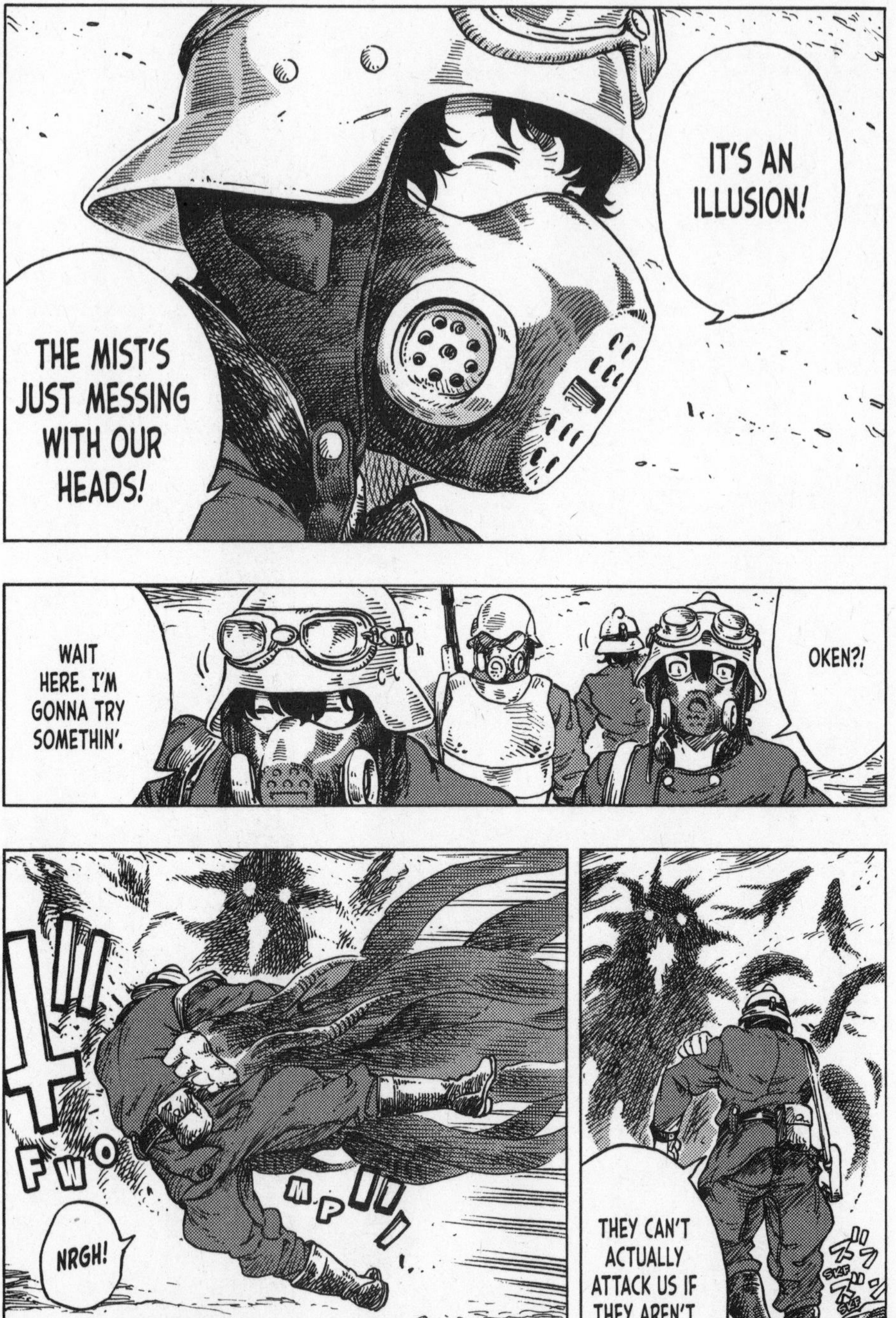
IT'S AN ILLUSION!
THE MIST'S JUST MESSING WITH OUR HEADS!
OKEN?!
WAIT HERE. I'M GONNA TRY SOMETHIN'.
THEY CAN'T ACTUALLY ATTACK US IF THEY AREN'T EVEN REA-
SKF SKF
FWOMP
NRGH!

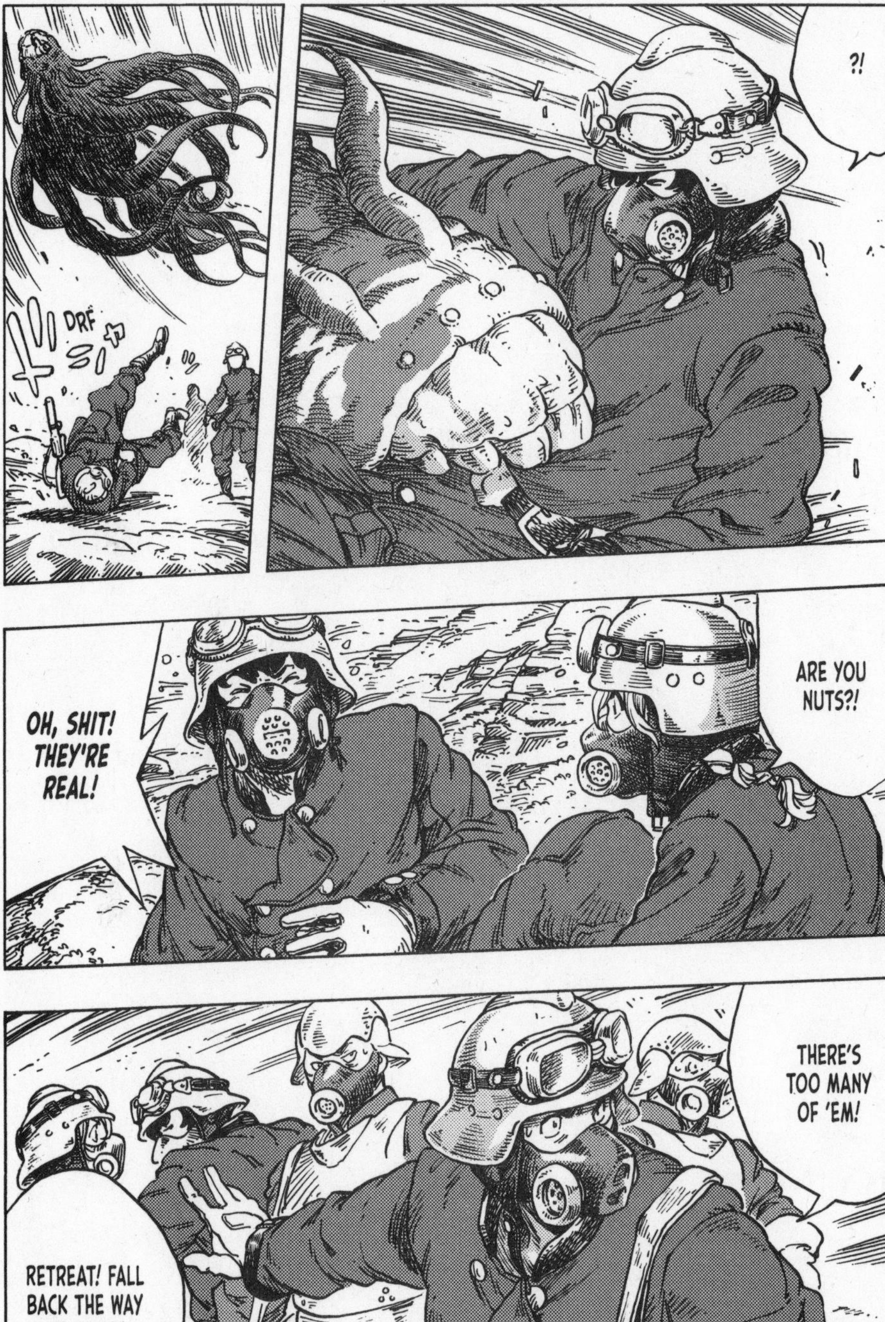
?!
DRF
ARE YOU NUTS?!
OH, SHIT! THEY'RE REAL!
THERE'S TOO MANY OF 'EM!
RETREAT! FALL BACK THE WAY WE CAME!

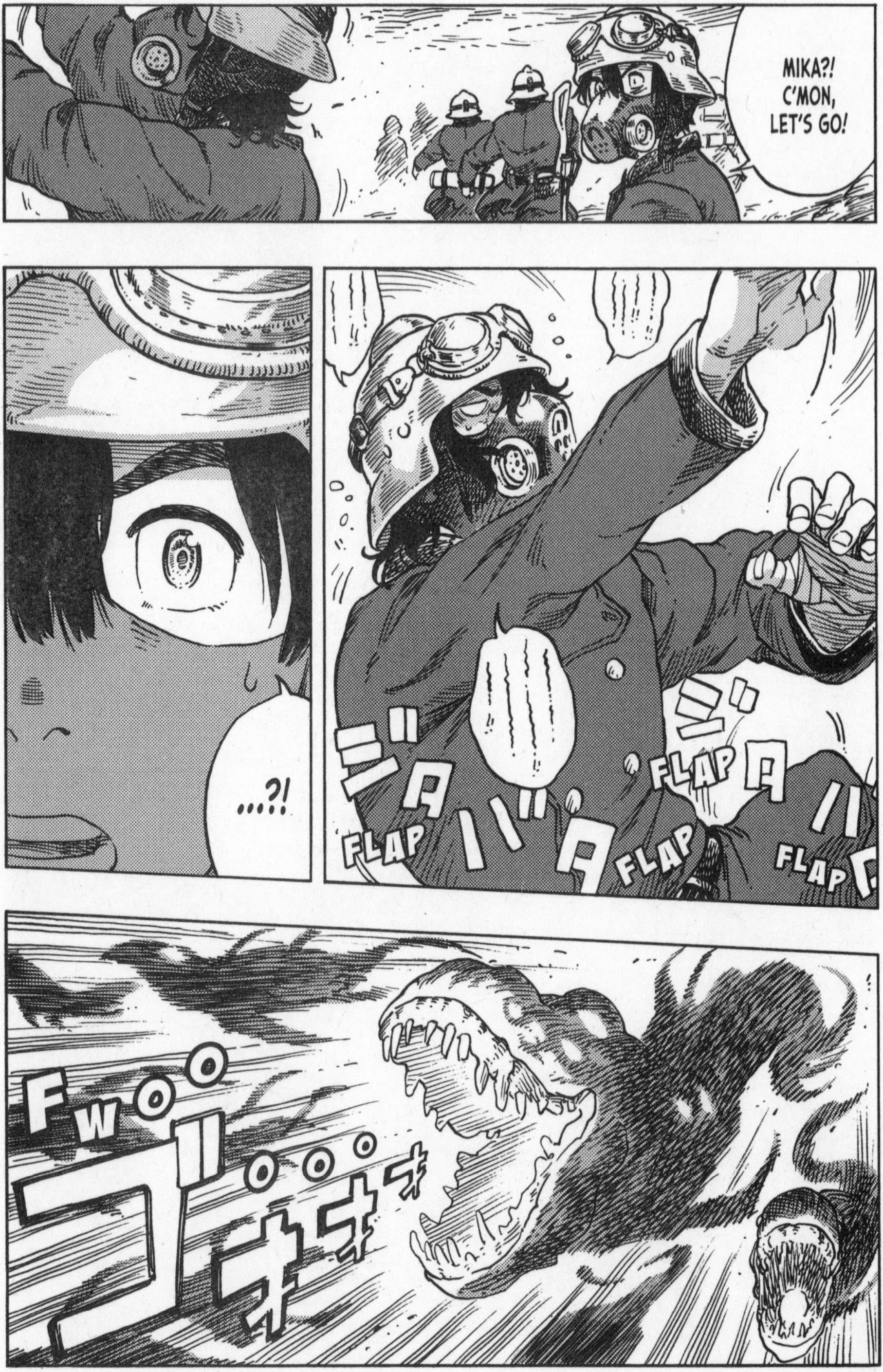
MIKA?! C'MON, LET'S GO!
ジタ ジタ バタ バタ
FLAP FLAP FLAP FLAP
...?!
ゴオオオ
FWOOOOO

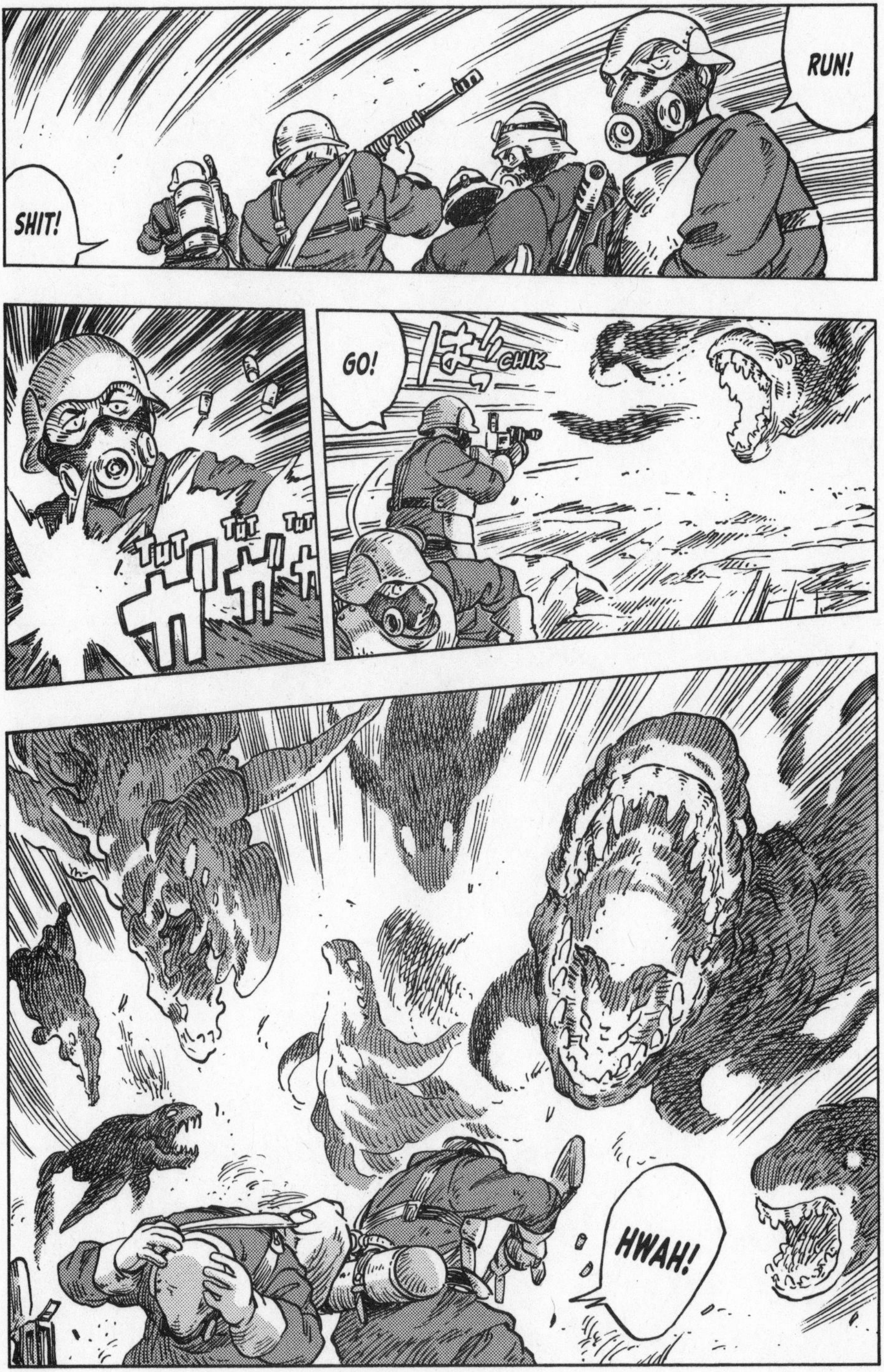
RUN!
SHIT!
GO!
CHIK
TUT TUT TUT
HWAH!

MIKA! WHAT'RE YOU DOING?!
RUFL
GET A HOLD OF YOURSELF!
RUFL
NRBLRB... 'ELB ME...
CAN'T BREATHE...
I DON'T WANNA DROWN...
HUH?
WHAT DO YOU MEAN, DROWN?
AHB...
HRB...

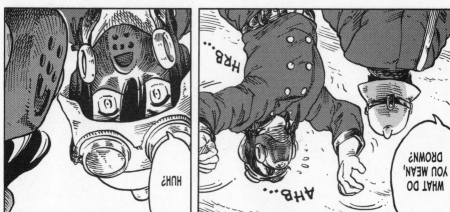

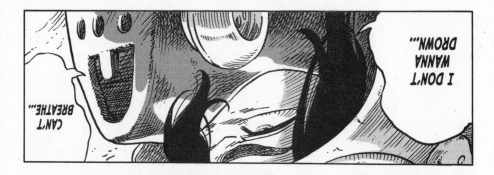

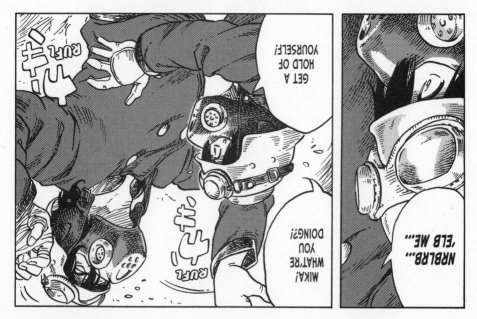

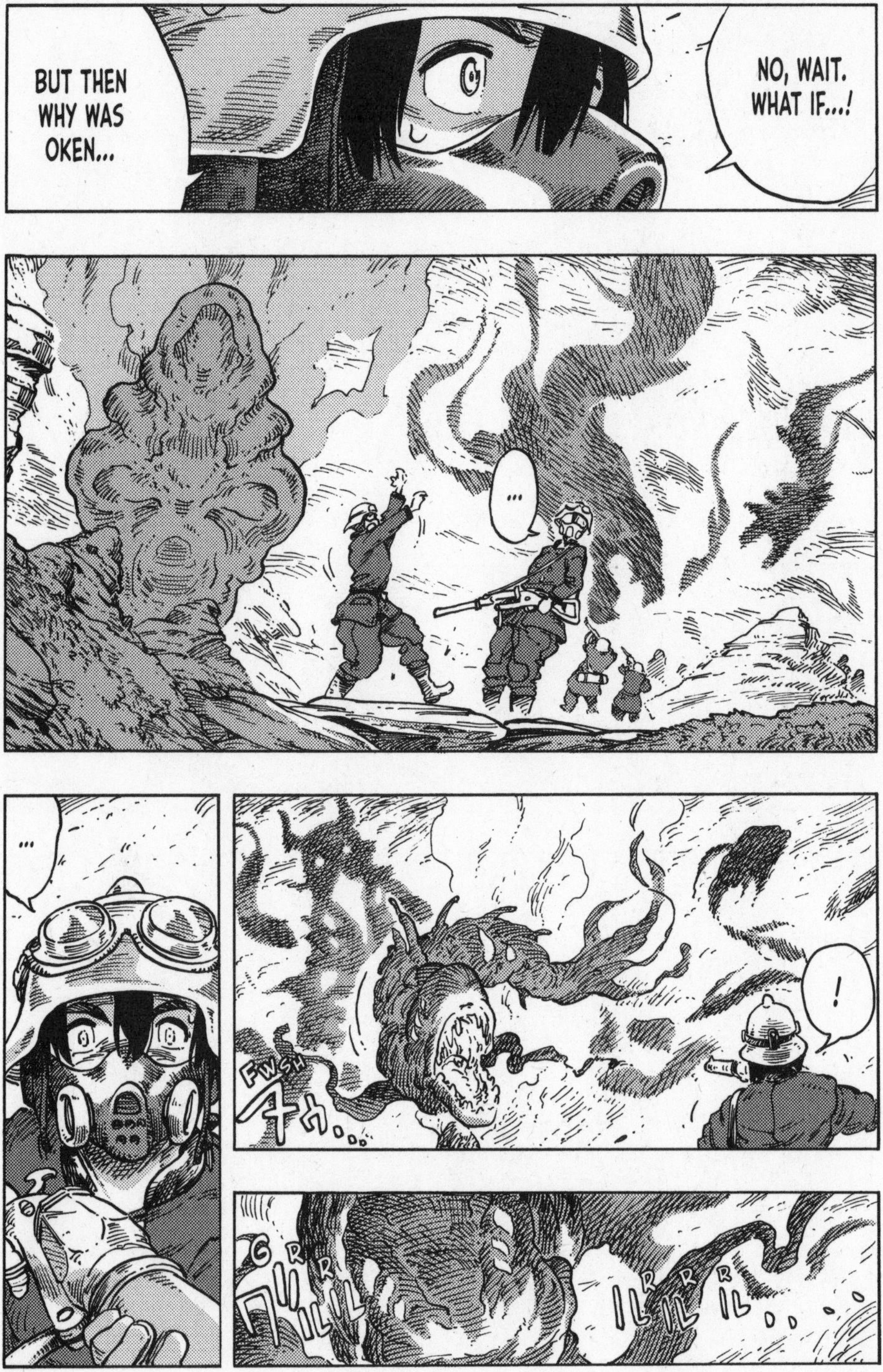
NO, WAIT. WHAT IF...!
BUT THEN WHY WAS OKEN...
...
!
FWSH
GRRRRR
...

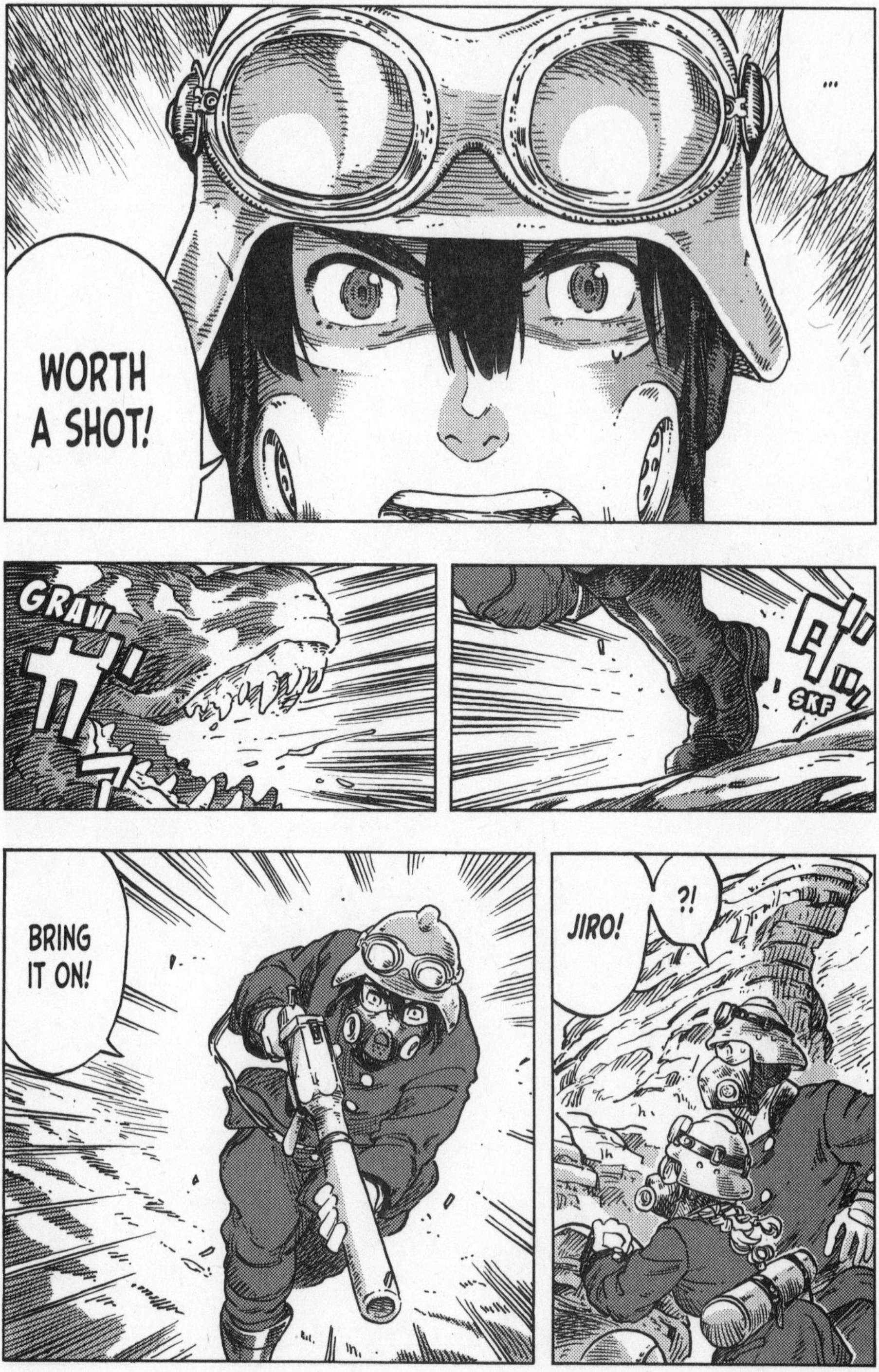
...
WORTH A SHOT!
SKF
GRAW
?!
JIRO!
BRING IT ON!

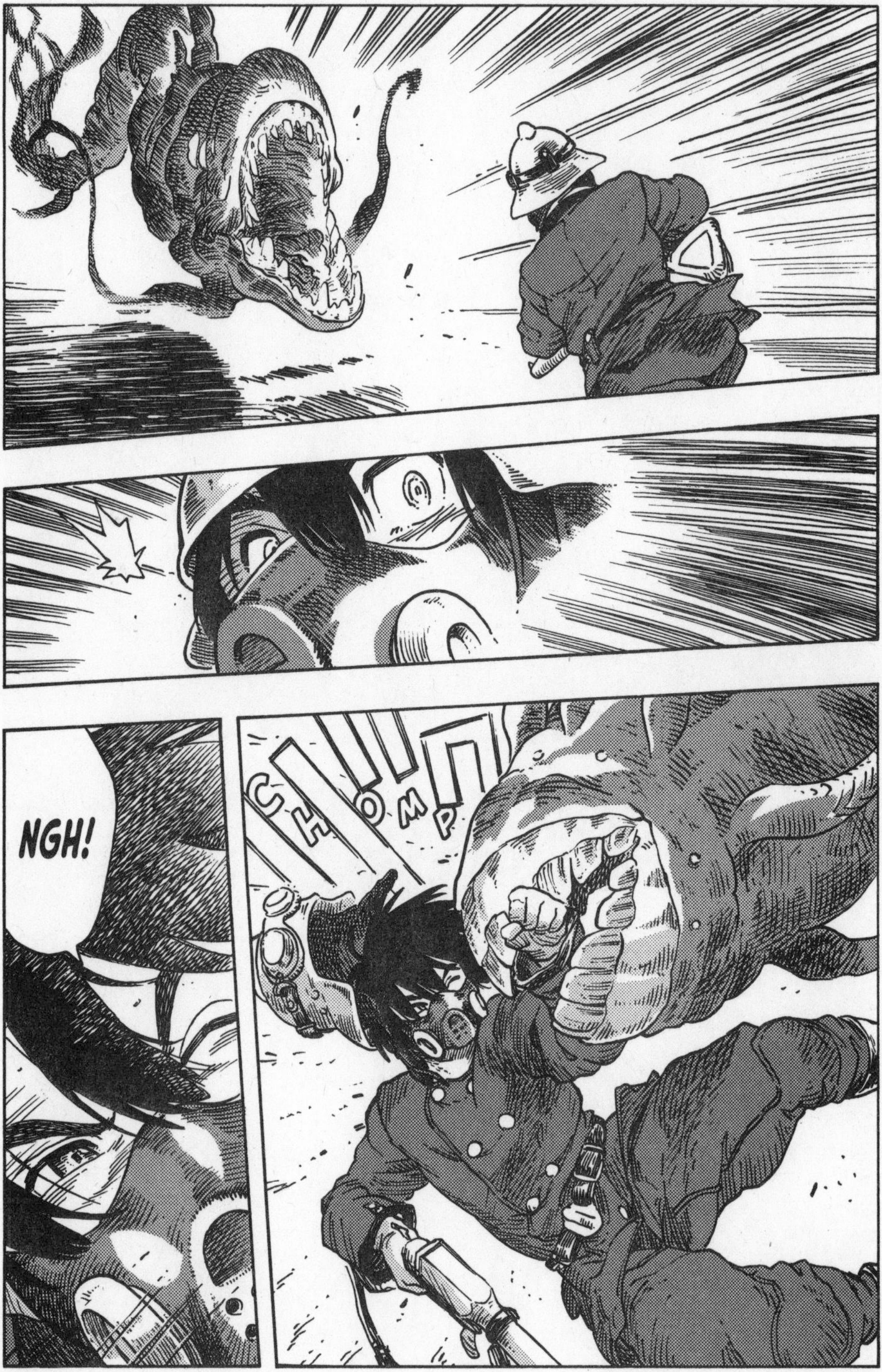
CHOMP
NGH!

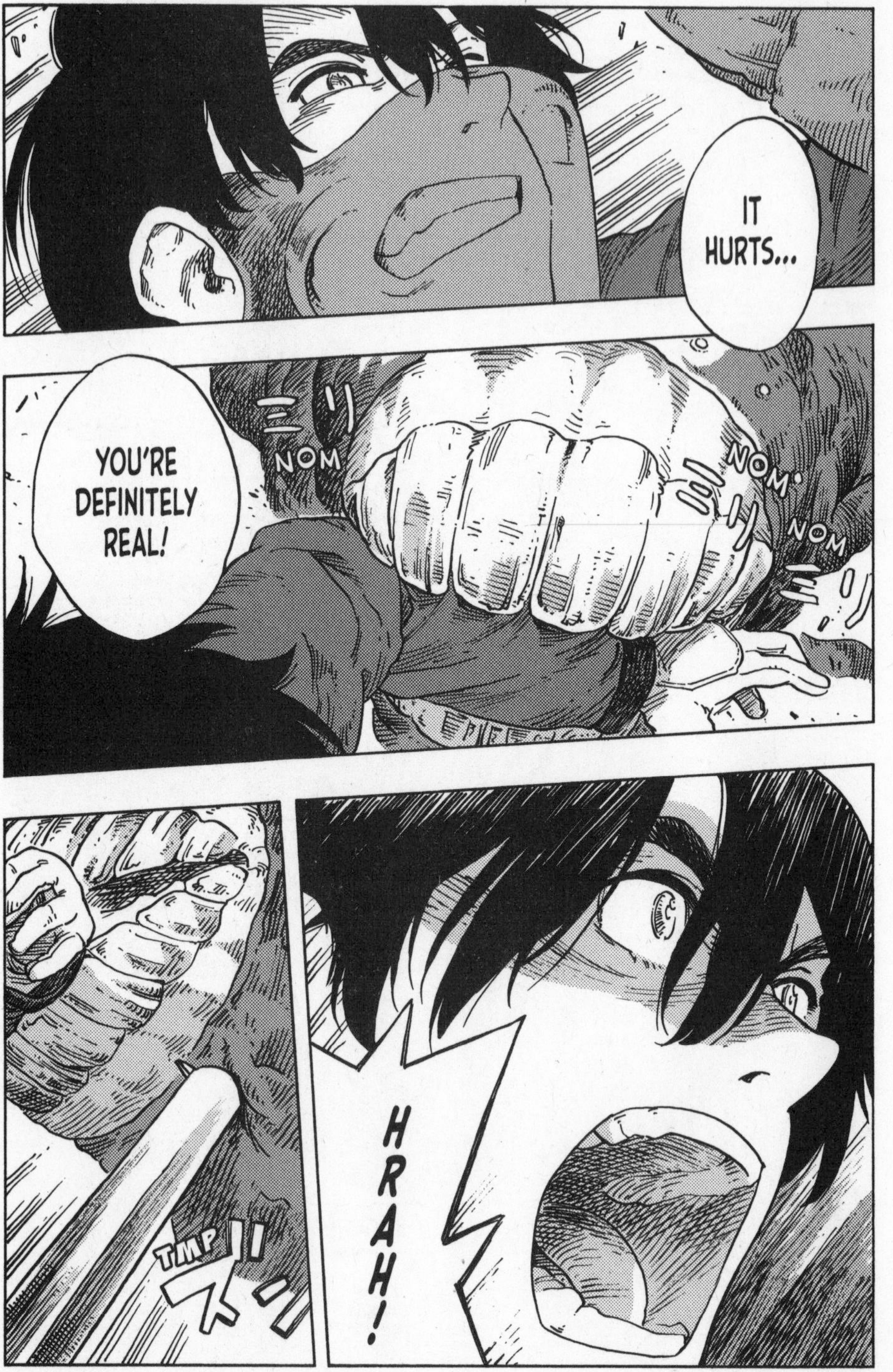
IT HURTS...
NOM NOM
NOM
YOU'RE DEFINITELY REAL!
HRAH!
TMP

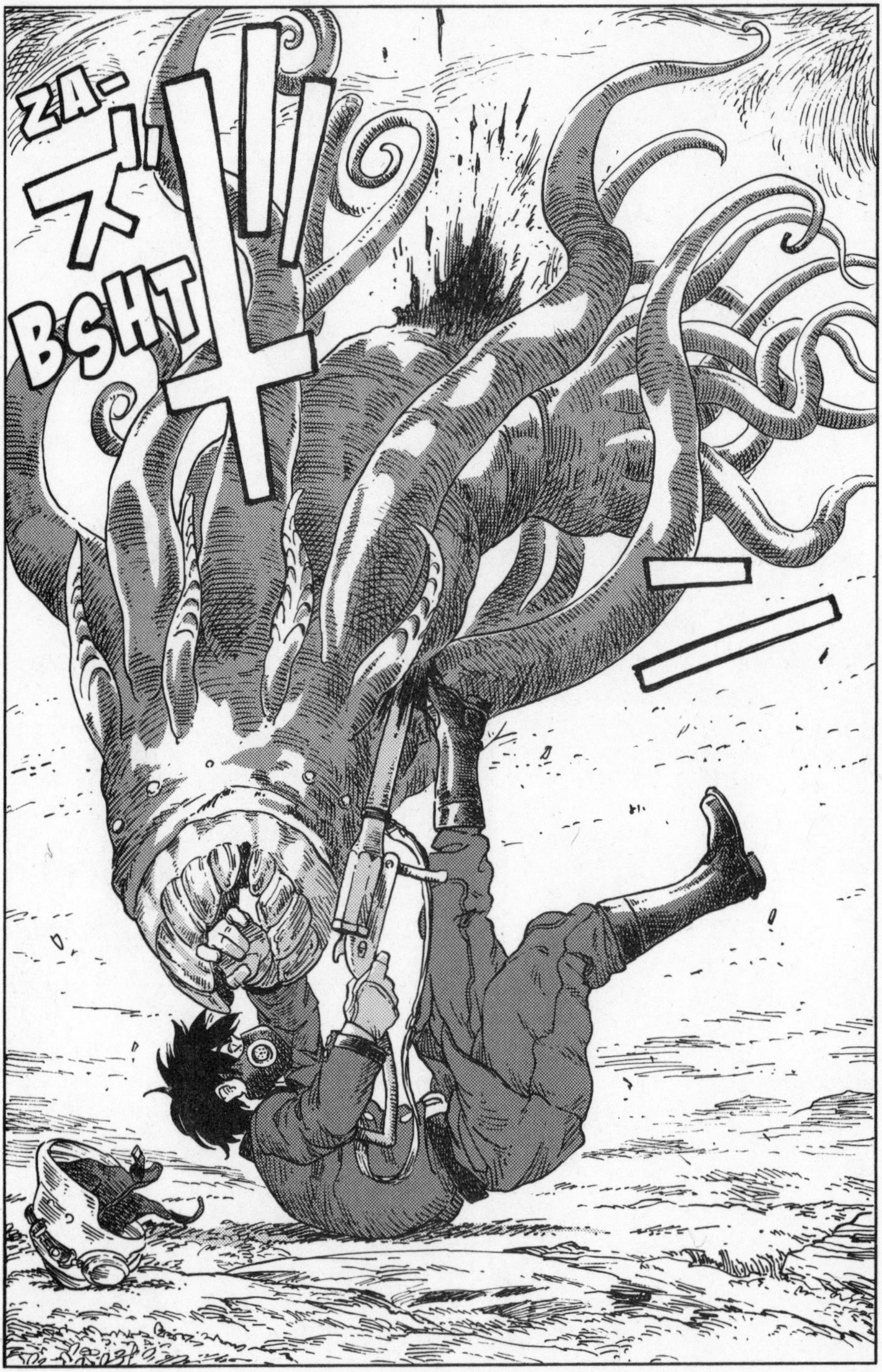
ZA-BSHT

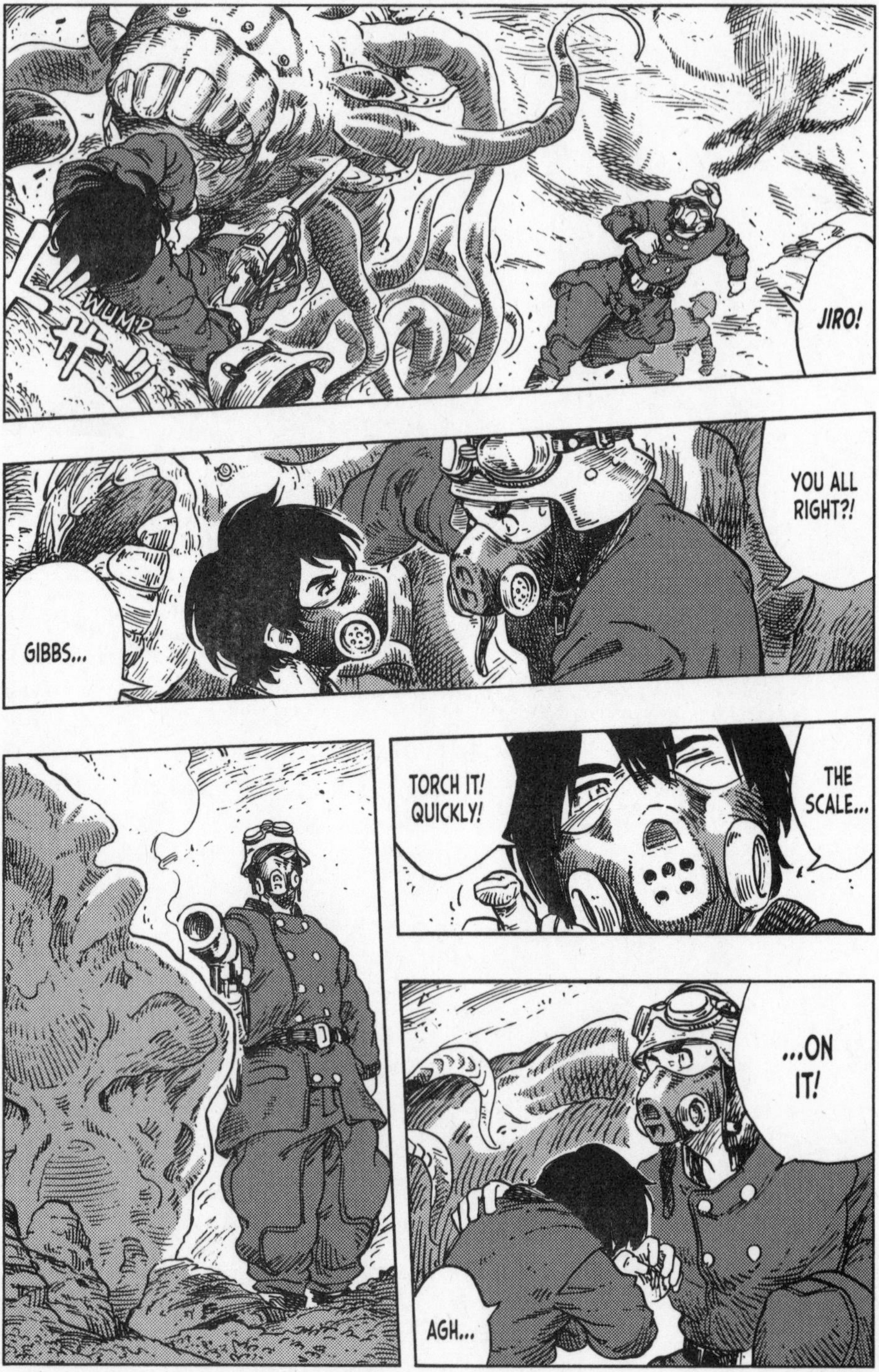
JIRO!
WUMP
YOU ALL RIGHT?!
GIBBS...
THE SCALE...
TORCH IT! QUICKLY!
...ON IT!
AGH...

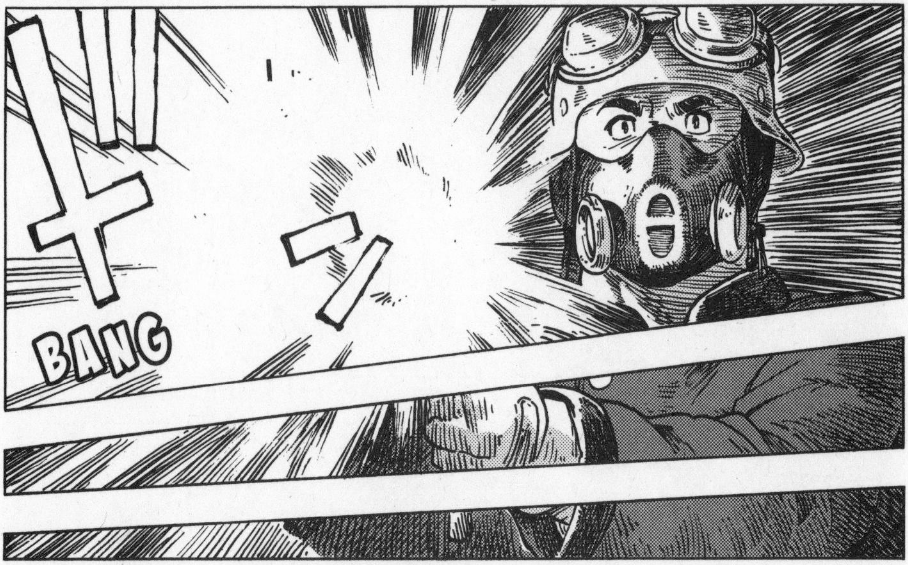
BANG

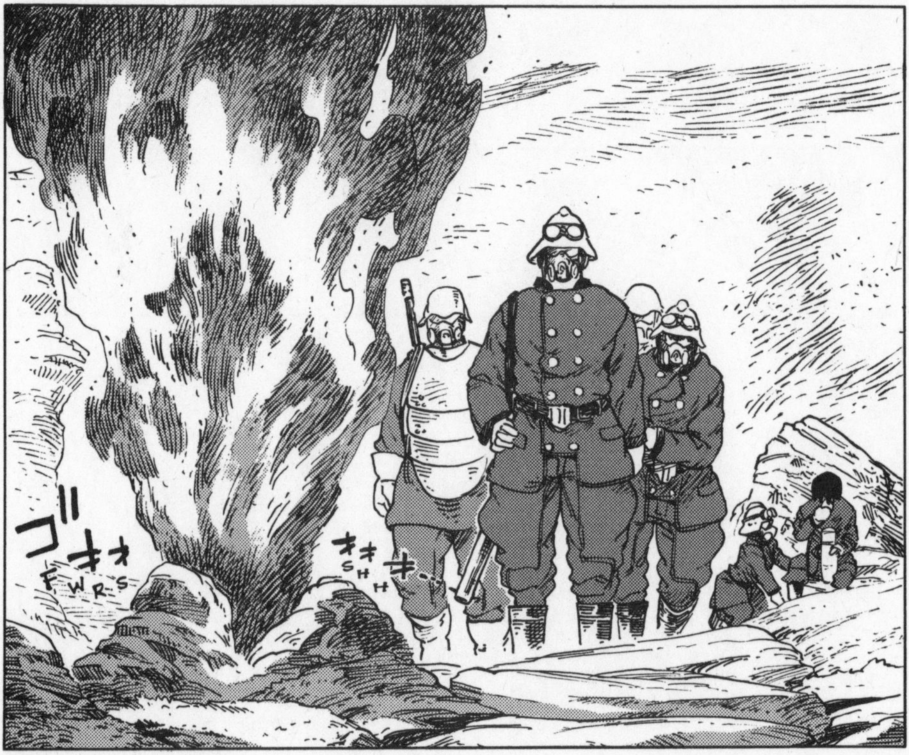
FWRS
SHH

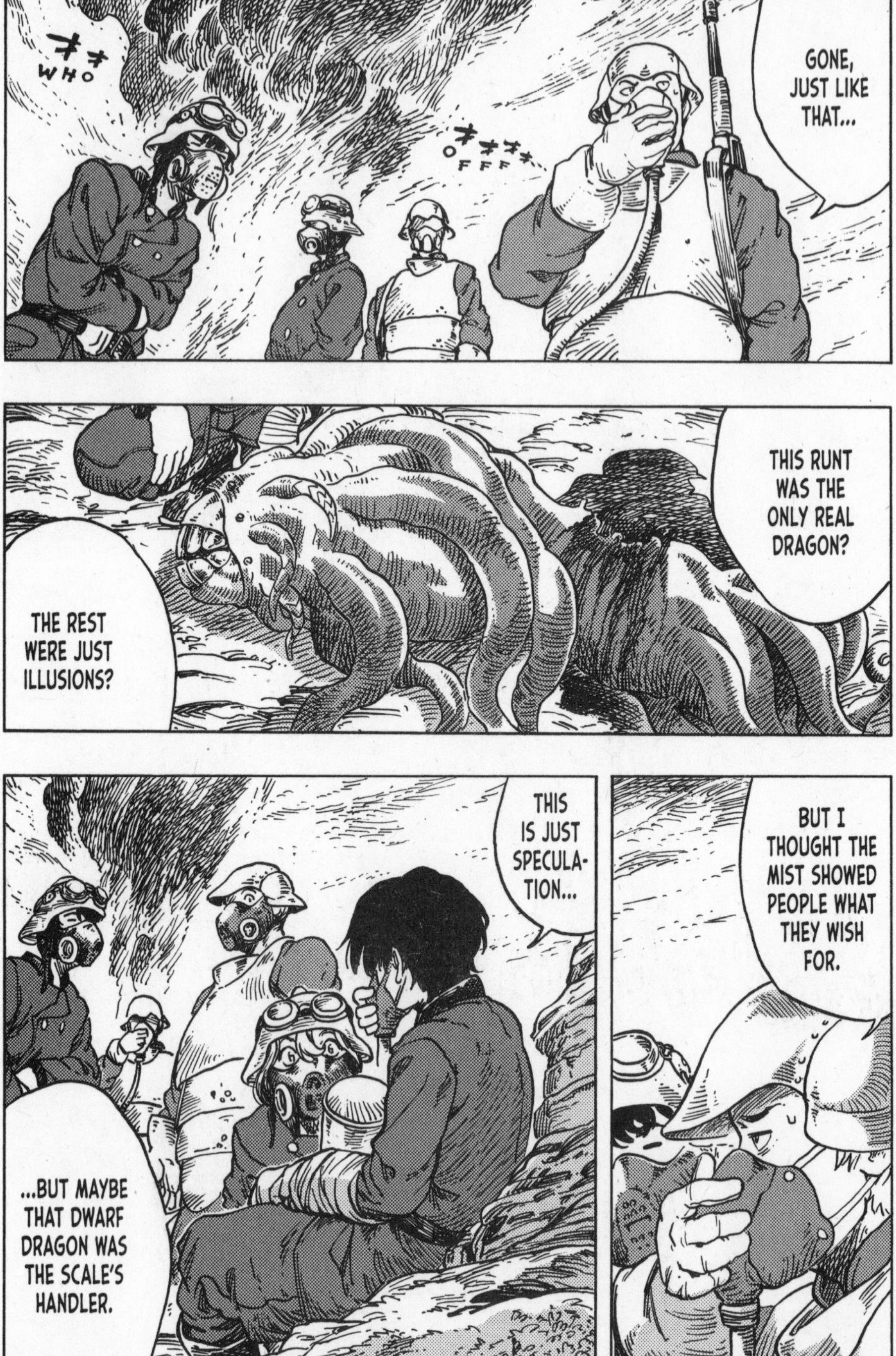
GONE, JUST LIKE THAT...
オォォォォ OFFF
オォ WHO
THIS RUNT WAS THE ONLY REAL DRAGON?
THE REST WERE JUST ILLUSIONS?
BUT I THOUGHT THE MIST SHOWED PEOPLE WHAT THEY WISH FOR.
THIS IS JUST SPECULA-TION...
...BUT MAYBE THAT DWARF DRAGON WAS THE SCALE'S HANDLER.

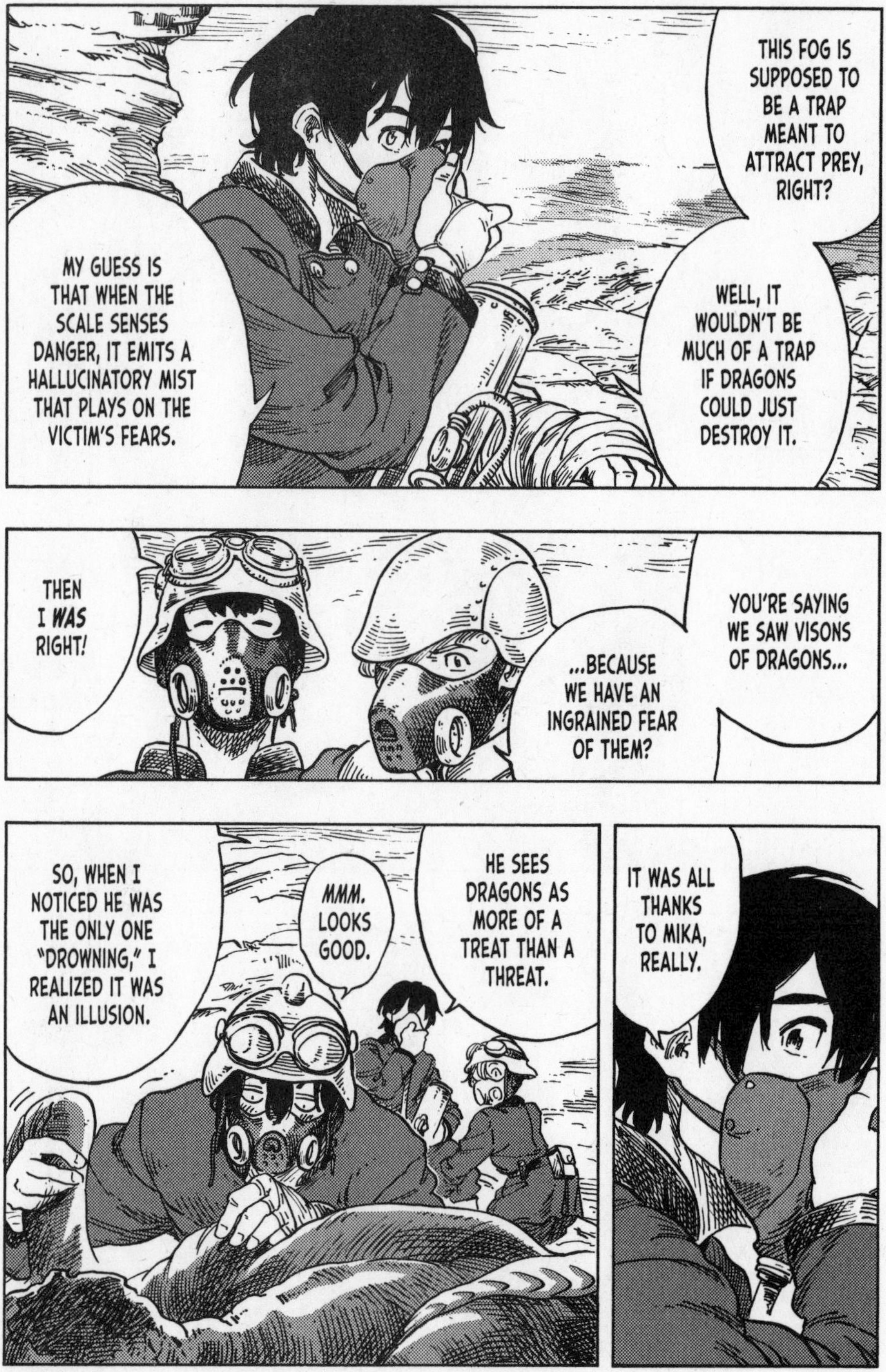
THIS FOG IS SUPPOSED TO BE A TRAP MEANT TO ATTRACT PREY, RIGHT?
WELL, IT WOULDN'T BE MUCH OF A TRAP IF DRAGONS COULD JUST DESTROY IT.
MY GUESS IS THAT WHEN THE SCALE SENSES DANGER, IT EMITS A HALLUCINATORY MIST THAT PLAYS ON THE VICTIM'S FEARS.
YOU'RE SAYING WE SAW VISONS OF DRAGONS...
...BECAUSE WE HAVE AN INGRAINED FEAR OF THEM?
THEN I *WAS* RIGHT!
IT WAS ALL THANKS TO MIKA, REALLY.
HE SEES DRAGONS AS MORE OF A TREAT THAN A THREAT.
MMM. LOOKS GOOD.
SO, WHEN I NOTICED HE WAS THE ONLY ONE "DROWNING," I REALIZED IT WAS AN ILLUSION.

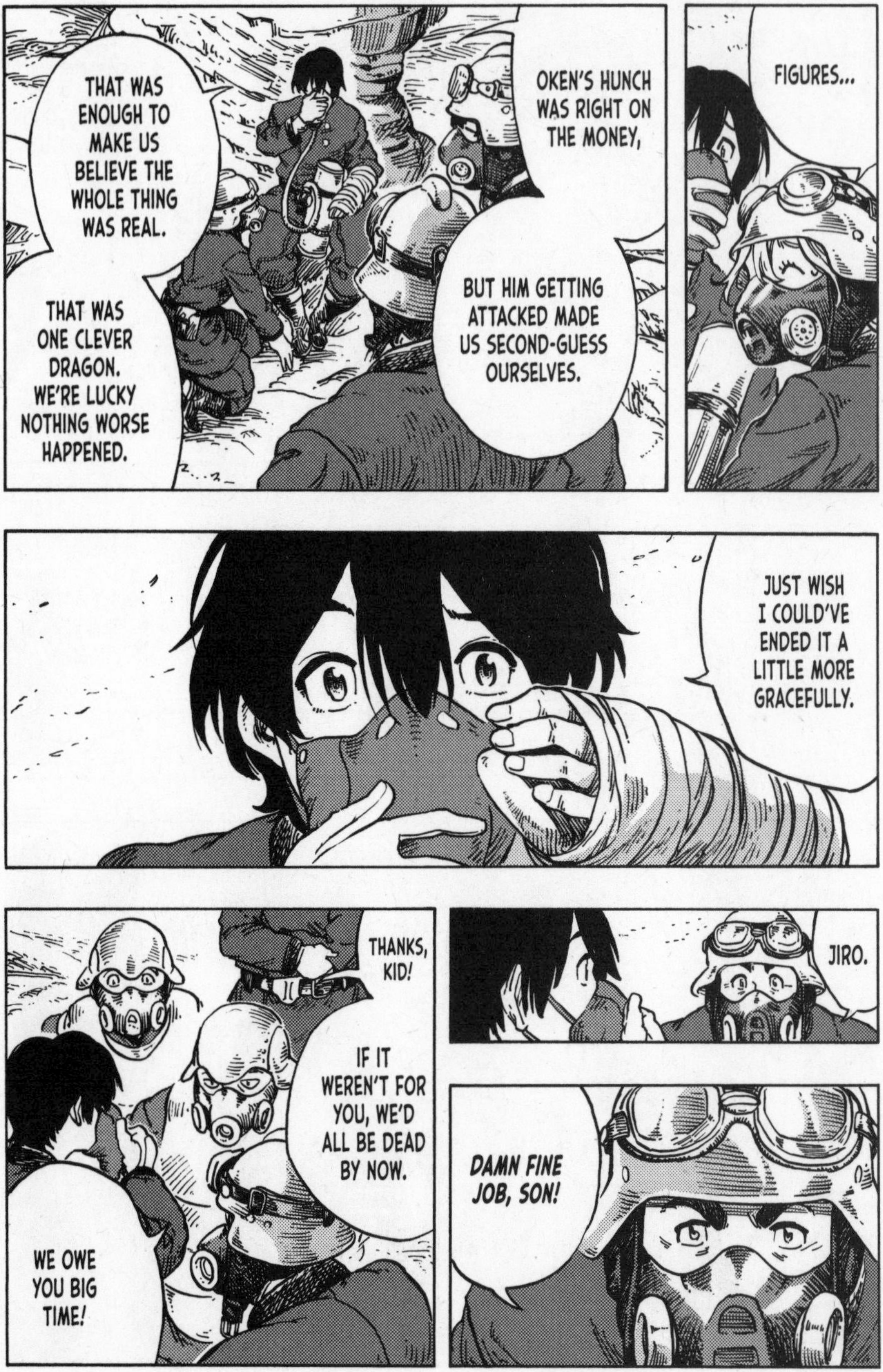
FIGURES...
OKEN'S HUNCH WAS RIGHT ON THE MONEY,
BUT HIM GETTING ATTACKED MADE US SECOND-GUESS OURSELVES.
THAT WAS ENOUGH TO MAKE US BELIEVE THE WHOLE THING WAS REAL.
THAT WAS ONE CLEVER DRAGON. WE'RE LUCKY NOTHING WORSE HAPPENED.
JUST WISH I COULD'VE ENDED IT A LITTLE MORE GRACEFULLY.
JIRO.
DAMN FINE JOB, SON!
THANKS, KID!
IF IT WEREN'T FOR YOU, WE'D ALL BE DEAD BY NOW.
WE OWE YOU BIG TIME!

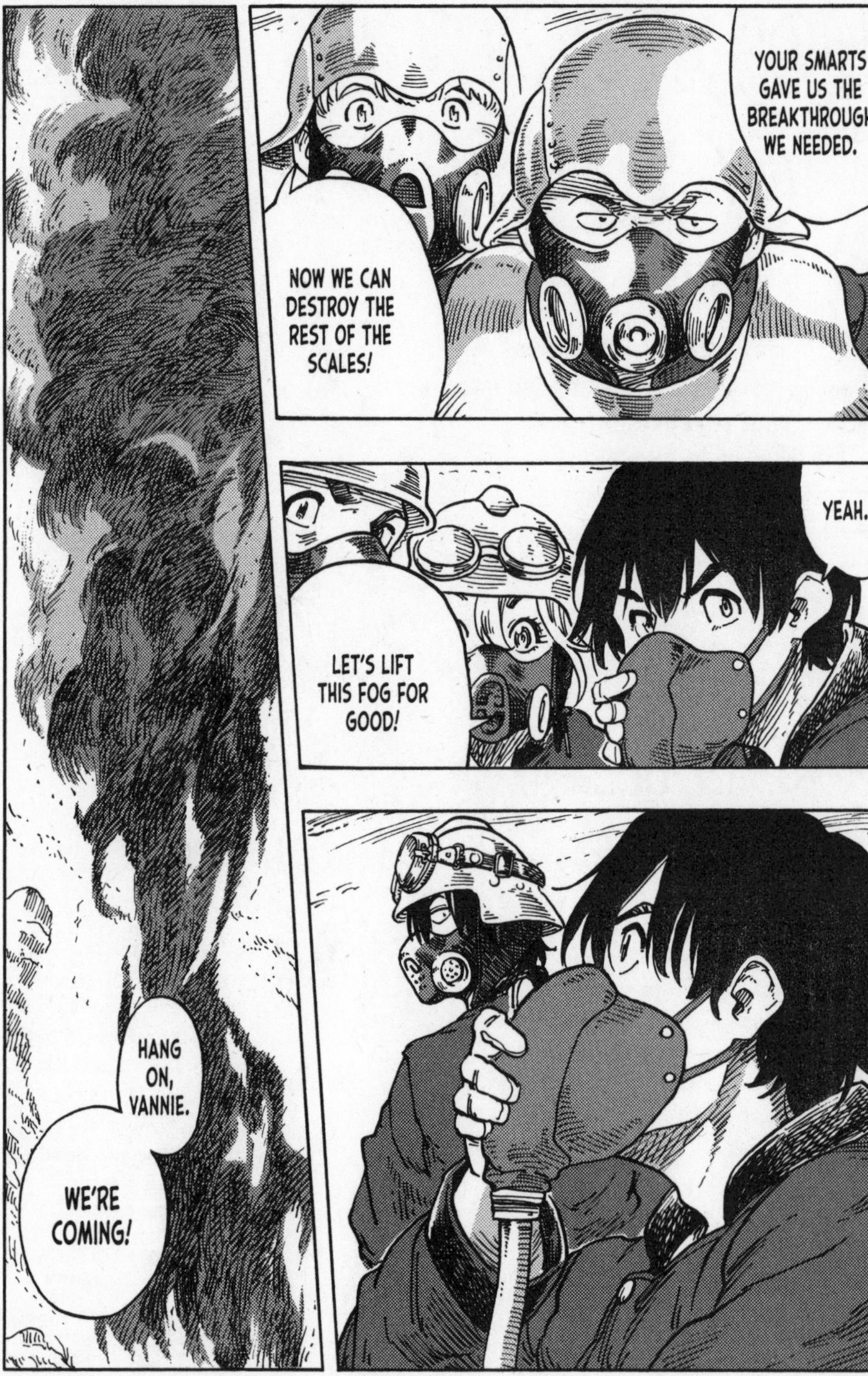
YOUR SMARTS GAVE US THE BREAKTHROUGH WE NEEDED.
NOW WE CAN DESTROY THE REST OF THE SCALES!
YEAH.
LET'S LIFT THIS FOG FOR GOOD!
HANG ON, VANNIE.
WE'RE COMING!

"DRAGON CORE"

TAKITA'S GUIDE TO DRAGONS 5

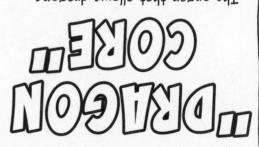

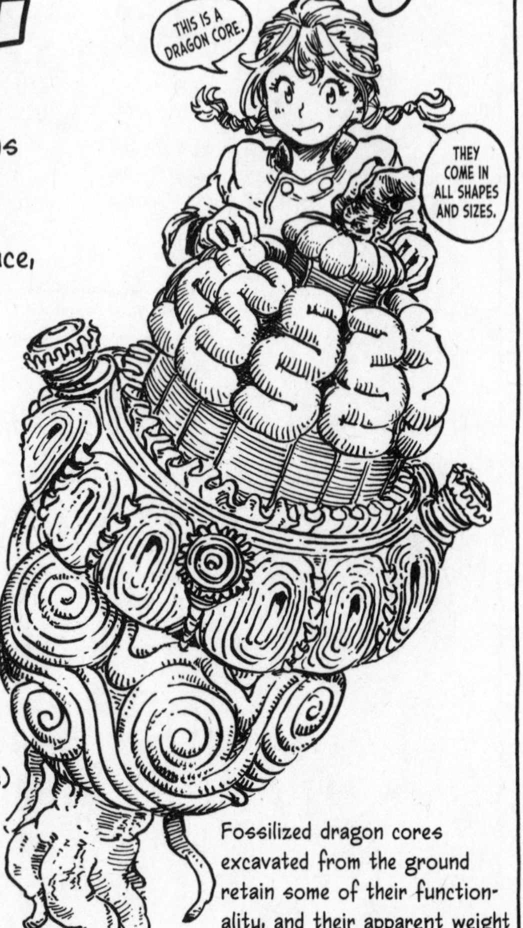
THIS IS A DRAGON CORE.
THEY COME IN ALL SHAPES AND SIZES.

The organ that allows dragons to fly.
It has long been believed that dragons fly by distorting space, generating a repulsion field, which they ride like a wave.
However, this idea is more myth than anything. The actual principle behind their flight is still unclear.
Dragon cores are very hard and inedible.

CORE BALLAST

Airships remain aloft using buoyancy created by lifting gas. When taking off, weights (ballasts) are dropped to lighten the hull and achieve lift, while landing is done by releasing lifting gas to make the hull slightly too heavy. Core ballasts make it possible to take off and land without the need for conventional ballasts or gas releases.

Fossilized dragon cores excavated from the ground retain some of their functionality, and their apparent weight changes when subjected to a magnetic field of a certain frequency. Airship load manipulation technology is based off of these properties.
(See vol. 10, p. 47)

- Increased core ballast output
  ↳ Ship ascends.
- Hull weight = buoyancy (equilibrium)
  ↳ Ship remains stationary aloft.
- Decreased core ballast output
  ↳ Ship descends.

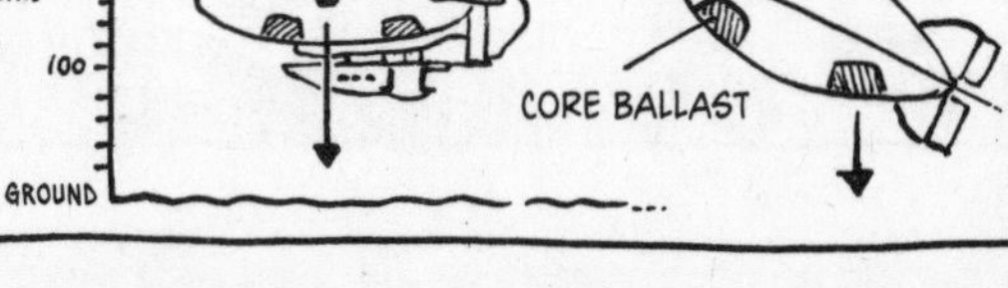
300
200
100
GROUND
CORE BALLAST

It is also possible to control the ship's posture by changing the weight of the ballasts in the front and rear.

Flight 58 Tzita

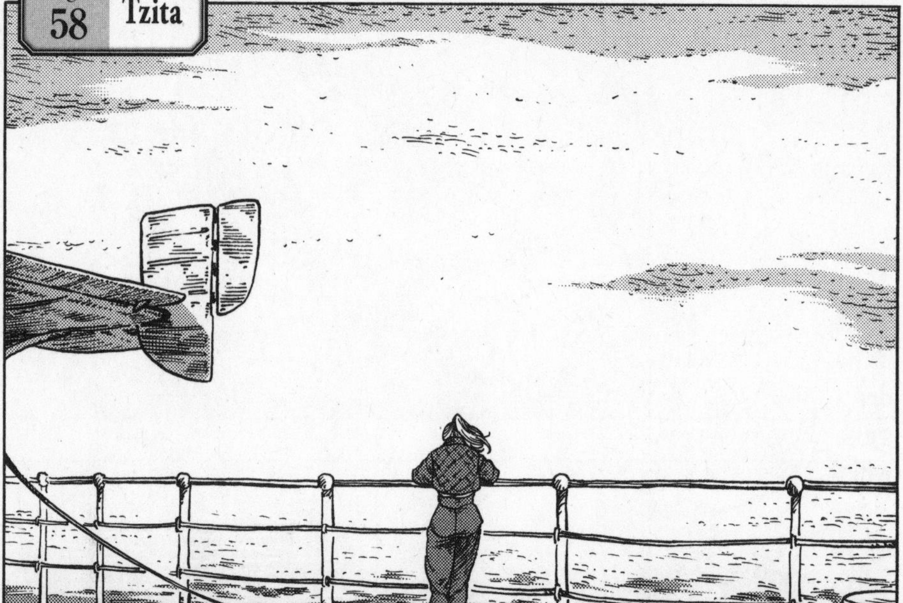

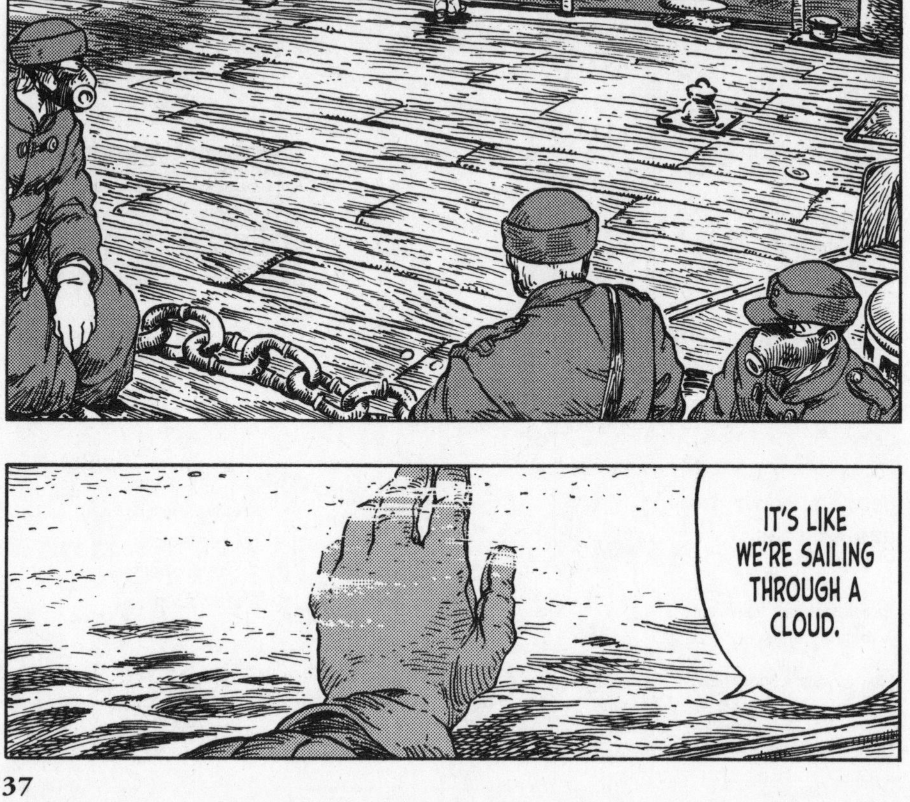
IT'S LIKE WE'RE SAILING THROUGH A CLOUD.

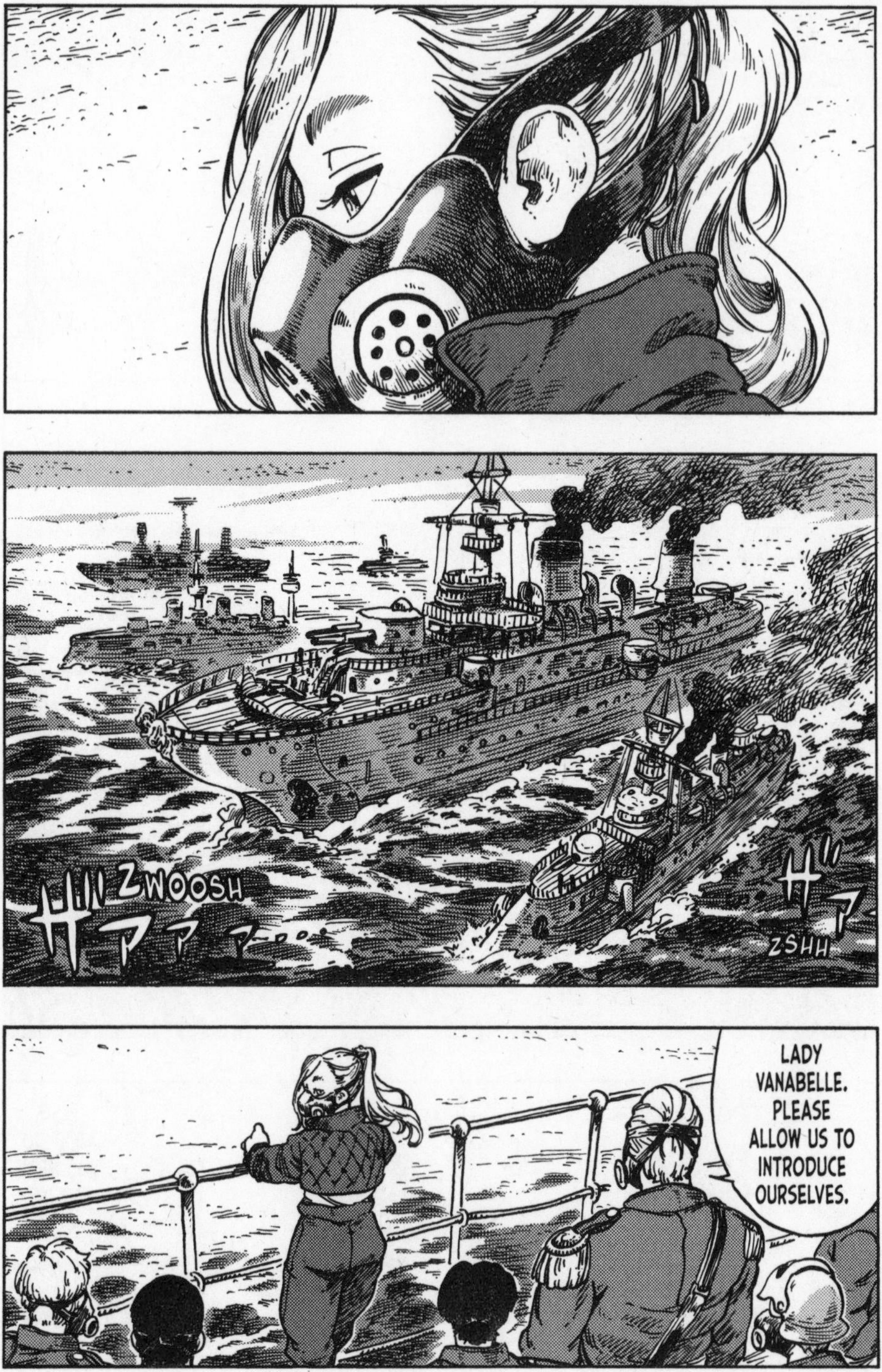
ZSHH
ZWOOSH
LADY VANABELLE. PLEASE ALLOW US TO INTRODUCE OURSELVES.

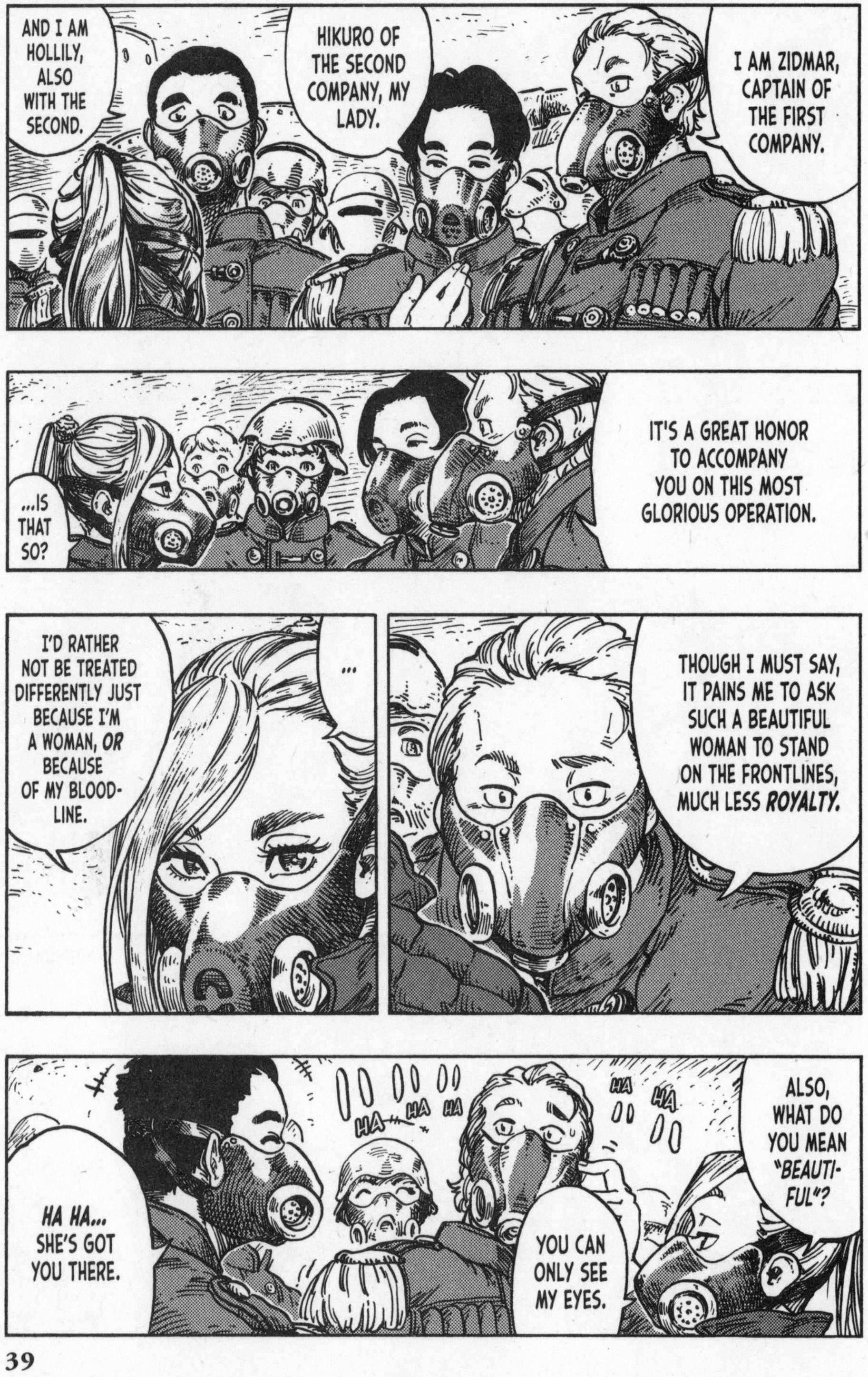
I AM ZIDMAR, CAPTAIN OF THE FIRST COMPANY.
HIKURO OF THE SECOND COMPANY, MY LADY.
AND I AM HOLLILY, ALSO WITH THE SECOND.
IT'S A GREAT HONOR TO ACCOMPANY YOU ON THIS MOST GLORIOUS OPERATION.
...IS THAT SO?
THOUGH I MUST SAY, IT PAINS ME TO ASK SUCH A BEAUTIFUL WOMAN TO STAND ON THE FRONTLINES, MUCH LESS *ROYALTY*.
...
I'D RATHER NOT BE TREATED DIFFERENTLY JUST BECAUSE I'M A WOMAN, *OR* BECAUSE OF MY BLOOD-LINE.
ALSO, WHAT DO YOU MEAN *"BEAUTI-FUL"*?
YOU CAN ONLY SEE MY EYES.
HA HA
HA HA HA
HA HA... SHE'S GOT YOU THERE.

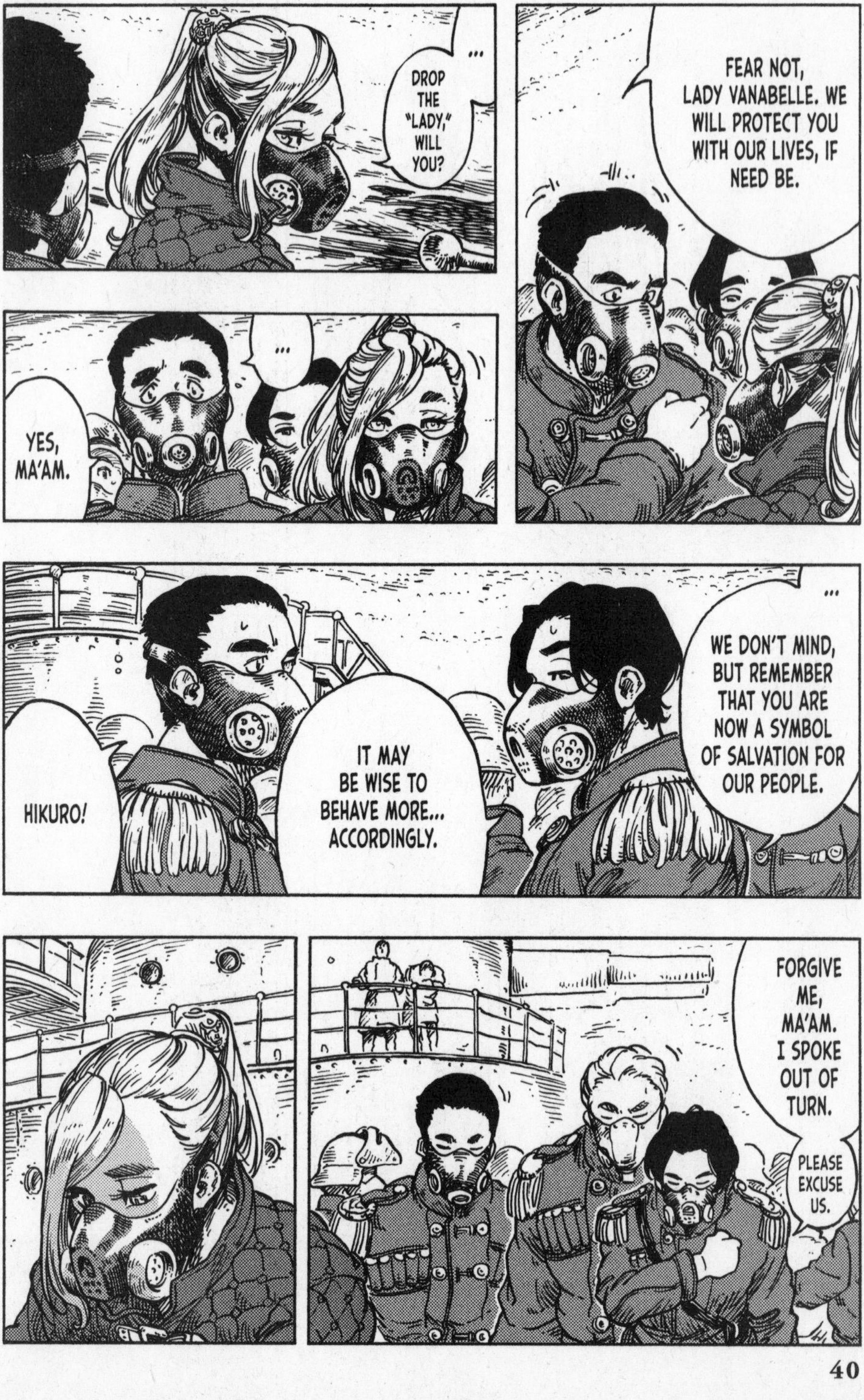
FEAR NOT, LADY VANABELLE. WE WILL PROTECT YOU WITH OUR LIVES, IF NEED BE.
...
DROP THE "LADY," WILL YOU?
...
YES, MA'AM.
...
WE DON'T MIND, BUT REMEMBER THAT YOU ARE NOW A SYMBOL OF SALVATION FOR OUR PEOPLE.
IT MAY BE WISE TO BEHAVE MORE... ACCORDINGLY.
HIKURO!
FORGIVE ME, MA'AM. I SPOKE OUT OF TURN.
PLEASE EXCUSE US.

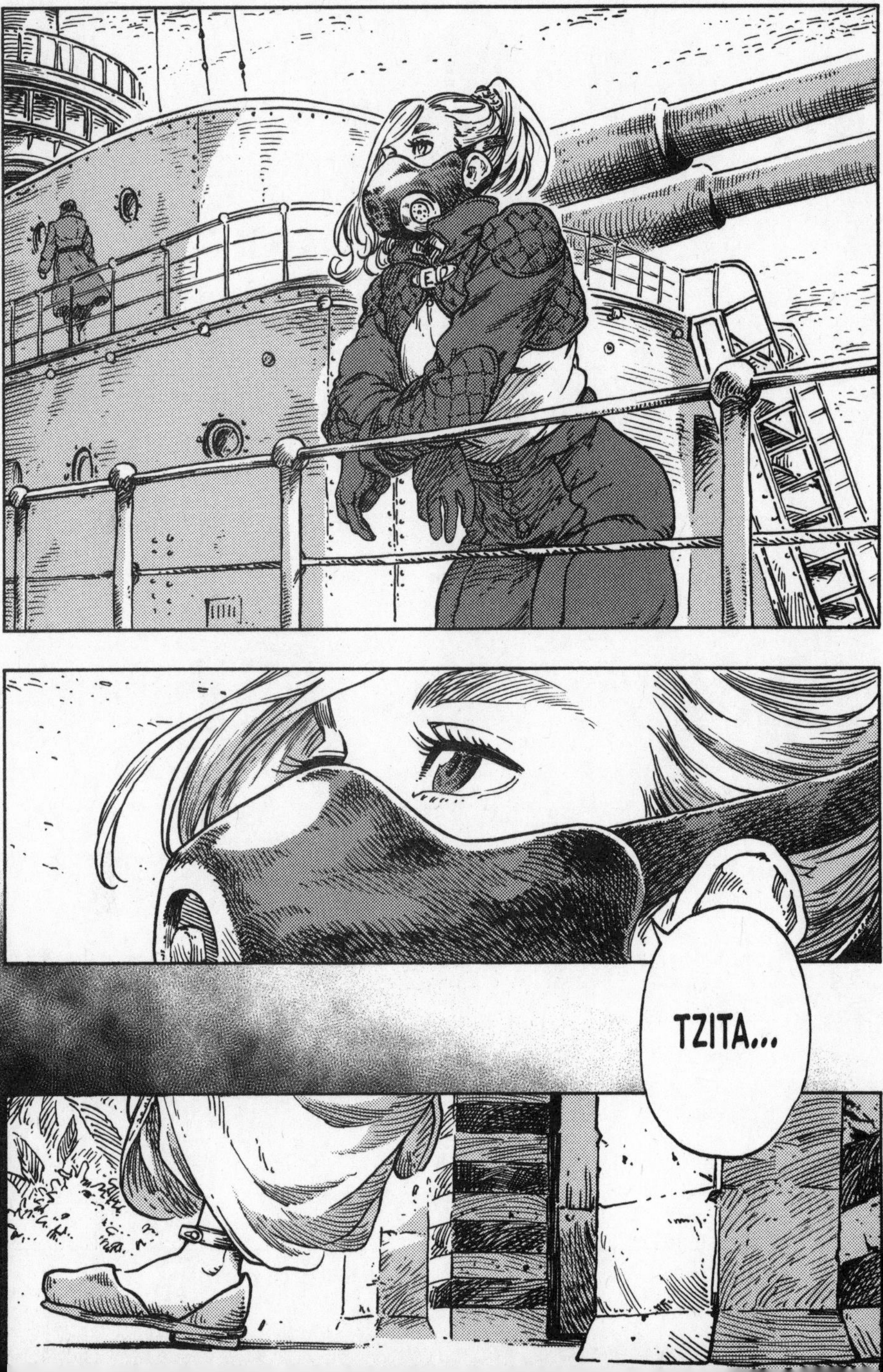
TZITA...

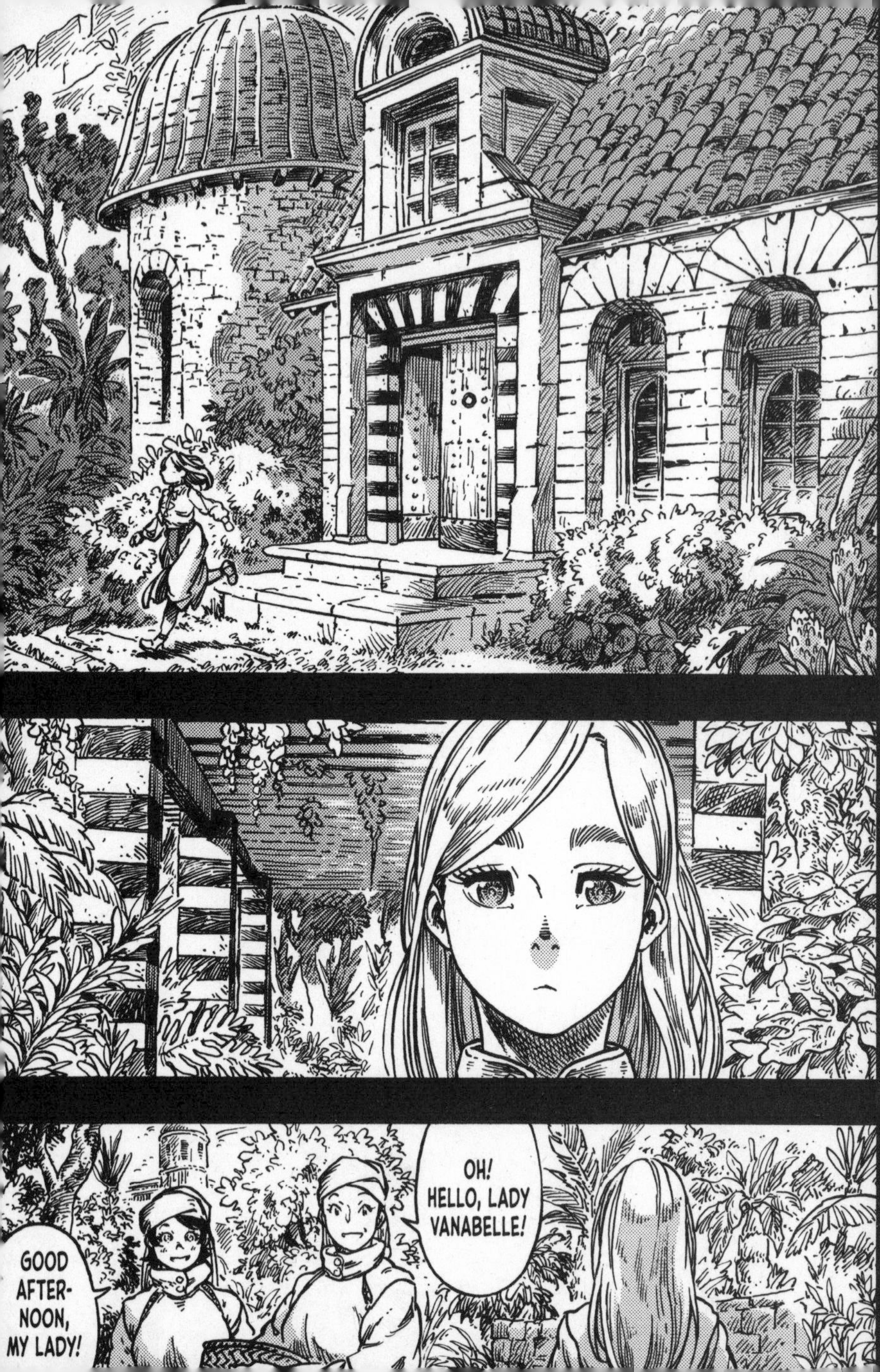
OH! HELLO, LADY VANABELLE!
GOOD AFTER-NOON, MY LADY!

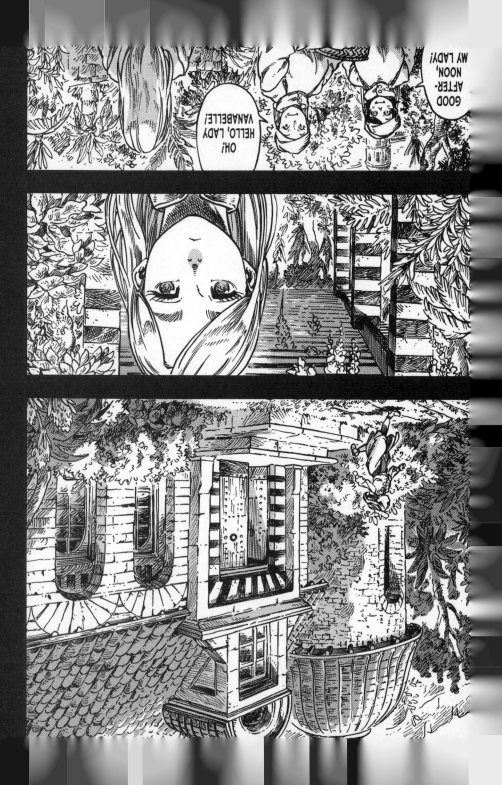

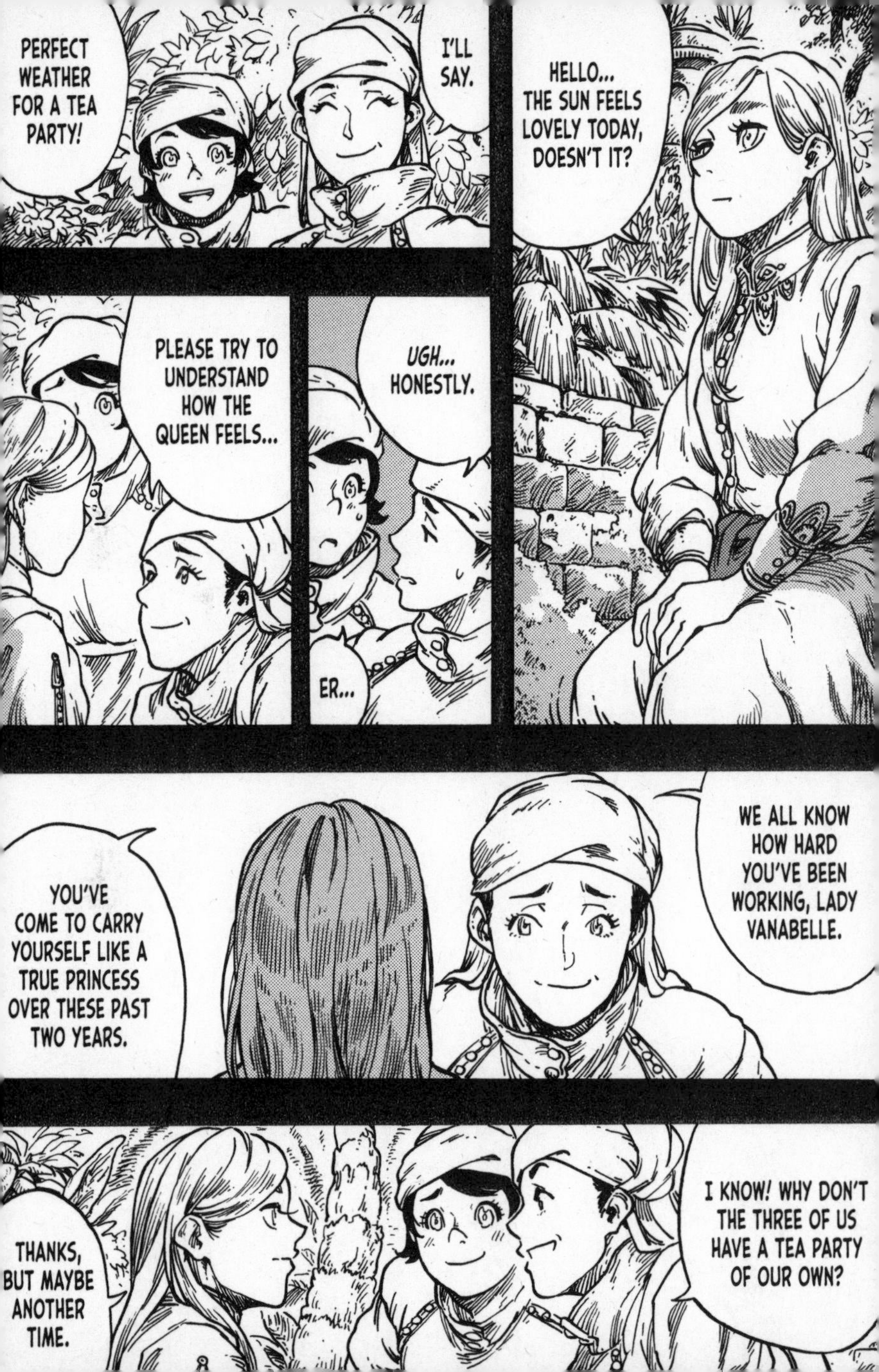
HELLO... THE SUN FEELS LOVELY TODAY, DOESN'T IT?
PERFECT WEATHER FOR A TEA PARTY!
I'LL SAY.
UGH... HONESTLY.
ER...
PLEASE TRY TO UNDERSTAND HOW THE QUEEN FEELS...
WE ALL KNOW HOW HARD YOU'VE BEEN WORKING, LADY VANABELLE.
YOU'VE COME TO CARRY YOURSELF LIKE A TRUE PRINCESS OVER THESE PAST TWO YEARS.
I KNOW! WHY DON'T THE THREE OF US HAVE A TEA PARTY OF OUR OWN?
THANKS, BUT MAYBE ANOTHER TIME.

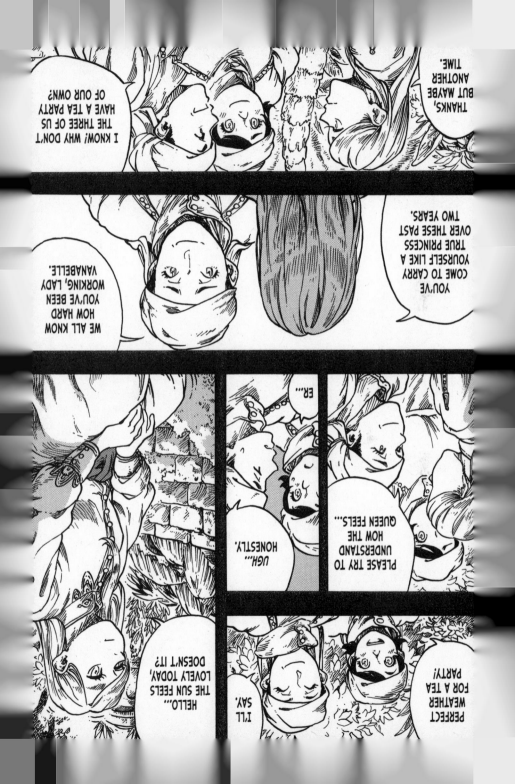

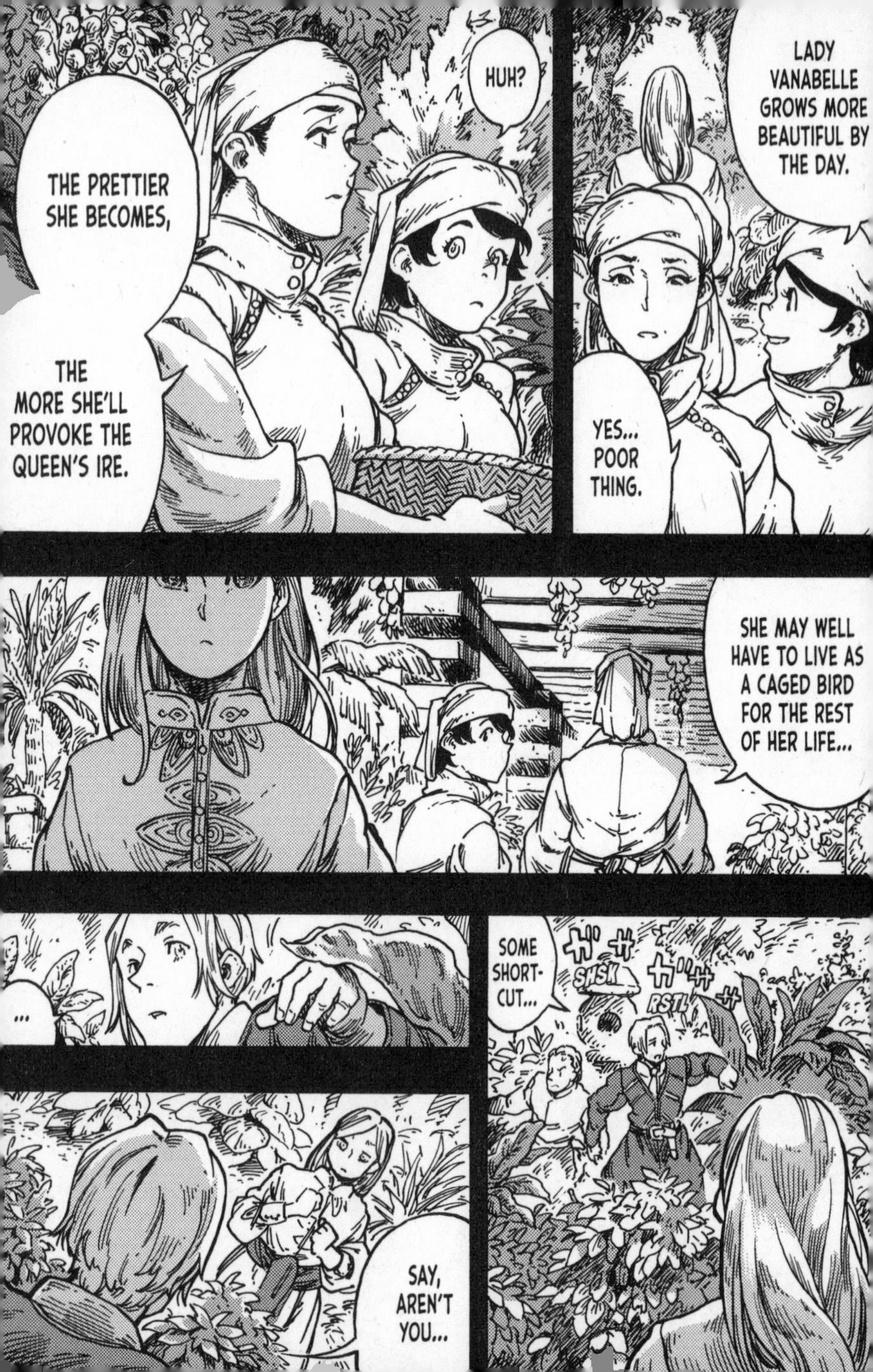
LADY VANABELLE GROWS MORE BEAUTIFUL BY THE DAY.
YES... POOR THING.
HUH?
THE PRETTIER SHE BECOMES,
THE MORE SHE'LL PROVOKE THE QUEEN'S IRE.
SHE MAY WELL HAVE TO LIVE AS A CAGED BIRD FOR THE REST OF HER LIFE...
SOME SHORT-CUT...
SHSK
RSTL
...
SAY, AREN'T YOU...

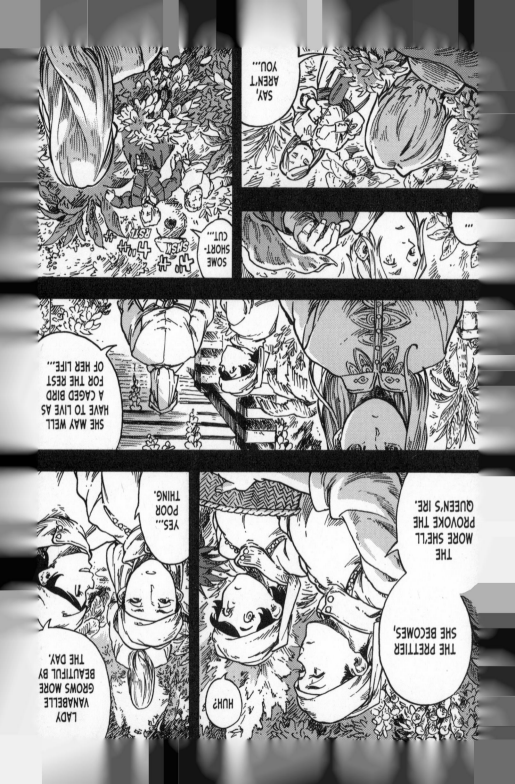

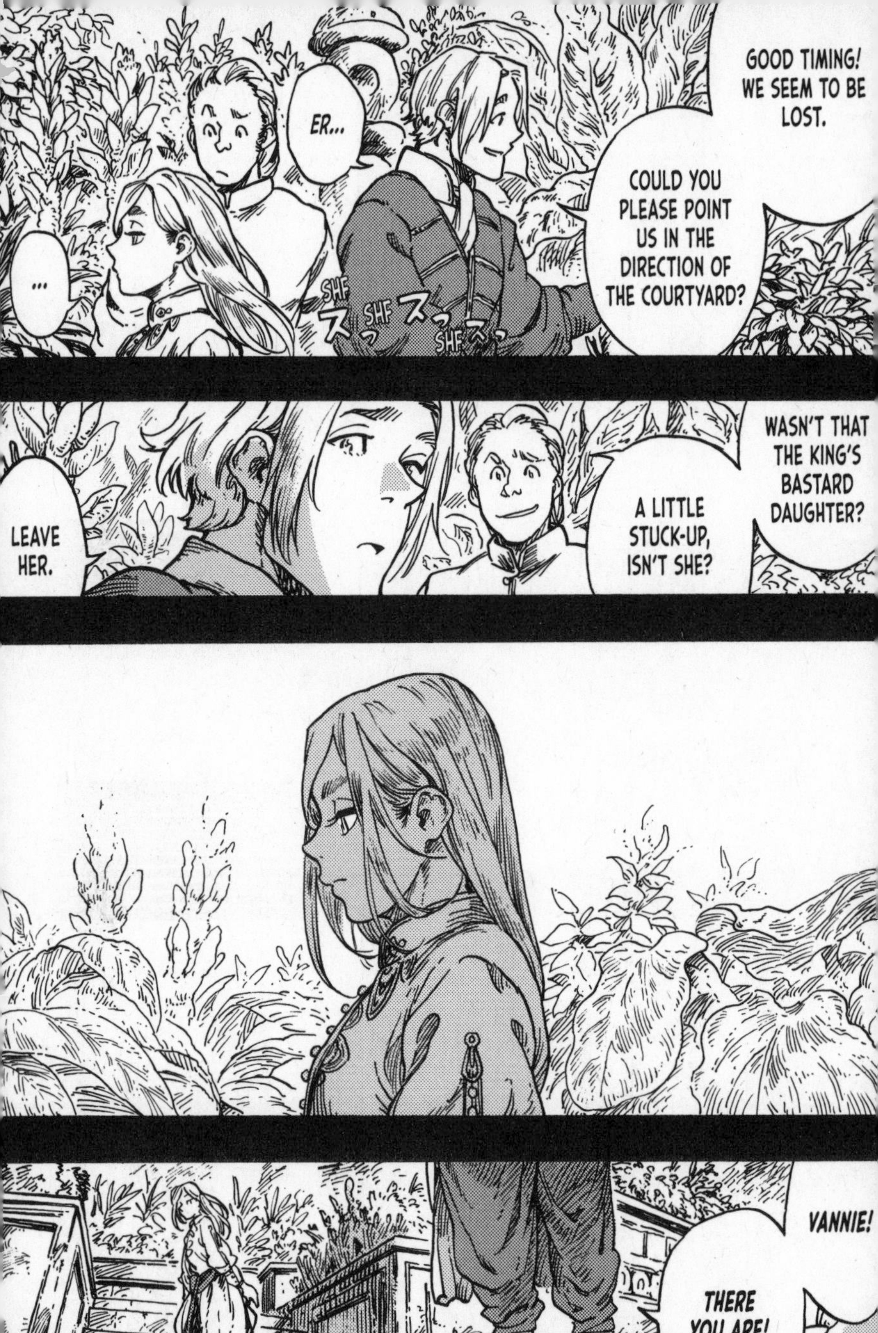
GOOD TIMING! WE SEEM TO BE LOST.
COULD YOU PLEASE POINT US IN THE DIRECTION OF THE COURTYARD?
ER...
SHF SHF SHF
...
WASN'T THAT THE KING'S BASTARD DAUGHTER?
A LITTLE STUCK-UP, ISN'T SHE?
LEAVE HER.
VANNIE!
THERE YOU ARE!

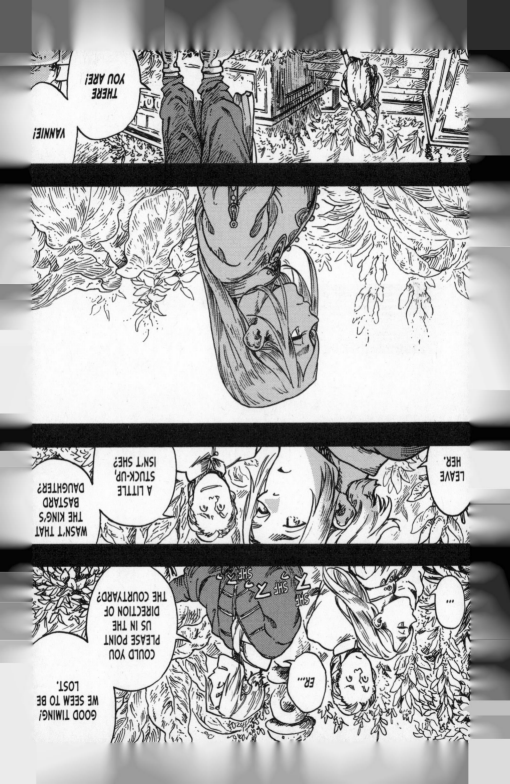

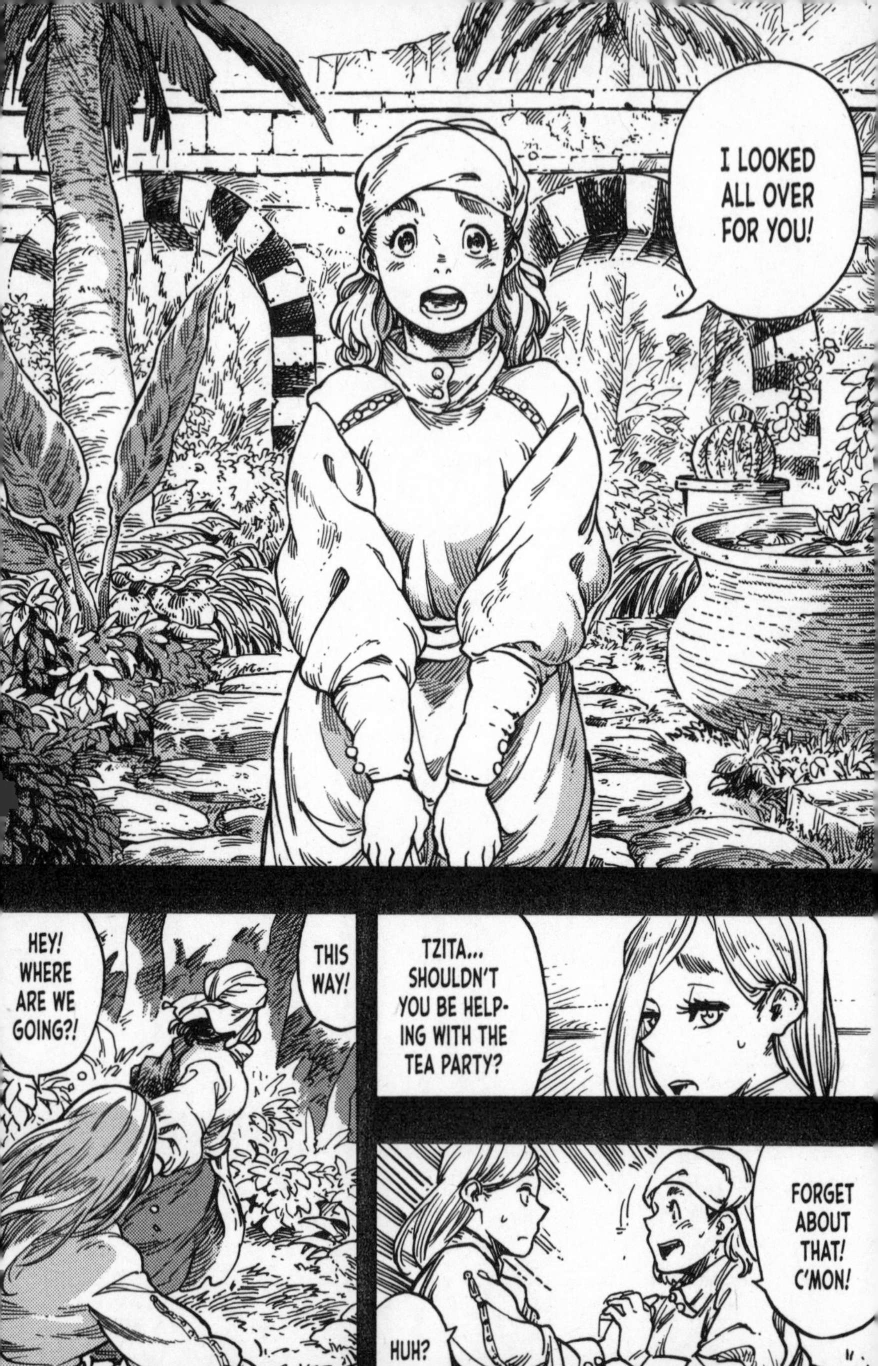
I LOOKED ALL OVER FOR YOU!
TZITA... SHOULDN'T YOU BE HELP-ING WITH THE TEA PARTY?
FORGET ABOUT THAT! C'MON!
HUH?
THIS WAY!
HEY! WHERE ARE WE GOING?!

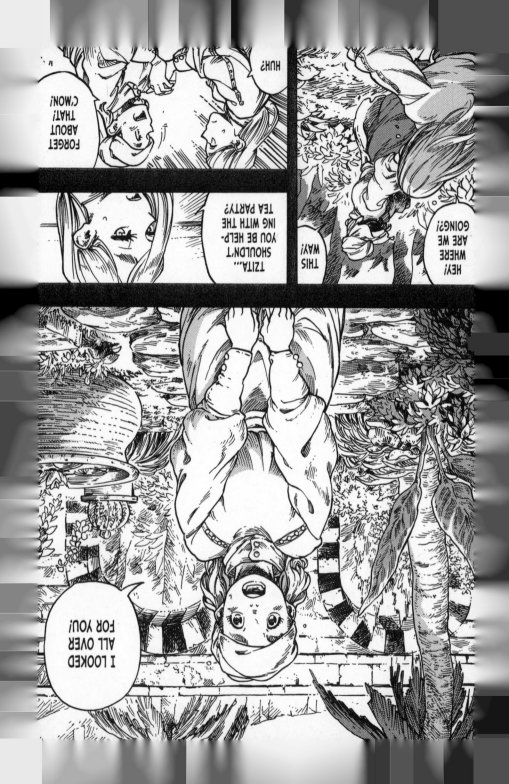

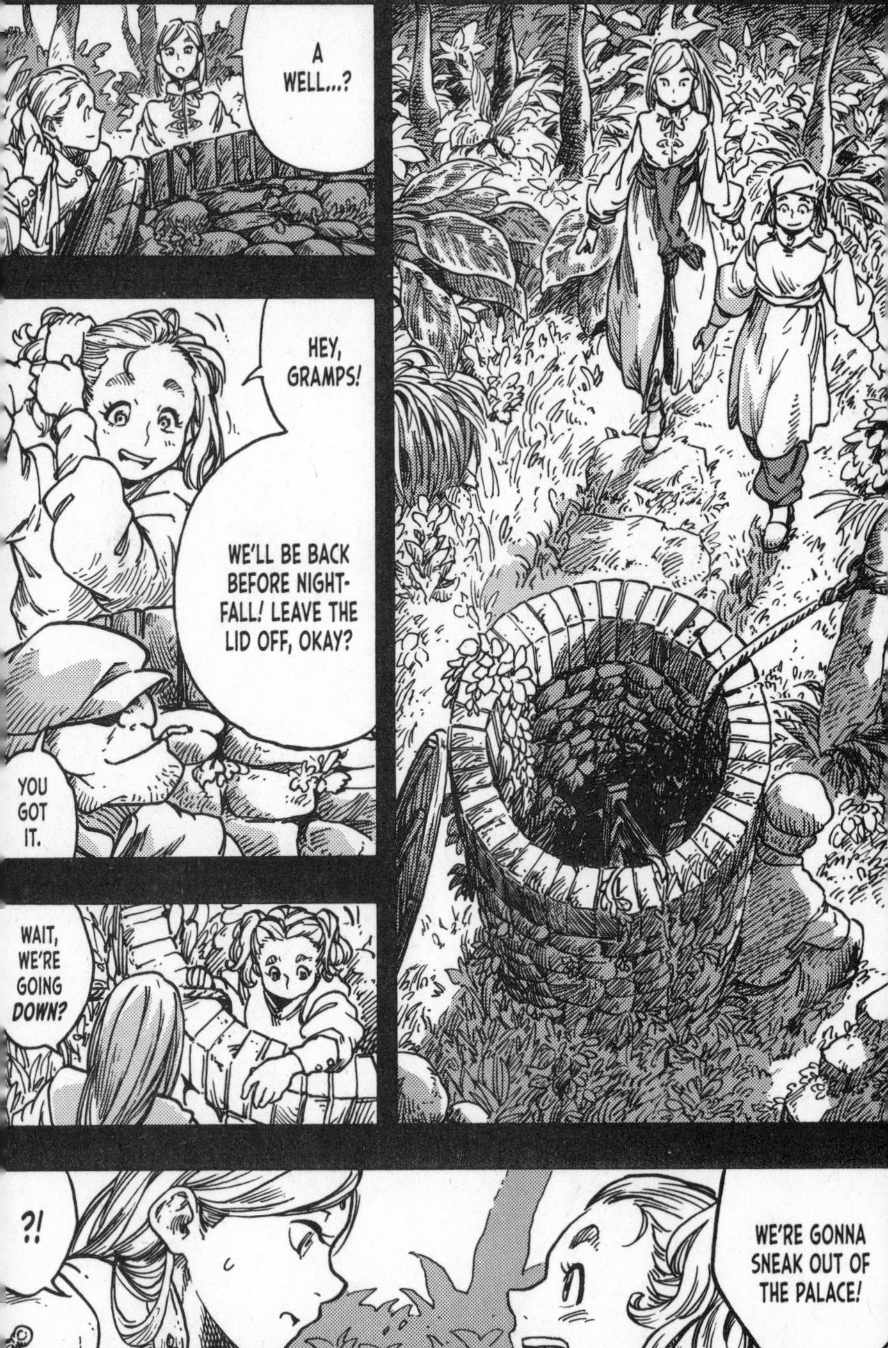
A WELL...?
HEY, GRAMPS!
WE'LL BE BACK BEFORE NIGHT-FALL! LEAVE THE LID OFF, OKAY?
YOU GOT IT.
WAIT, WE'RE GOING *DOWN*?
WE'RE GONNA SNEAK OUT OF THE PALACE!
?!

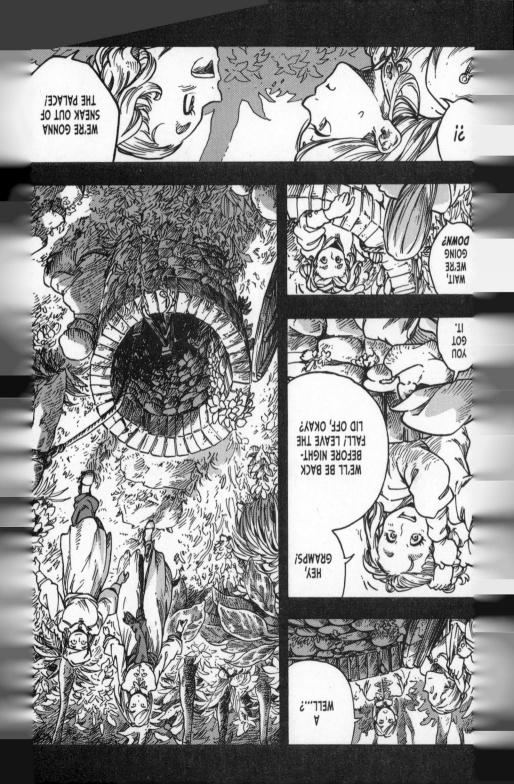

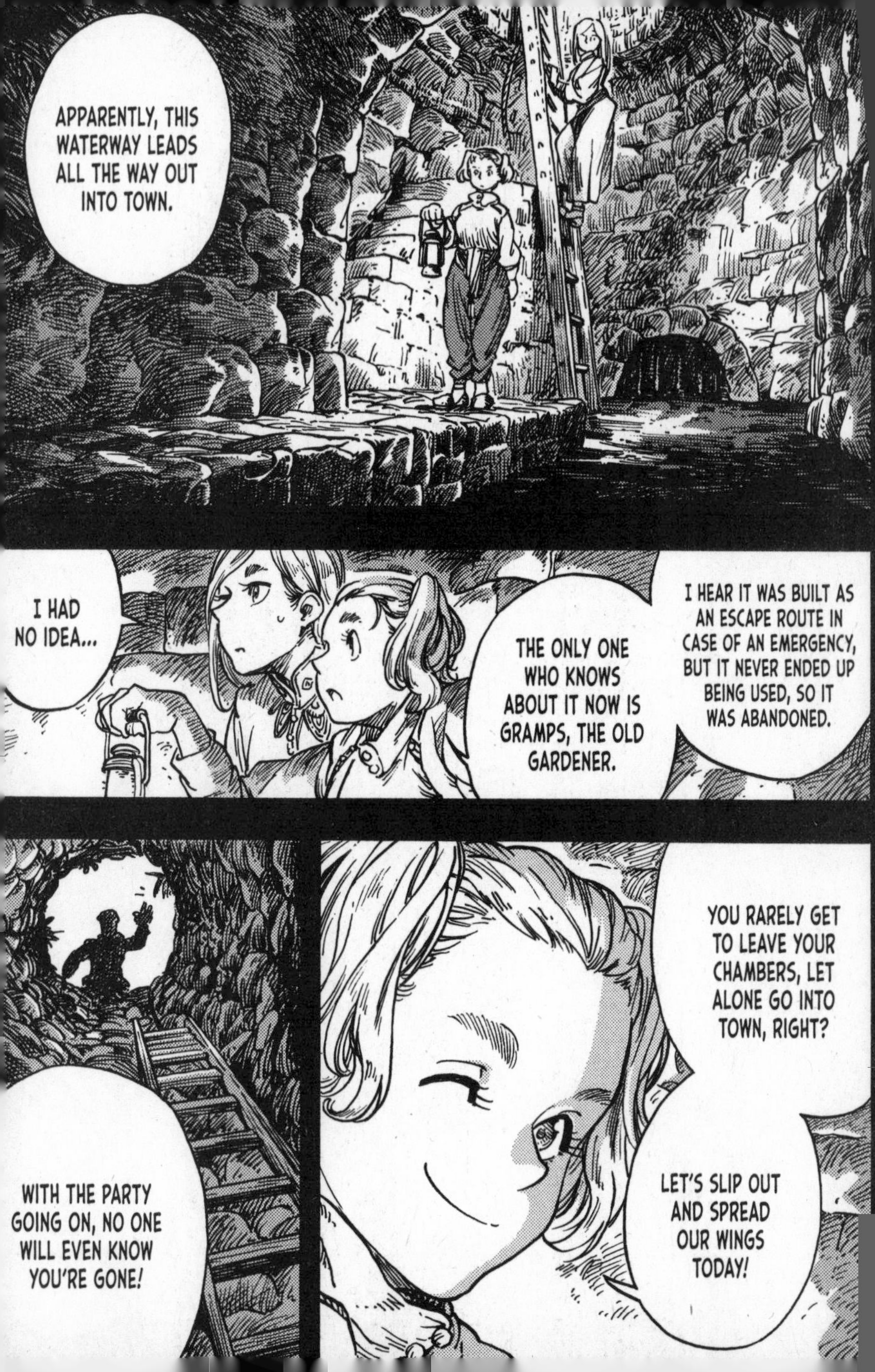
APPARENTLY, THIS WATERWAY LEADS ALL THE WAY OUT INTO TOWN.
I HEAR IT WAS BUILT AS AN ESCAPE ROUTE IN CASE OF AN EMERGENCY, BUT IT NEVER ENDED UP BEING USED, SO IT WAS ABANDONED.
THE ONLY ONE WHO KNOWS ABOUT IT NOW IS GRAMPS, THE OLD GARDENER.
I HAD NO IDEA...
YOU RARELY GET TO LEAVE YOUR CHAMBERS, LET ALONE GO INTO TOWN, RIGHT?
LET'S SLIP OUT AND SPREAD OUR WINGS TODAY!
WITH THE PARTY GOING ON, NO ONE WILL EVEN KNOW YOU'RE GONE!

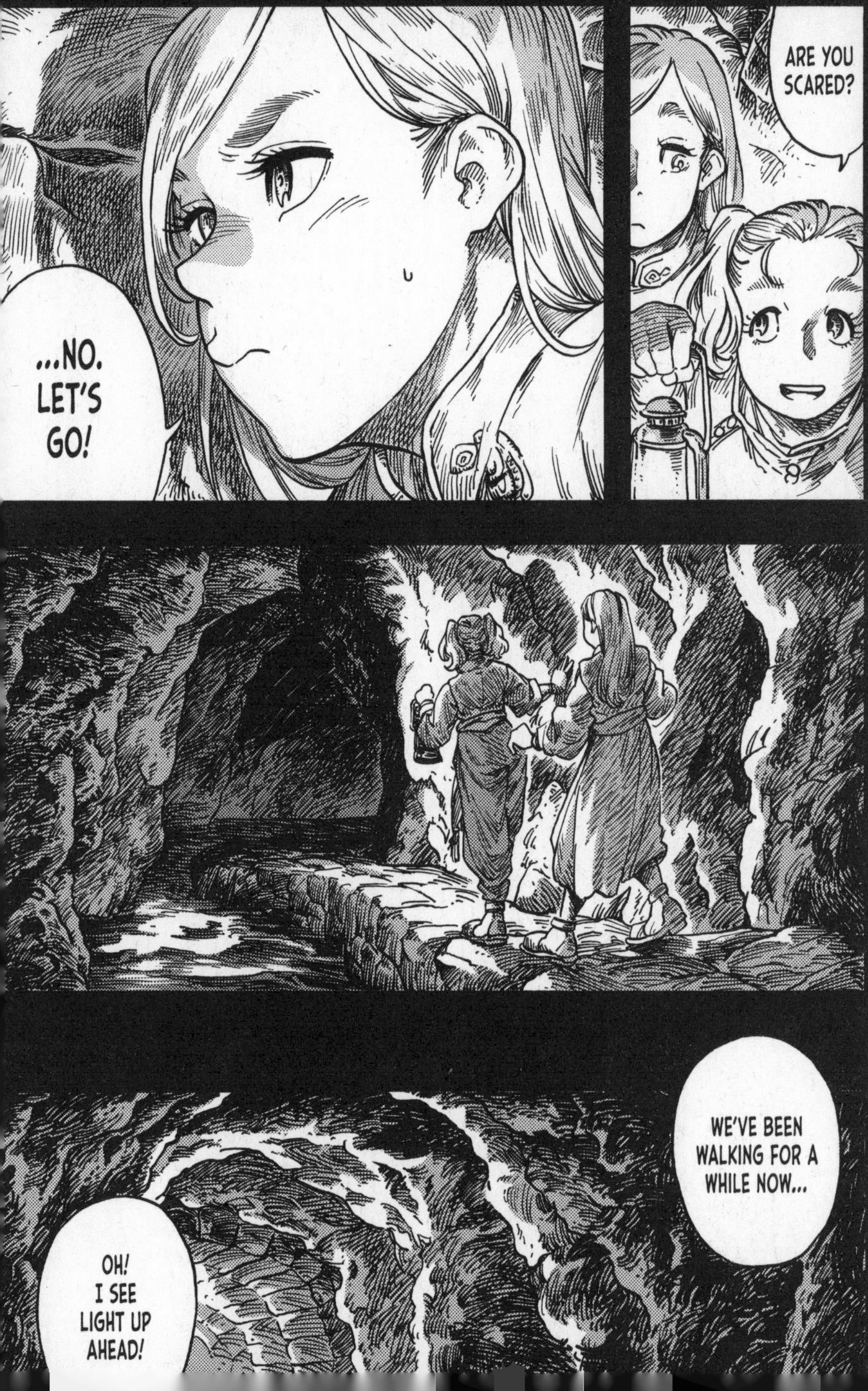
ARE YOU SCARED?
...NO. LET'S GO!
WE'VE BEEN WALKING FOR A WHILE NOW...
OH! I SEE LIGHT UP AHEAD!

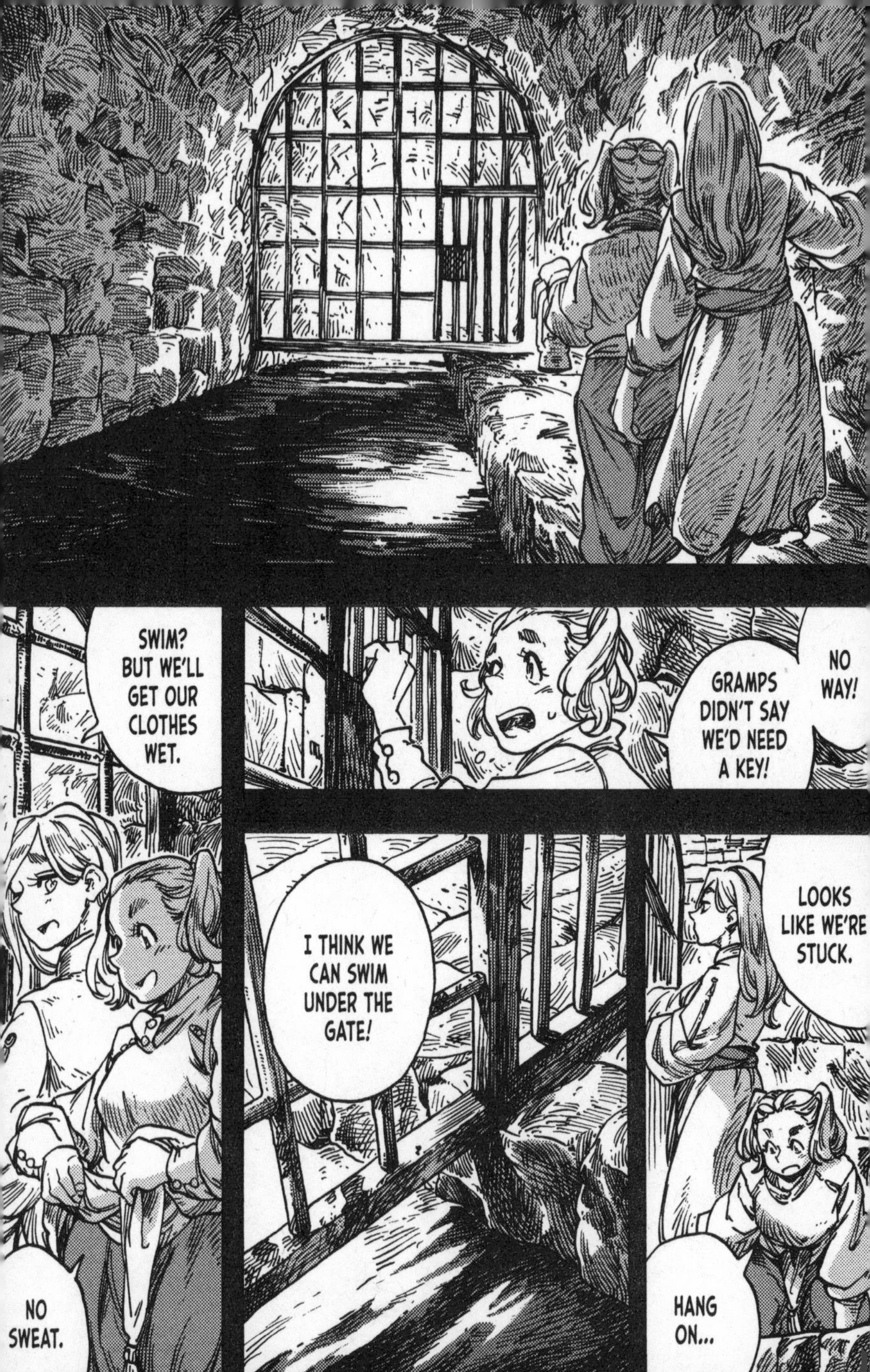
NO WAY!
GRAMPS DIDN'T SAY WE'D NEED A KEY!
SWIM? BUT WE'LL GET OUR CLOTHES WET.
LOOKS LIKE WE'RE STUCK.
HANG ON...
I THINK WE CAN SWIM UNDER THE GATE!
NO SWEAT.

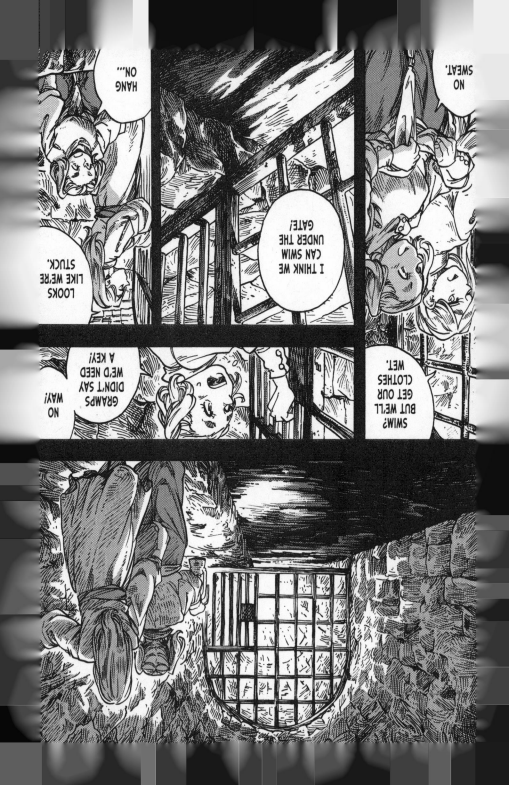

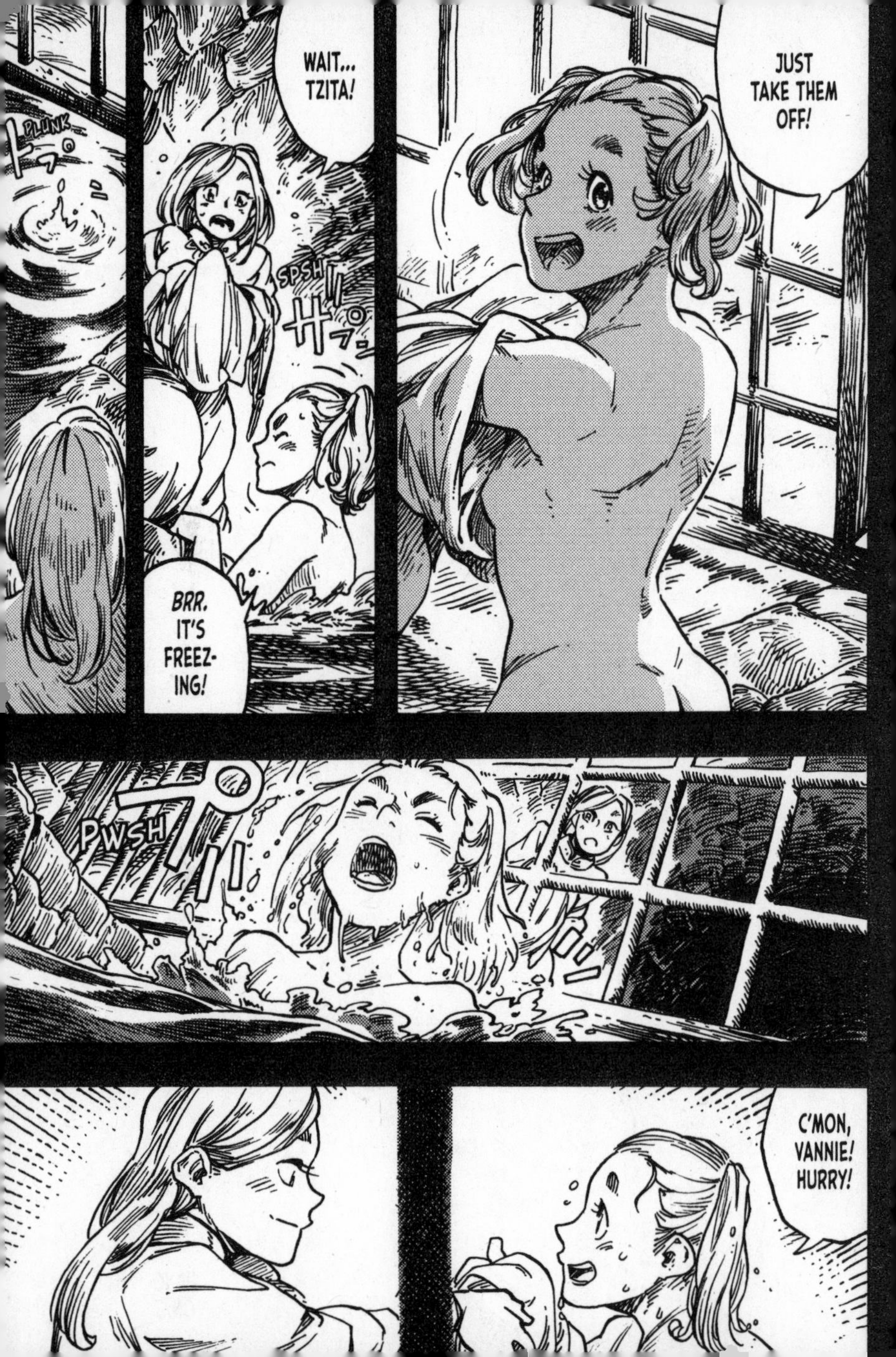
JUST TAKE THEM OFF!
WAIT... TZITA!
SPSH
BRR. IT'S FREEZ-ING!
PLUNK
PWSH
C'MON, VANNIE! HURRY!

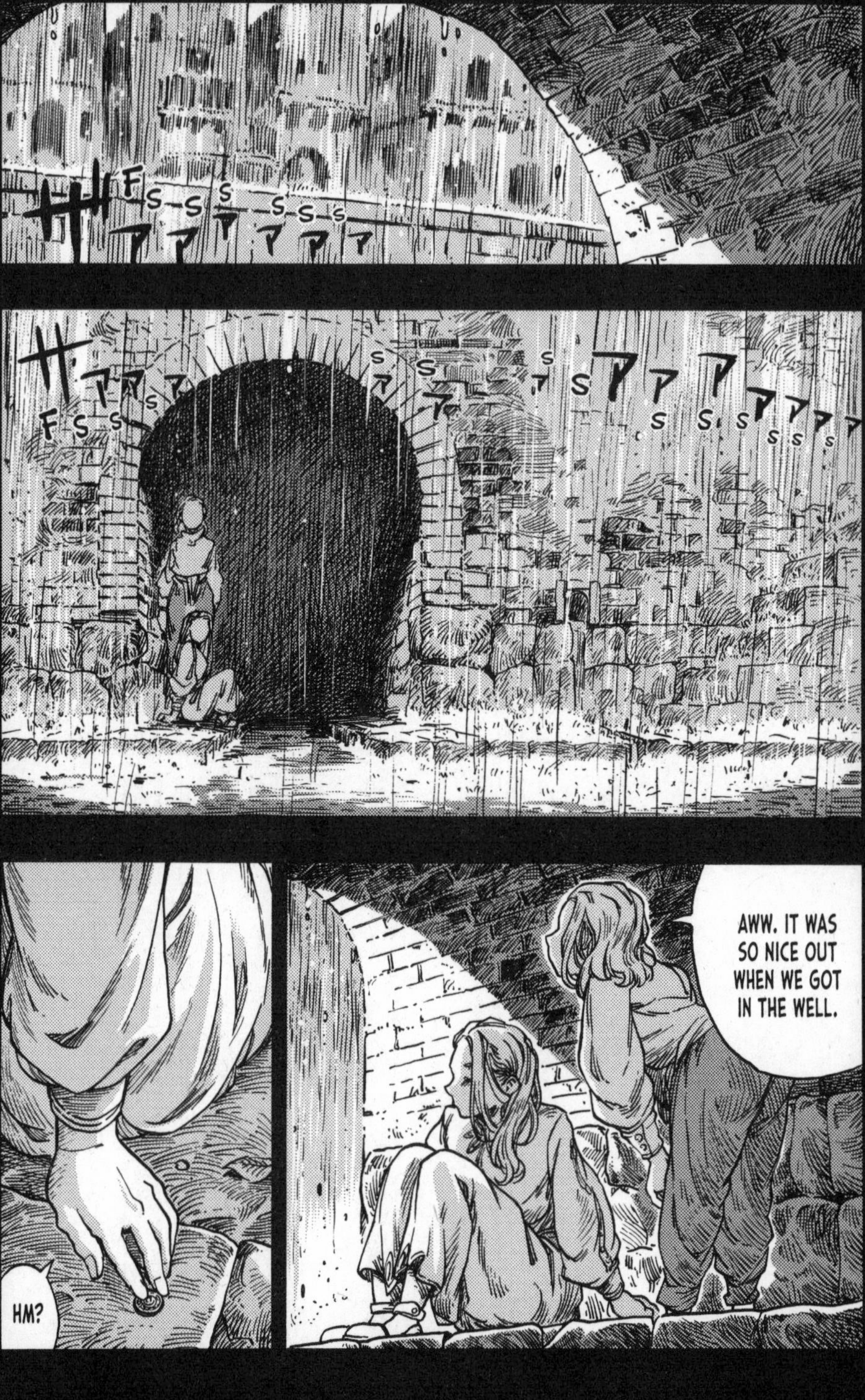
FSSSSSS
FSSSS
AWW. IT WAS SO NICE OUT WHEN WE GOT IN THE WELL.
HM?

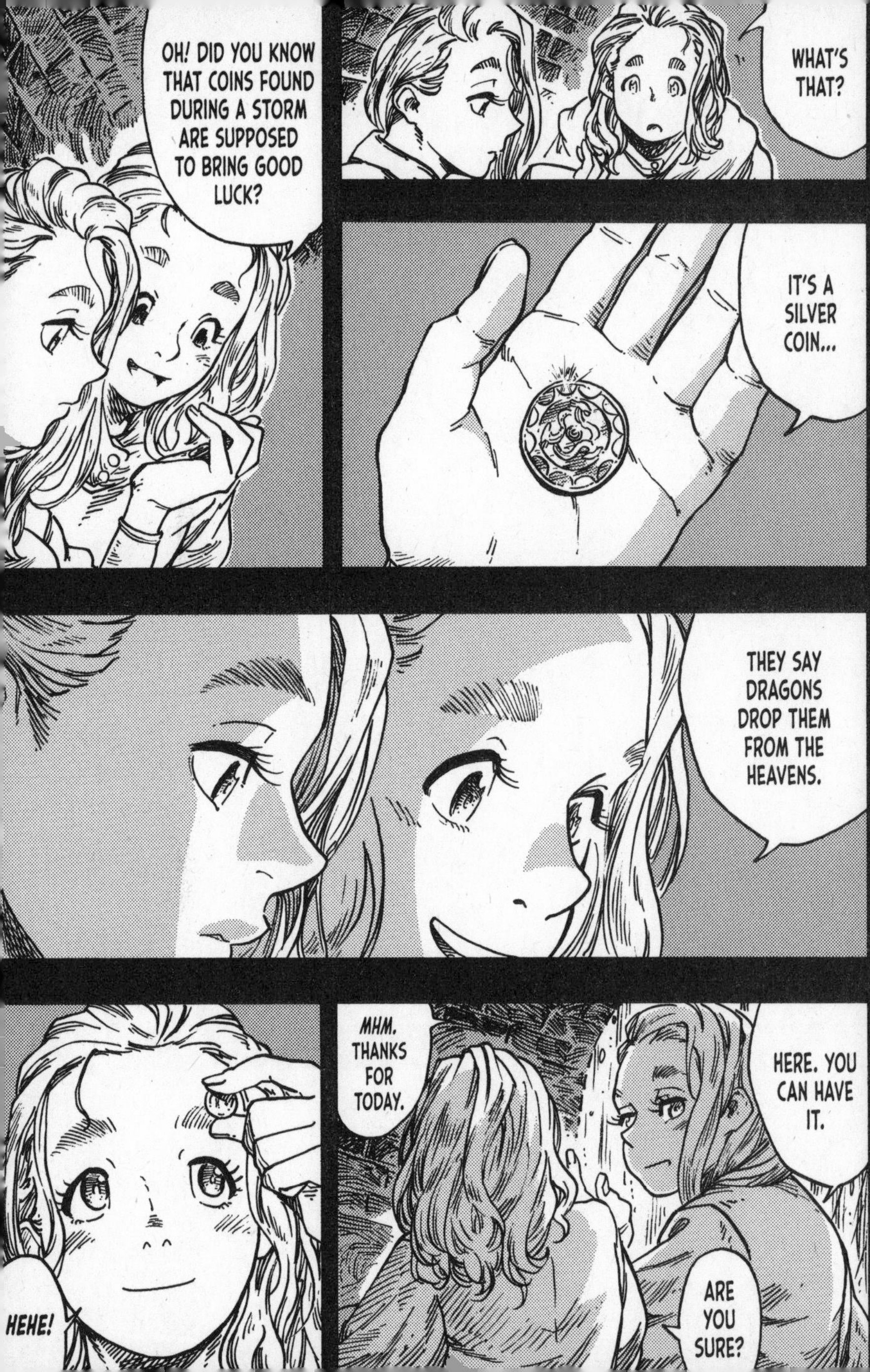
WHAT'S THAT?
IT'S A SILVER COIN...
OH! DID YOU KNOW THAT COINS FOUND DURING A STORM ARE SUPPOSED TO BRING GOOD LUCK?
THEY SAY DRAGONS DROP THEM FROM THE HEAVENS.
HERE. YOU CAN HAVE IT.
ARE YOU SURE?
MHM. THANKS FOR TODAY.
HEHE!

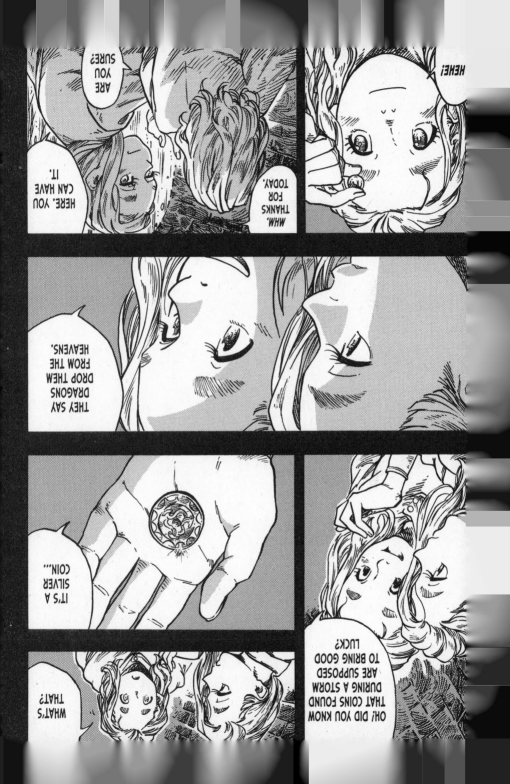

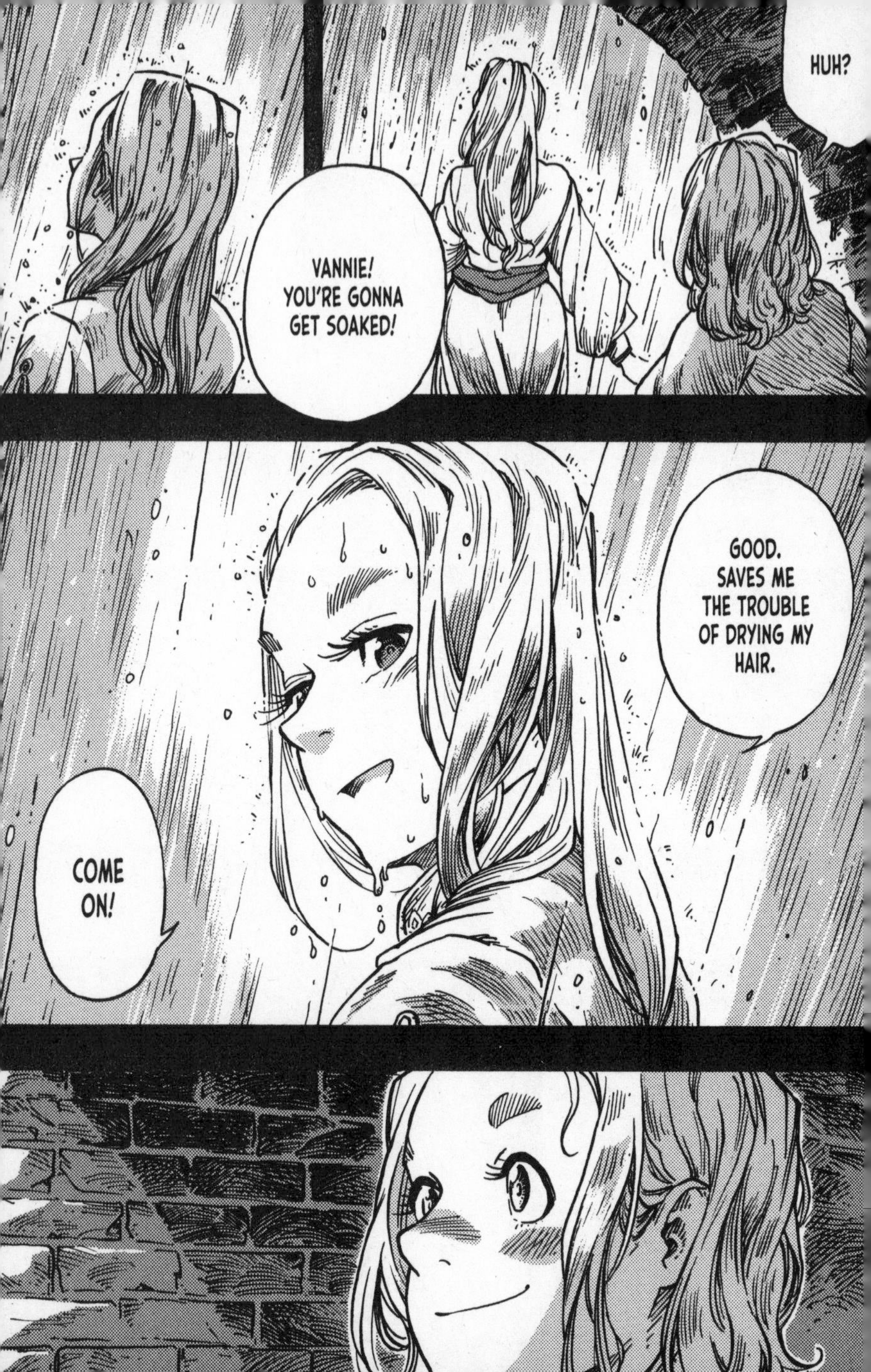
HUH?
VANNIE! YOU'RE GONNA GET SOAKED!
GOOD. SAVES ME THE TROUBLE OF DRYING MY HAIR.
COME ON!

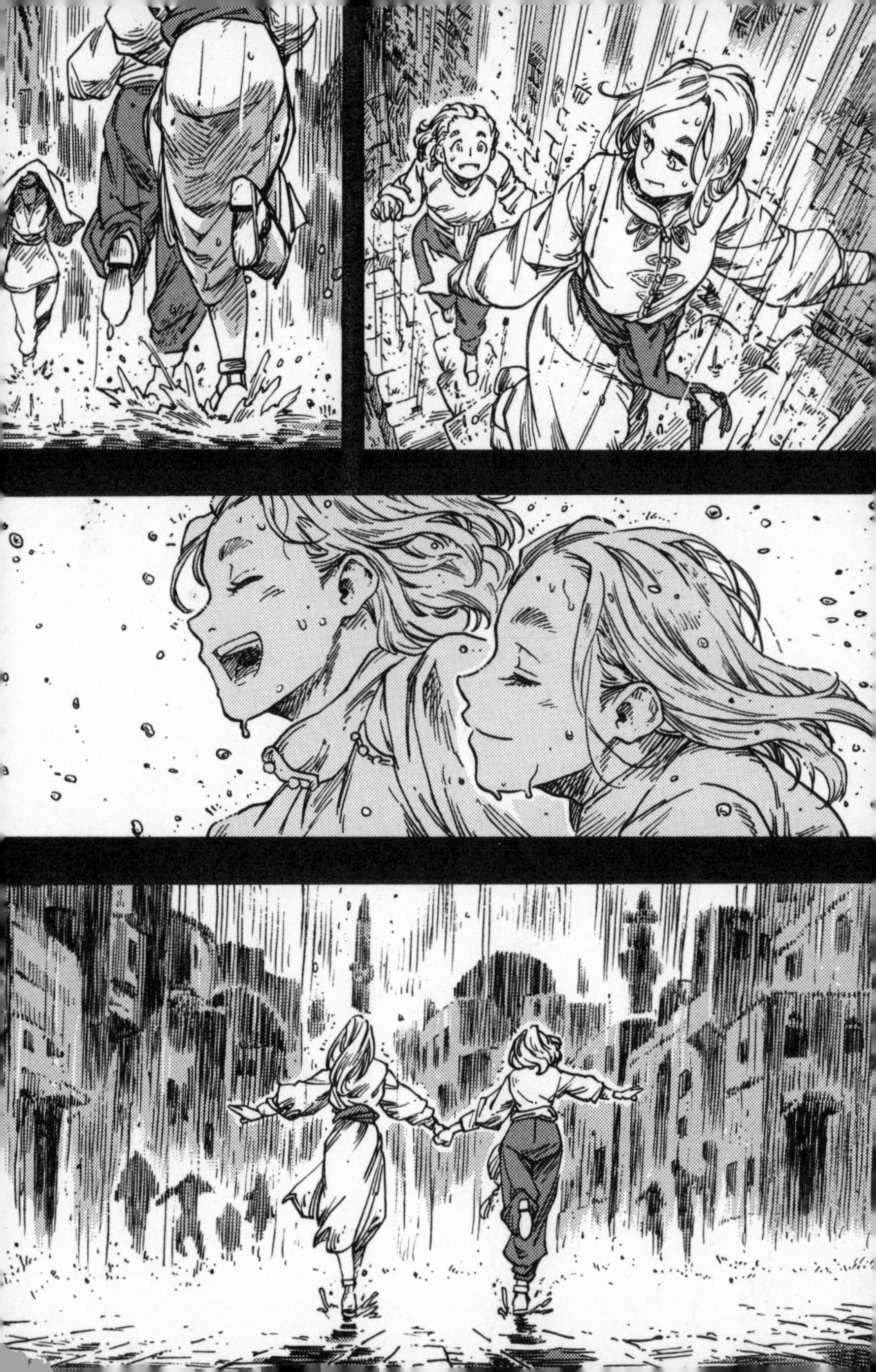

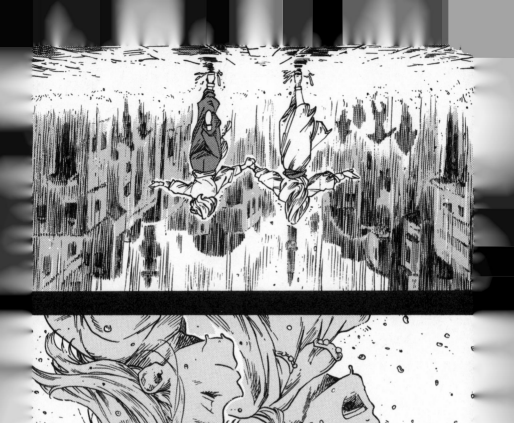

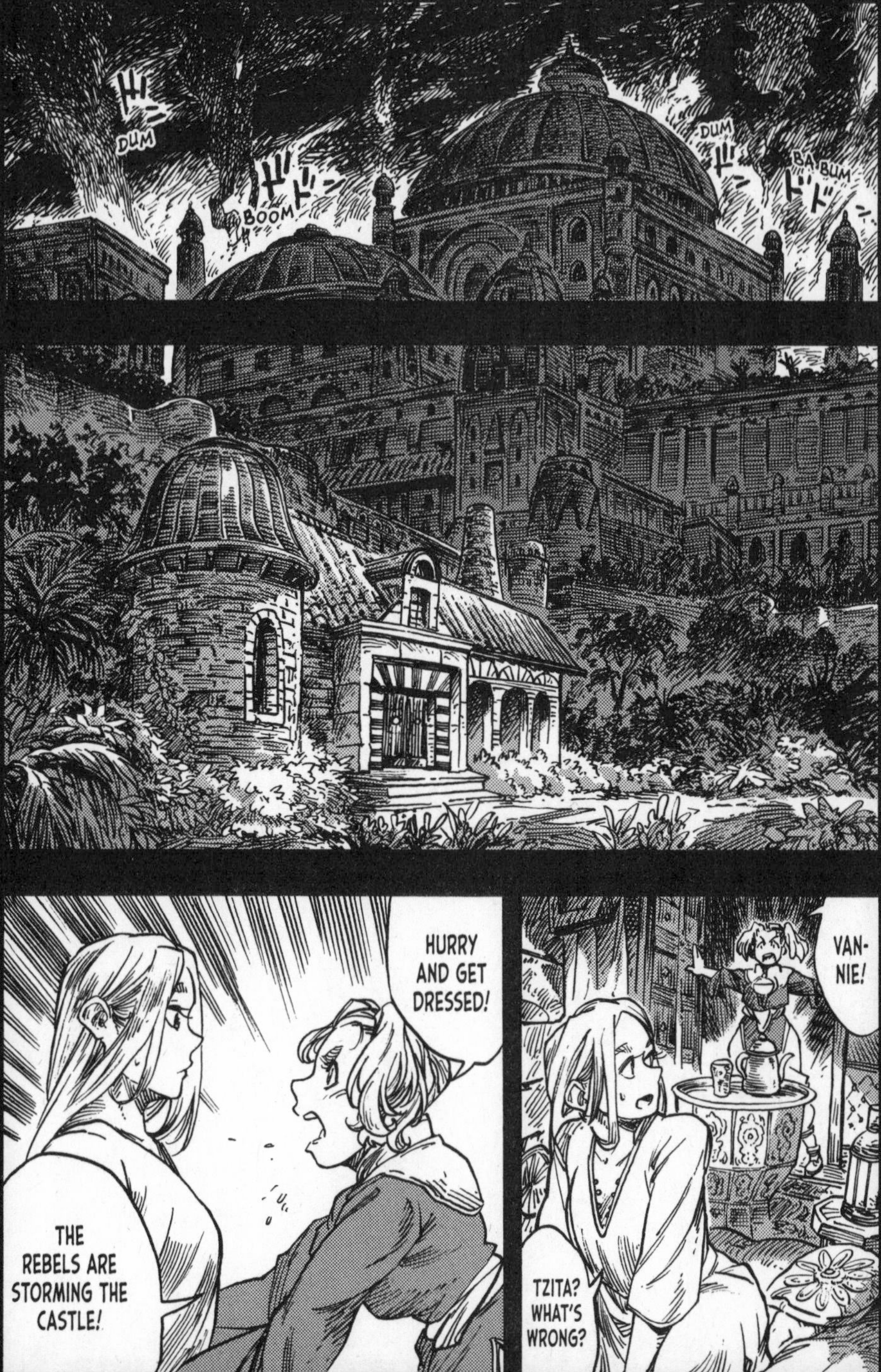
BA BUM
DUM
BOOM
DUM
VAN-NIE!
TZITA? WHAT'S WRONG?
HURRY AND GET DRESSED!
THE REBELS ARE STORMING THE CASTLE!

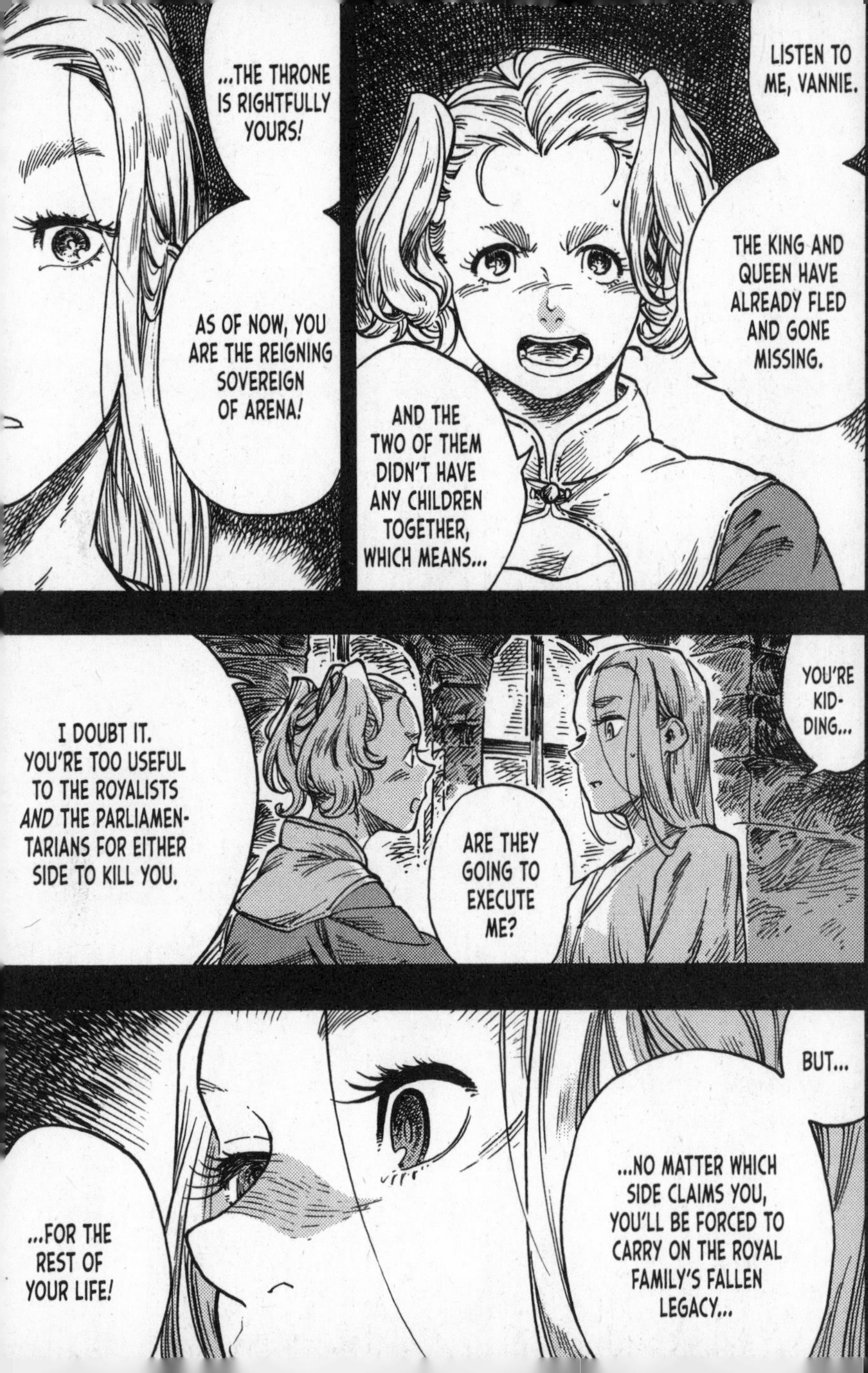
LISTEN TO ME, VANNIE.
THE KING AND QUEEN HAVE ALREADY FLED AND GONE MISSING.
AND THE TWO OF THEM DIDN'T HAVE ANY CHILDREN TOGETHER, WHICH MEANS...
AS OF NOW, YOU ARE THE REIGNING SOVEREIGN OF ARENA!
...THE THRONE IS RIGHTFULLY YOURS!
YOU'RE KID-DING...
ARE THEY GOING TO EXECUTE ME?
I DOUBT IT. YOU'RE TOO USEFUL TO THE ROYALISTS *AND* THE PARLIAMEN-TARIANS FOR EITHER SIDE TO KILL YOU.
BUT...
...NO MATTER WHICH SIDE CLAIMS YOU, YOU'LL BE FORCED TO CARRY ON THE ROYAL FAMILY'S FALLEN LEGACY...
...FOR THE REST OF YOUR LIFE!

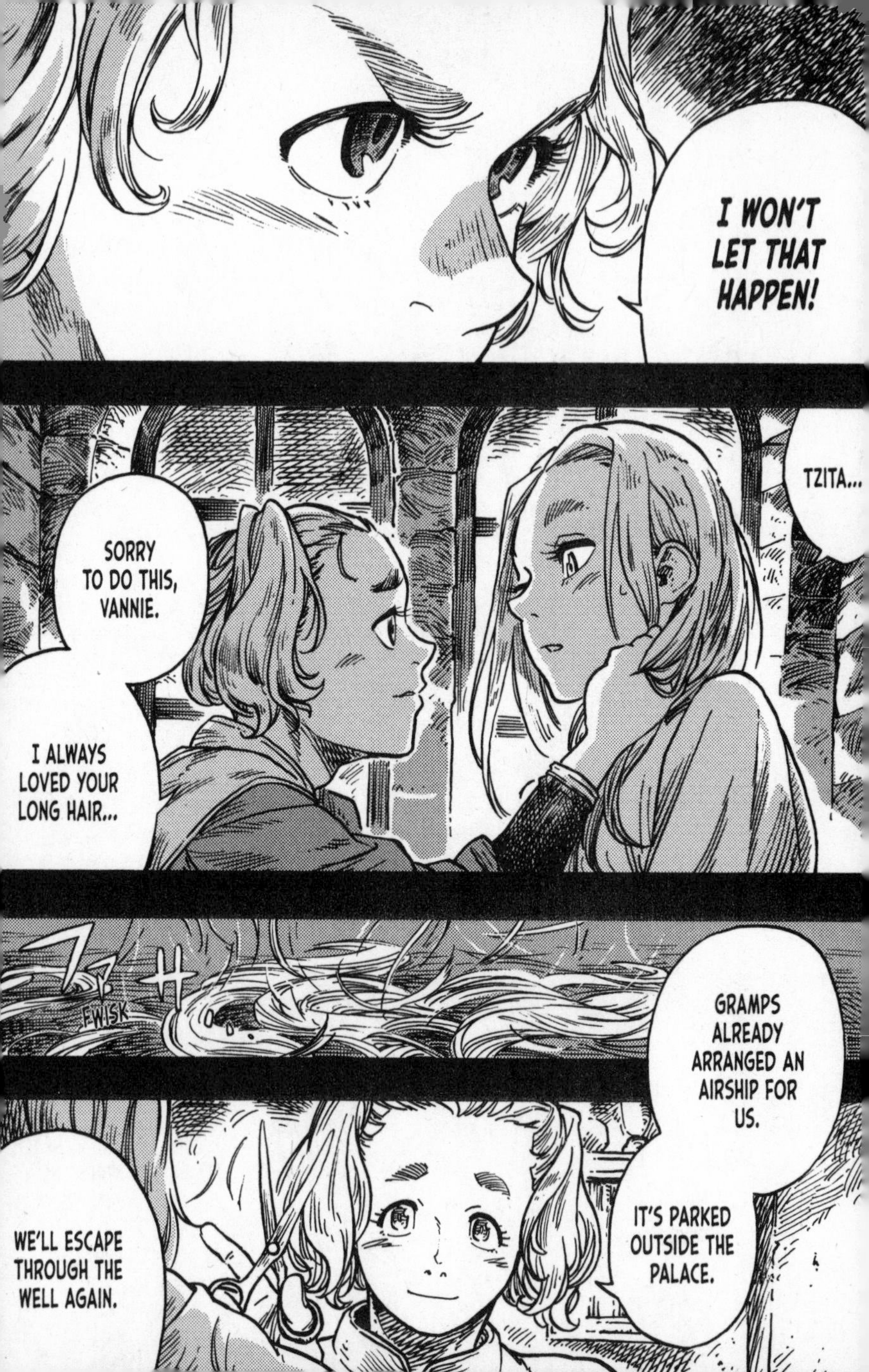
I WON'T LET THAT HAPPEN!
TZITA...
SORRY TO DO THIS, VANNIE.
I ALWAYS LOVED YOUR LONG HAIR...
FWISK
GRAMPS ALREADY ARRANGED AN AIRSHIP FOR US.
IT'S PARKED OUTSIDE THE PALACE.
WE'LL ESCAPE THROUGH THE WELL AGAIN.

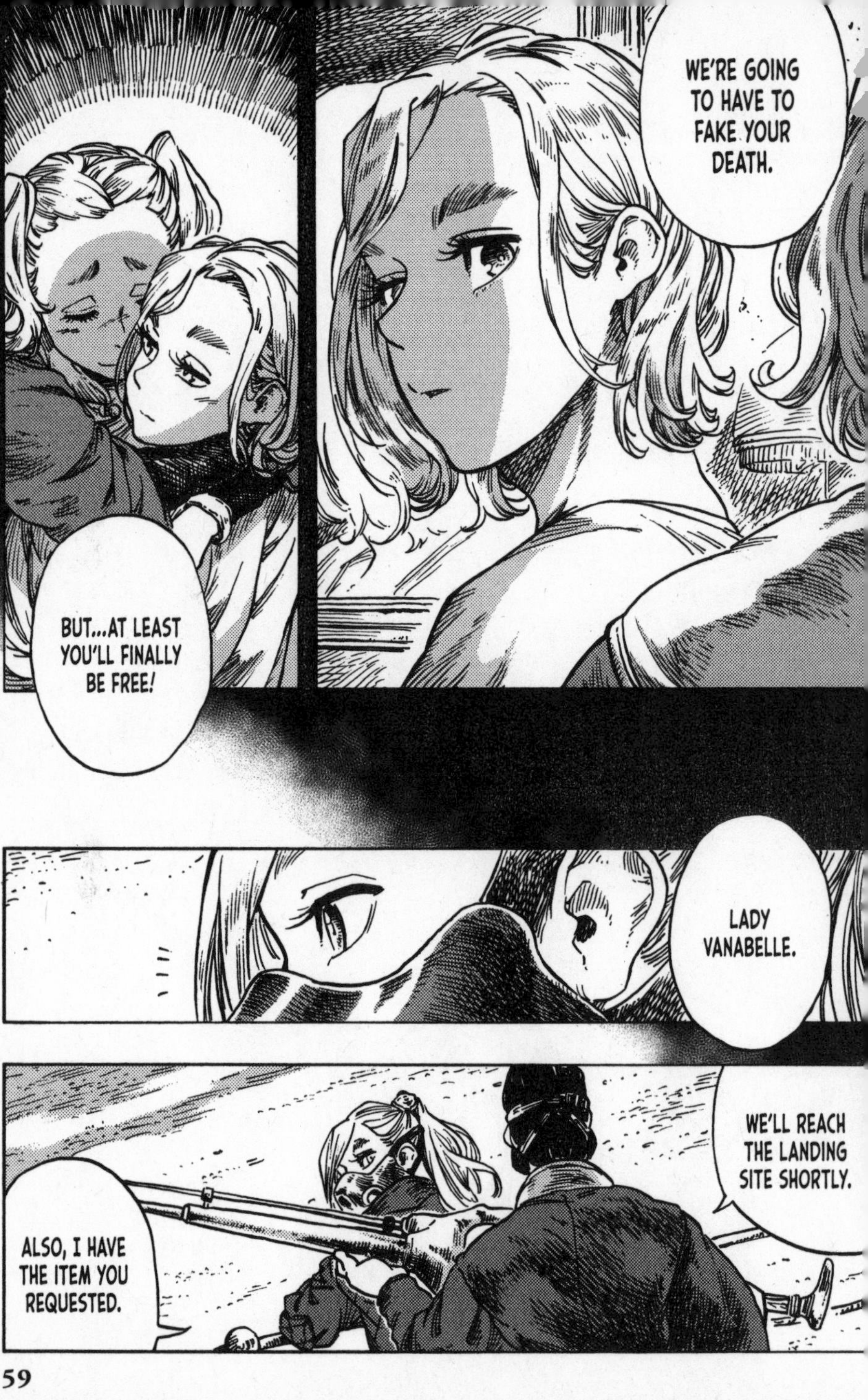
WE'RE GOING TO HAVE TO FAKE YOUR DEATH.
BUT...AT LEAST YOU'LL FINALLY BE FREE!
LADY VANABELLE.
WE'LL REACH THE LANDING SITE SHORTLY.
ALSO, I HAVE THE ITEM YOU REQUESTED.

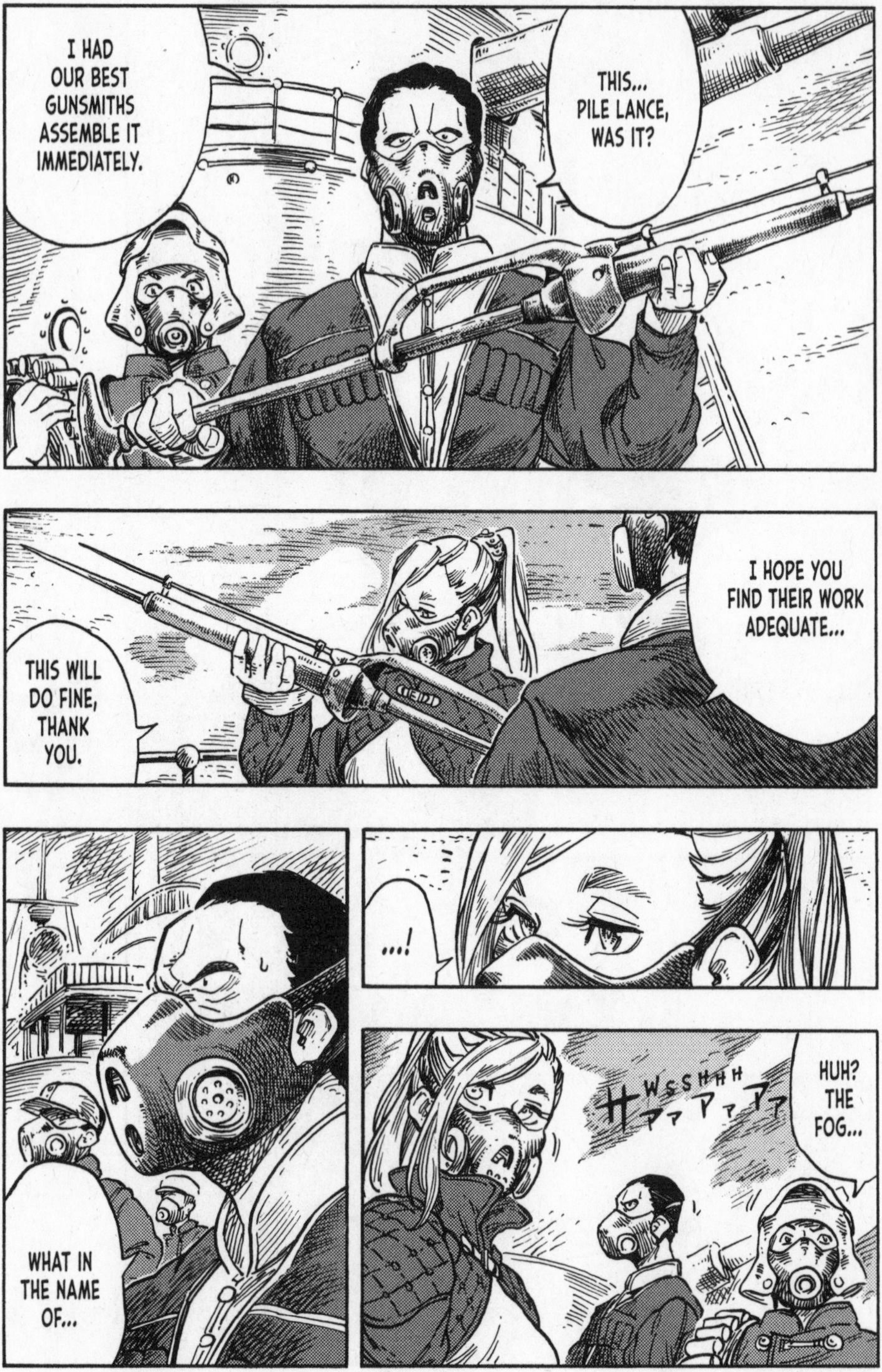
THIS... PILE LANCE, WAS IT?
I HAD OUR BEST GUNSMITHS ASSEMBLE IT IMMEDIATELY.
I HOPE YOU FIND THEIR WORK ADEQUATE...
THIS WILL DO FINE, THANK YOU.
...!
HUH? THE FOG...
WSSHHH
WHAT IN THE NAME OF...

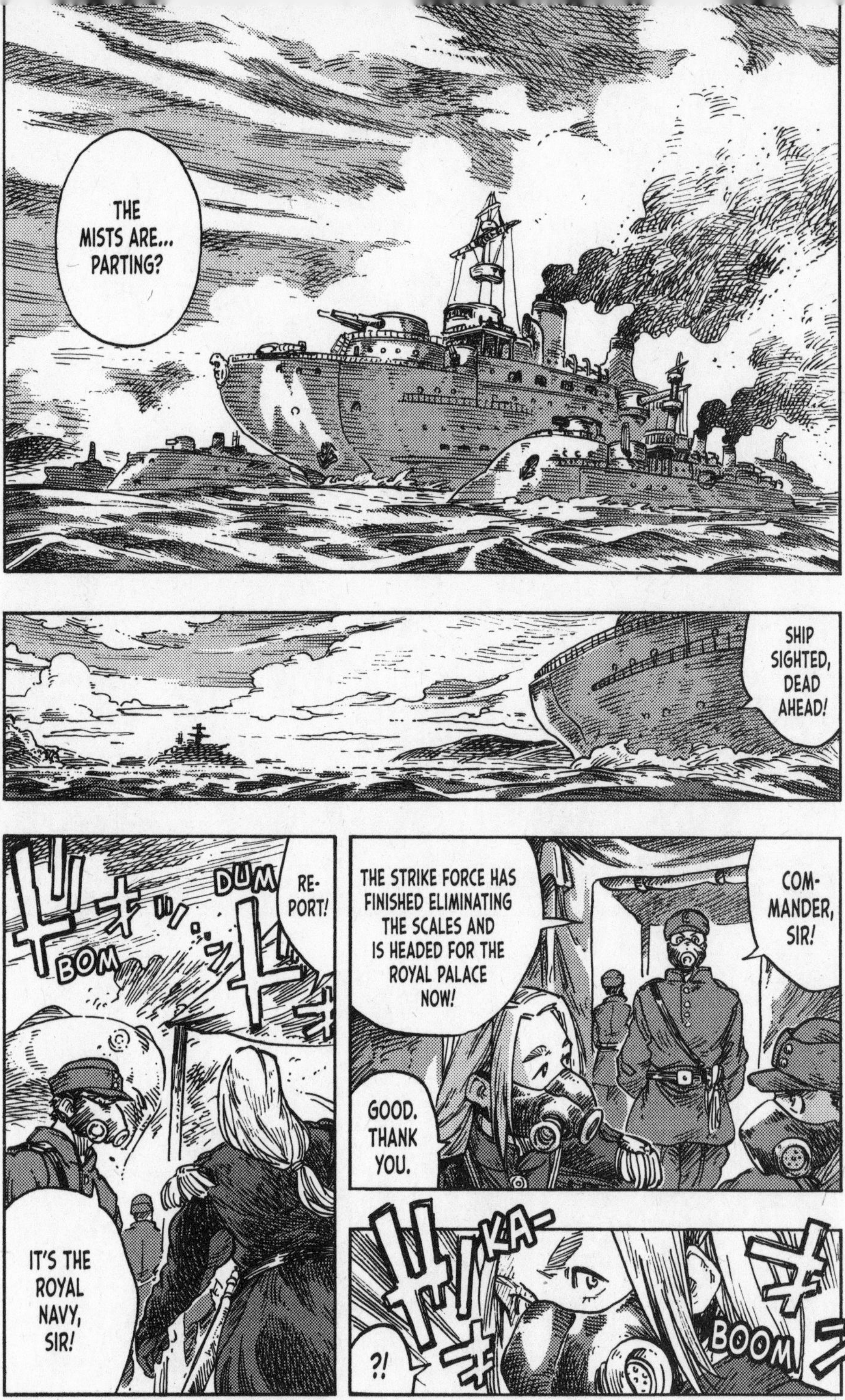
THE MISTS ARE... PARTING?
SHIP SIGHTED, DEAD AHEAD!
COM-MANDER, SIR!
THE STRIKE FORCE HAS FINISHED ELIMINATING THE SCALES AND IS HEADED FOR THE ROYAL PALACE NOW!
GOOD. THANK YOU.
BOOM
?!
KA-
RE-PORT!
DUM
BOM
IT'S THE ROYAL NAVY, SIR!

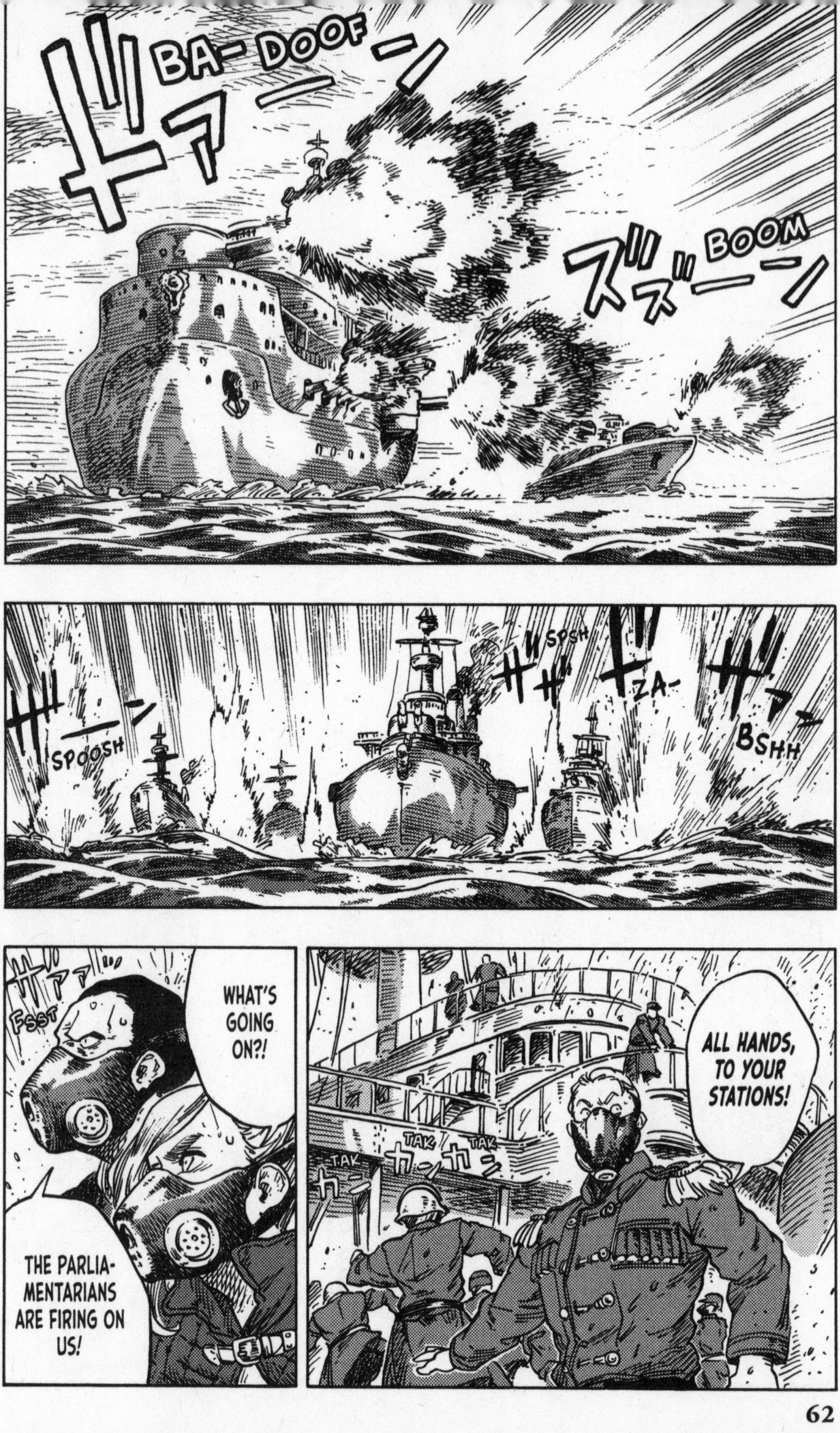
BA-DOOF
BOOM
SPOOSH
SPSH
ZA-
BSHH
ALL HANDS, TO YOUR STATIONS!
TAK
TAK
TAK
WHAT'S GOING ON?!
FSST
THE PARLIA-MENTARIANS ARE FIRING ON US!

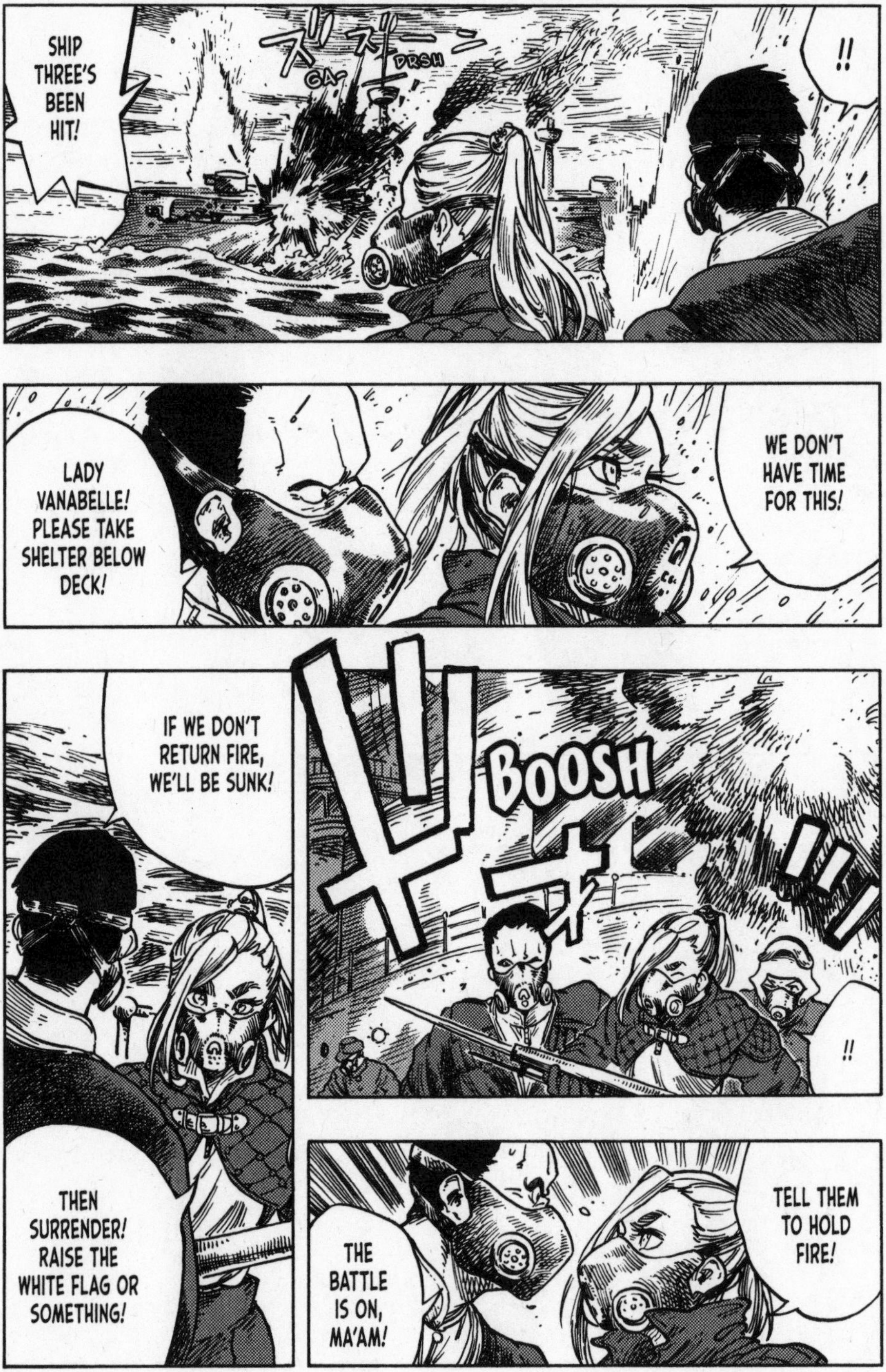
!!
GA-
DRSH
SHIP THREE'S BEEN HIT!
WE DON'T HAVE TIME FOR THIS!
LADY VANABELLE! PLEASE TAKE SHELTER BELOW DECK!
BOOSH
!!
TELL THEM TO HOLD FIRE!
THE BATTLE IS ON, MA'AM!
IF WE DON'T RETURN FIRE, WE'LL BE SUNK!
THEN SURRENDER! RAISE THE WHITE FLAG OR SOMETHING!

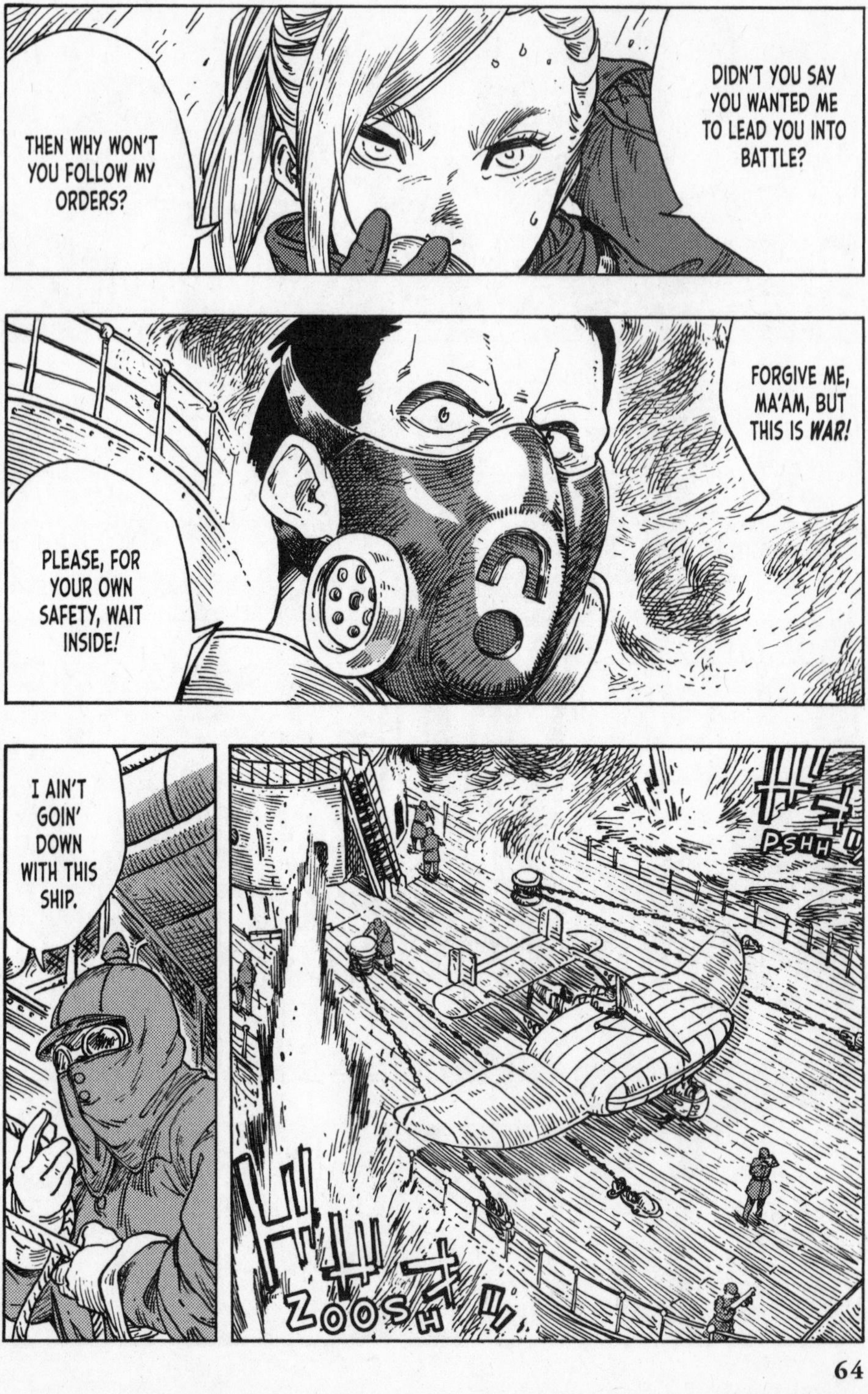
DIDN'T YOU SAY YOU WANTED ME TO LEAD YOU INTO BATTLE?
THEN WHY WON'T YOU FOLLOW MY ORDERS?
FORGIVE ME, MA'AM, BUT THIS IS *WAR!*
PLEASE, FOR YOUR OWN SAFETY, WAIT INSIDE!
PSHH!!
ZOOSH!!
I AIN'T GOIN' DOWN WITH THIS SHIP.

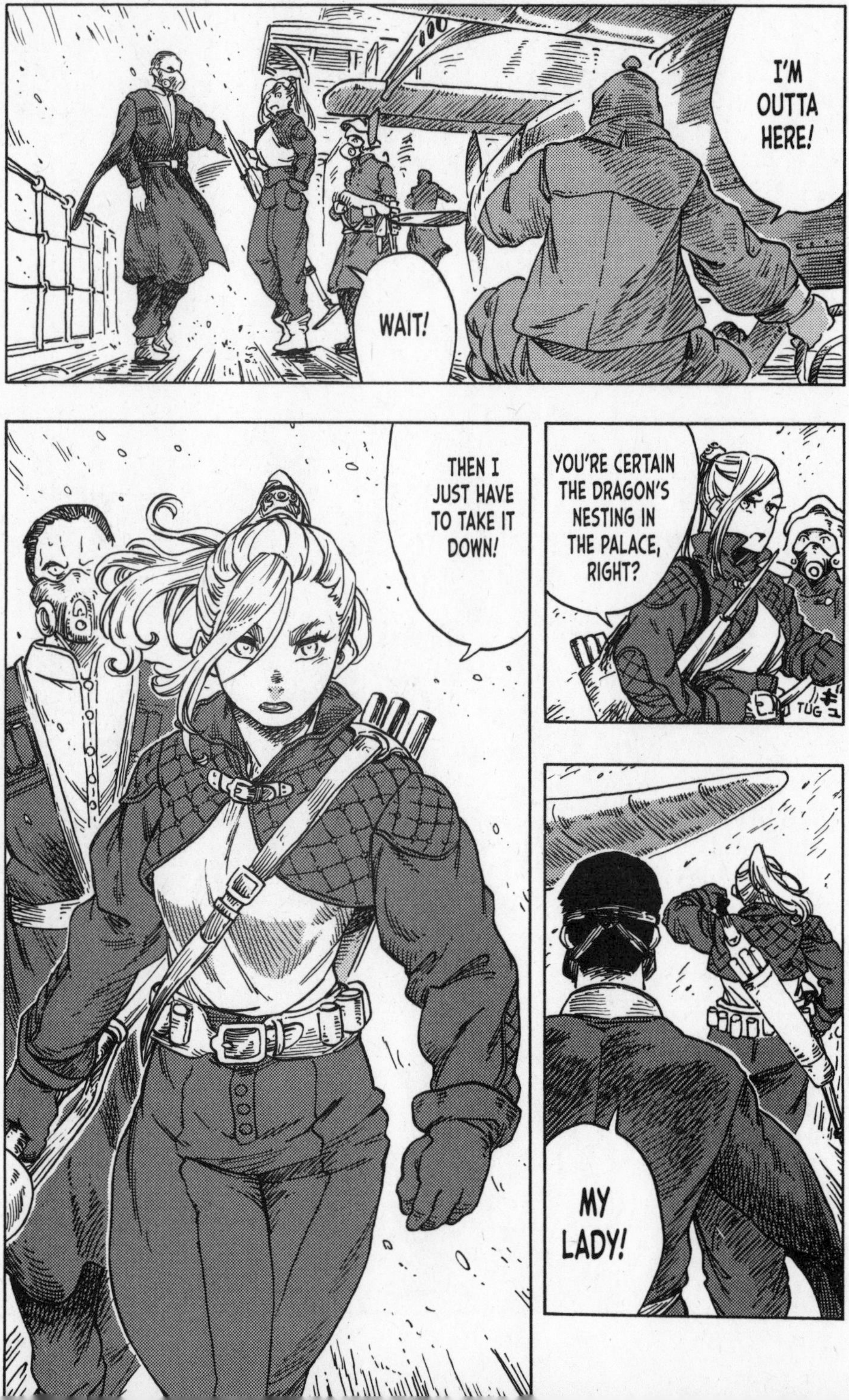
I'M OUTTA HERE!
WAIT!
YOU'RE CERTAIN THE DRAGON'S NESTING IN THE PALACE, RIGHT?
TUG
MY LADY!
THEN I JUST HAVE TO TAKE IT DOWN!

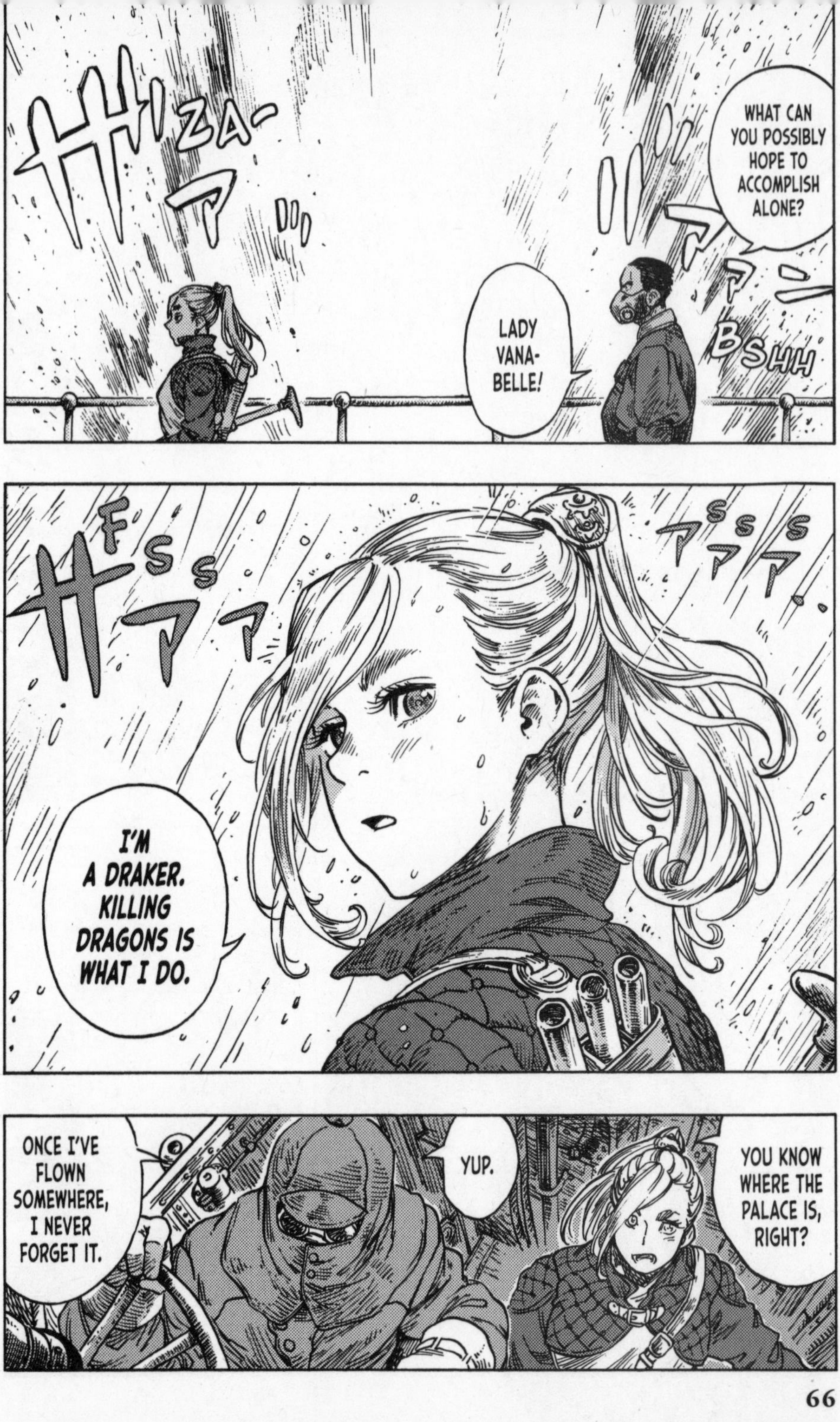
WHAT CAN YOU POSSIBLY HOPE TO ACCOMPLISH ALONE?
BSHH
LADY VANA-BELLE!
ZA-
FSS
SSS
I'M A DRAKER. KILLING DRAGONS IS WHAT I DO.
YOU KNOW WHERE THE PALACE IS, RIGHT?
YUP.
ONCE I'VE FLOWN SOMEWHERE, I NEVER FORGET IT.

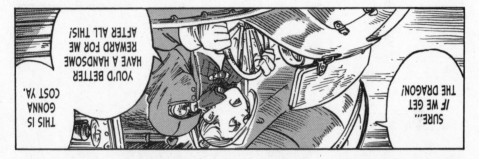

THIS IS GONNA COST YA.

YOU'D BETTER HAVE A HANDSOME REWARD FOR ME AFTER ALL THIS!

SURE.... IF WE GET THE DRAGON!

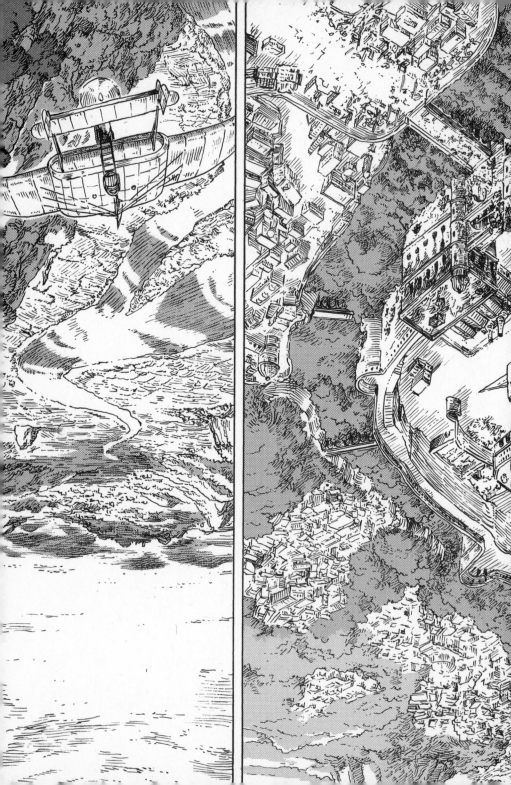

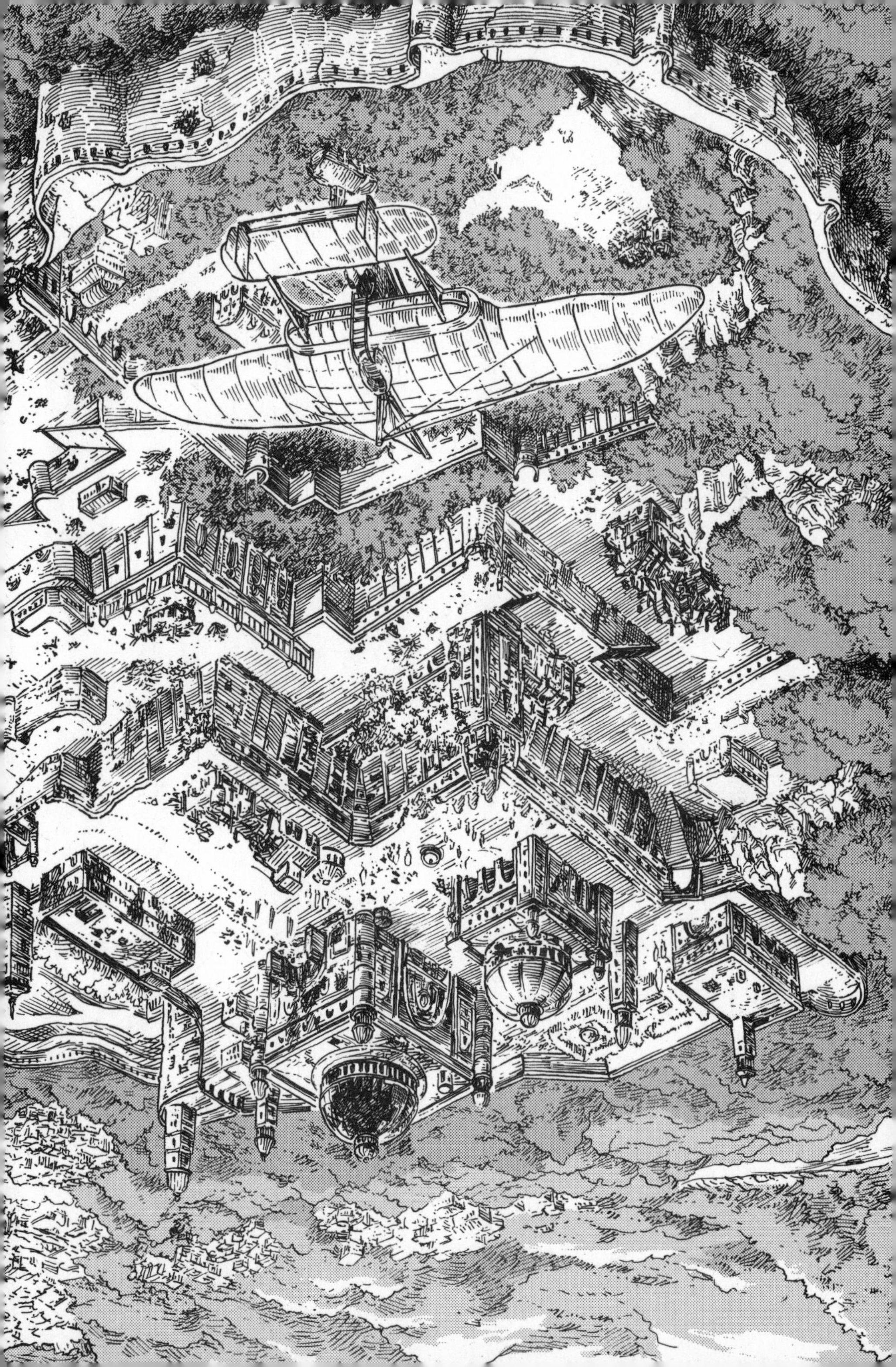

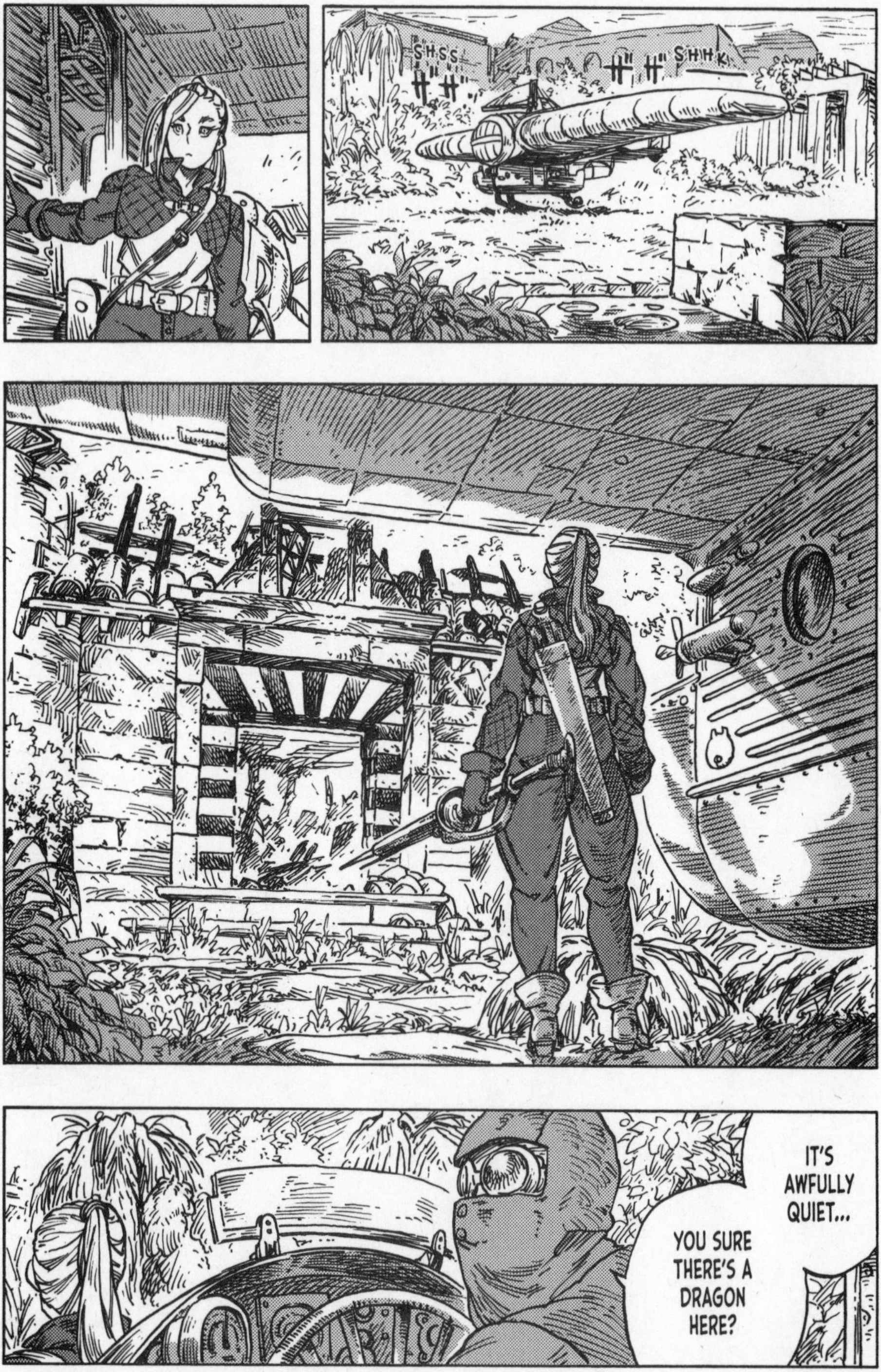
SHHK
SHSS
IT'S AWFULLY QUIET...
YOU SURE THERE'S A DRAGON HERE?

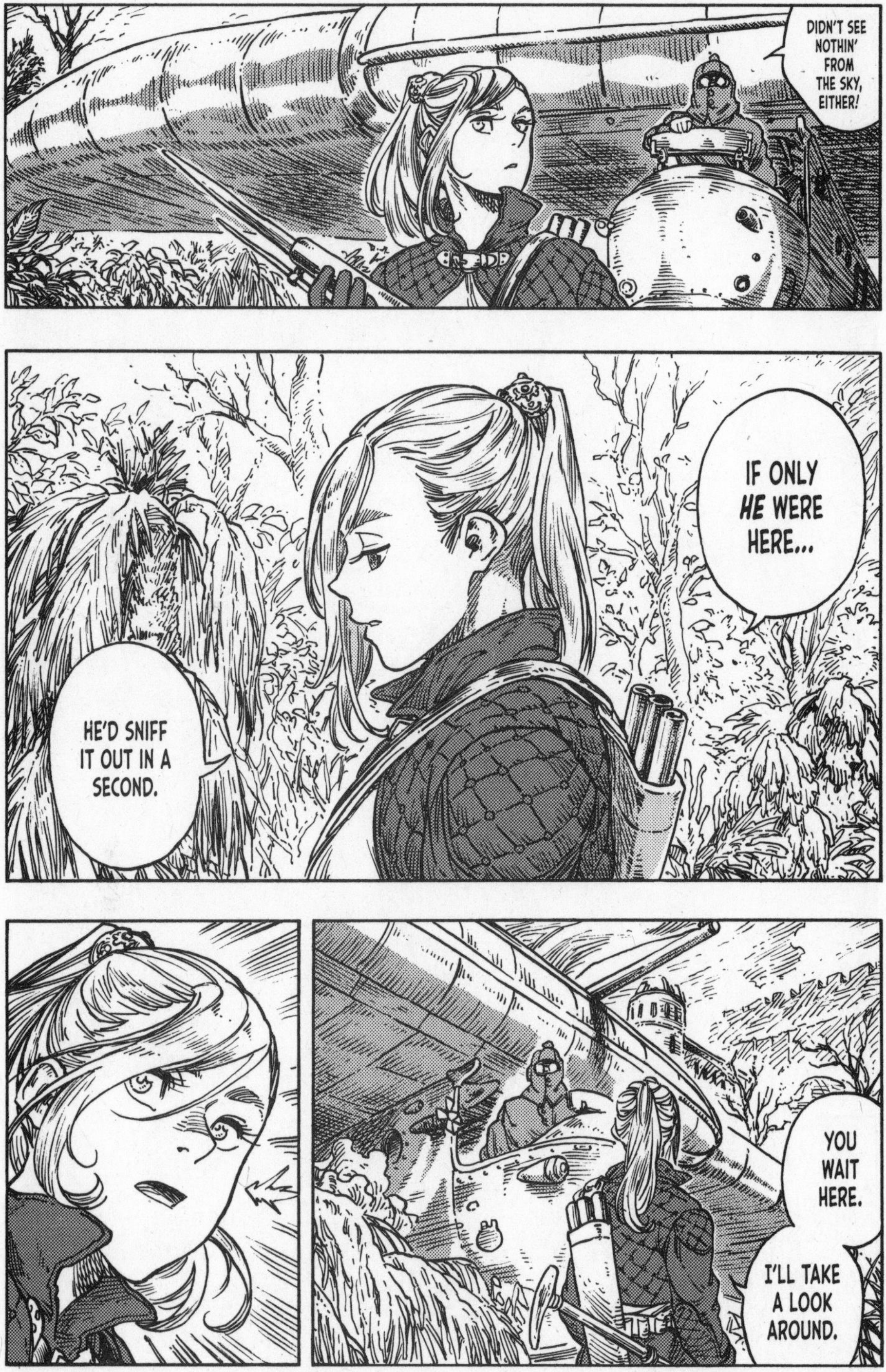
DIDN'T SEE NOTHIN' FROM THE SKY, EITHER!
IF ONLY *HE* WERE HERE...
HE'D SNIFF IT OUT IN A SECOND.
YOU WAIT HERE.
I'LL TAKE A LOOK AROUND.

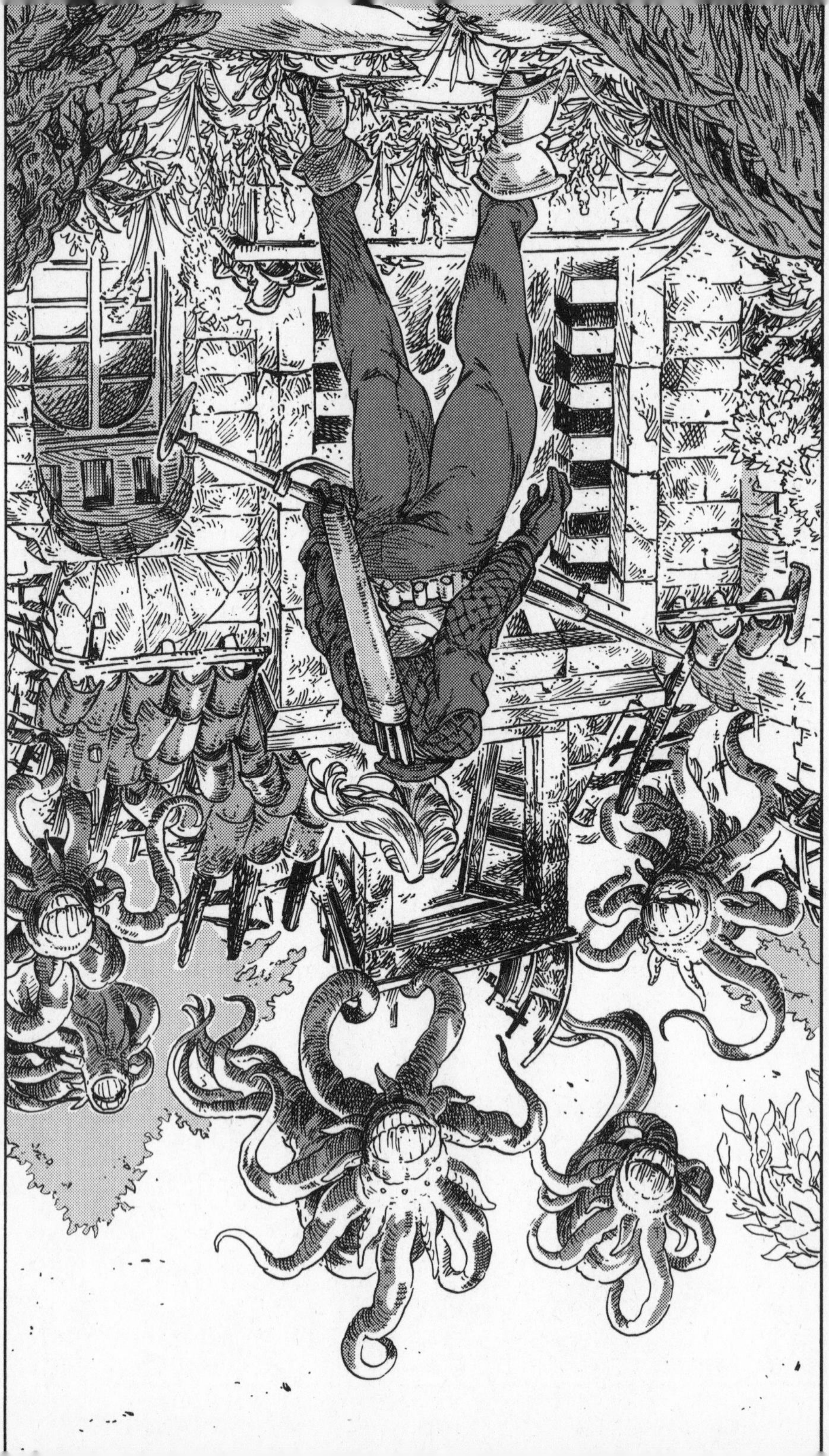

Flight 59 Solo Battle

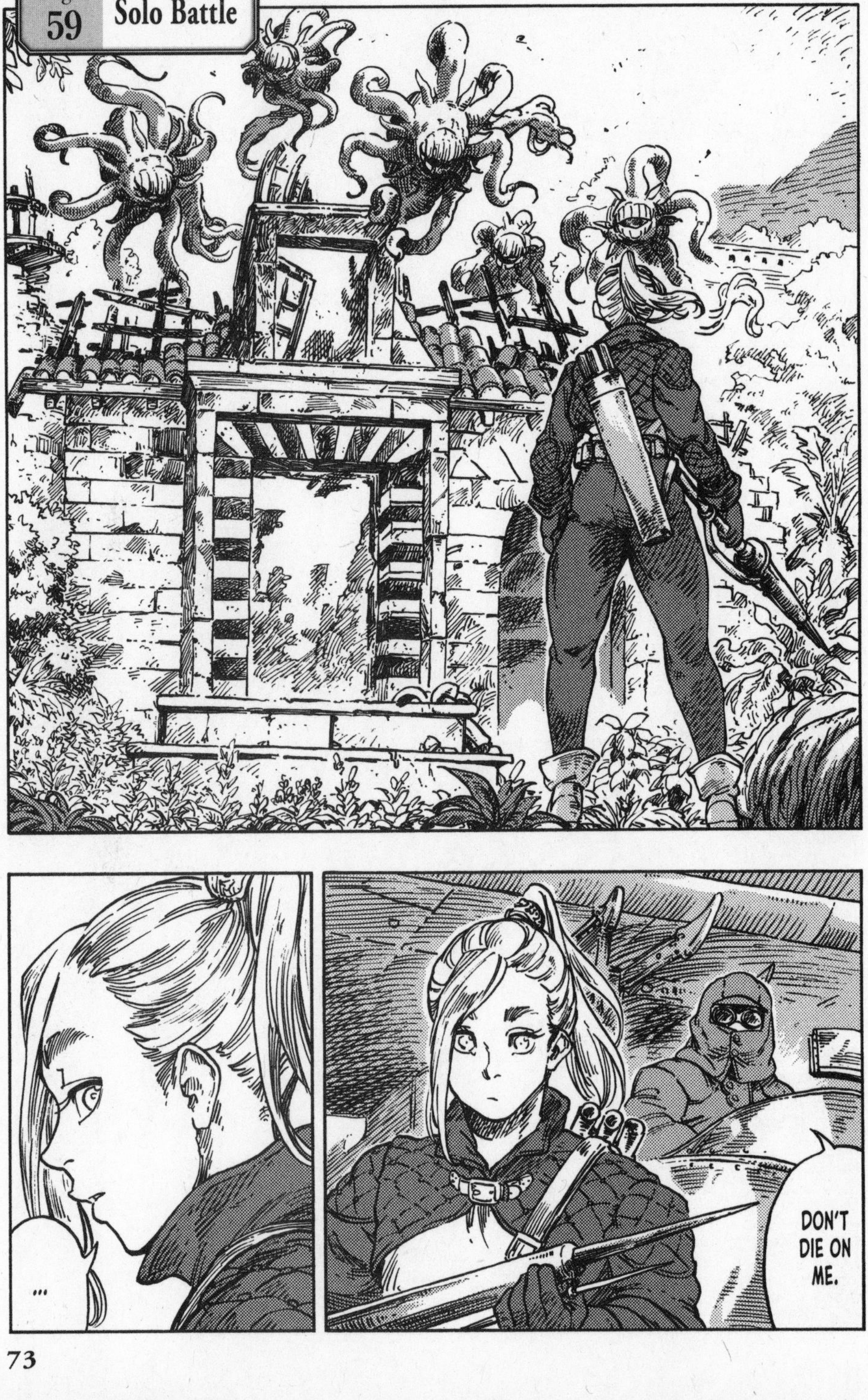
DON'T DIE ON ME.
...

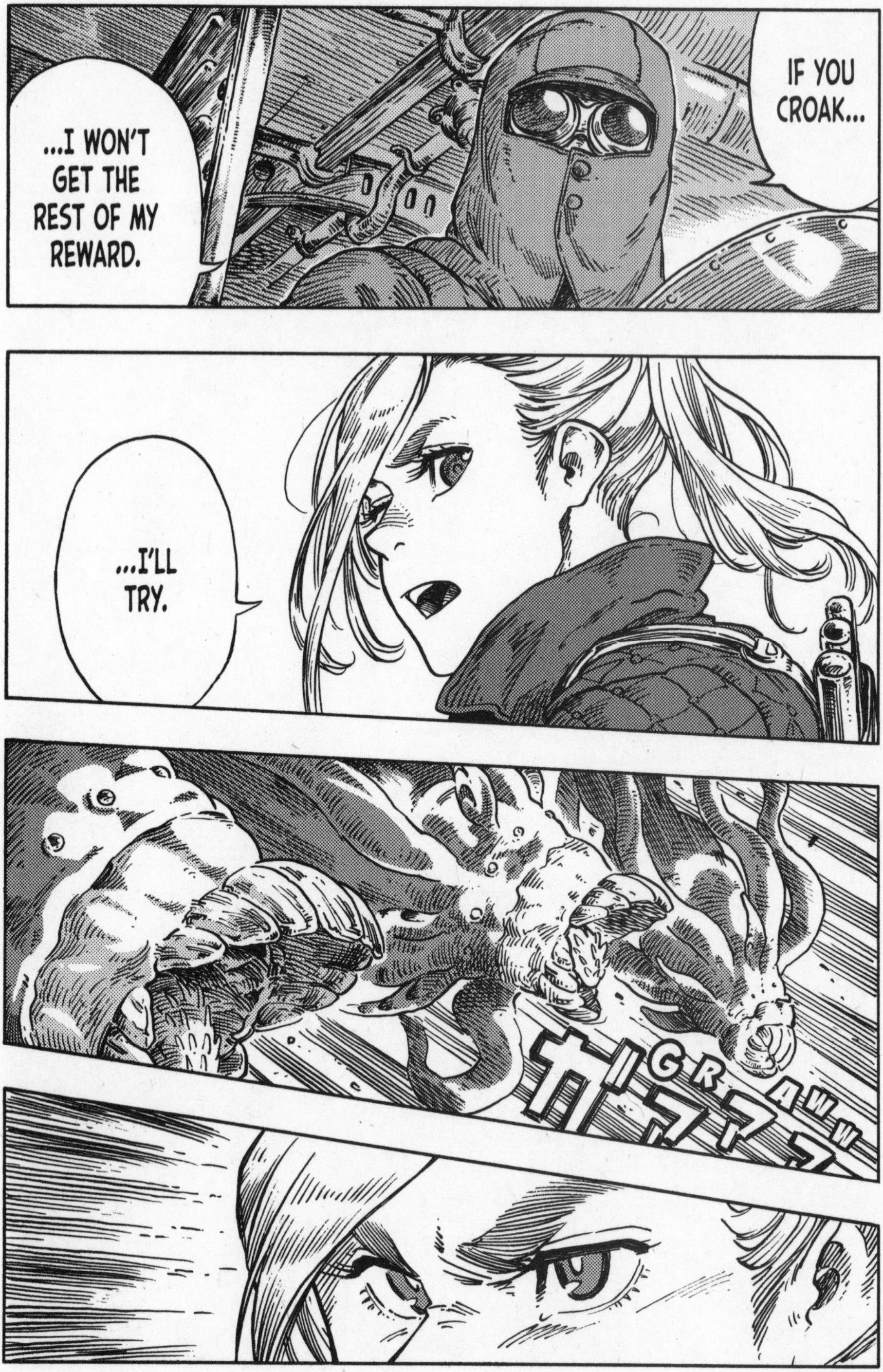
IF YOU CROAK...
...I WON'T GET THE REST OF MY REWARD.
...I'LL TRY.
GRAWW

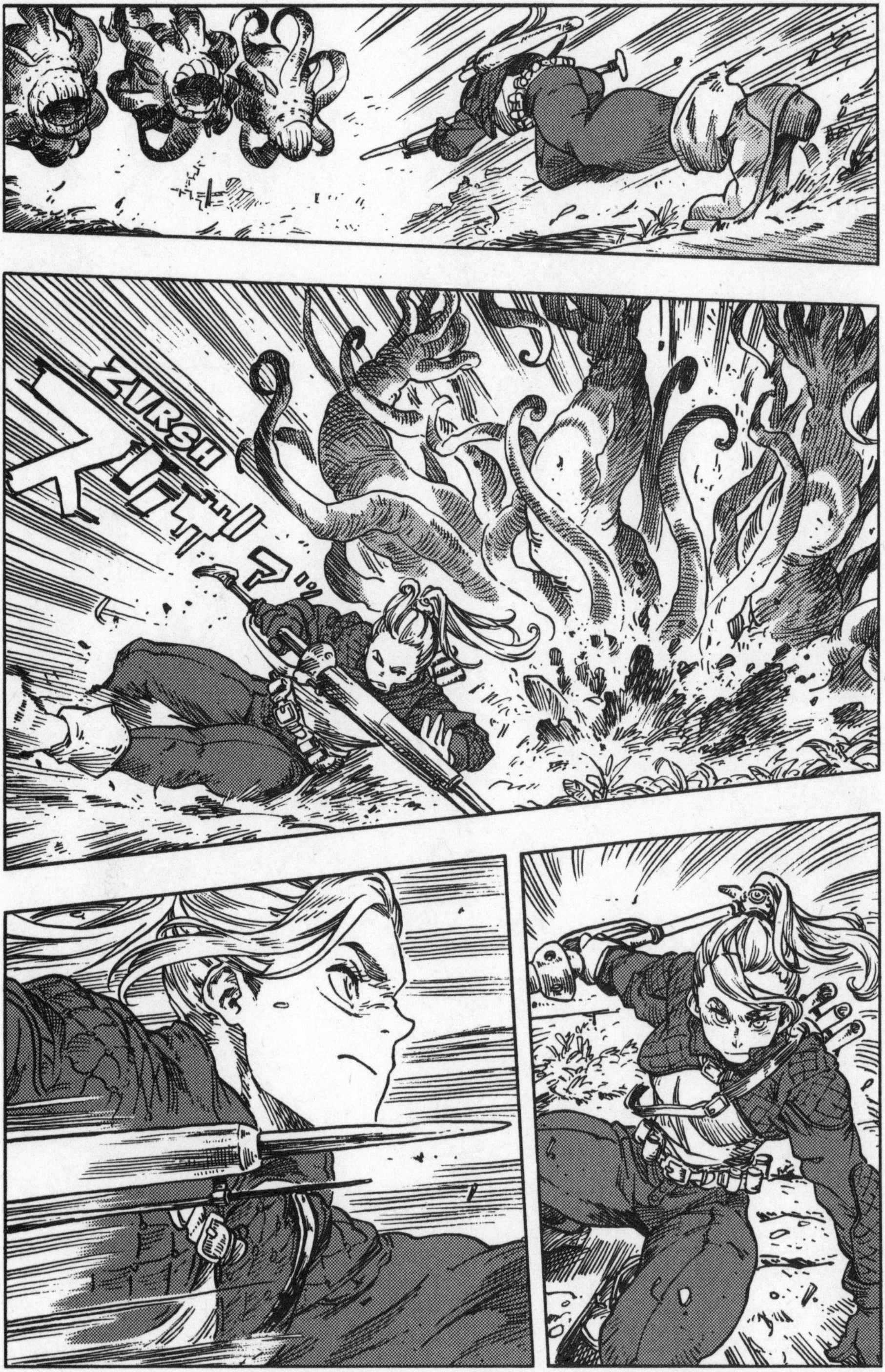
ZURSH

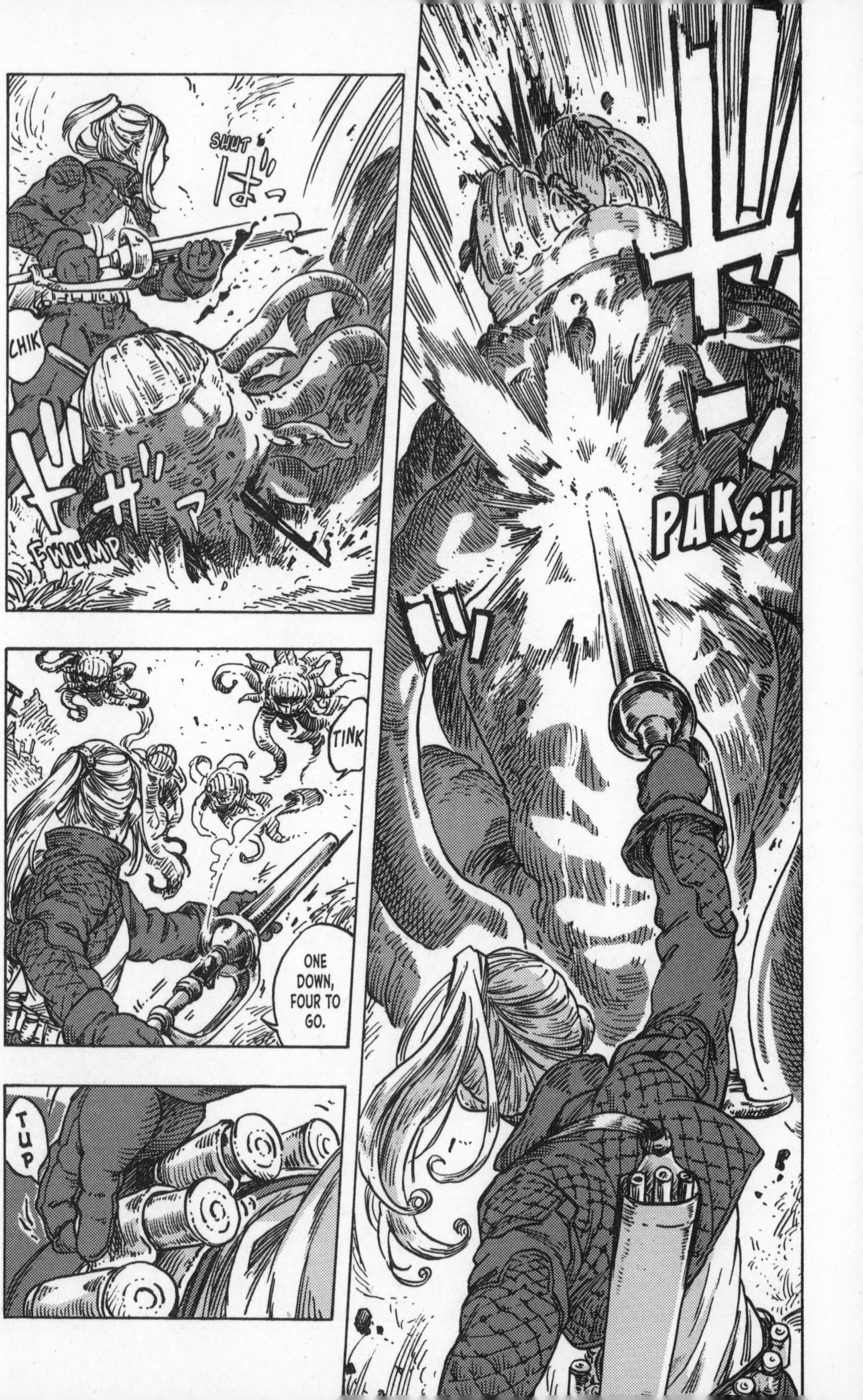
PAKSH
SHUT
ばっ
CHIK
FWUMP
TINK
ONE DOWN, FOUR TO GO.
TUP

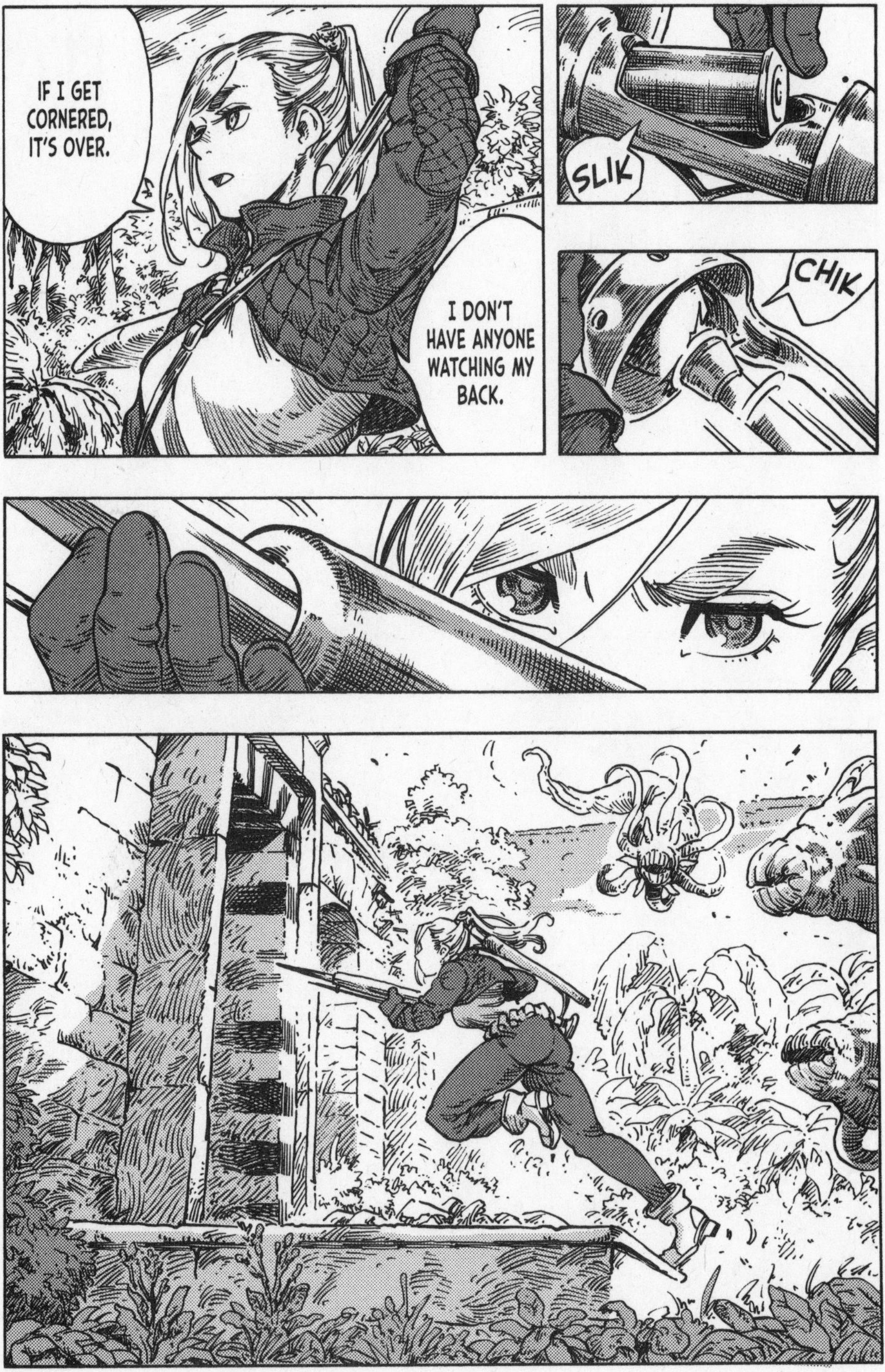
SLIK
CHIK
IF I GET CORNERED, IT'S OVER.
I DON'T HAVE ANYONE WATCHING MY BACK.

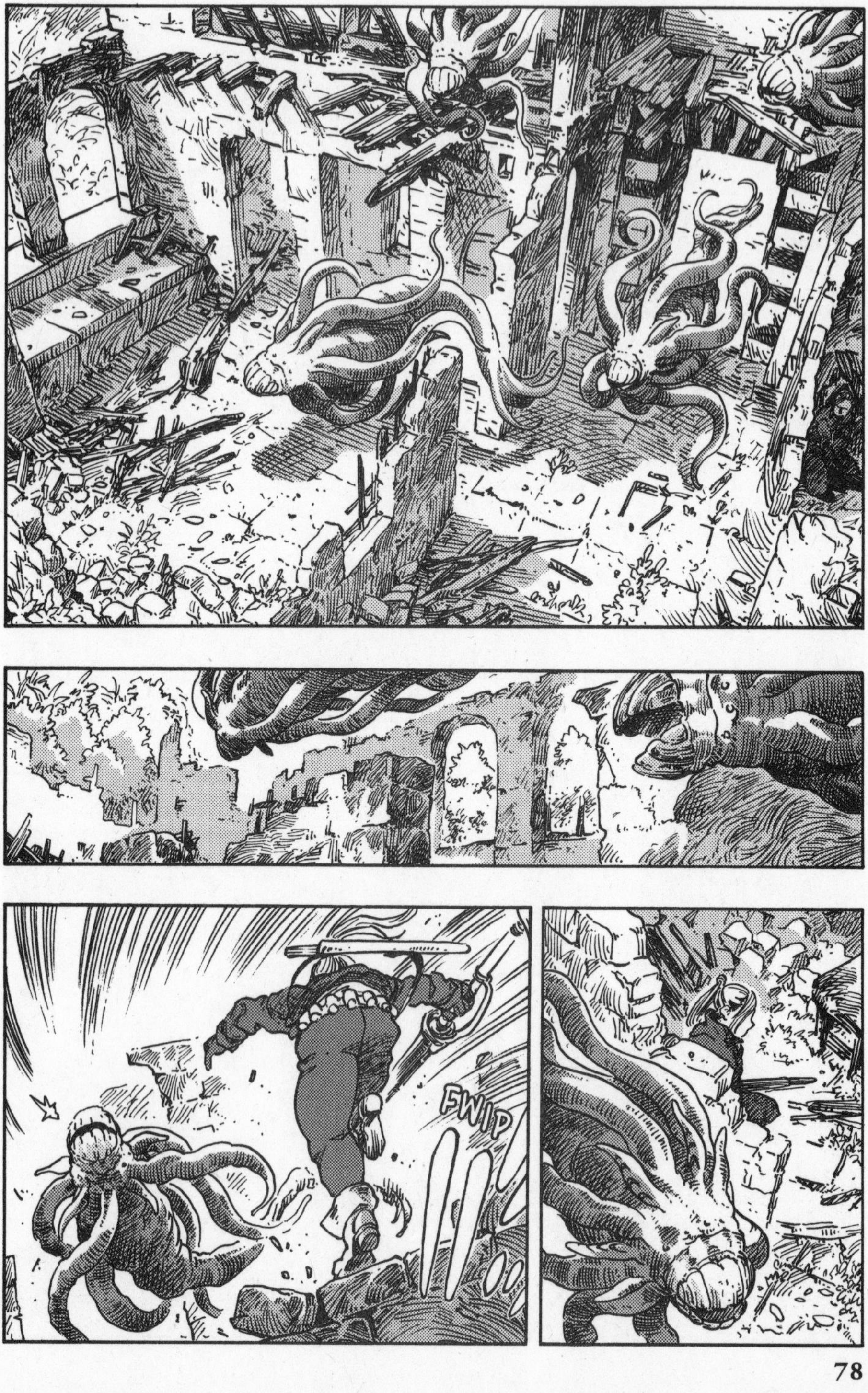
FWIP

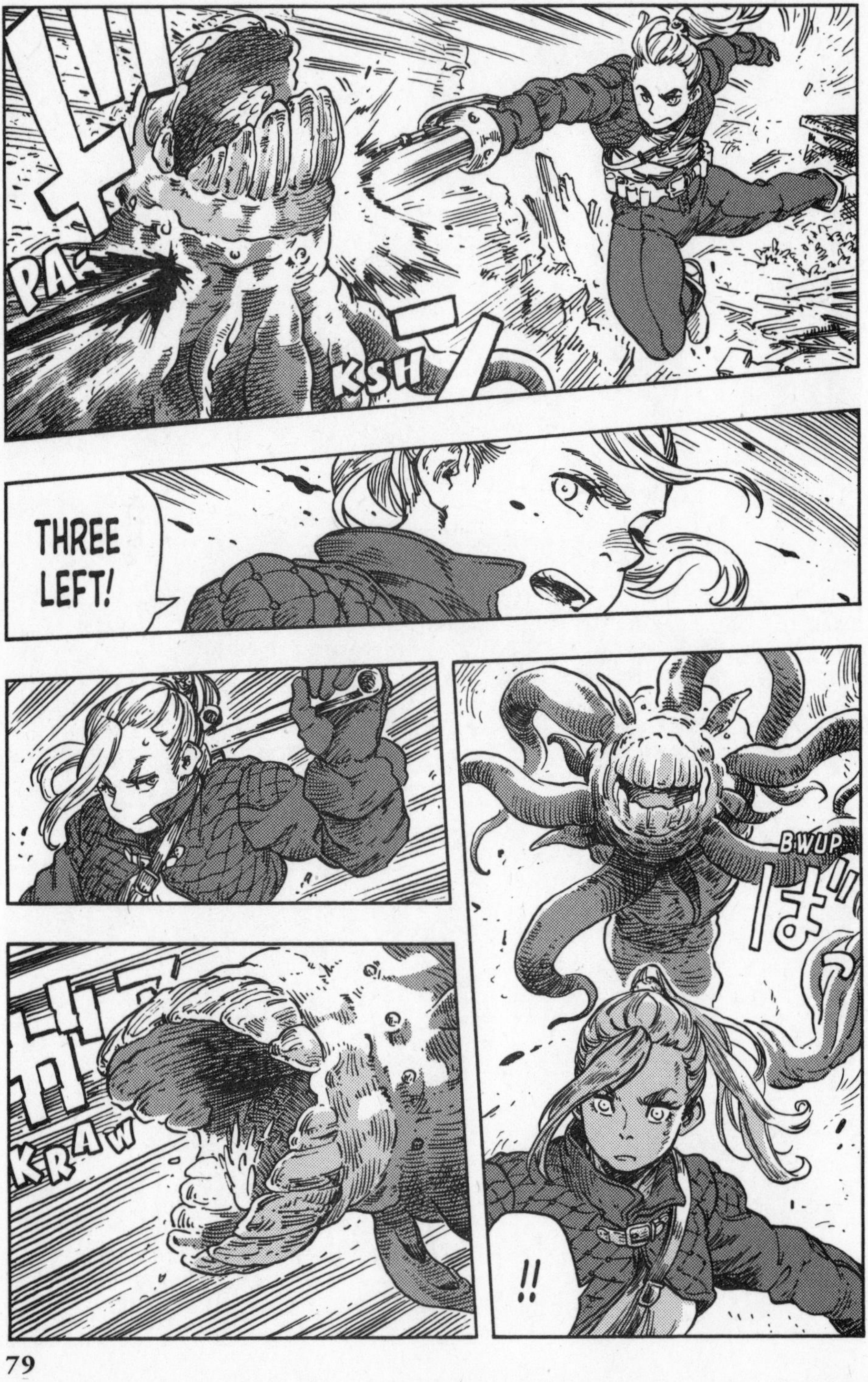
PA-
KSH
THREE LEFT!
BWUP
!!
KRAW

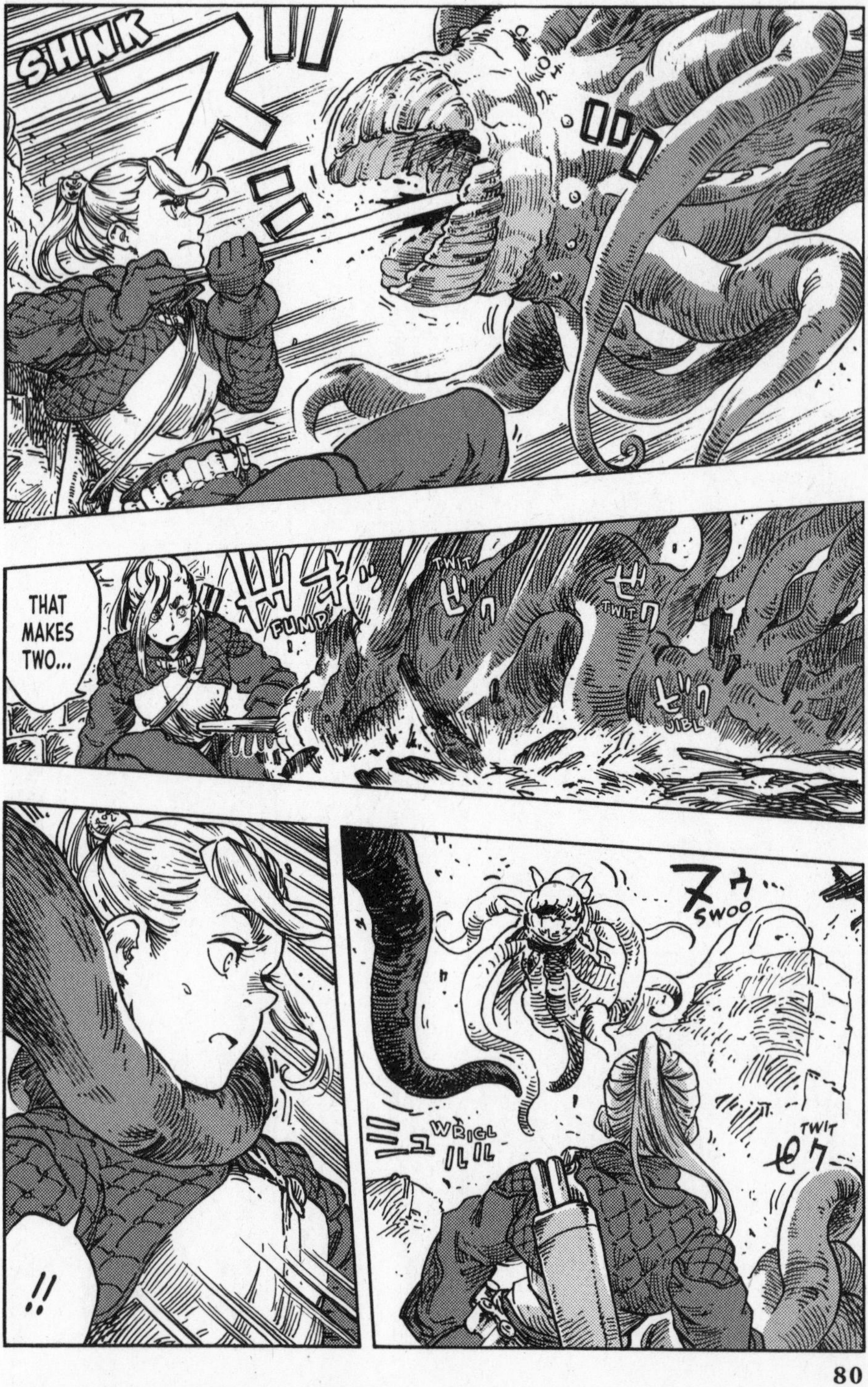
SHNK
THAT MAKES TWO...
FUMP
TWIT
TWIT
JIBL
SWOO
WRIGL
TWIT
!!

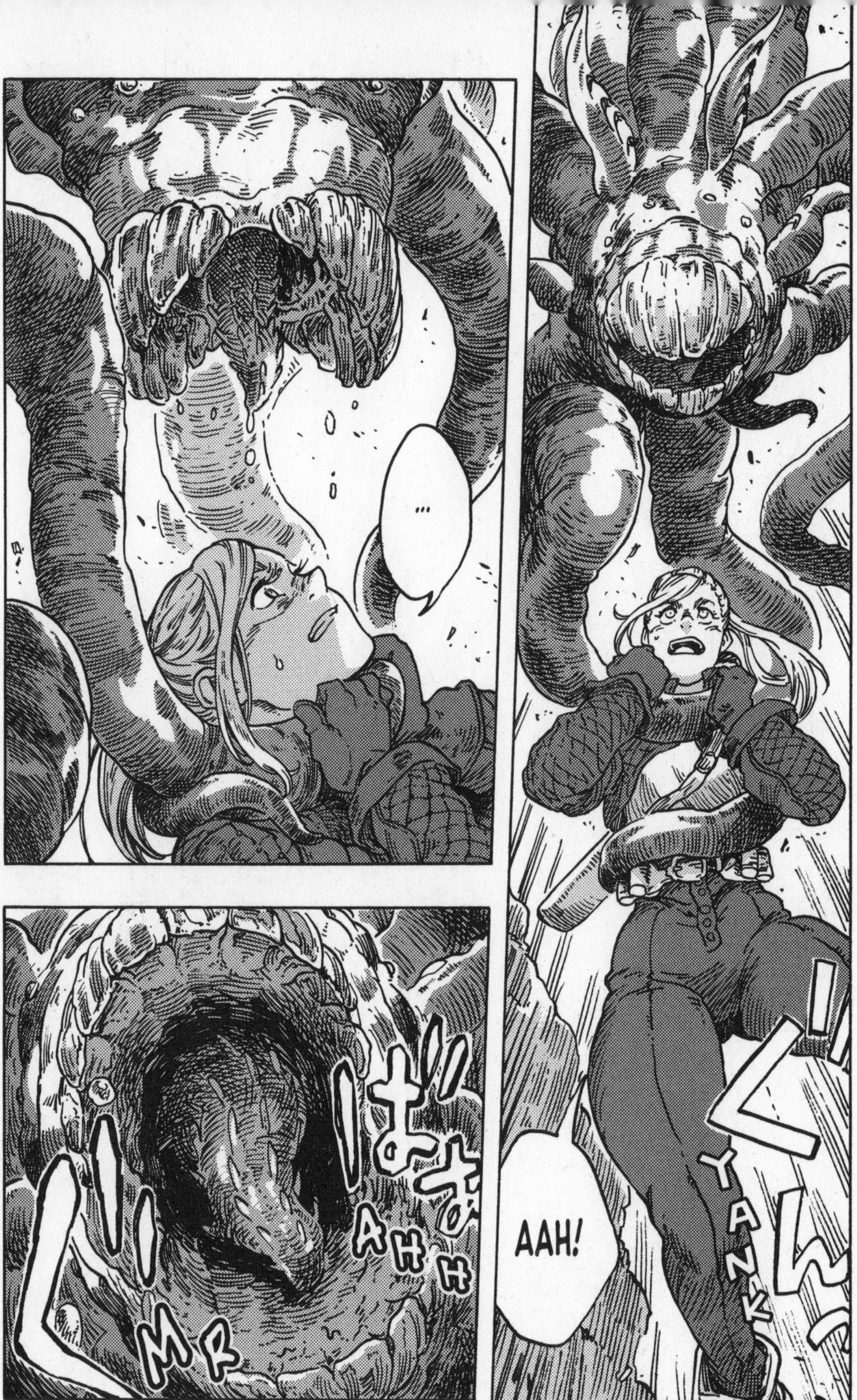
AAH!
YANK
...
AHH
MR

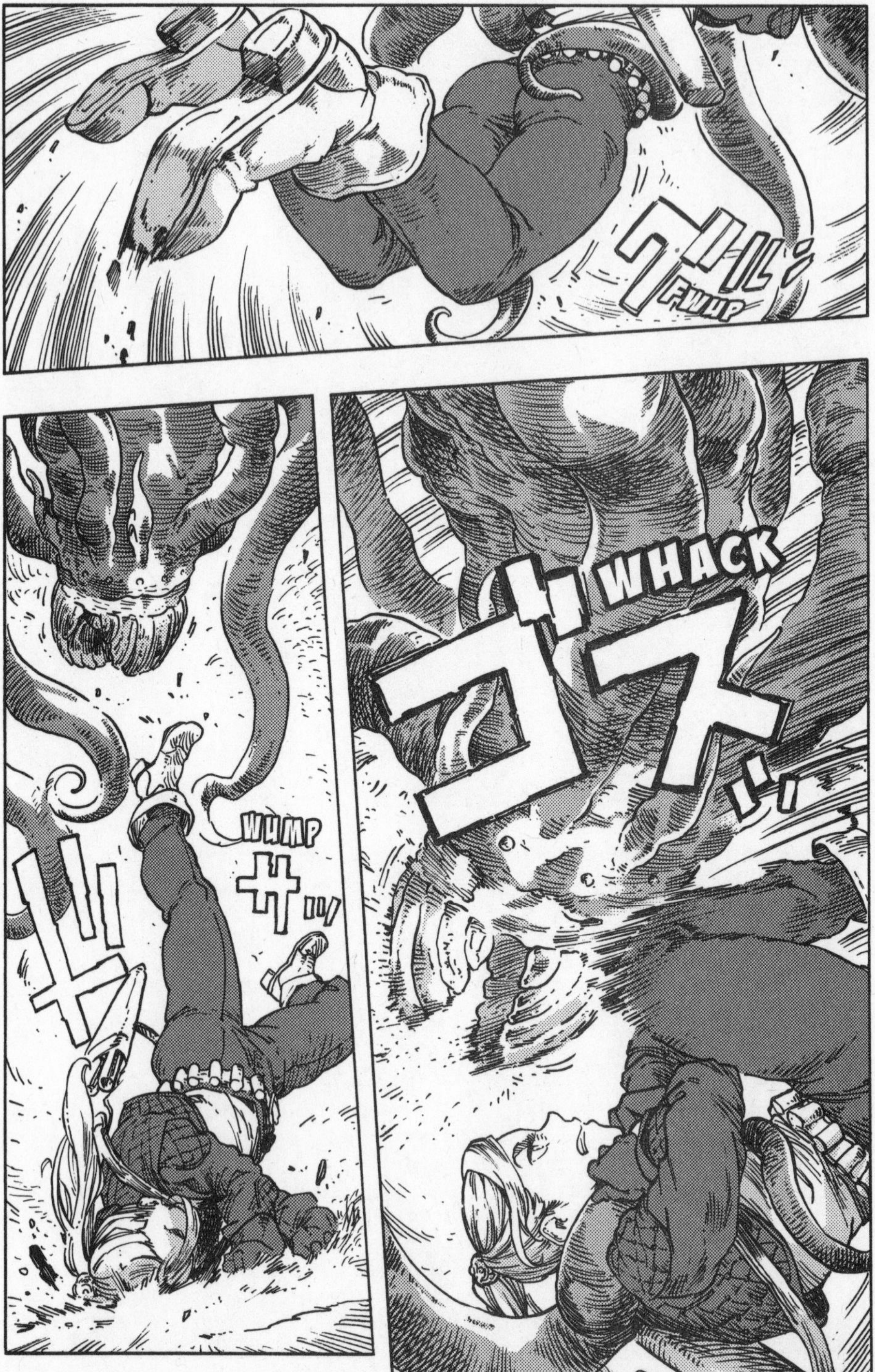
FWUP
WHACK
WUMP

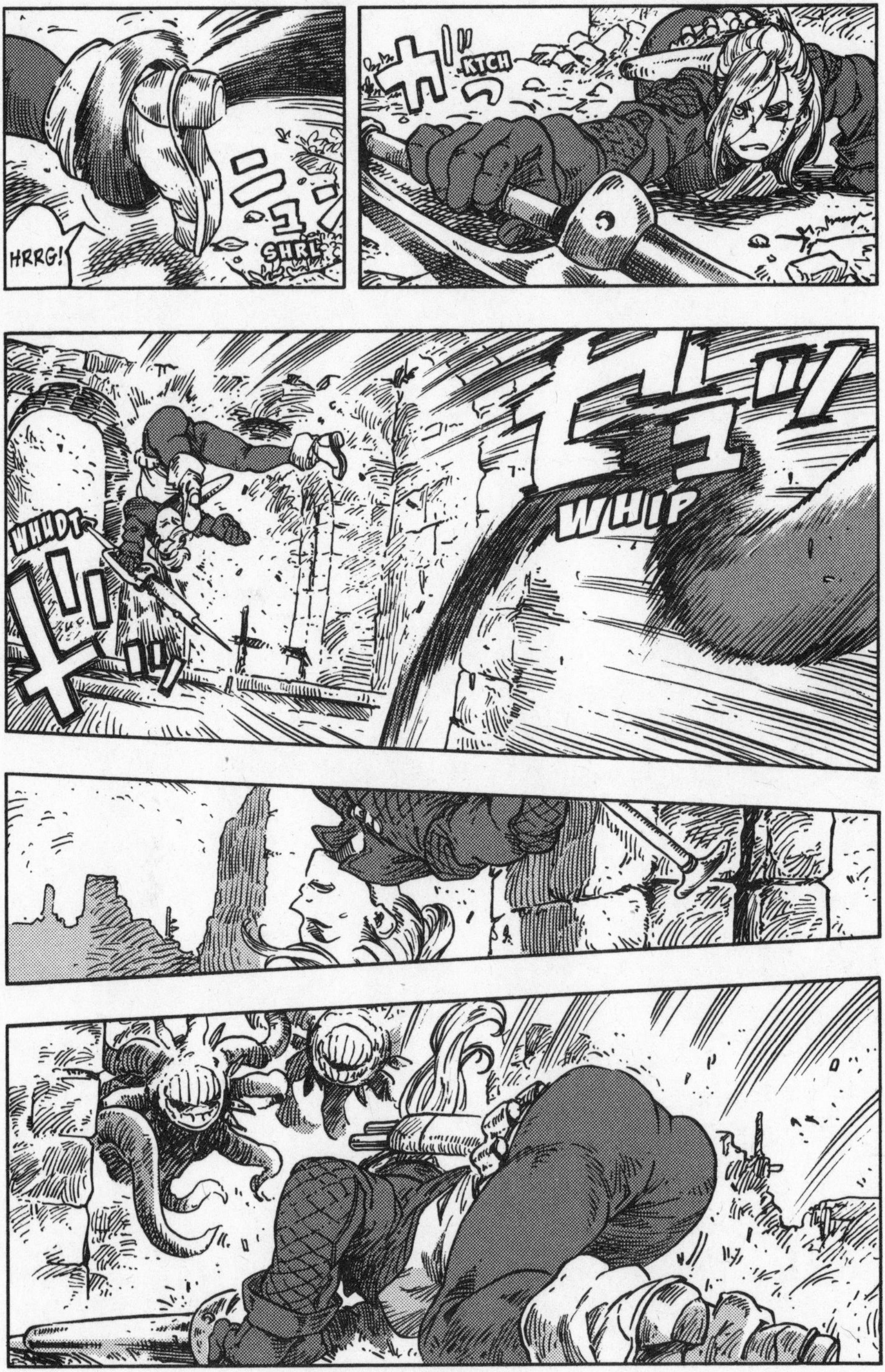
KTCH
SHRL
HRRG!
WHIP
WHUDT

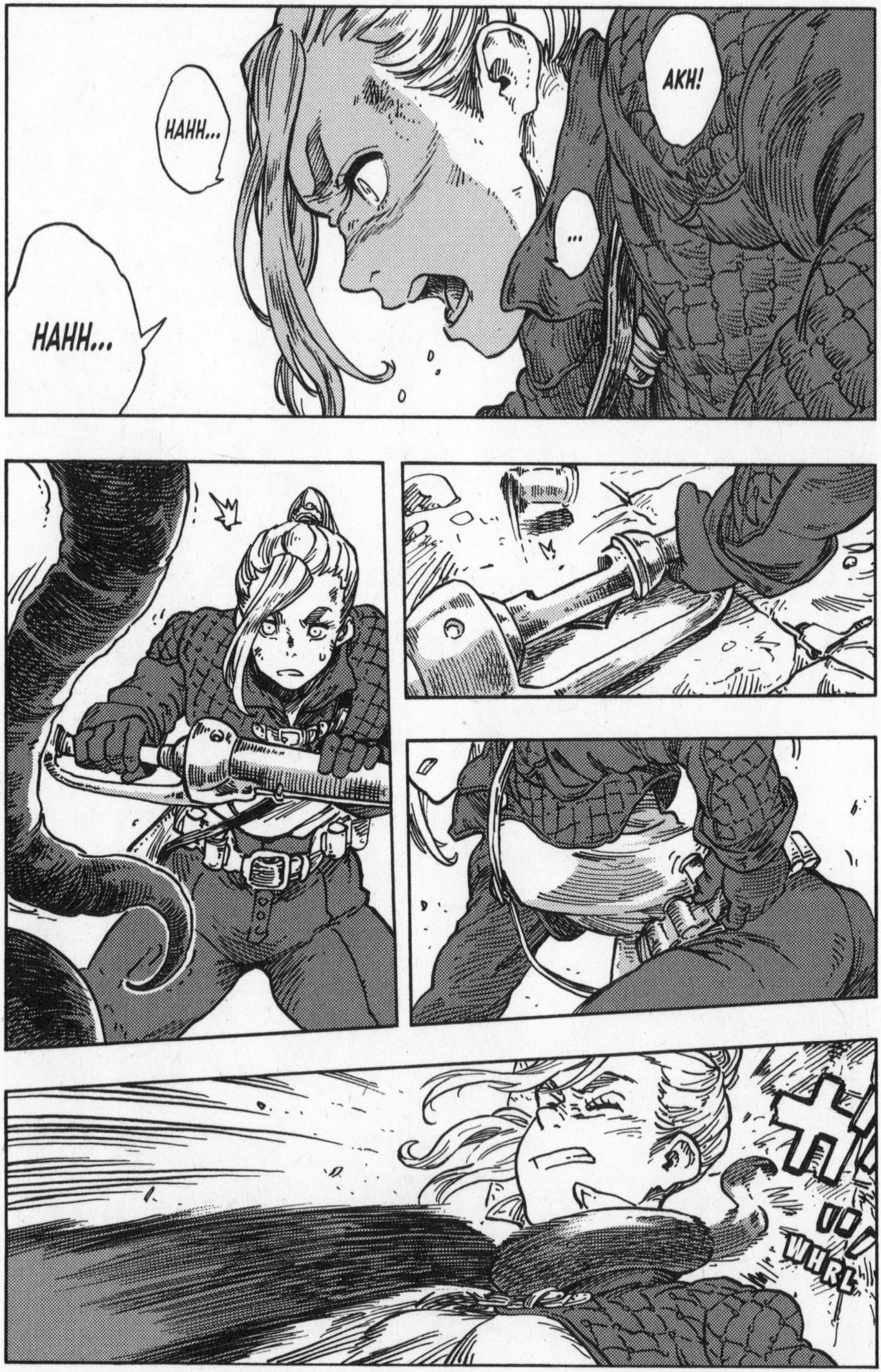
AKH!
...
HAHH...
HAHH...
WHRL

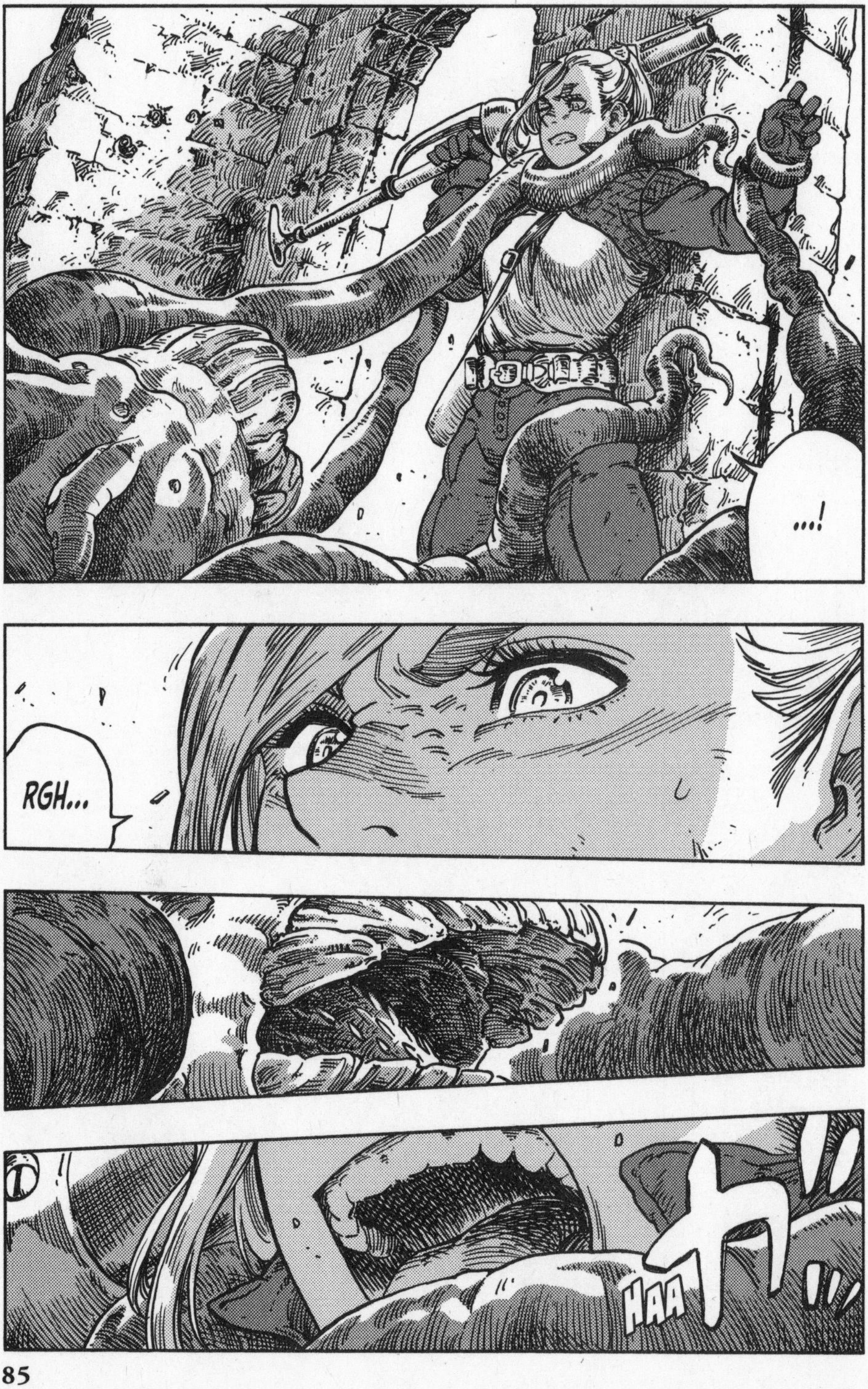
...!
RGH...
HAA

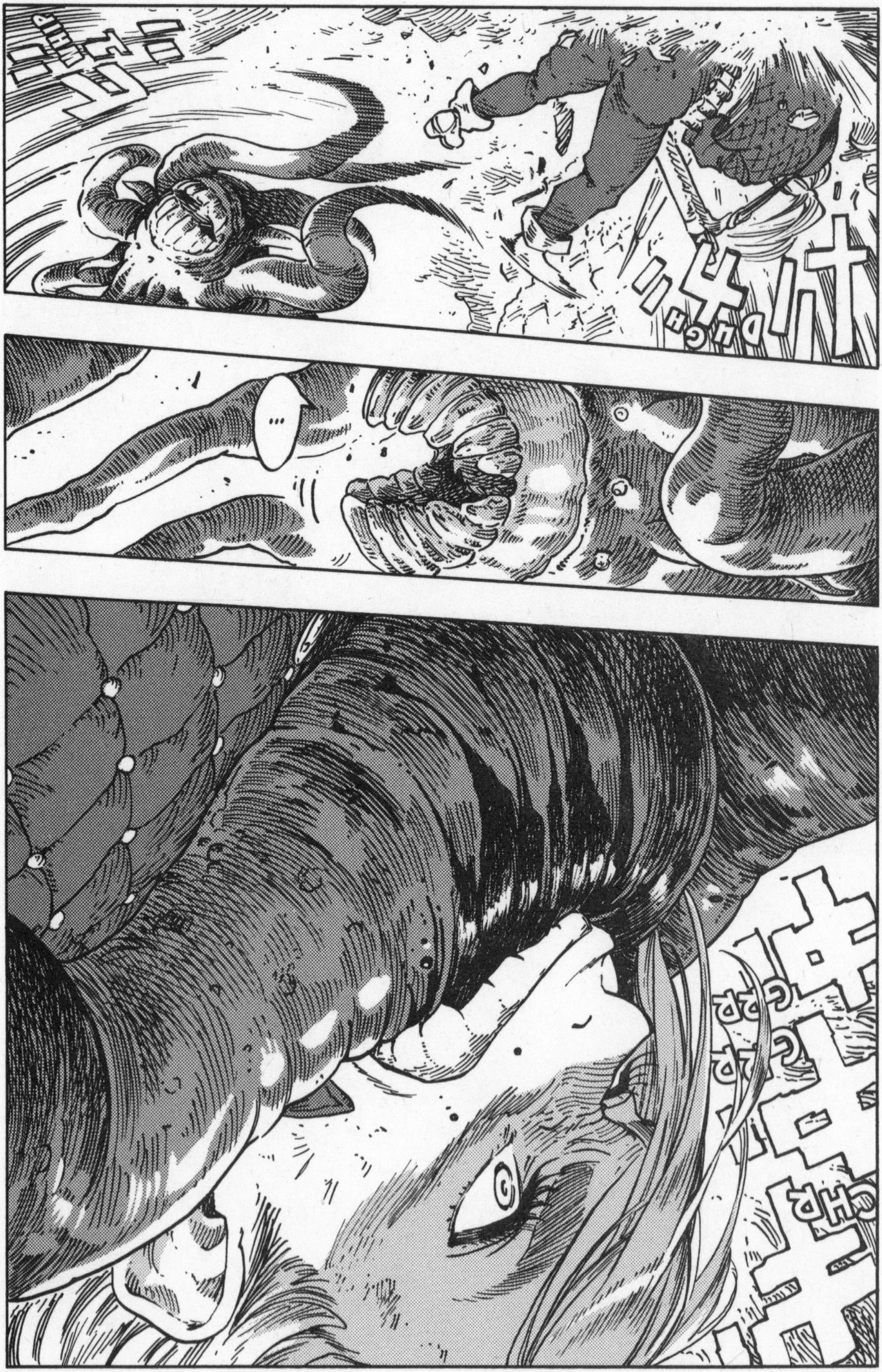
DUGH!!
...

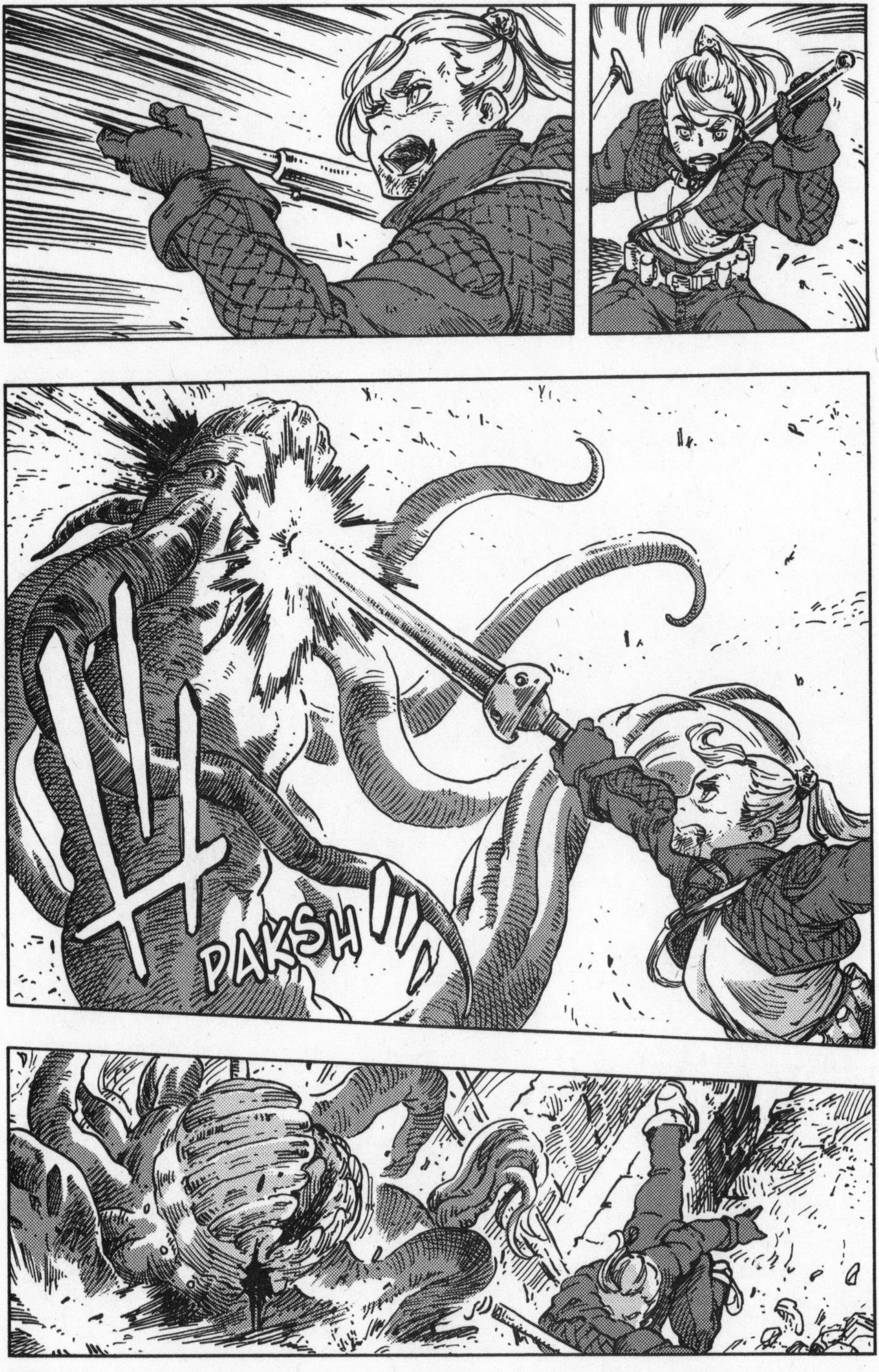
PAKSH

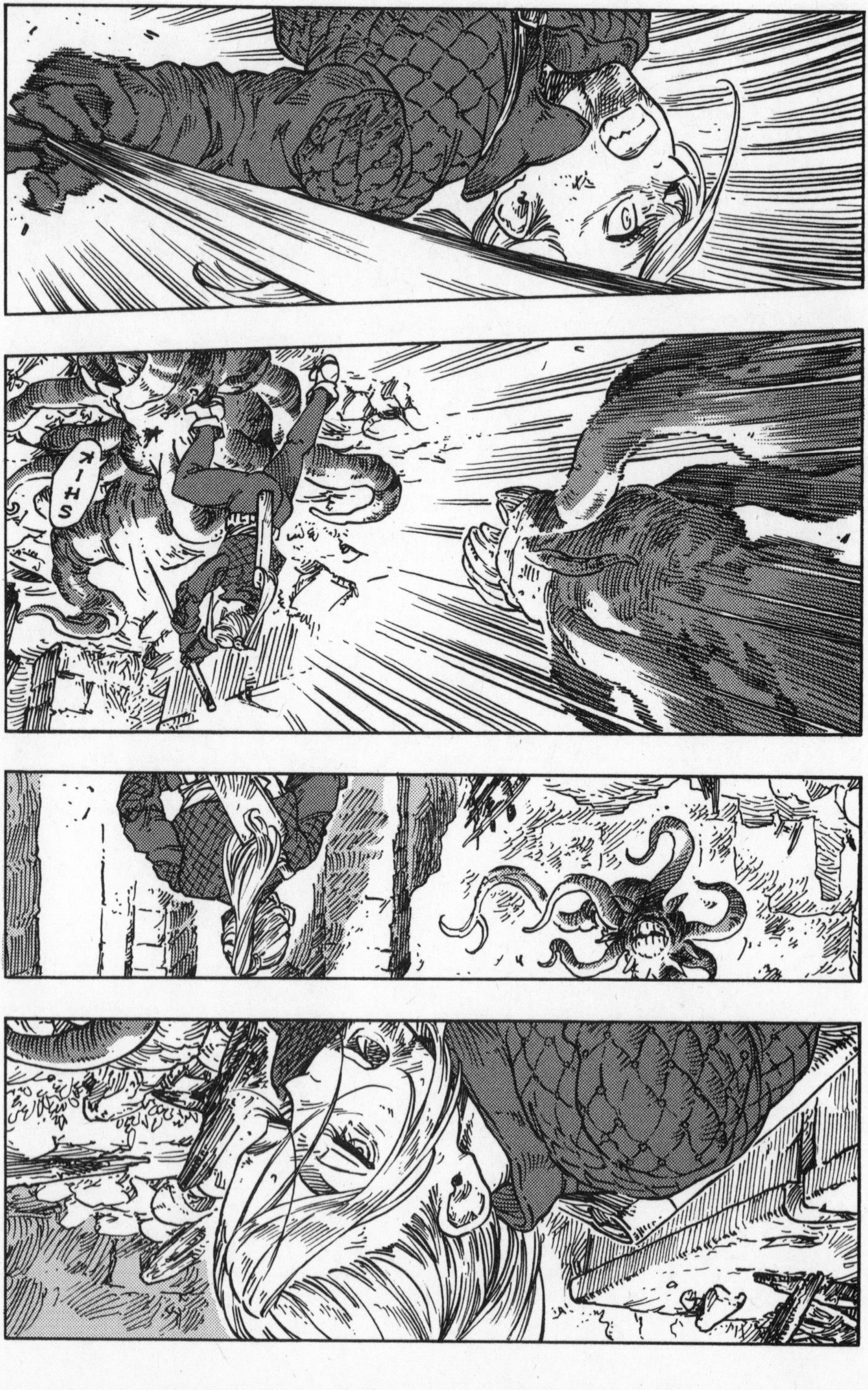
SHIK

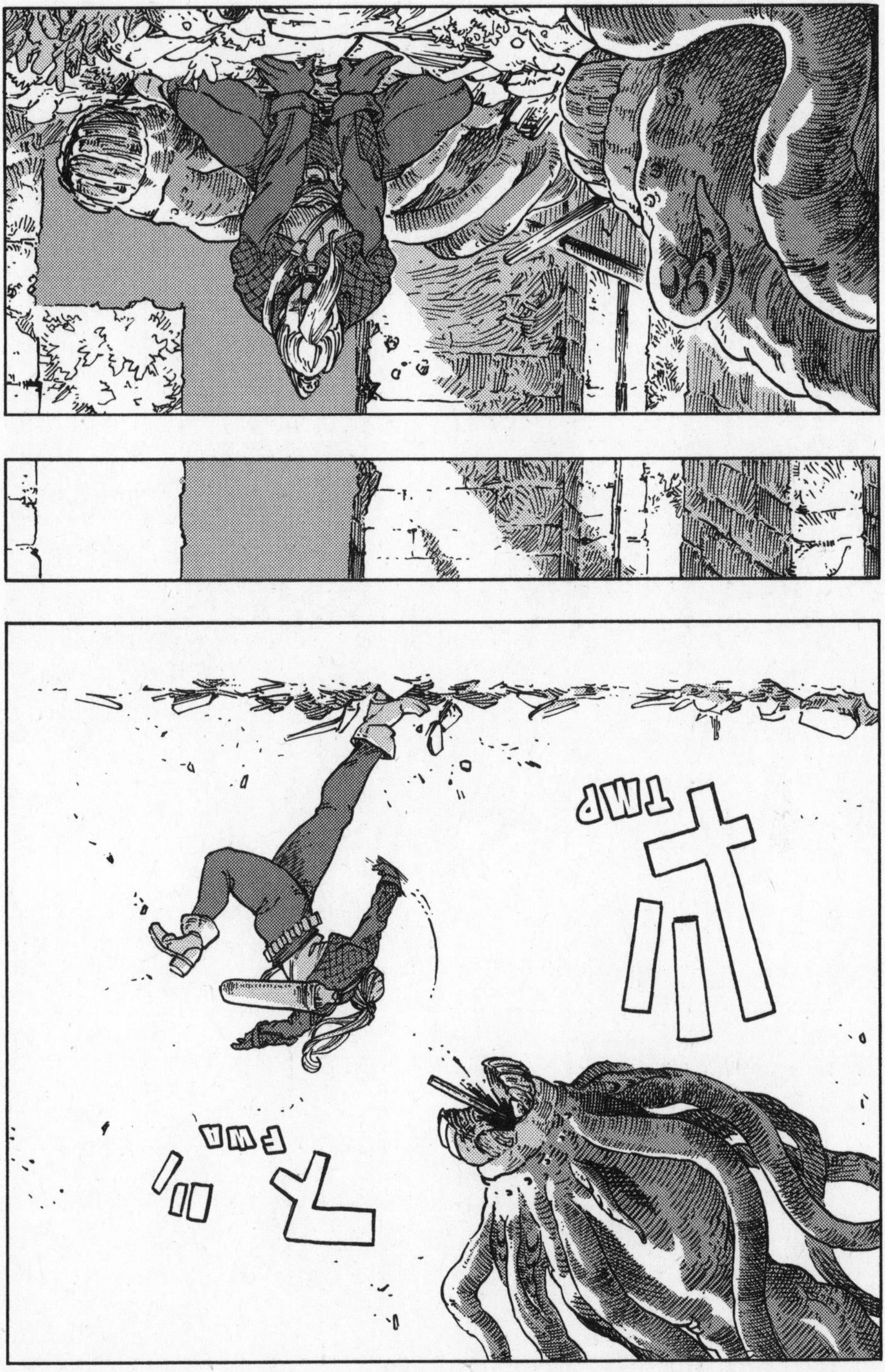
TMP
FWA

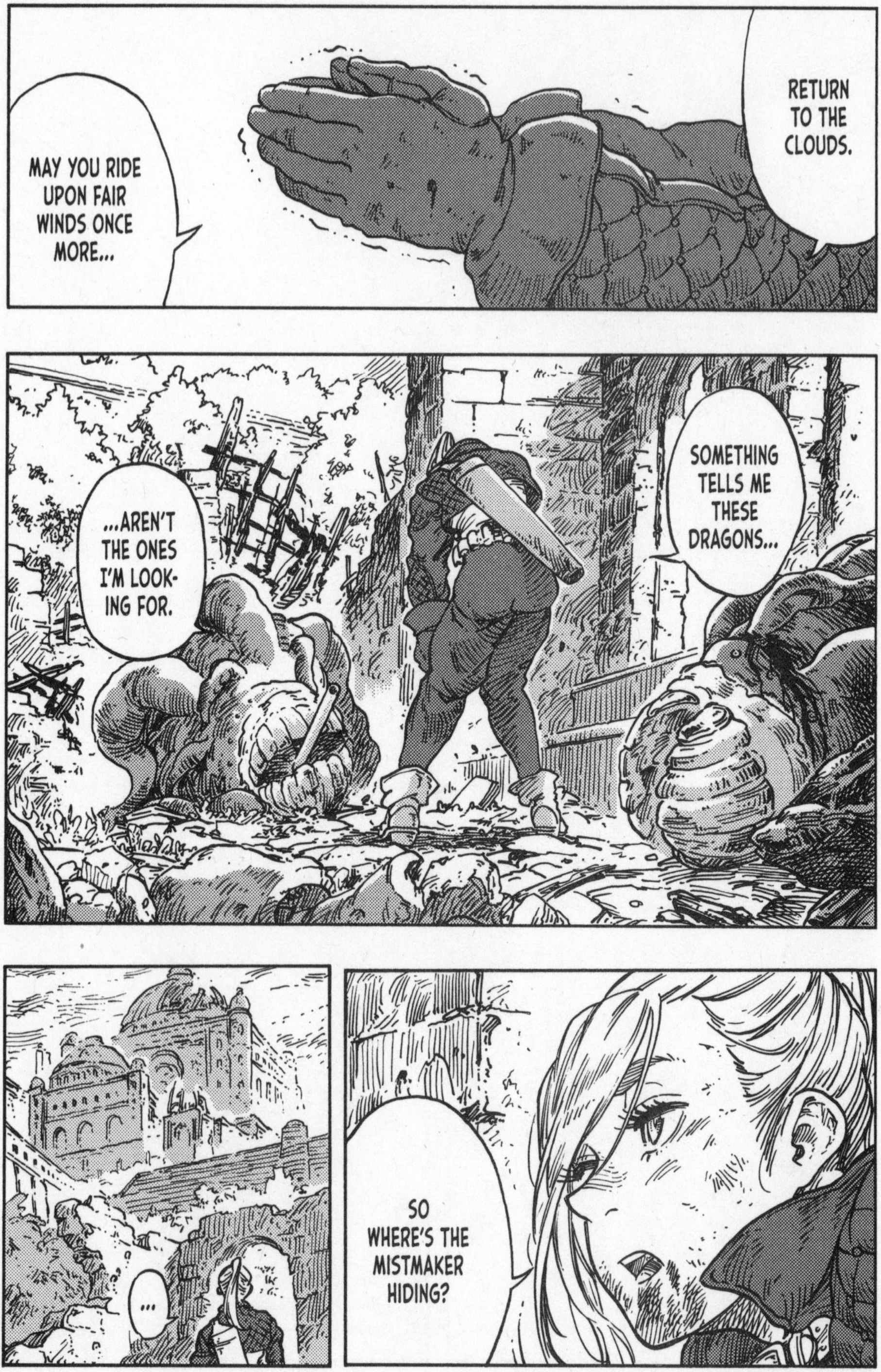
RETURN TO THE CLOUDS.
MAY YOU RIDE UPON FAIR WINDS ONCE MORE...
SOMETHING TELLS ME THESE DRAGONS...
...AREN'T THE ONES I'M LOOKING FOR.
SO WHERE'S THE MISTMAKER HIDING?
...

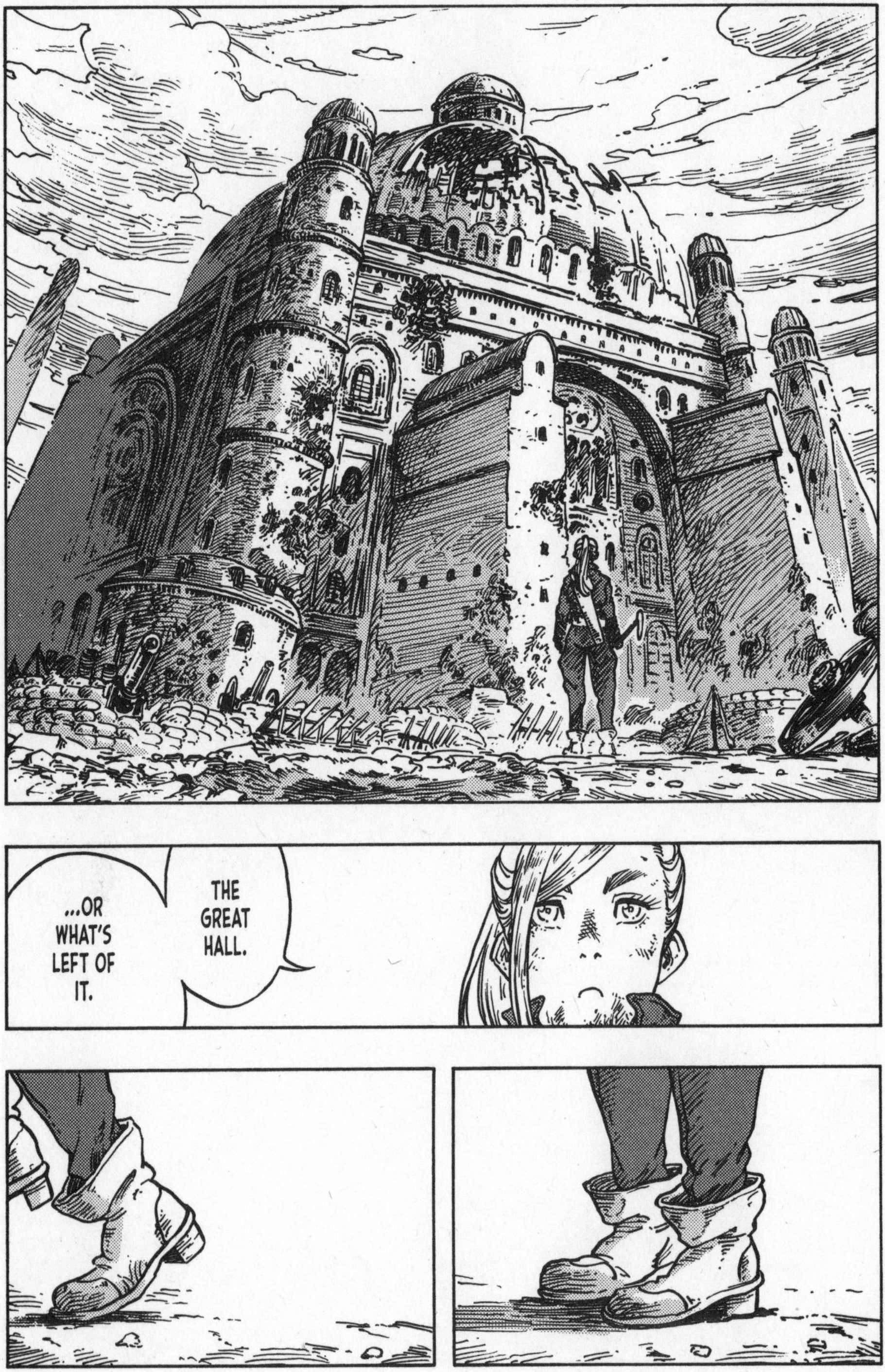
THE GREAT HALL.
...OR WHAT'S LEFT OF IT.

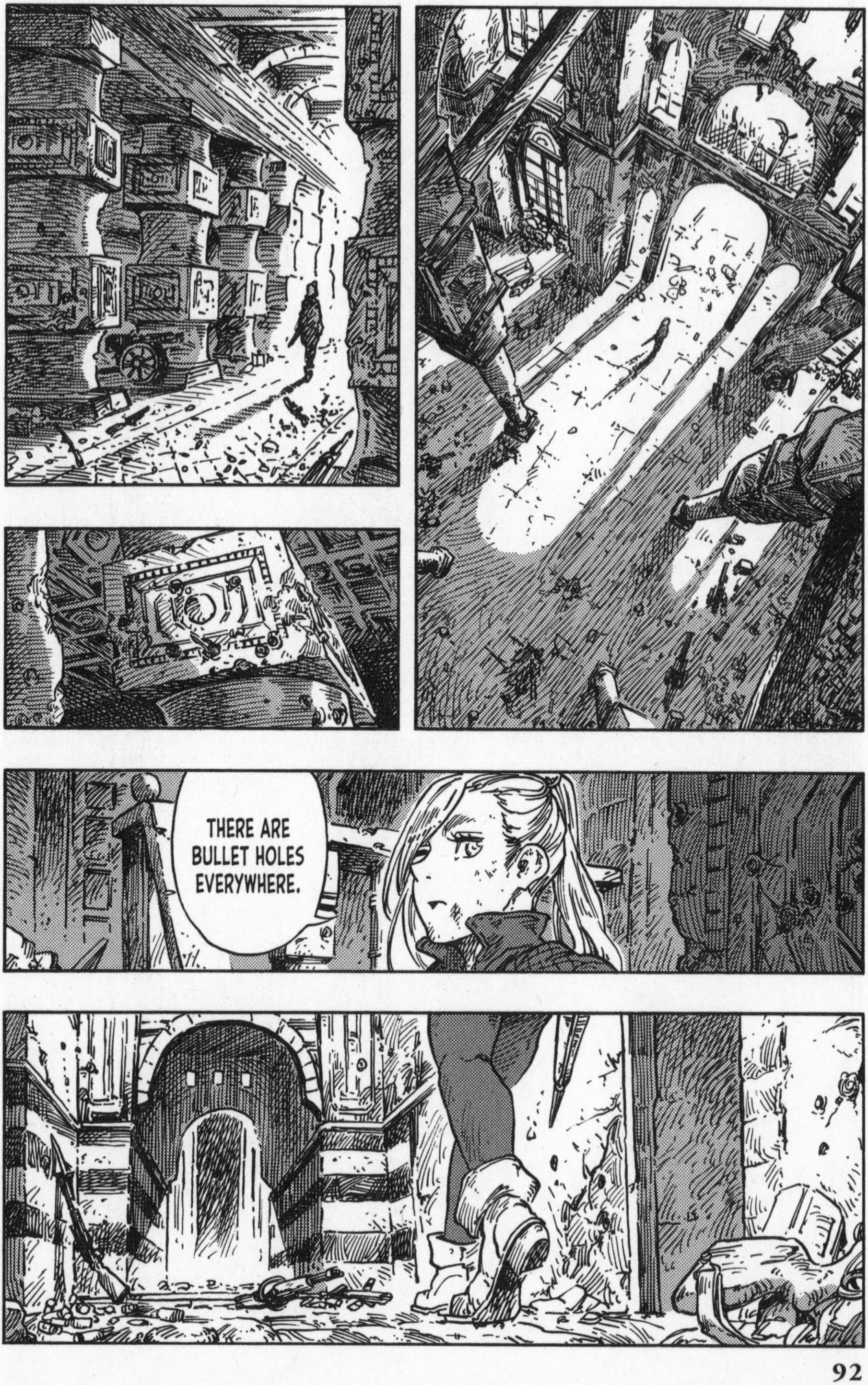
THERE ARE BULLET HOLES EVERYWHERE.

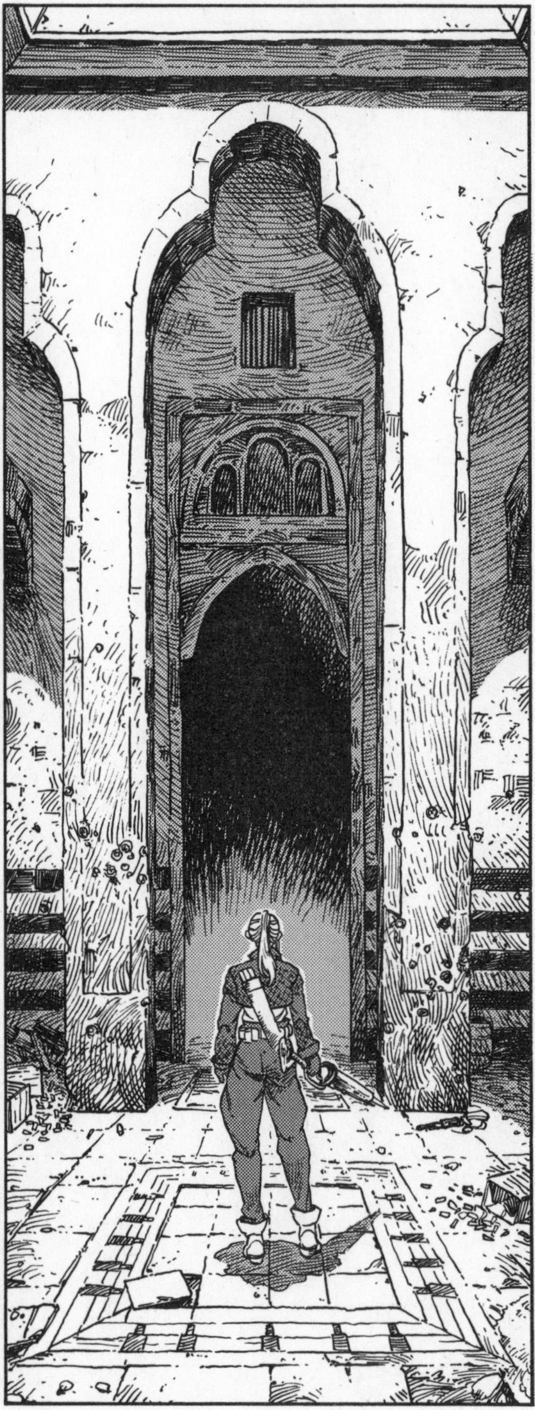
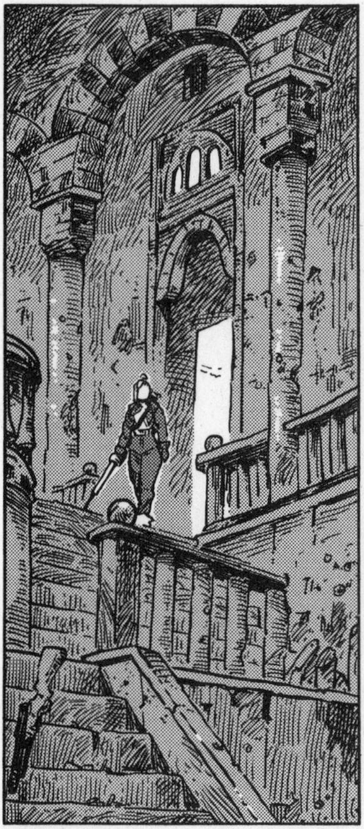
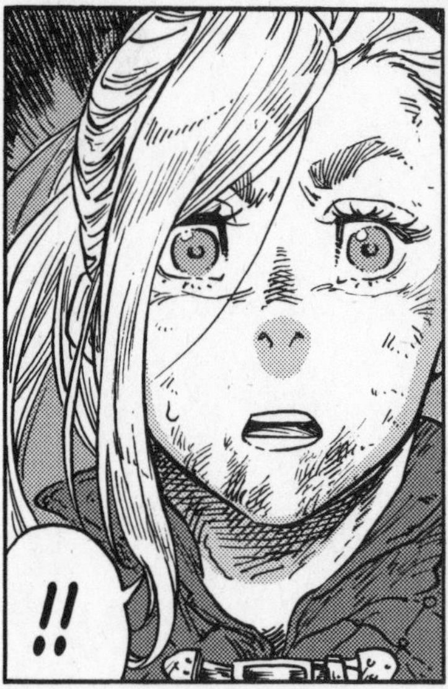
!!

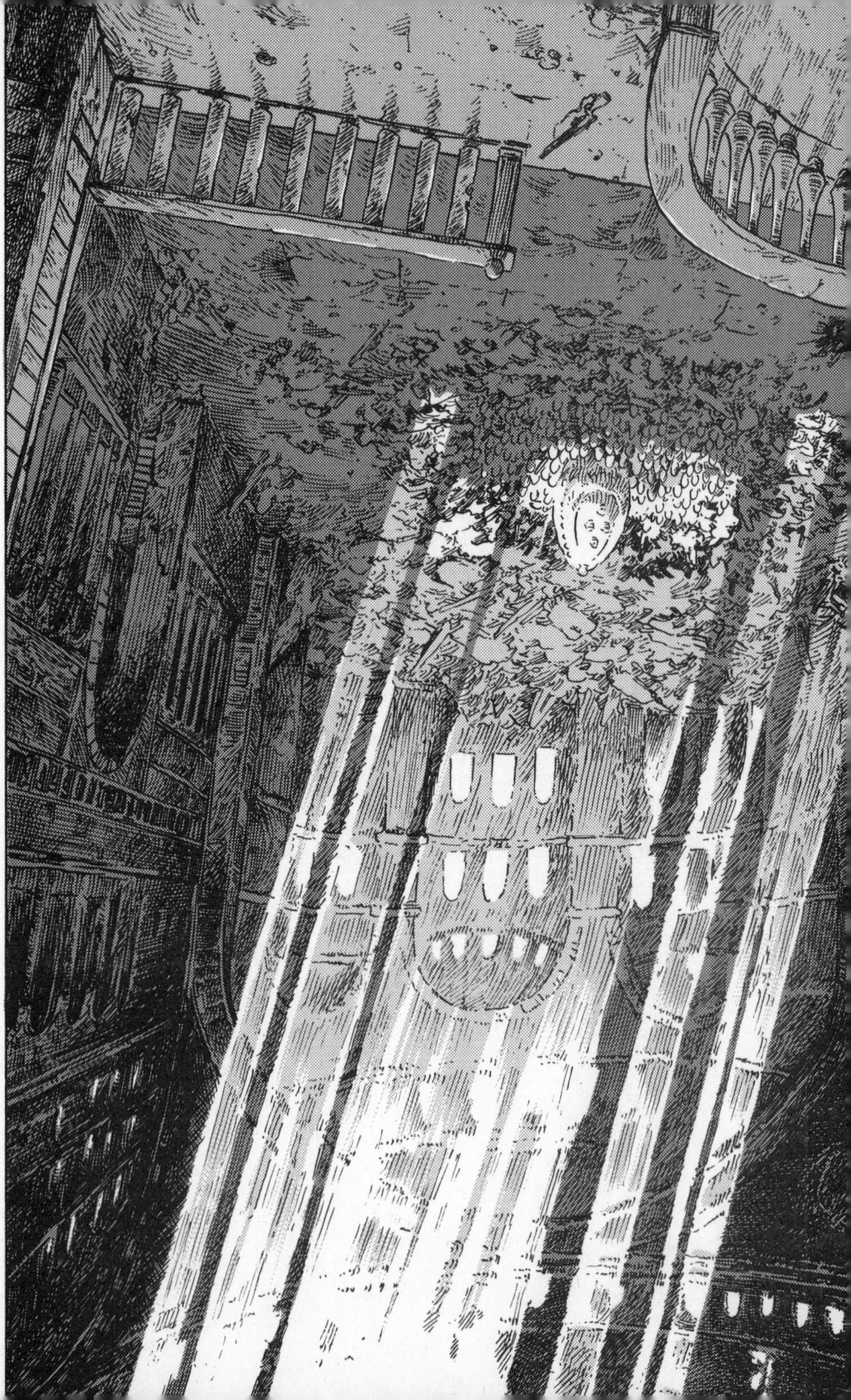

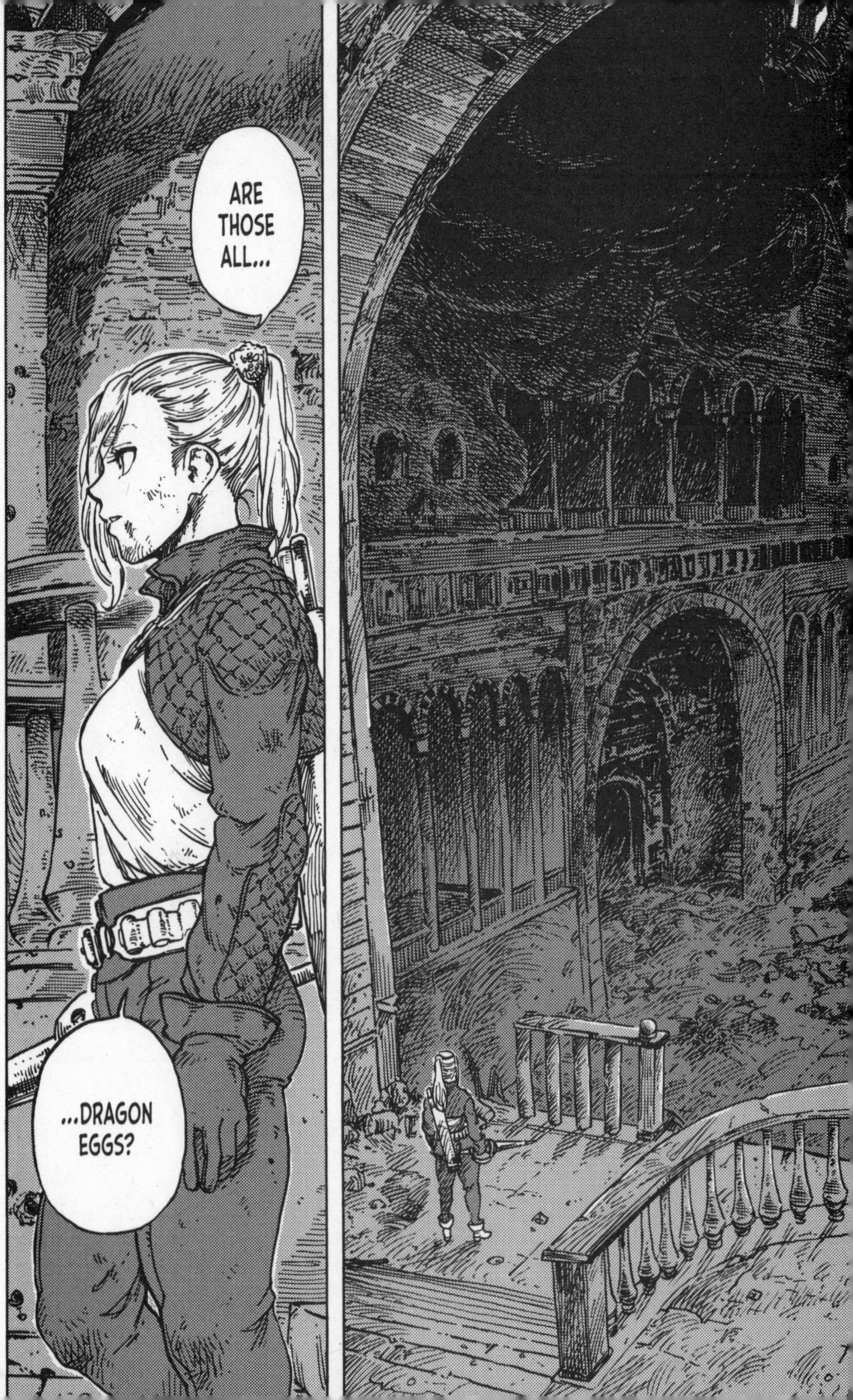
ARE THOSE ALL...
...DRAGON EGGS?

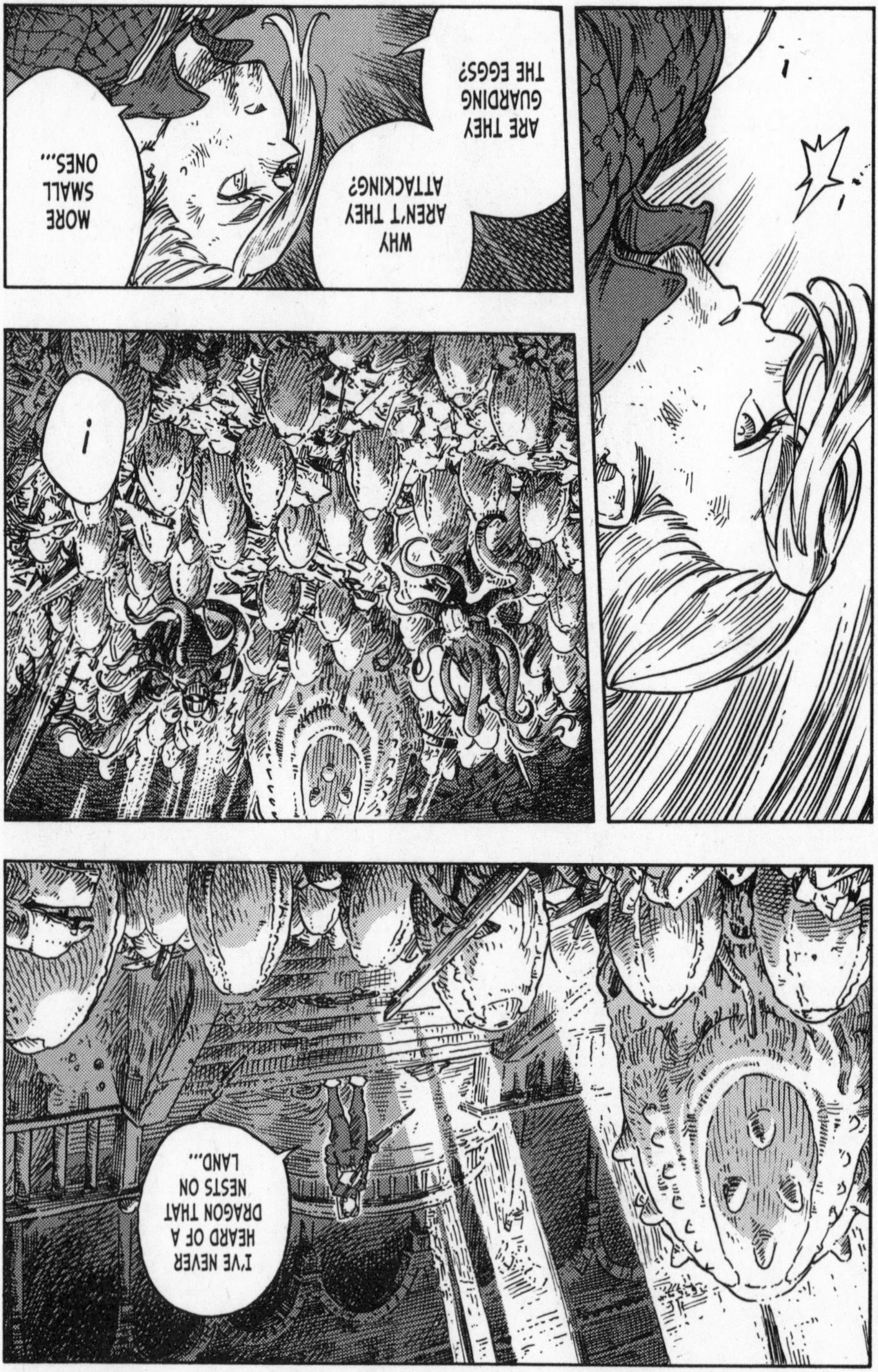
I'VE NEVER HEARD OF A DRAGON THAT NESTS ON LAND...
!
MORE SMALL ONES...
WHY AREN'T THEY ATTACKING?
ARE THEY GUARDING THE EGGS?

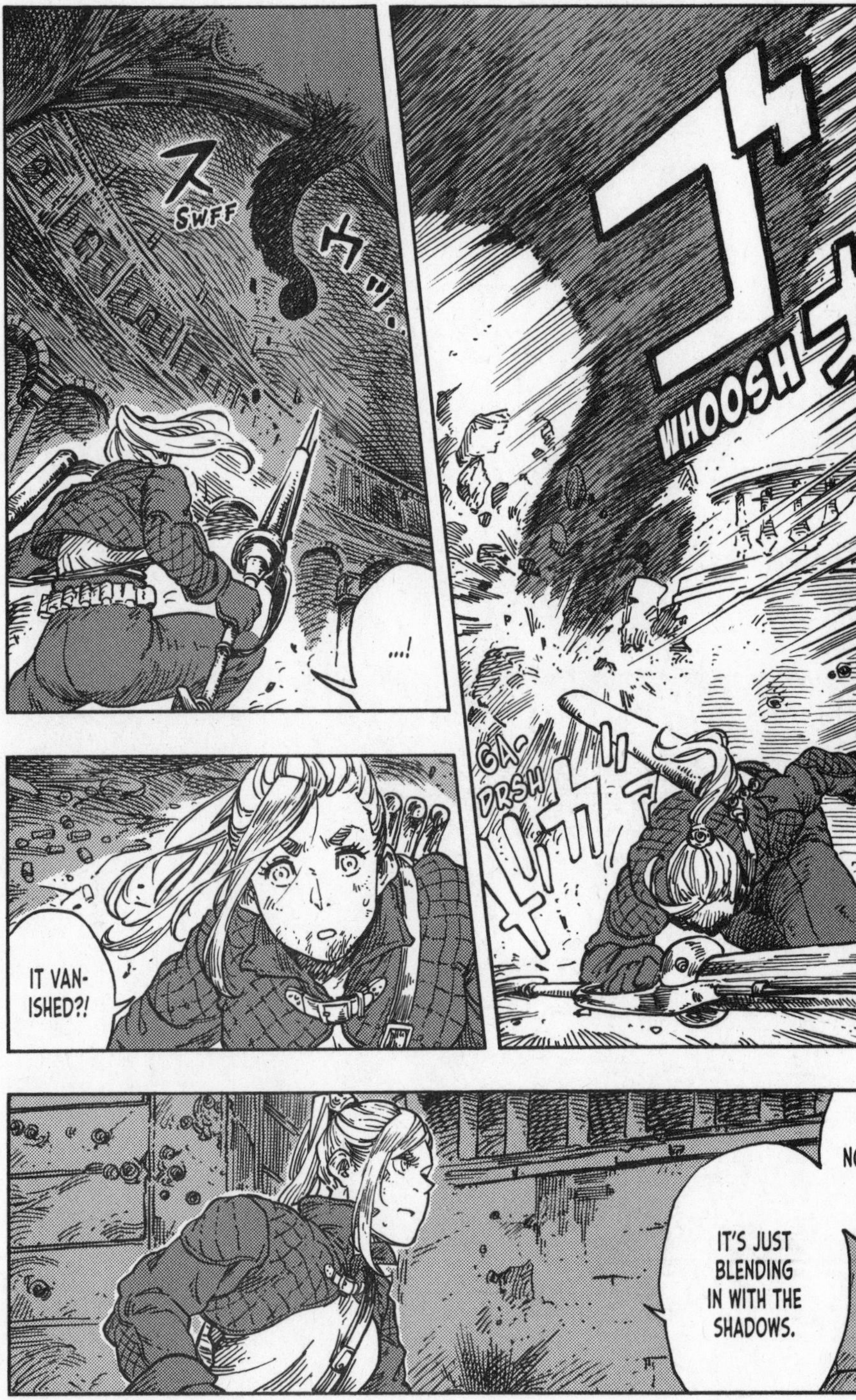
WHOOSH
GA-DRSH
SWFF
...!
IT VAN-ISHED?!
NO...
IT'S JUST BLENDING IN WITH THE SHADOWS.

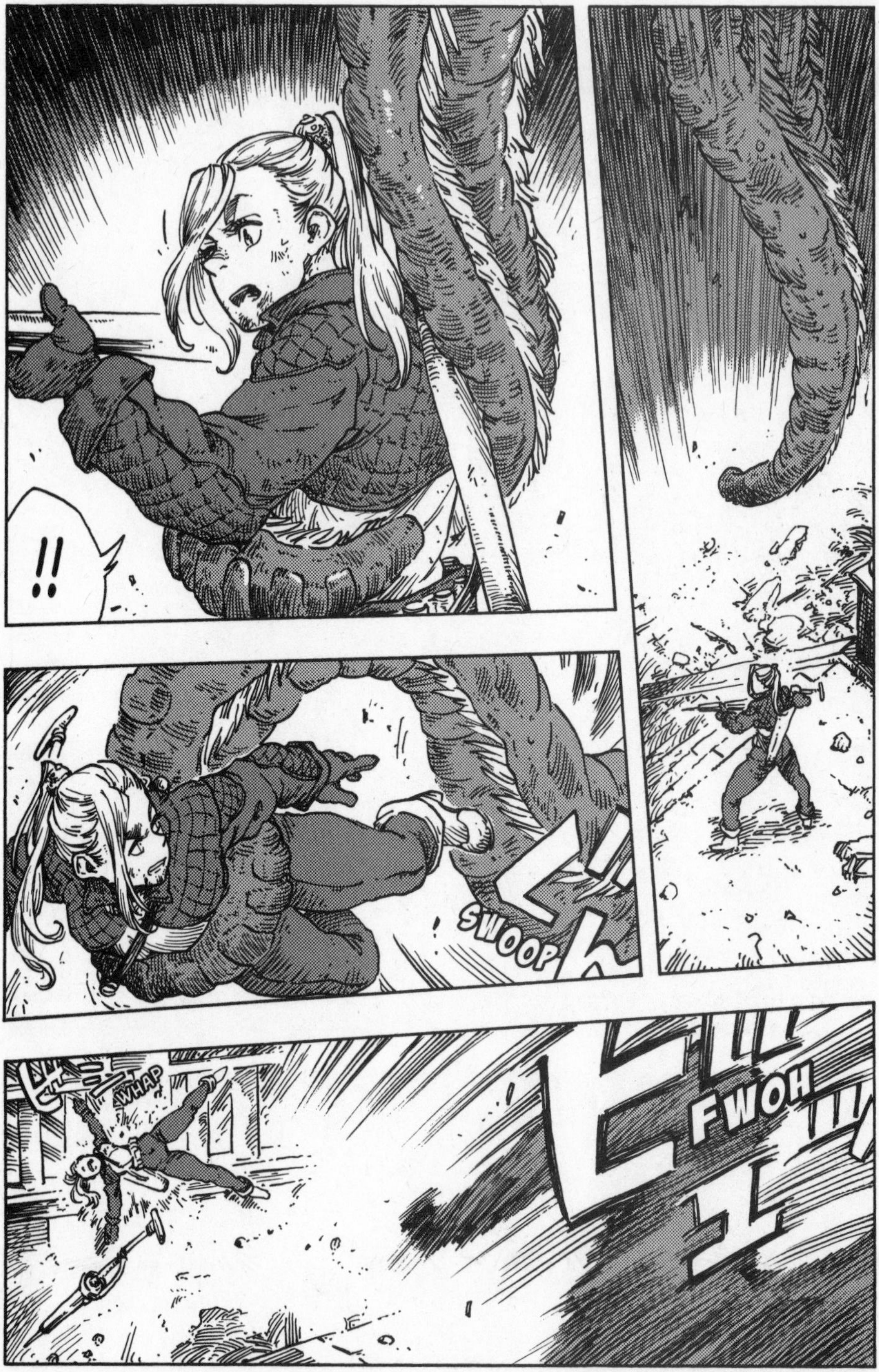
!!
SWOOP
FWOH
WHAP

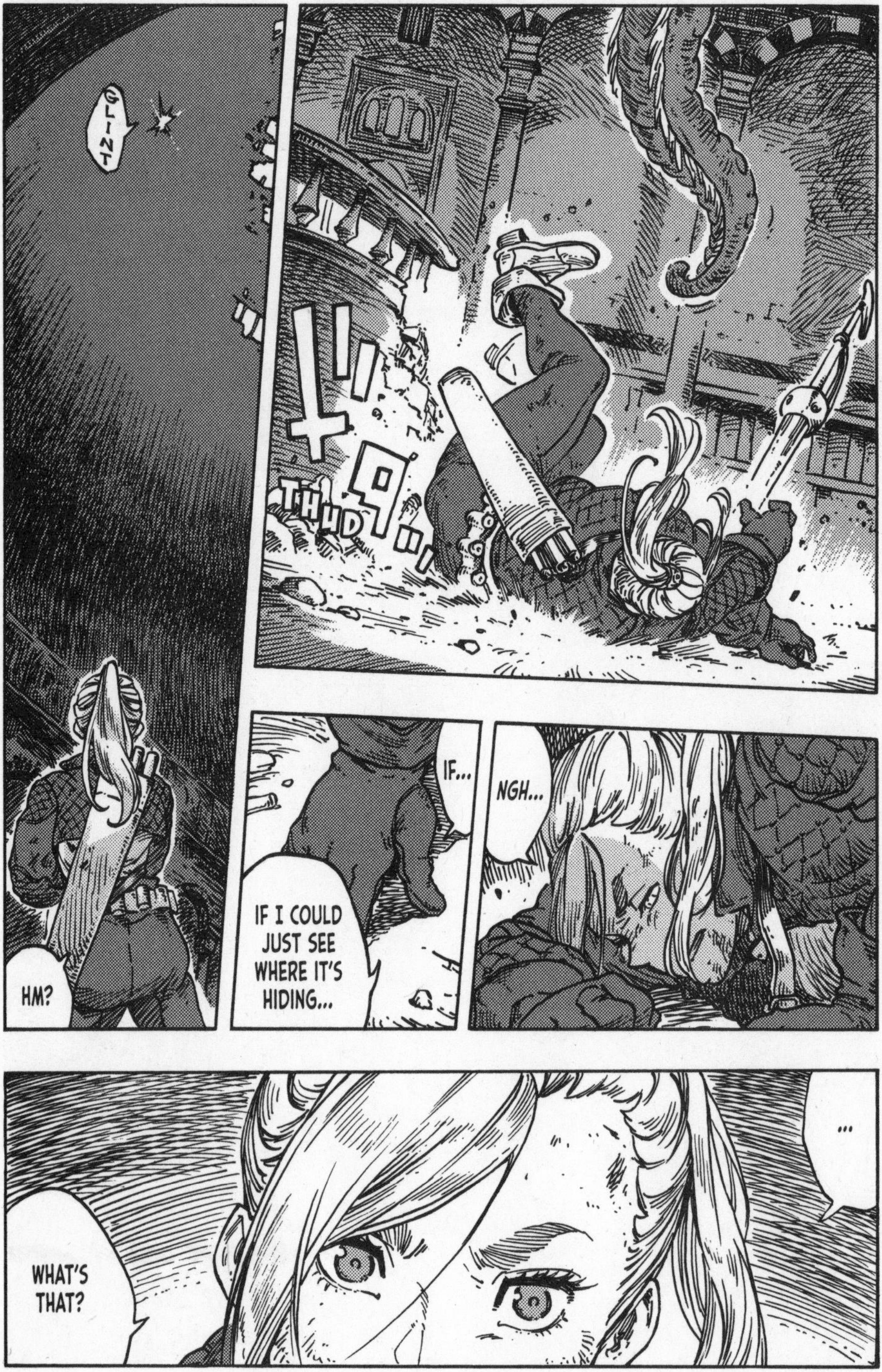
THUD
NGH...
IF...
IF I COULD JUST SEE WHERE IT'S HIDING...
GLINT
HM?
...
WHAT'S THAT?

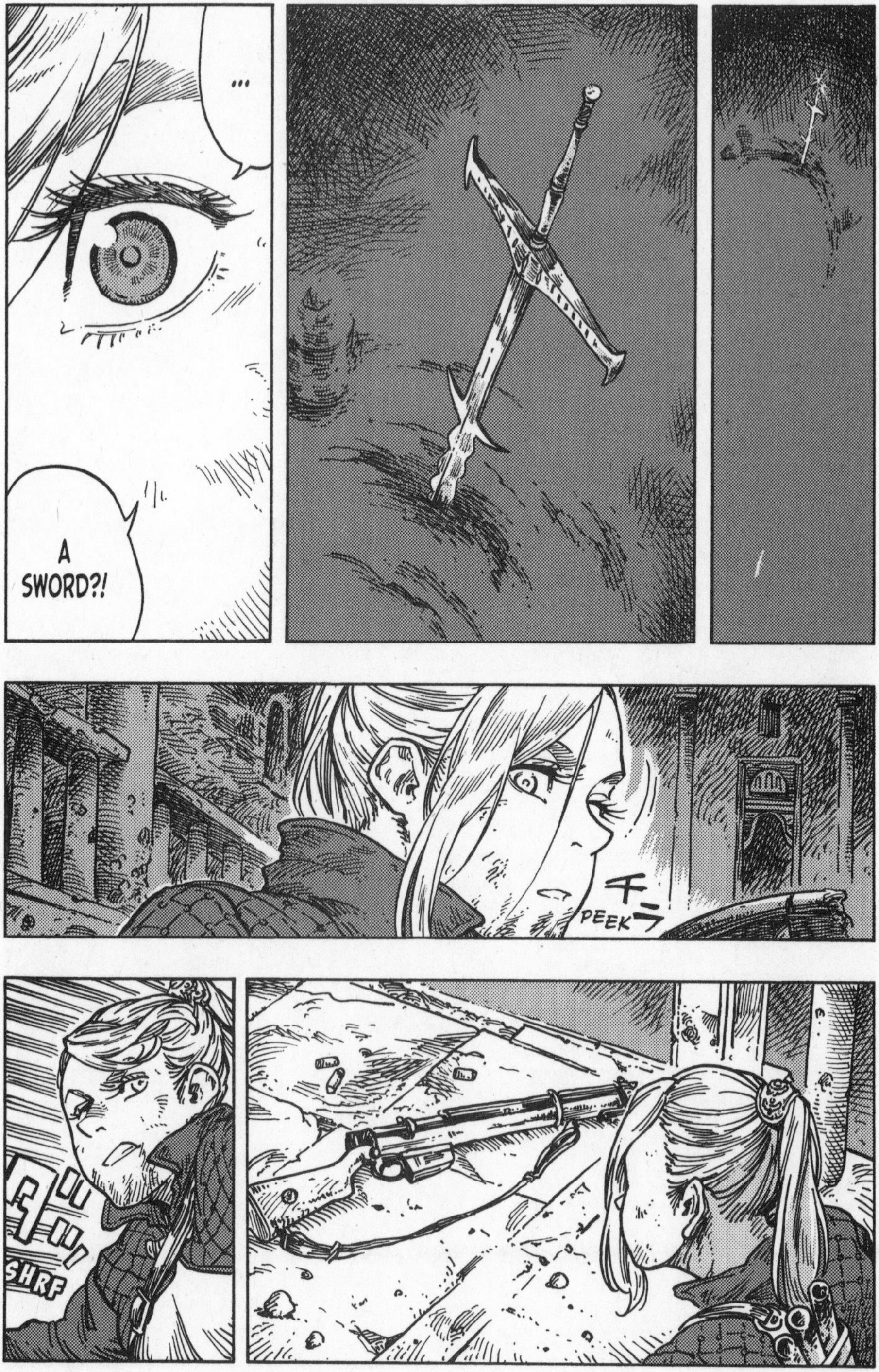
...
A SWORD?!
チラ
PEEK
SHRF

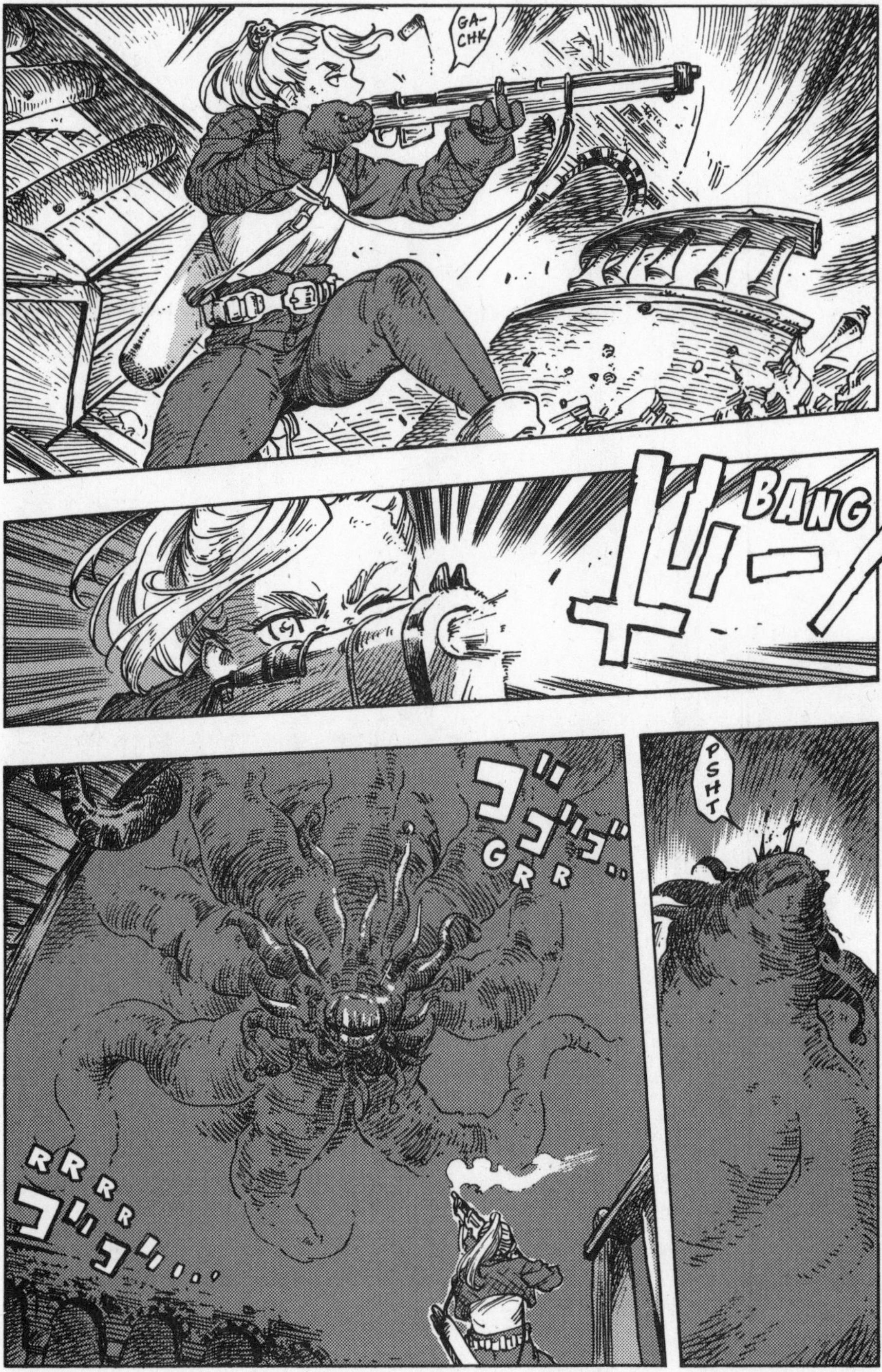
GA-
CHK
BANG
PSHT
GRR..
RRRR...

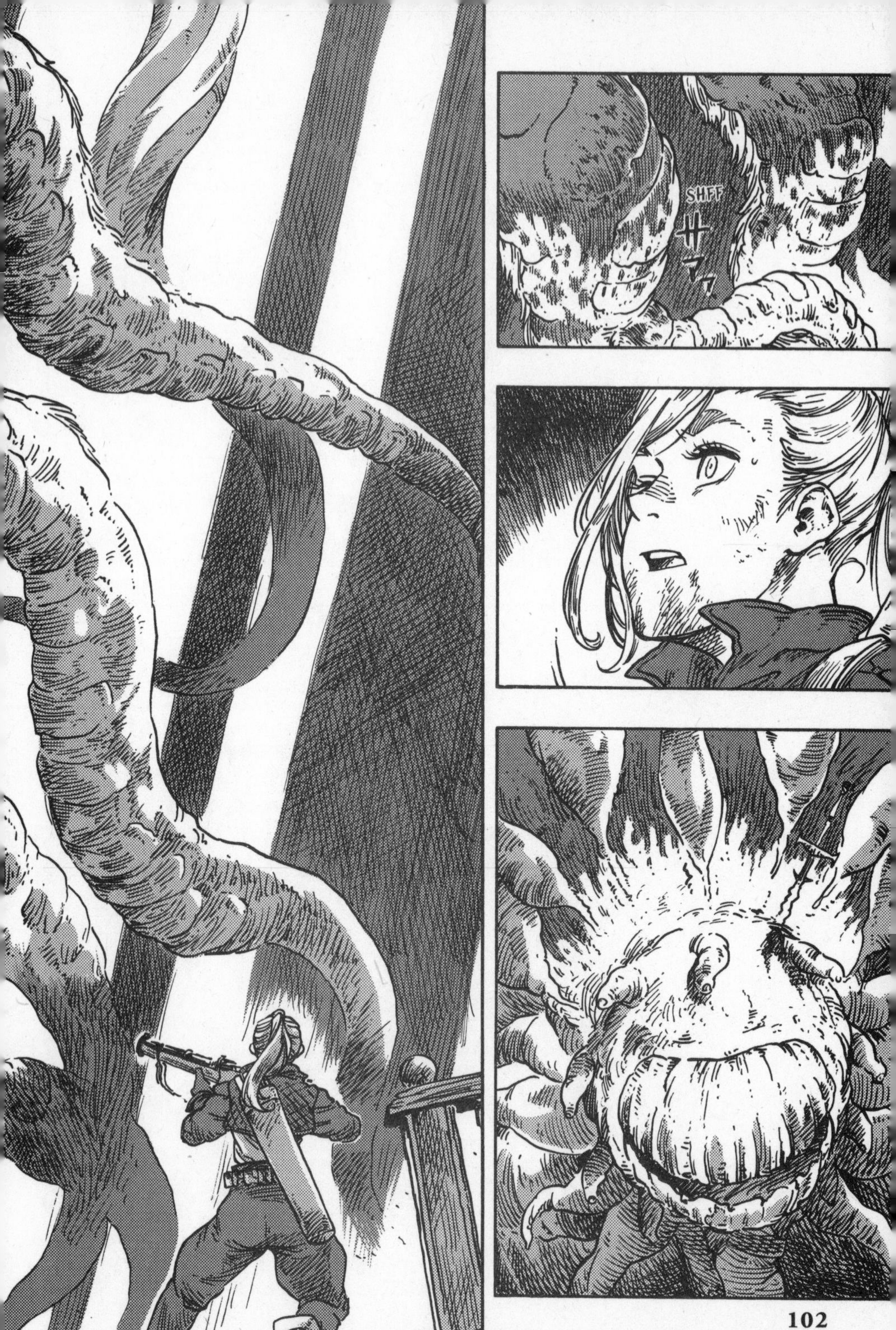
SHFF

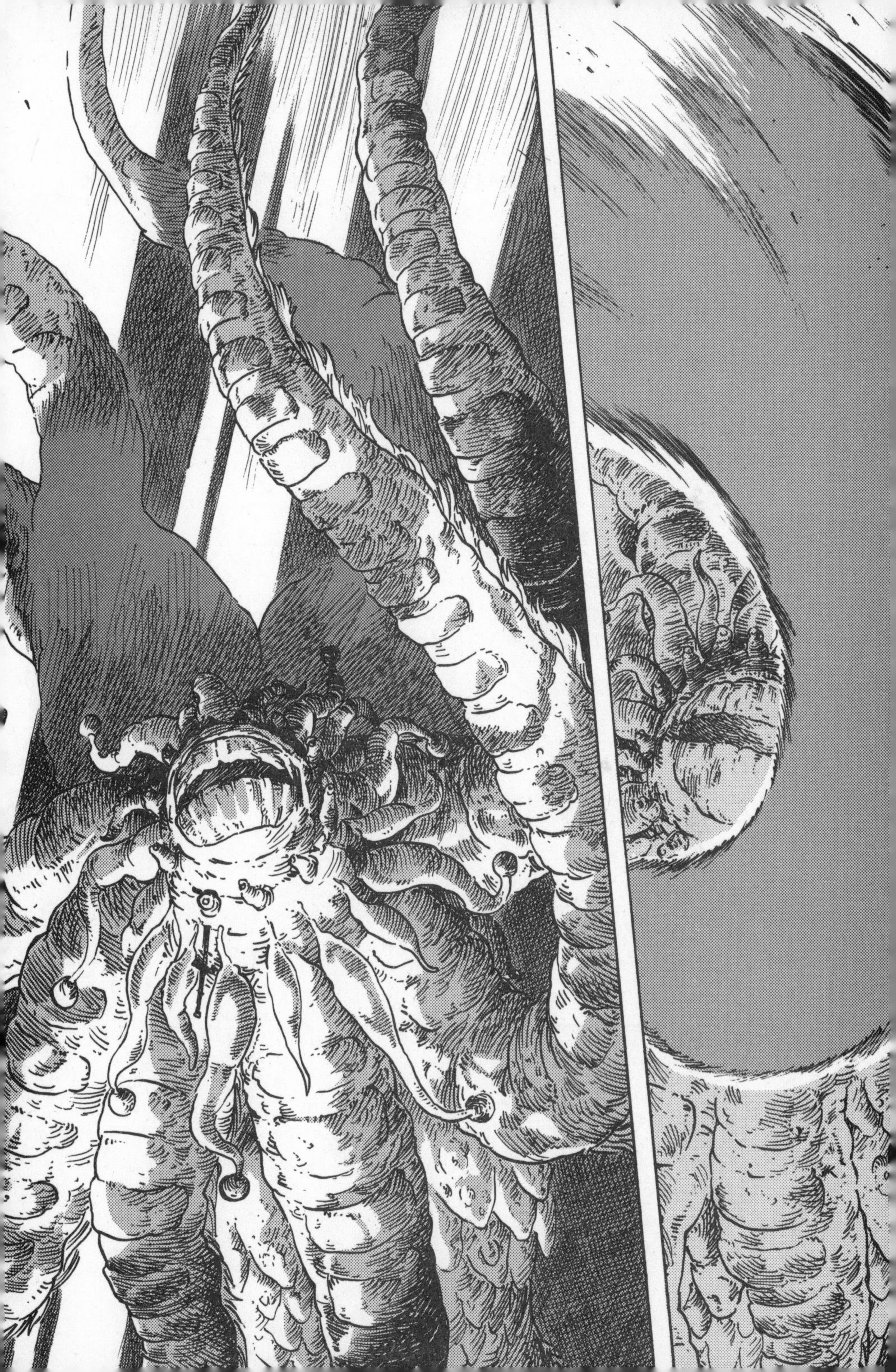

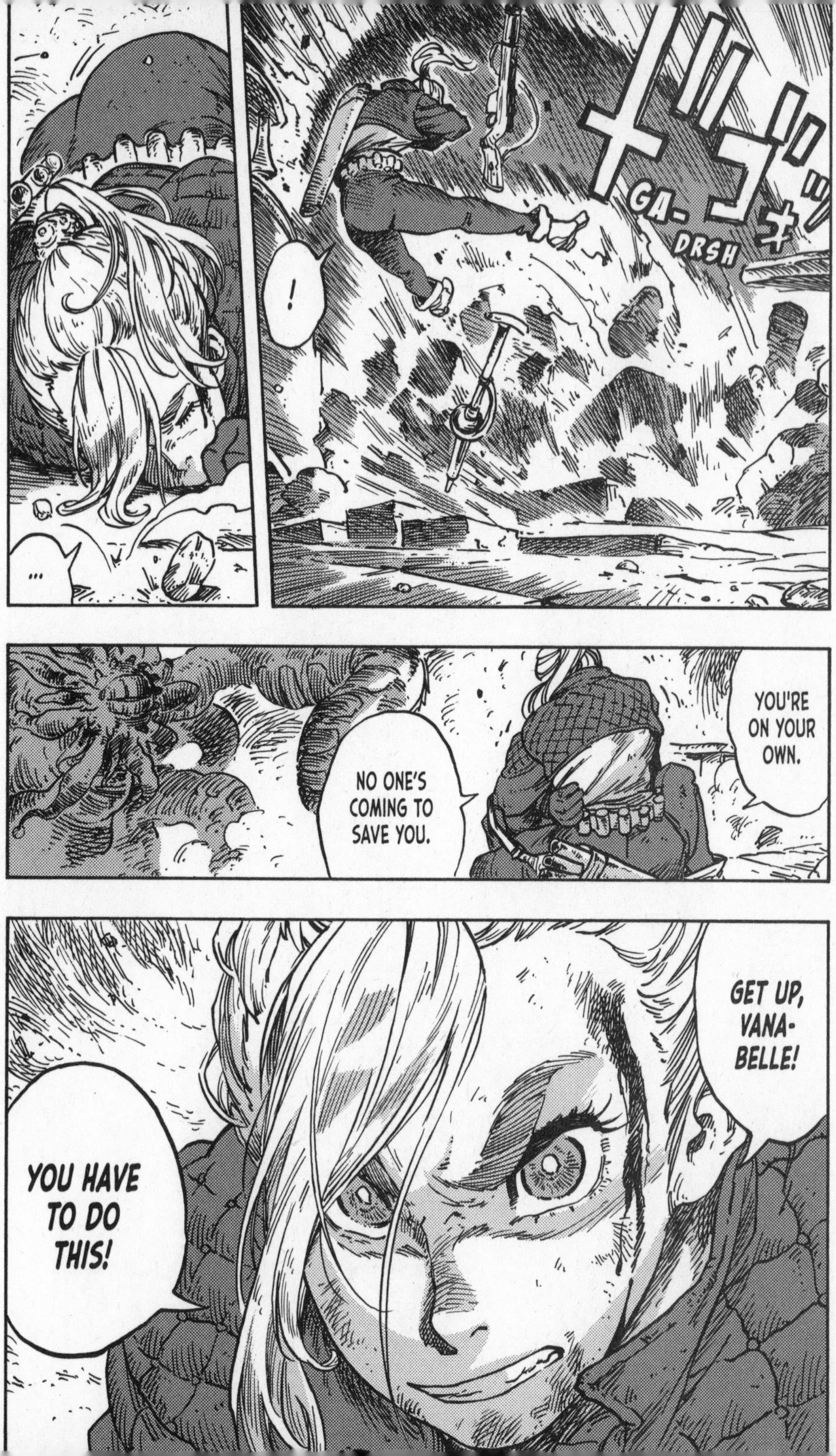
GA-DRSH
!
...
YOU'RE ON YOUR OWN.
NO ONE'S COMING TO SAVE YOU.
GET UP, VANA-BELLE!
YOU HAVE TO DO THIS!

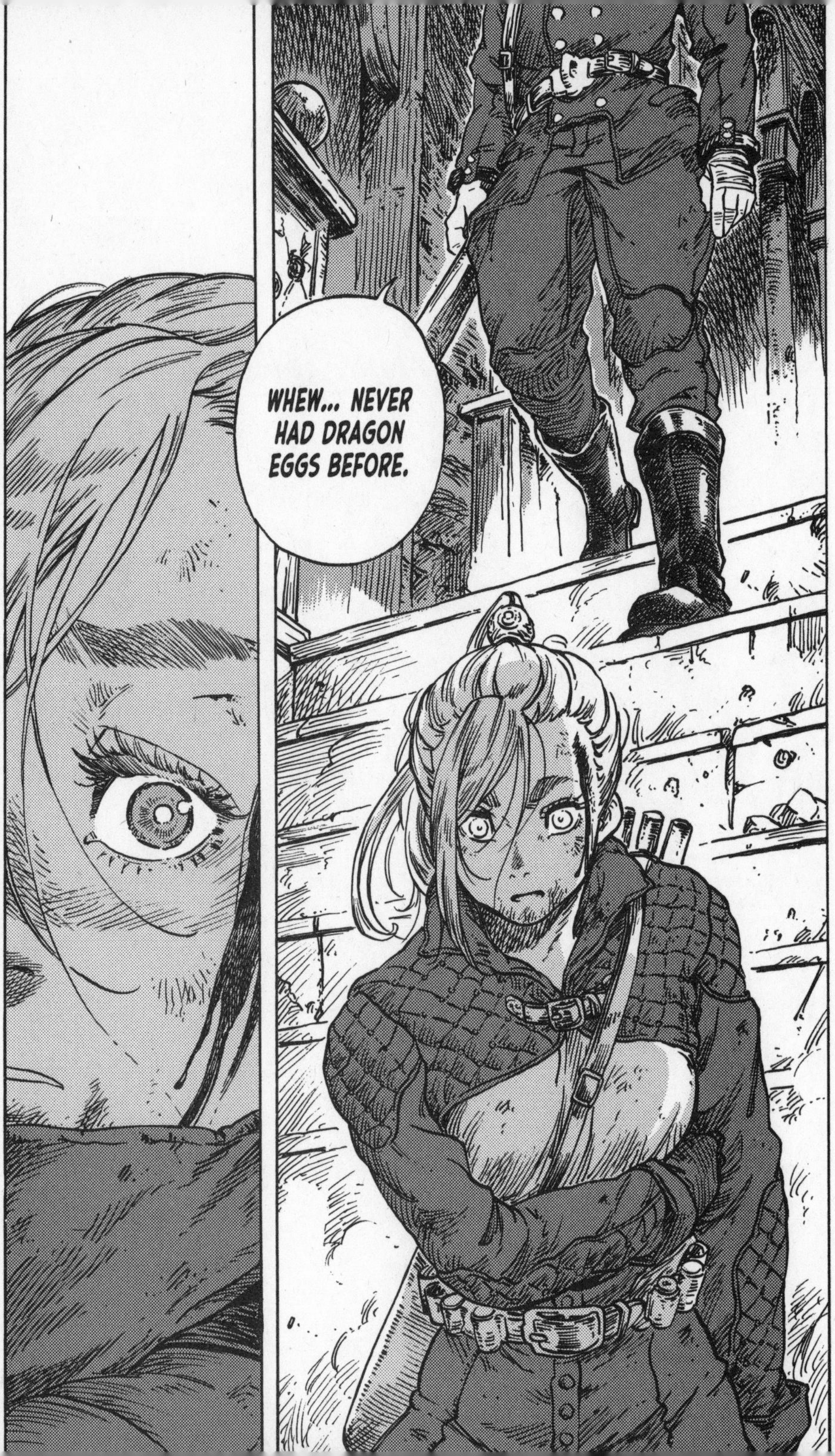
WHEW... NEVER HAD DRAGON EGGS BEFORE.

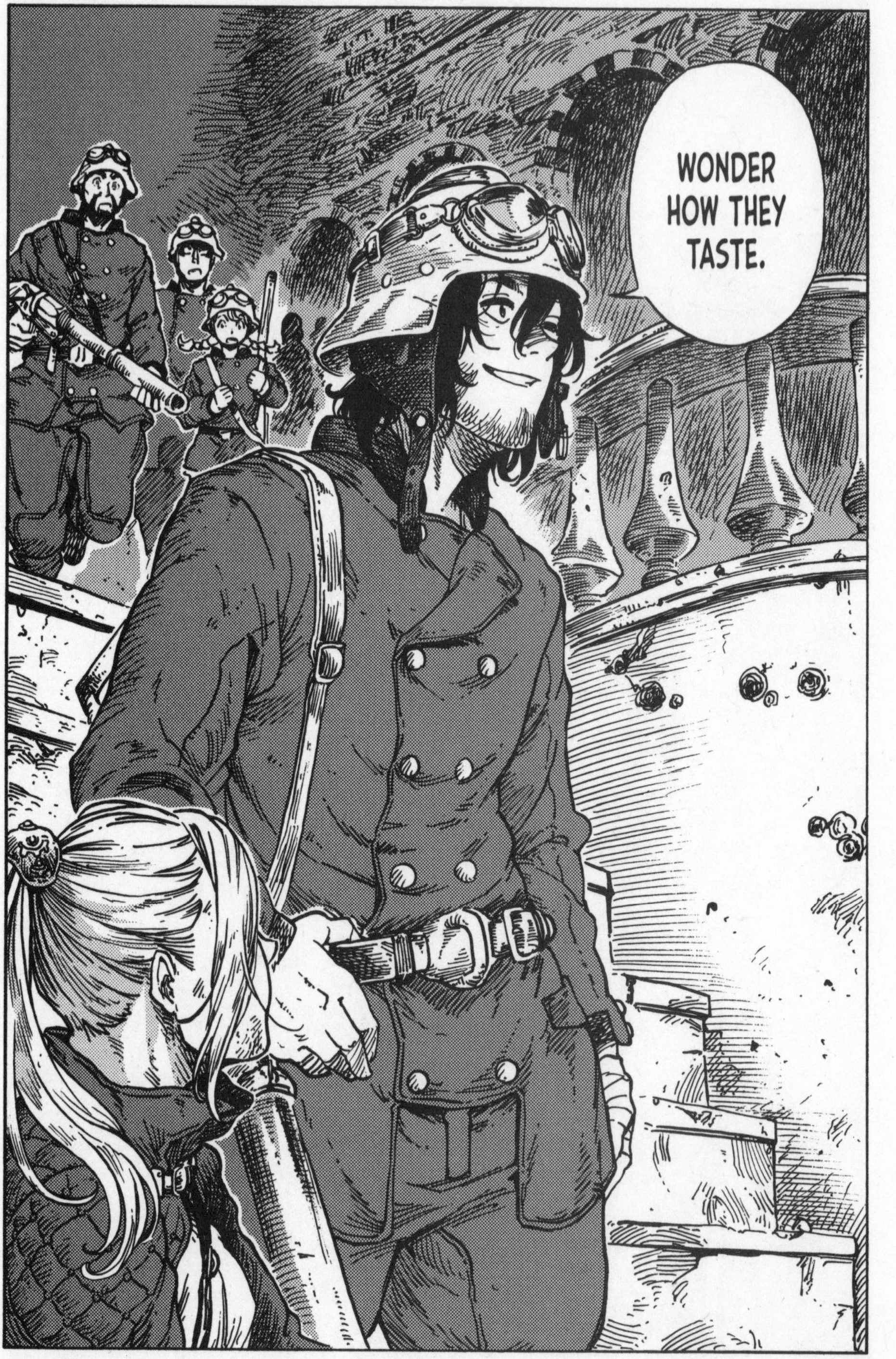
WONDER HOW THEY TASTE.

Flight 60 Beyond the Mists

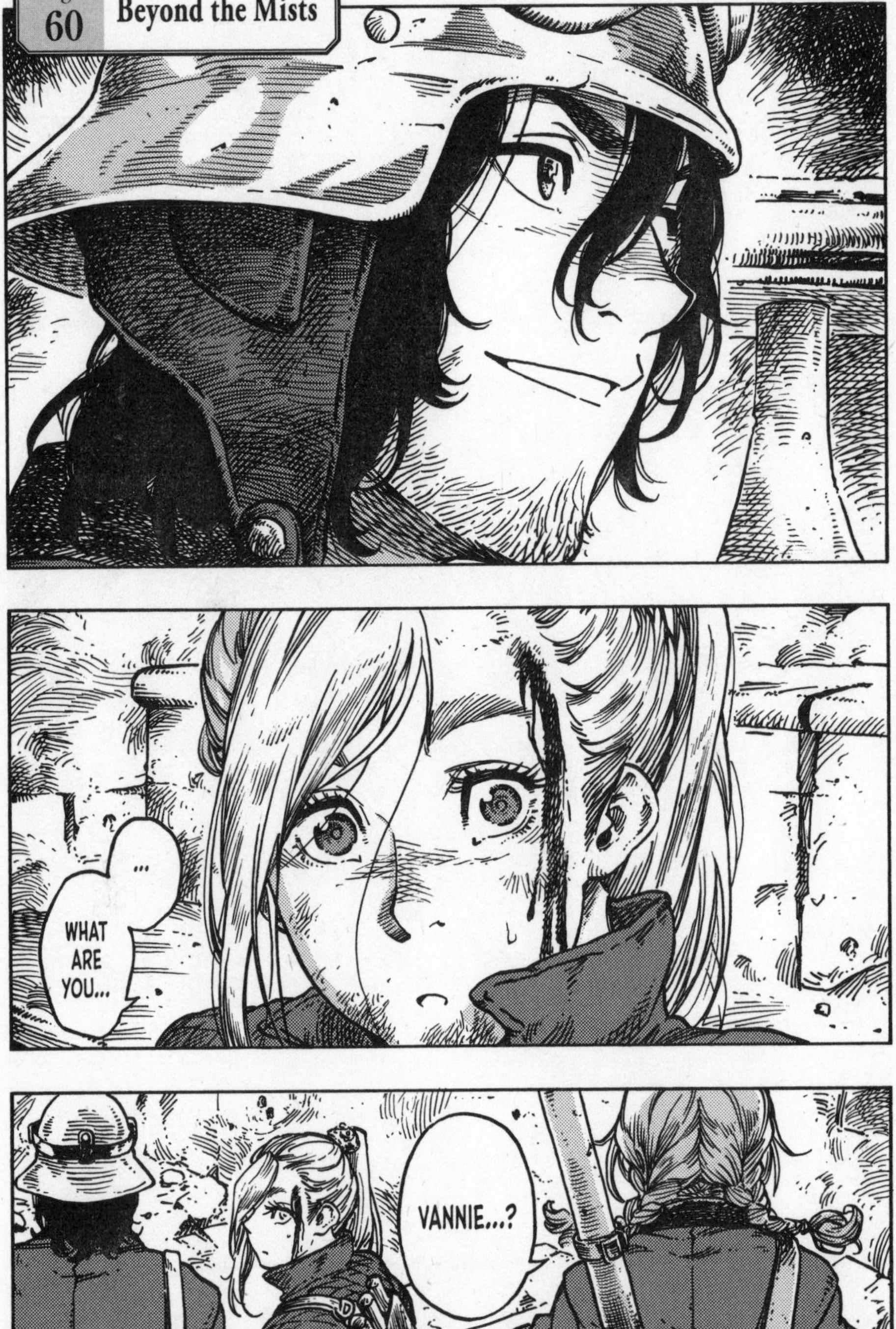
...
WHAT ARE YOU...
VANNIE...?

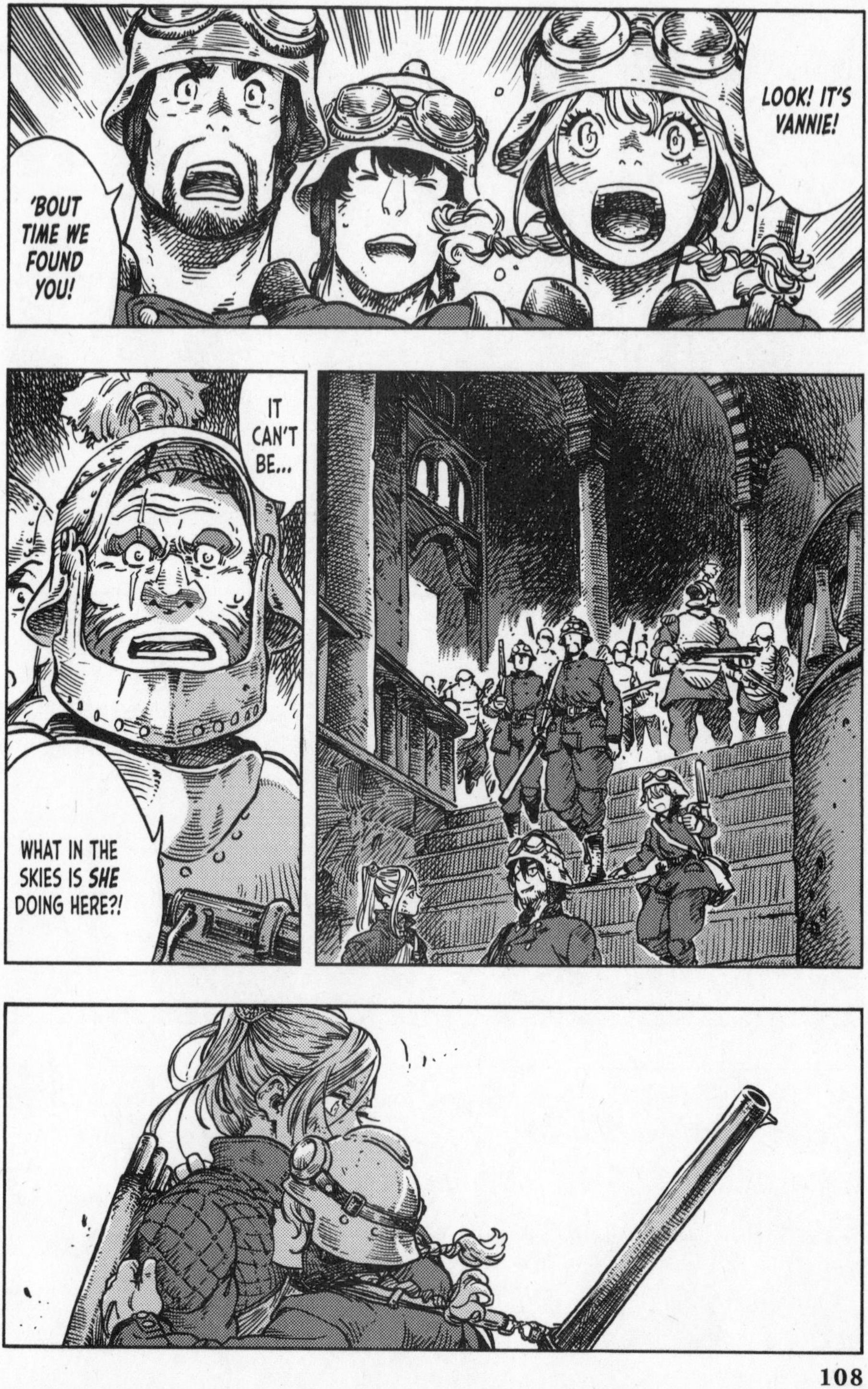
LOOK! IT'S VANNIE!
'BOUT TIME WE FOUND YOU!
IT CAN'T BE...
WHAT IN THE SKIES IS *SHE* DOING HERE?!

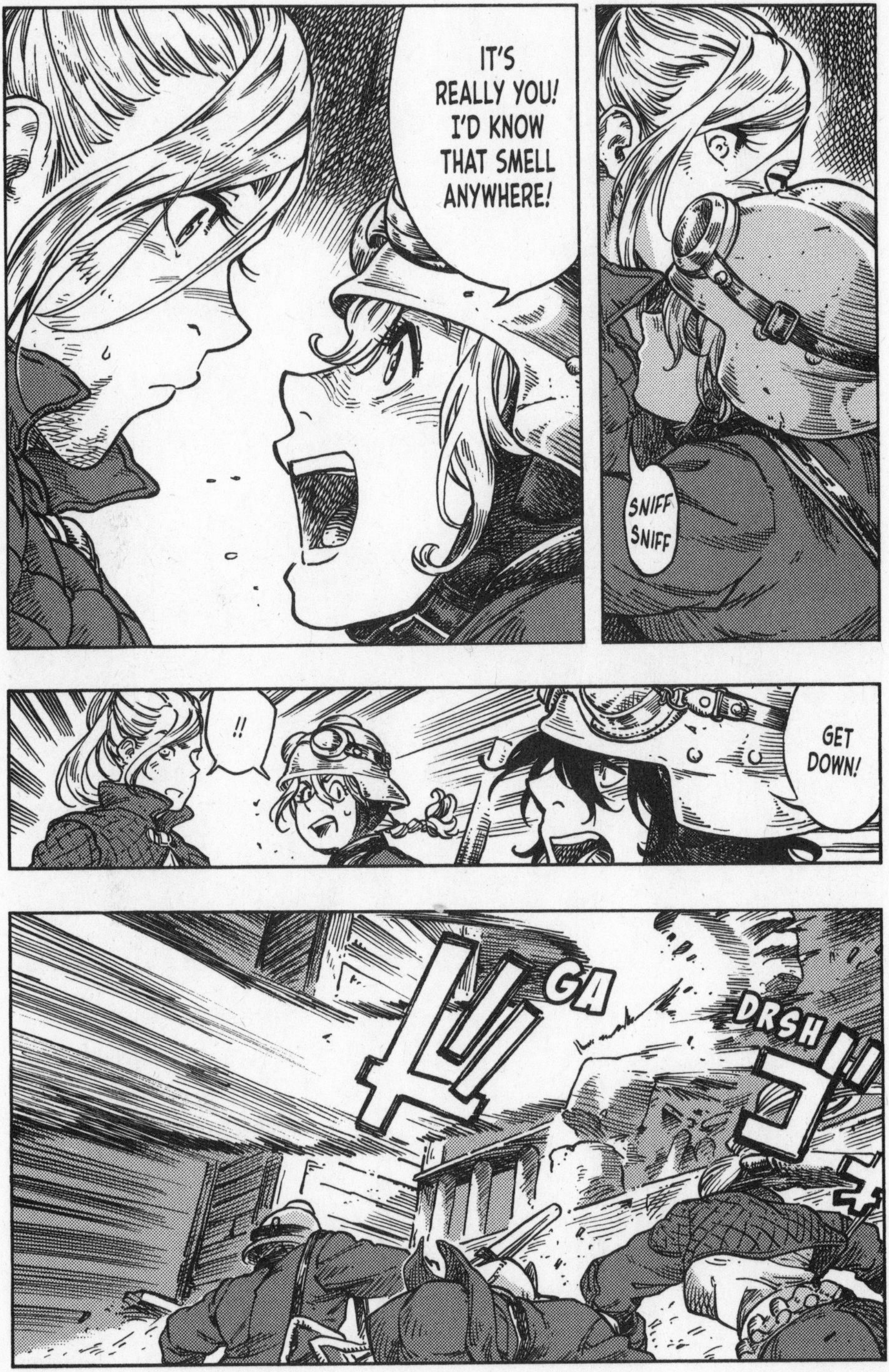
SNIFF SNIFF
IT'S REALLY YOU! I'D KNOW THAT SMELL ANYWHERE!
...
GET DOWN!
!!
DRSH
GA

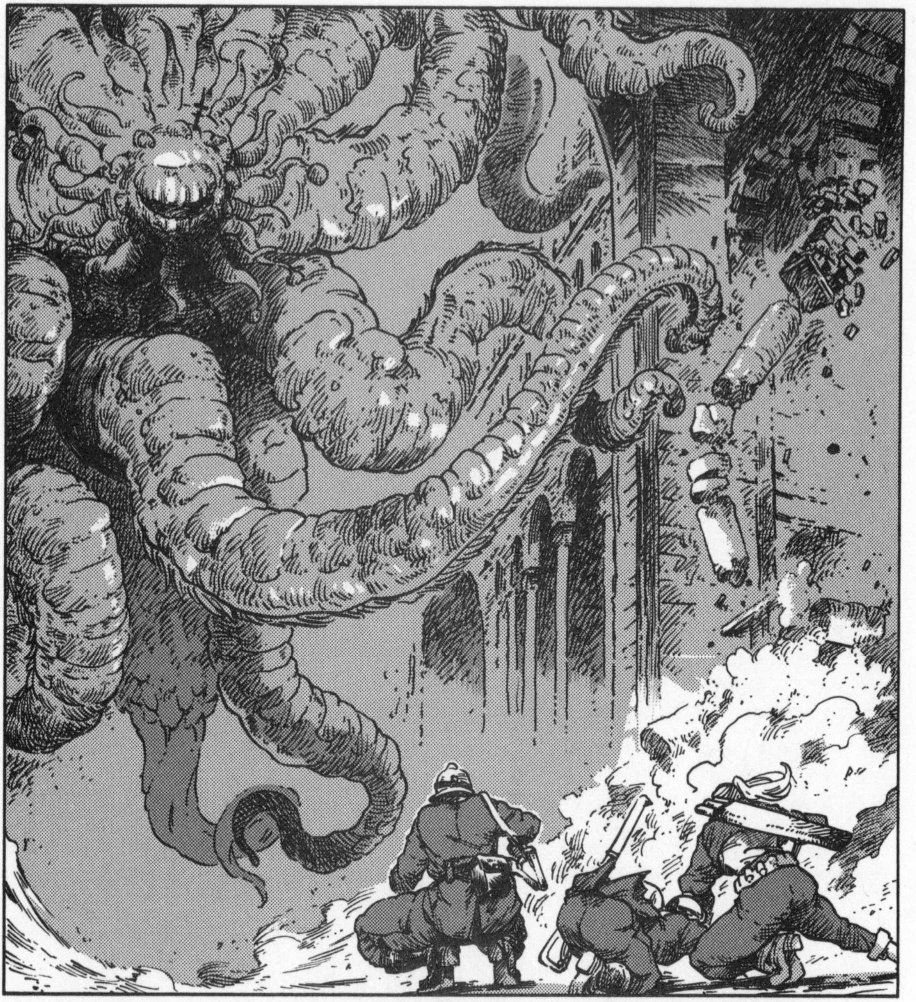

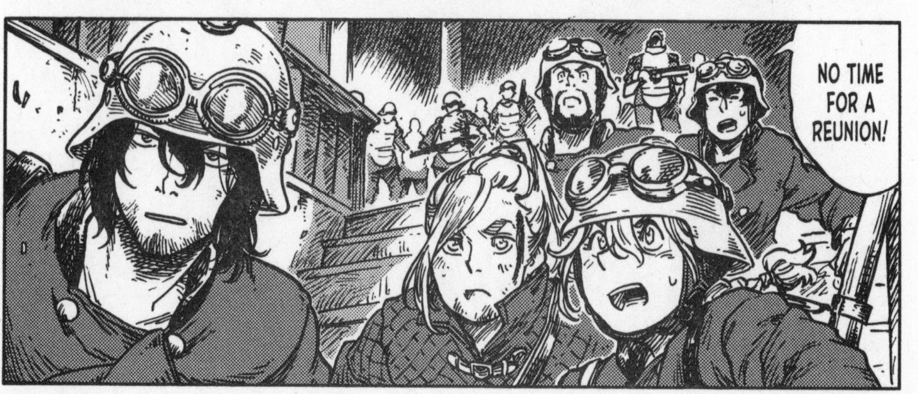
NO TIME FOR A REUNION!

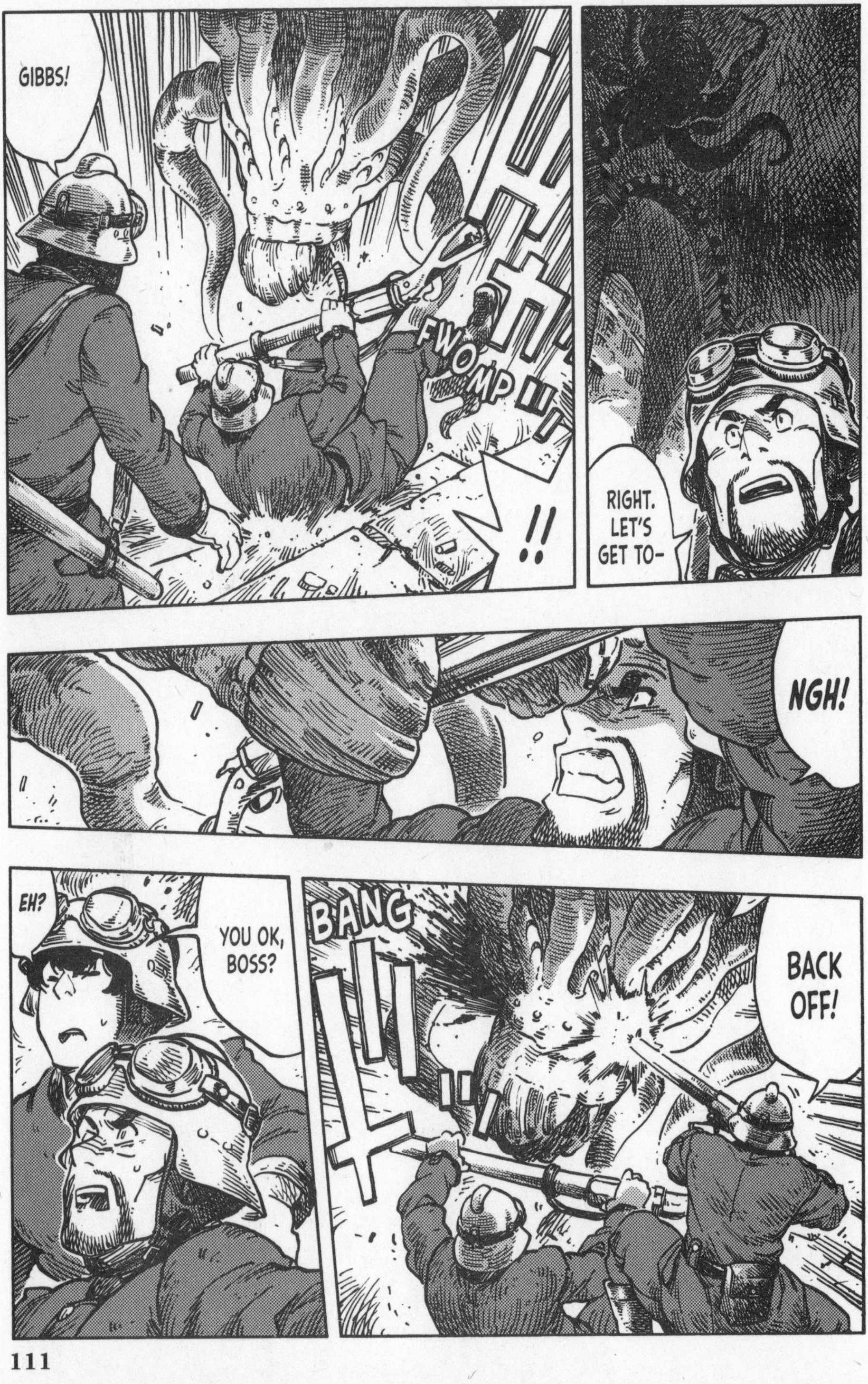
RIGHT. LET'S GET TO-
GIBBS!
FWOMP!!!
!!
NGH!
BACK OFF!
BANG
YOU OK, BOSS?
EH?

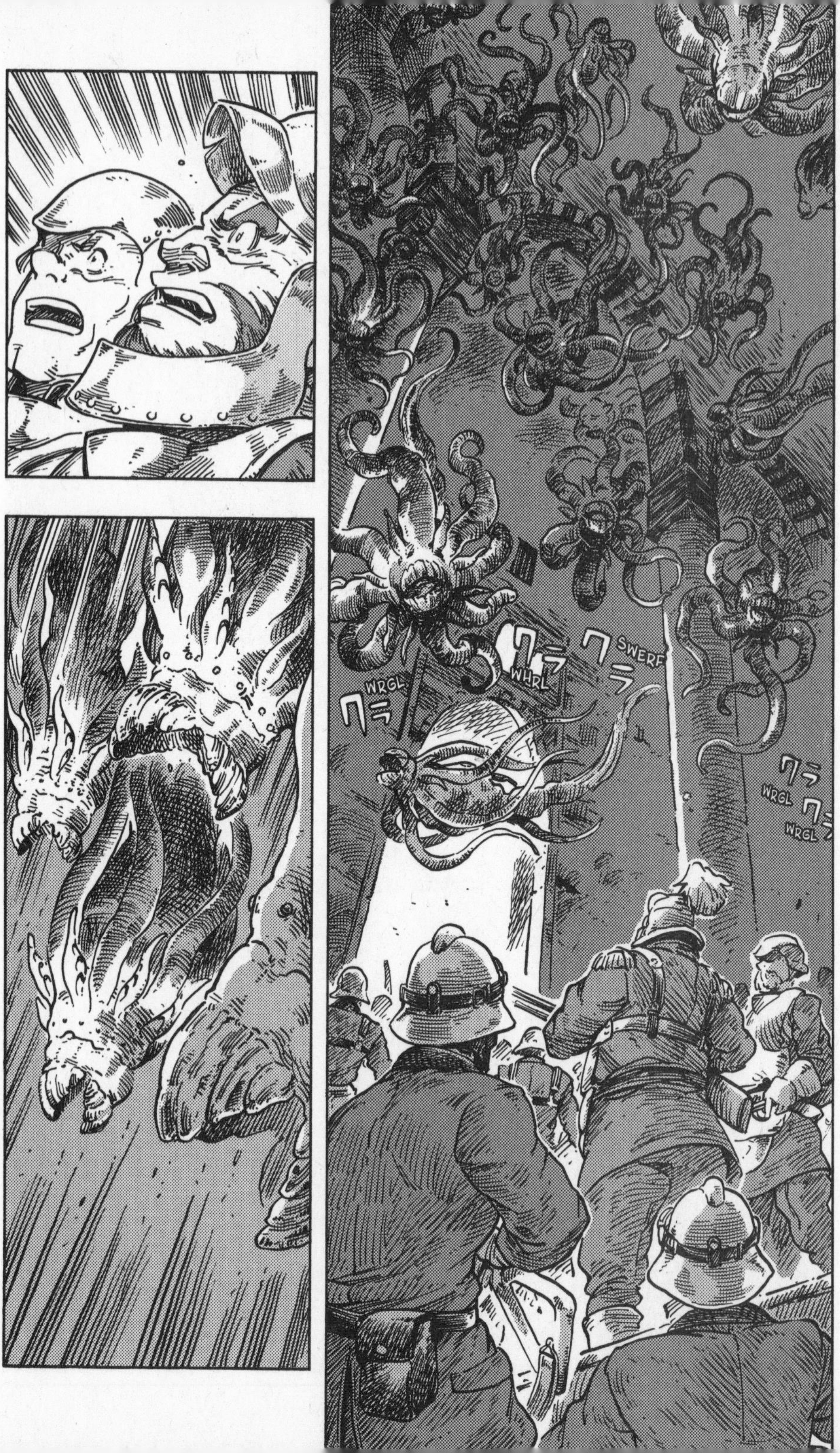
クラ SWERF
クラ WHRL
クラ WRGL
クラ WRGL
クラ WRGL

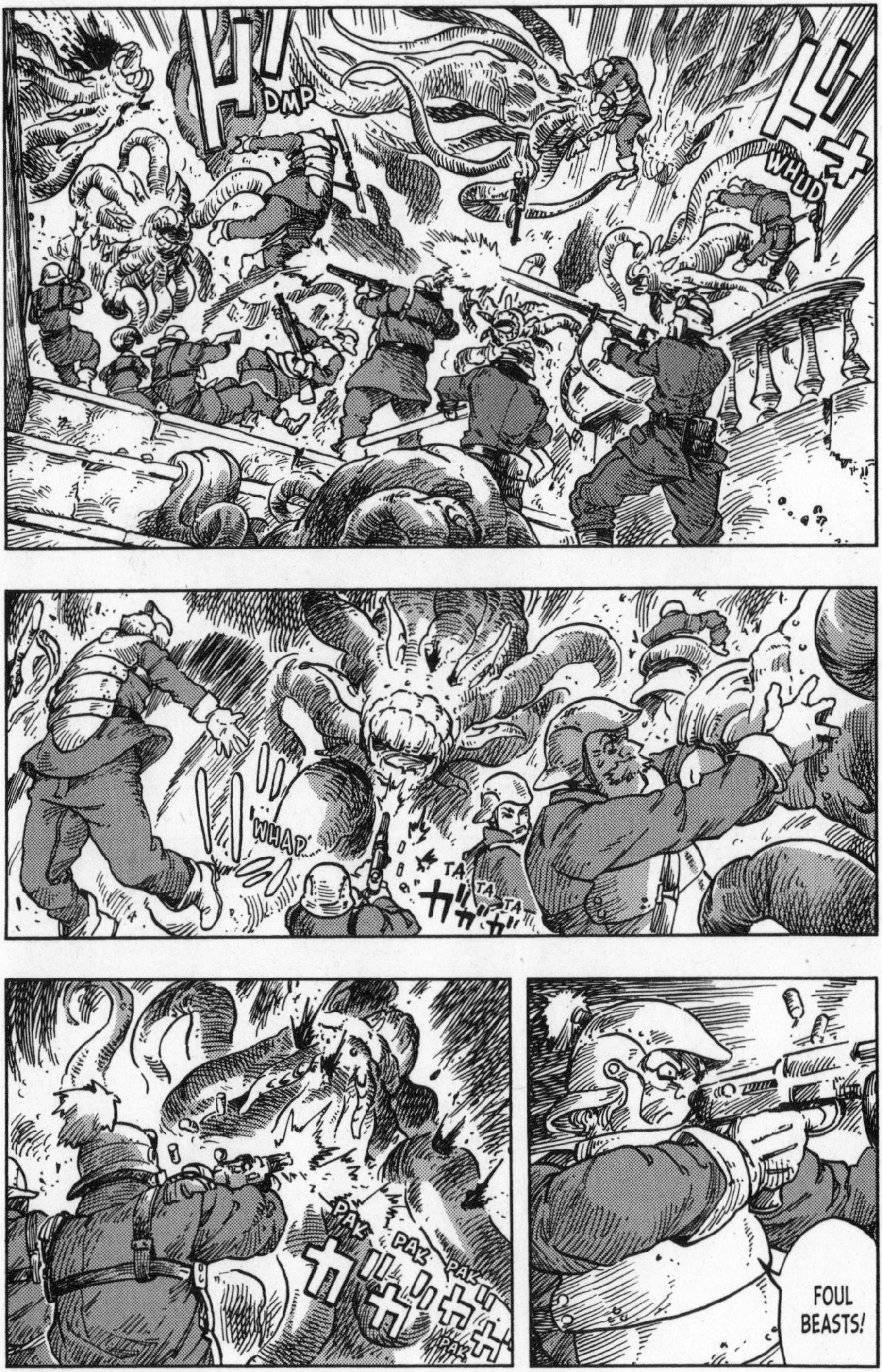
WHUD
DMP
TA TA TA
WHAP
FOUL BEASTS!
PAK PAK PAK PAK

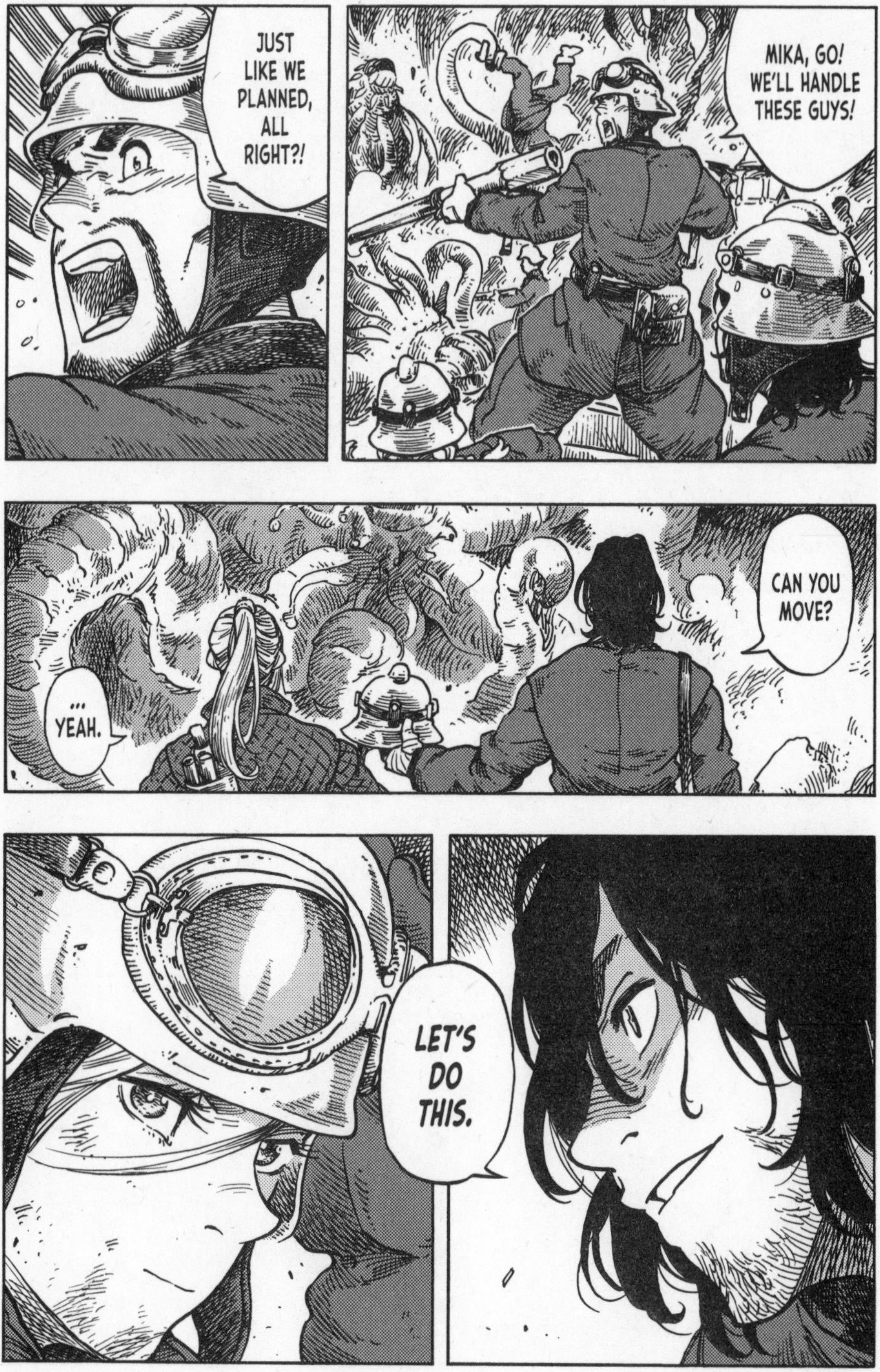
MIKA, GO! WE'LL HANDLE THESE GUYS!
JUST LIKE WE PLANNED, ALL RIGHT?!
CAN YOU MOVE?
... YEAH.
LET'S DO THIS.

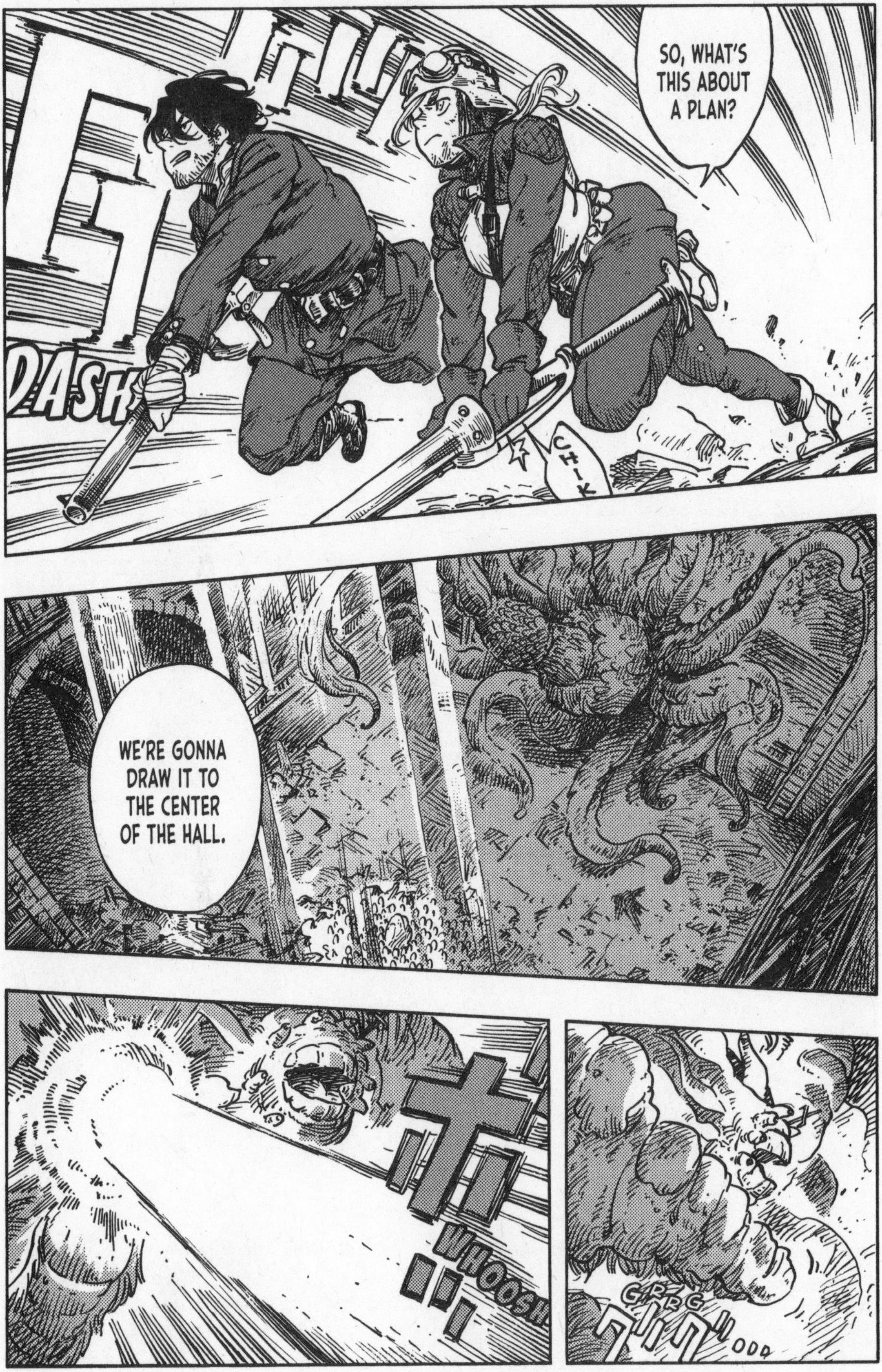
SO, WHAT'S THIS ABOUT A PLAN?
DASH
CHIK
WE'RE GONNA DRAW IT TO THE CENTER OF THE HALL.
GRRG
WHOOSH

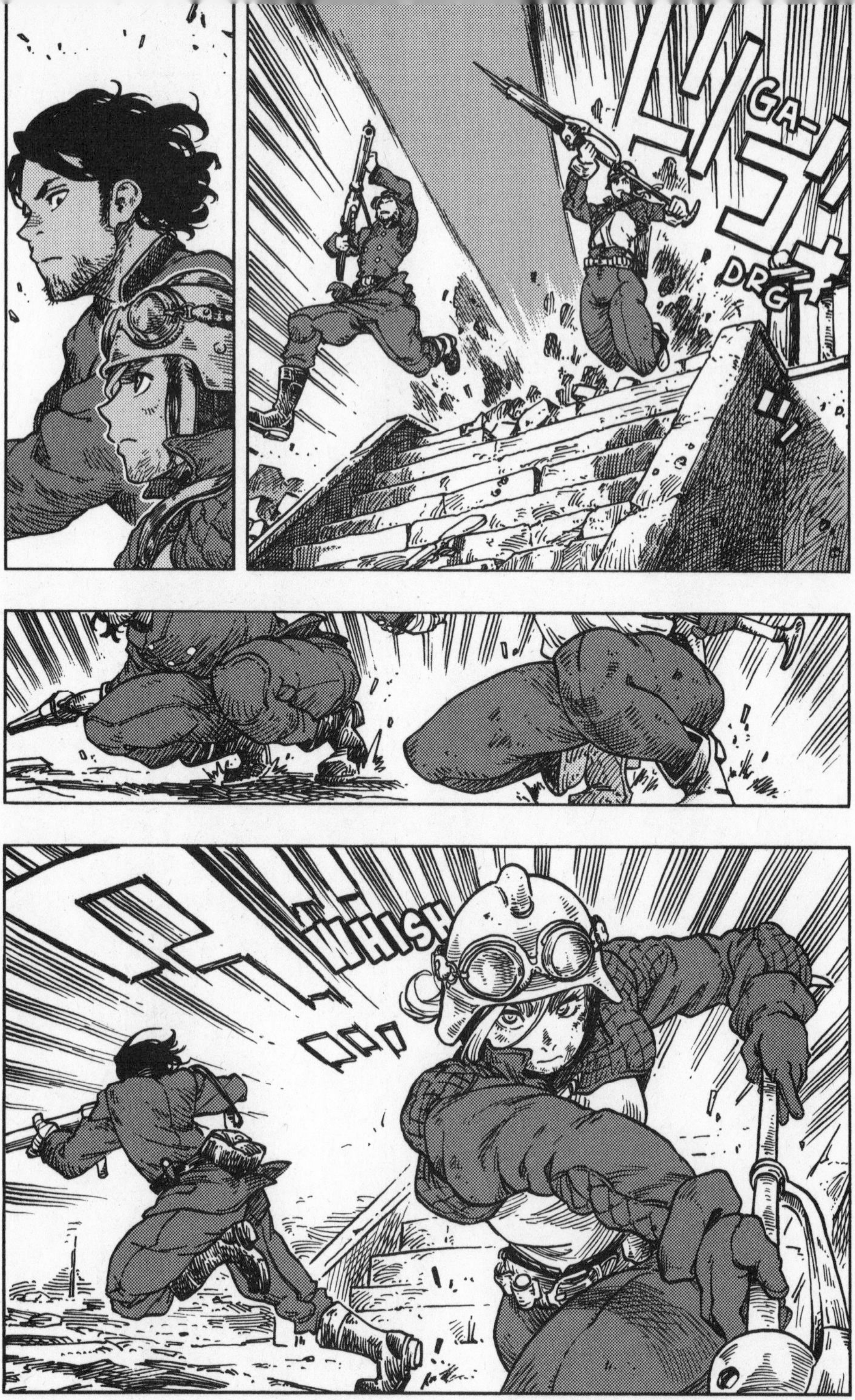
GA-
DRG
WHISH

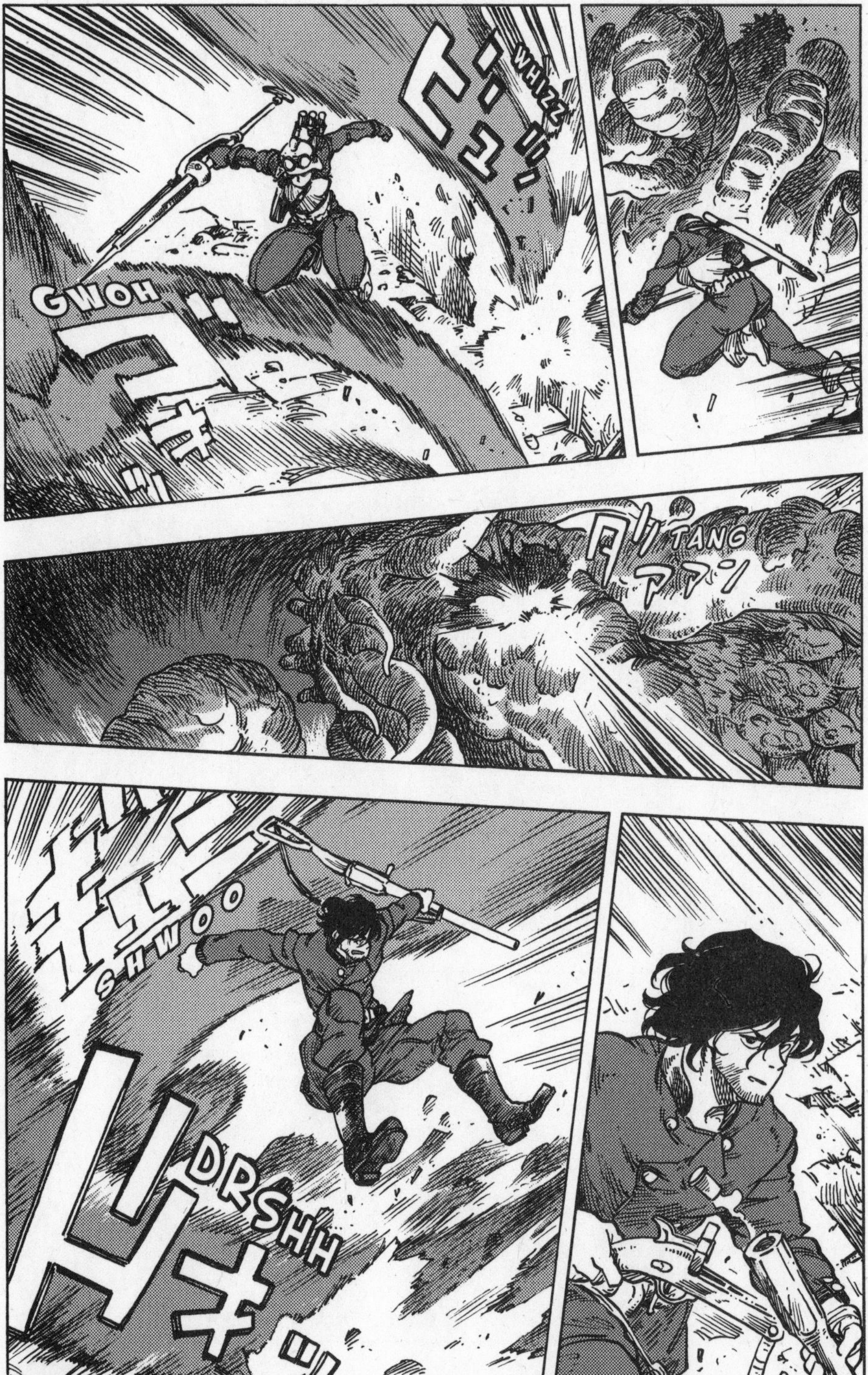
WHIZZ
GWOH
TANG
SHWOO
DRSHH

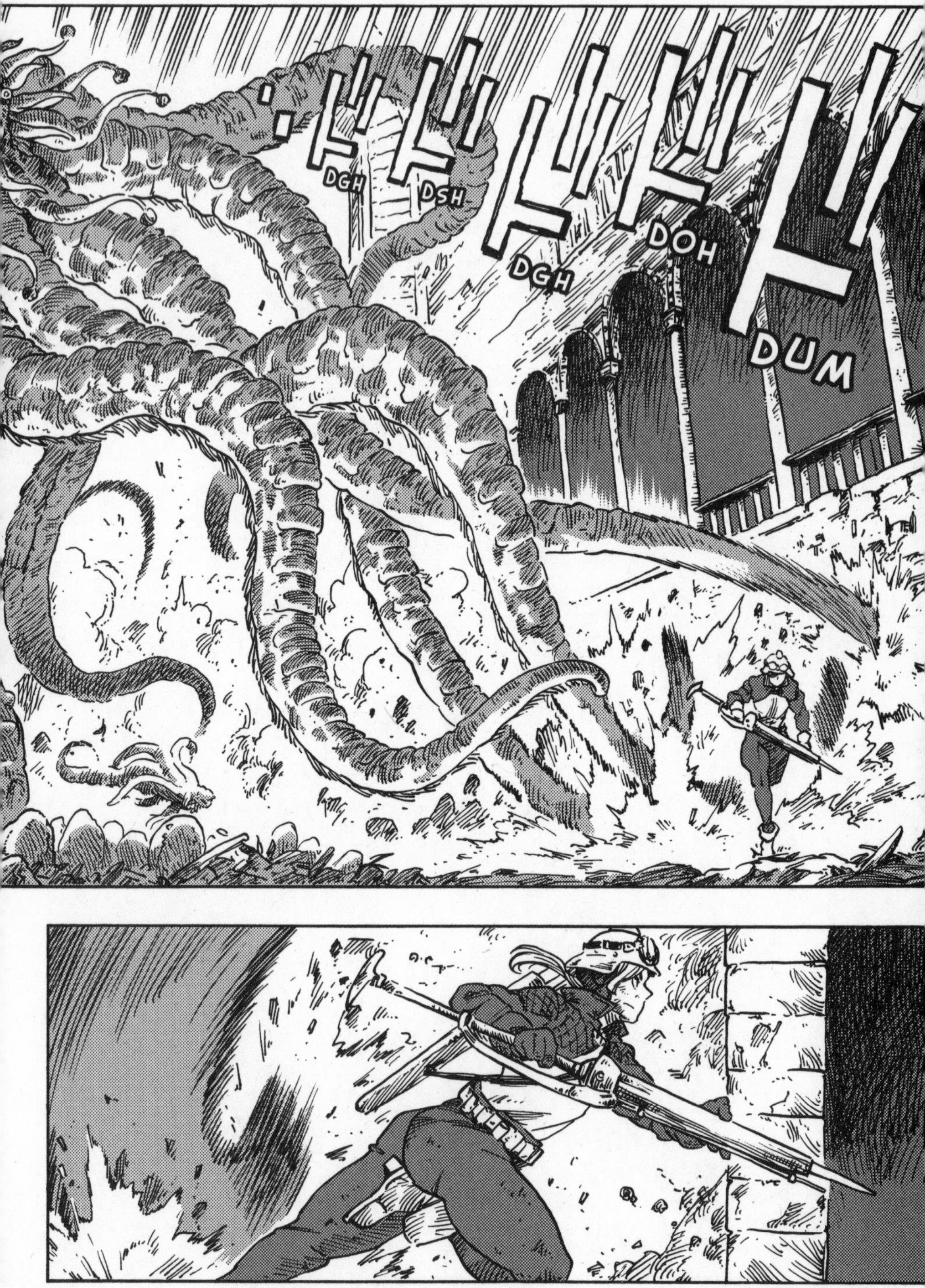
DUM
DOH
DGH
DSH
DGH

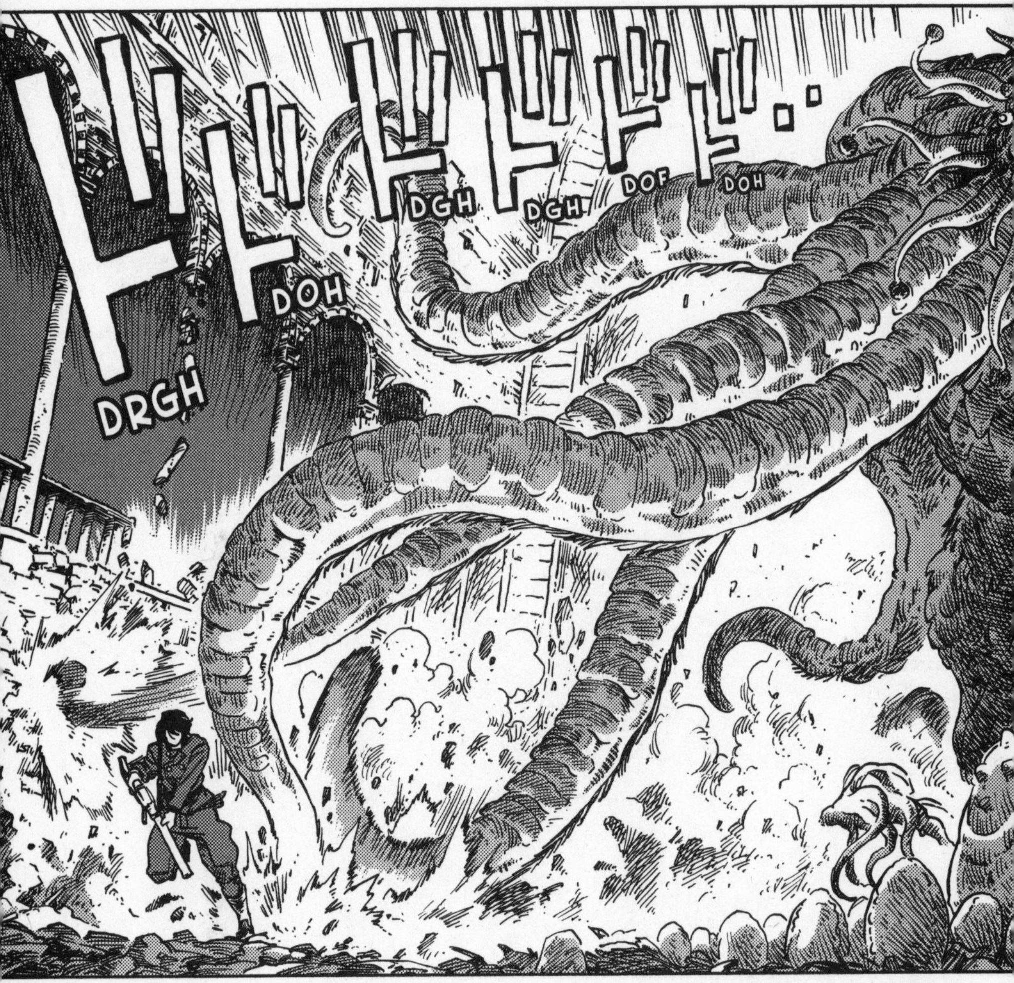
DRGH
DOH
DGH
DGH
DOF
DOH

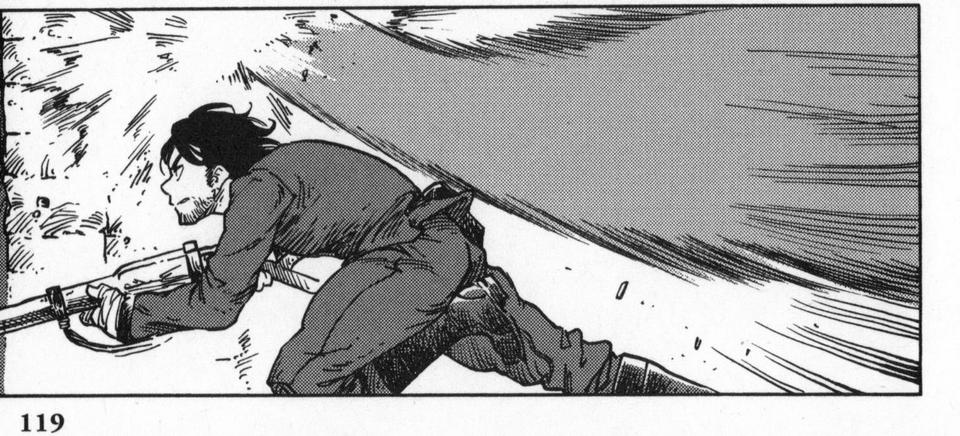

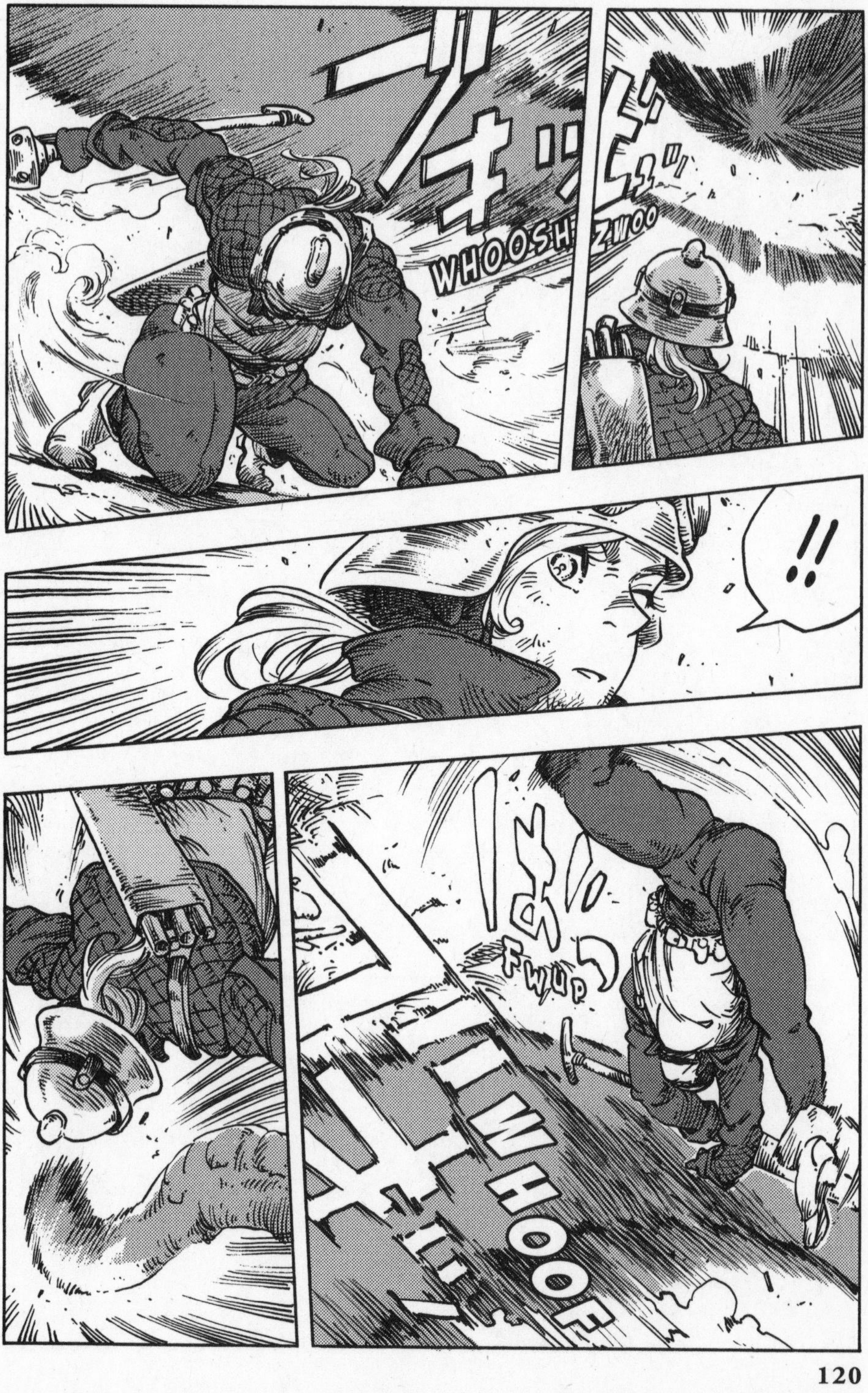
ZWOO
WHOOSH
!!
FWUP
WHOOF

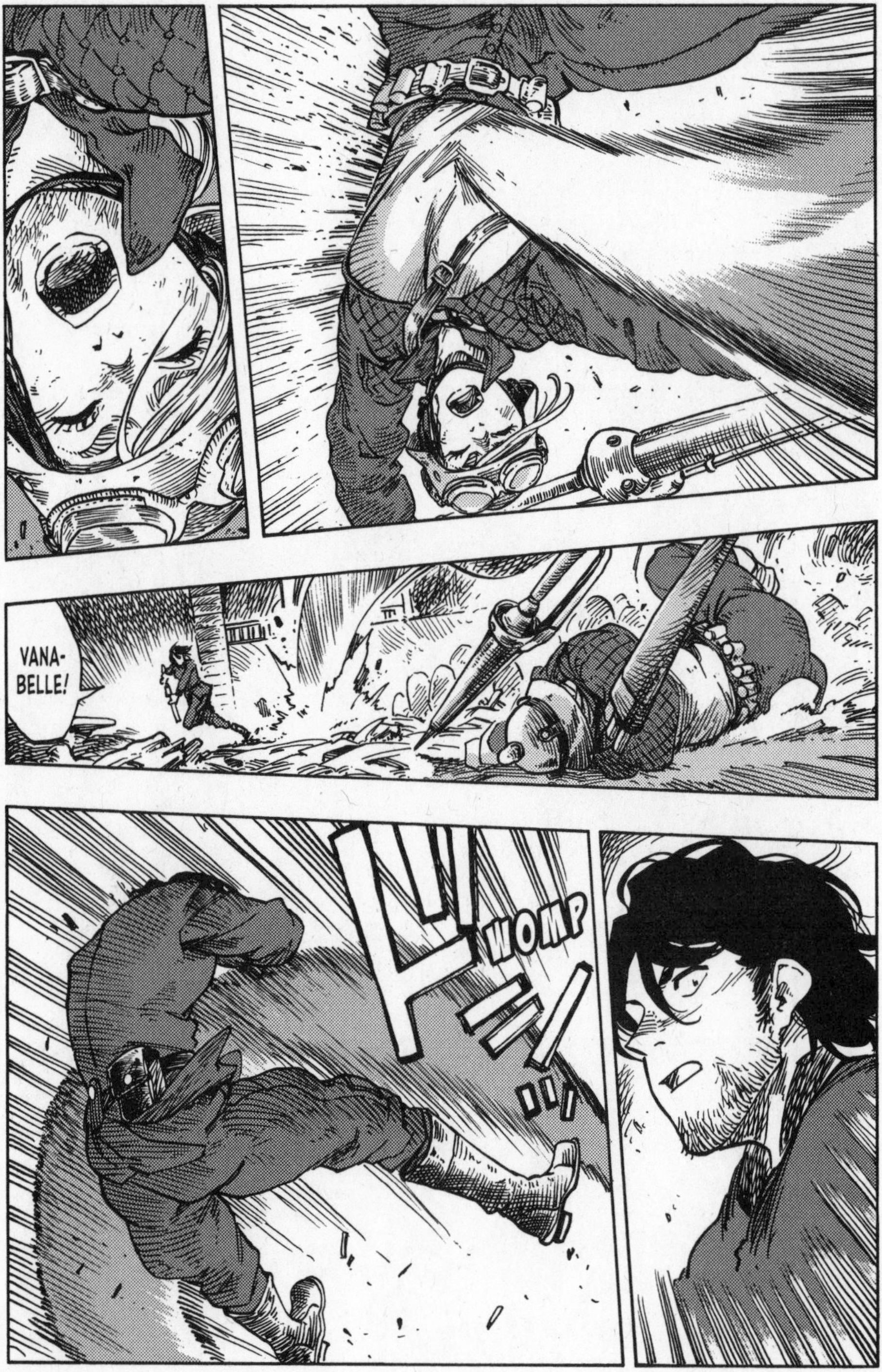
VANA-
BELLE!
WOMP

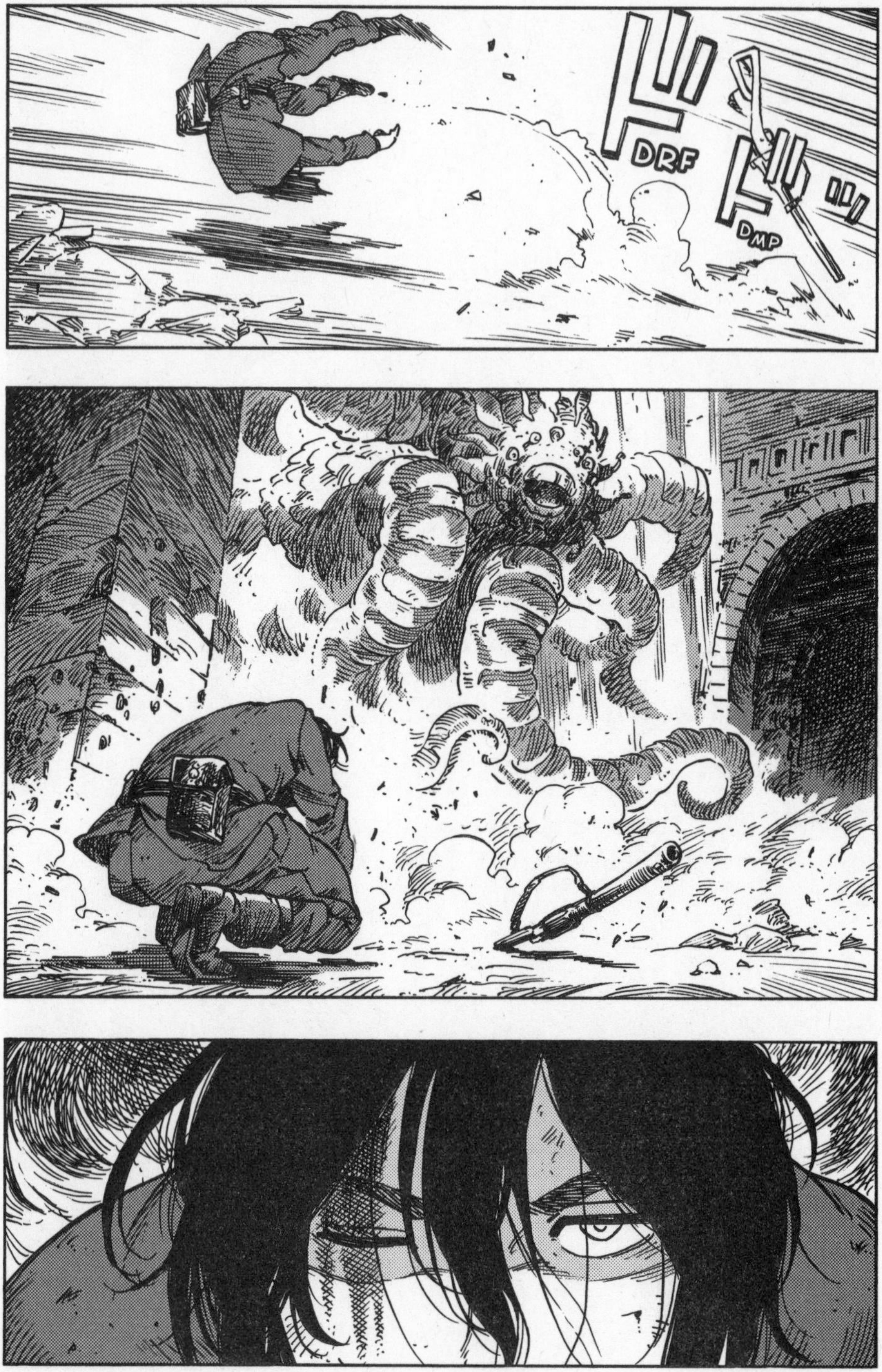
DRF
DMP

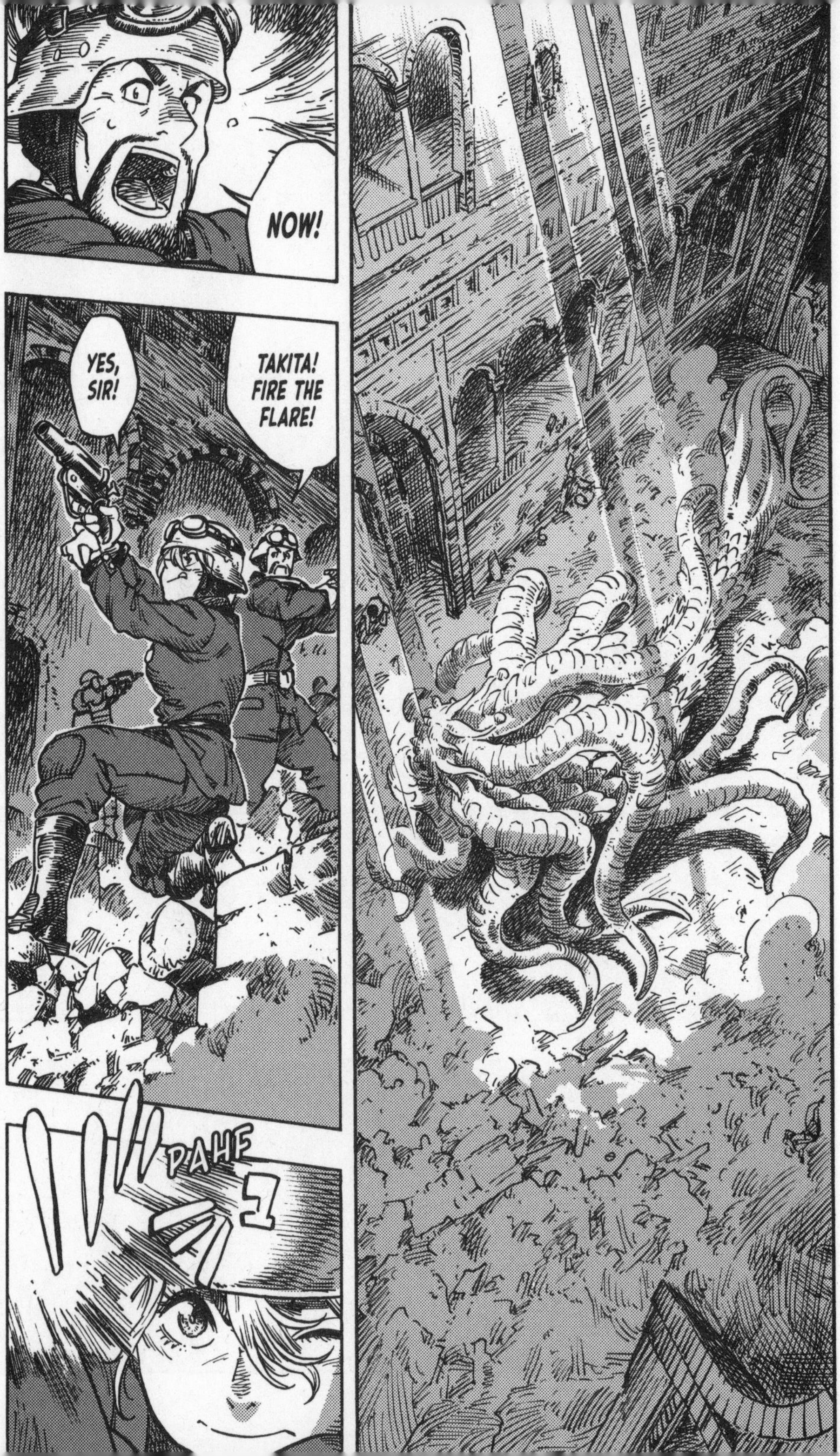
NOW!
TAKITA! FIRE THE FLARE!
YES, SIR!
PAHF

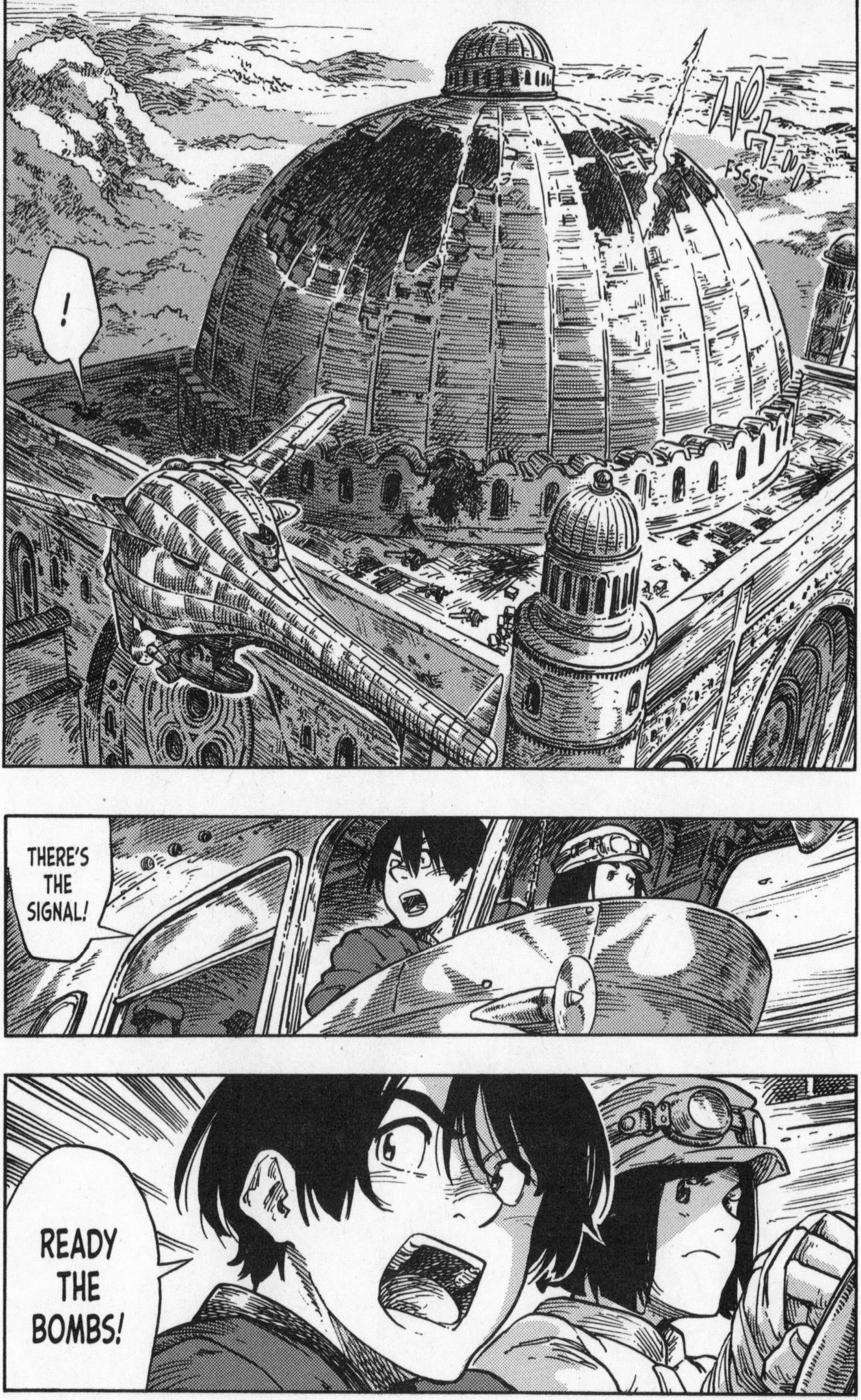
FSSST
!
THERE'S THE SIGNAL!
READY THE BOMBS!

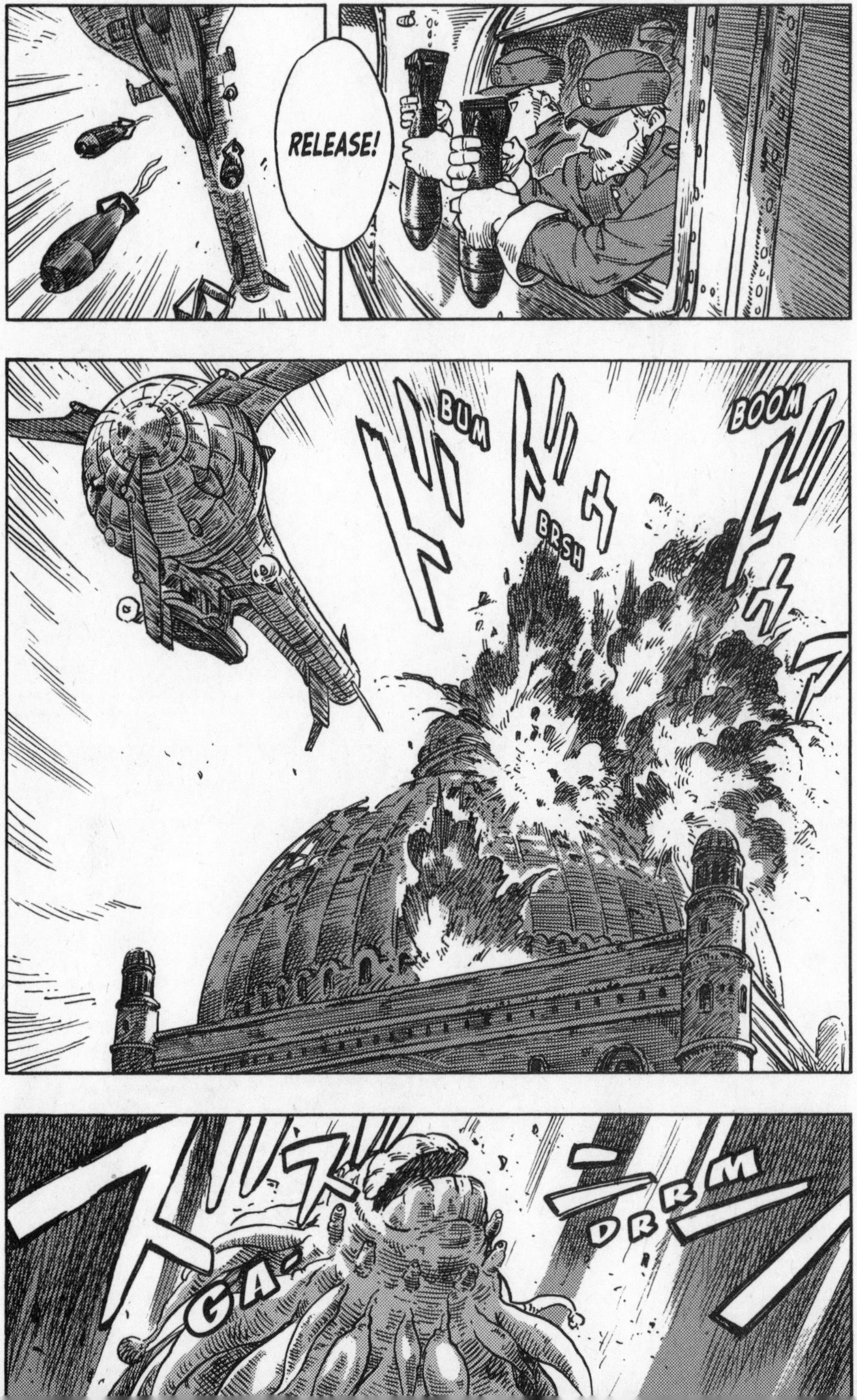
RELEASE!
BOOM
BUM
BRSH
DRRM
GA-

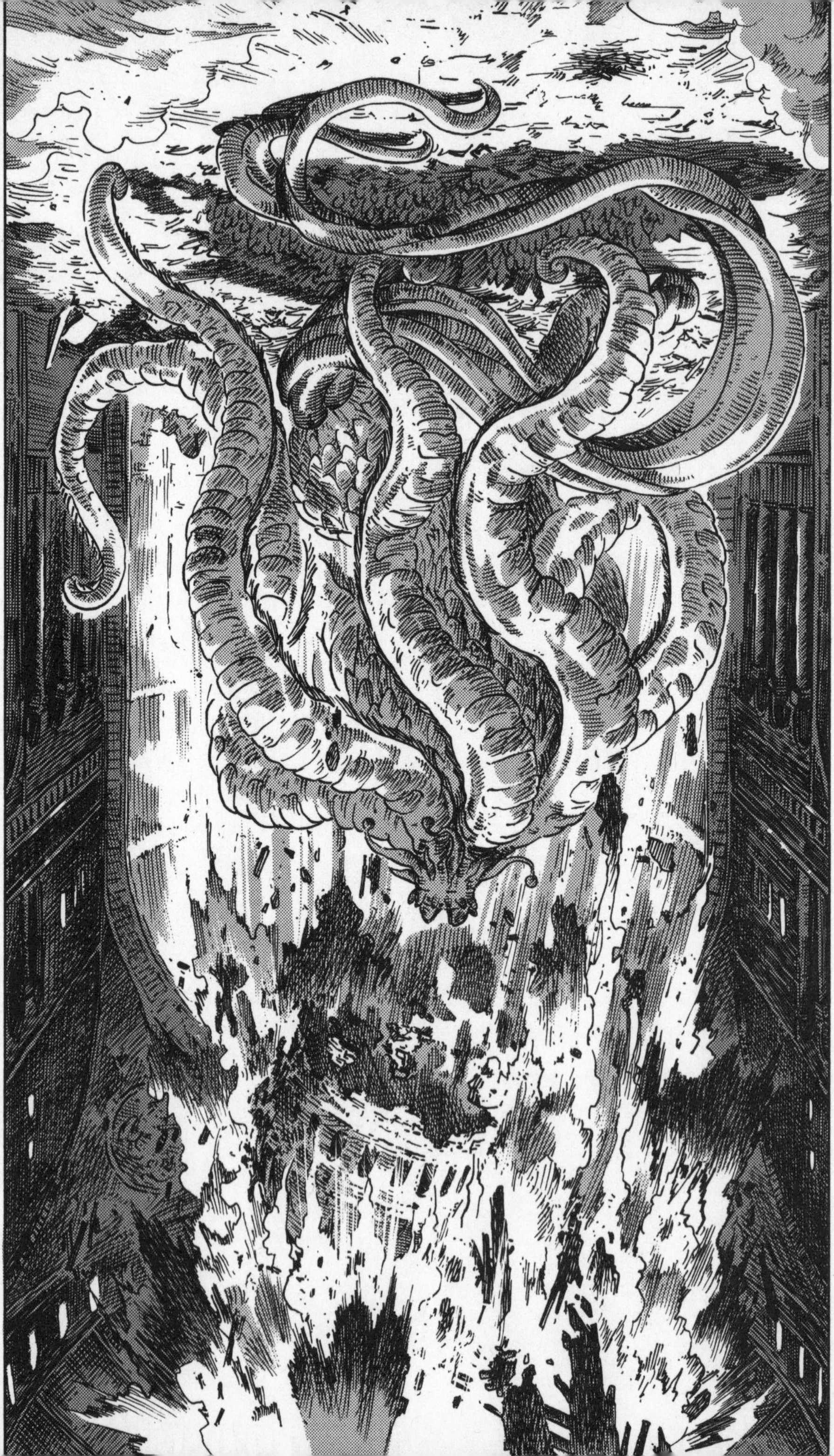

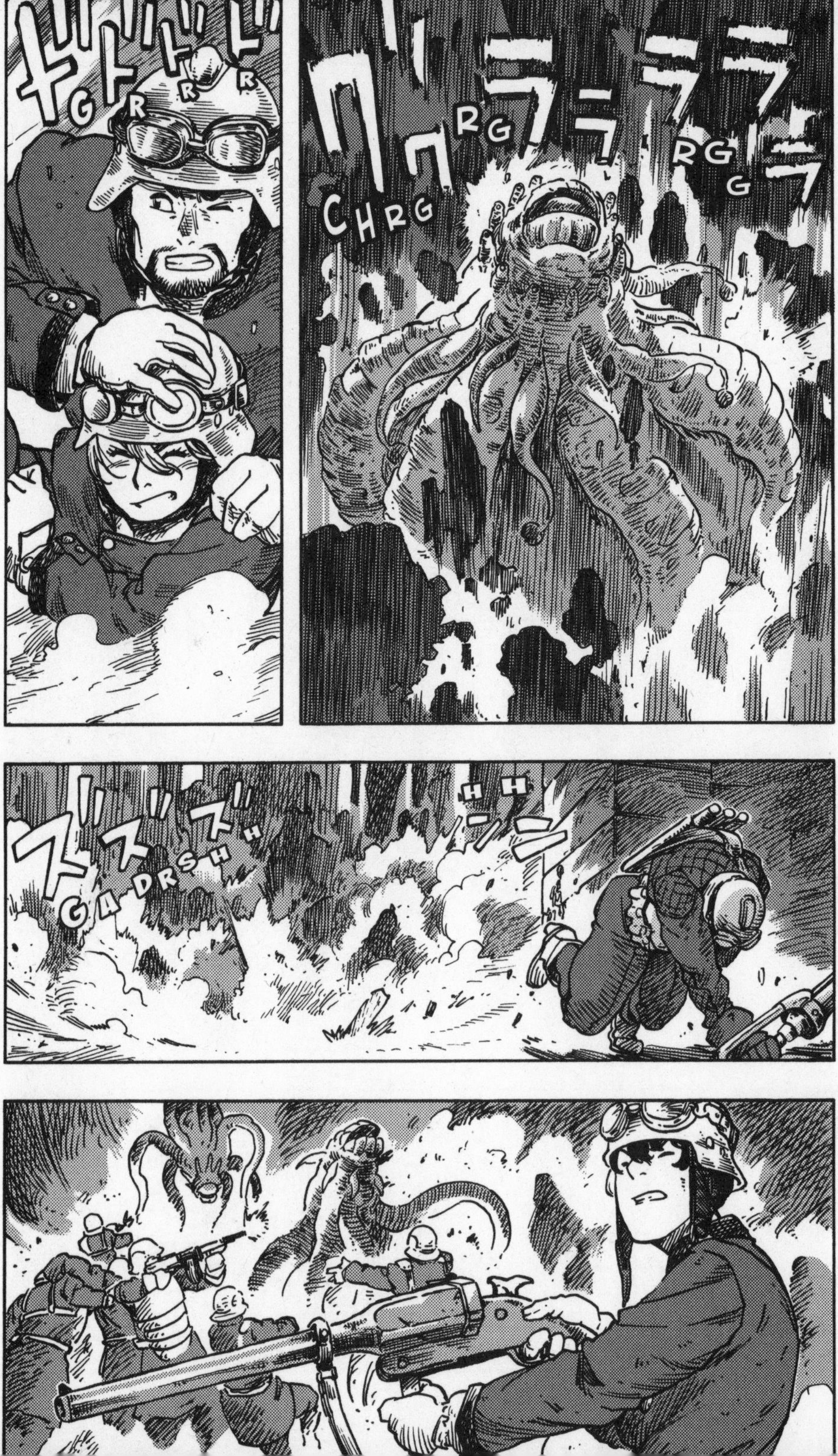
CHRG
RG
RGG
GRRR
GADRSHH
HH

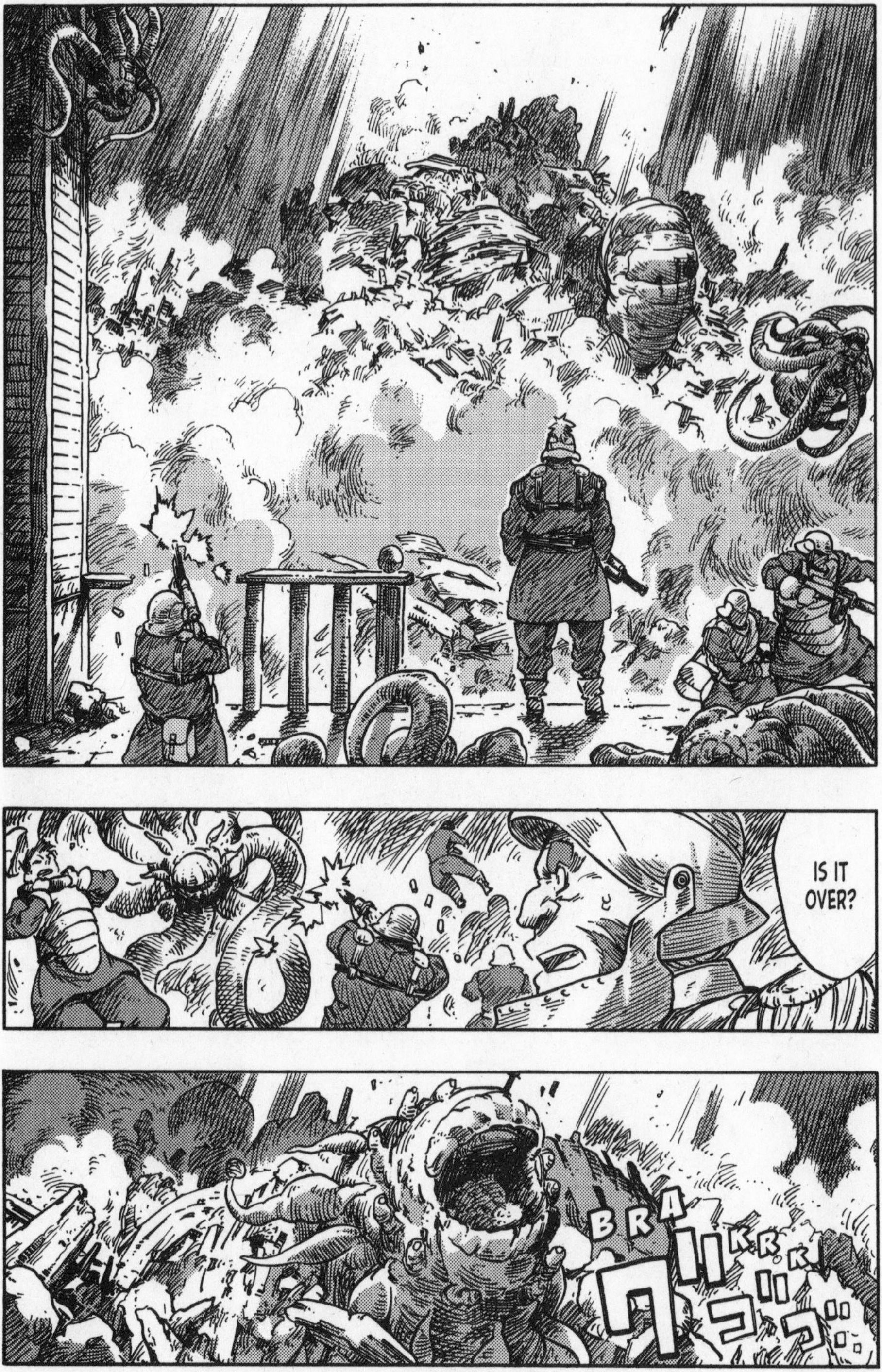
IS IT OVER?
BRAKRK

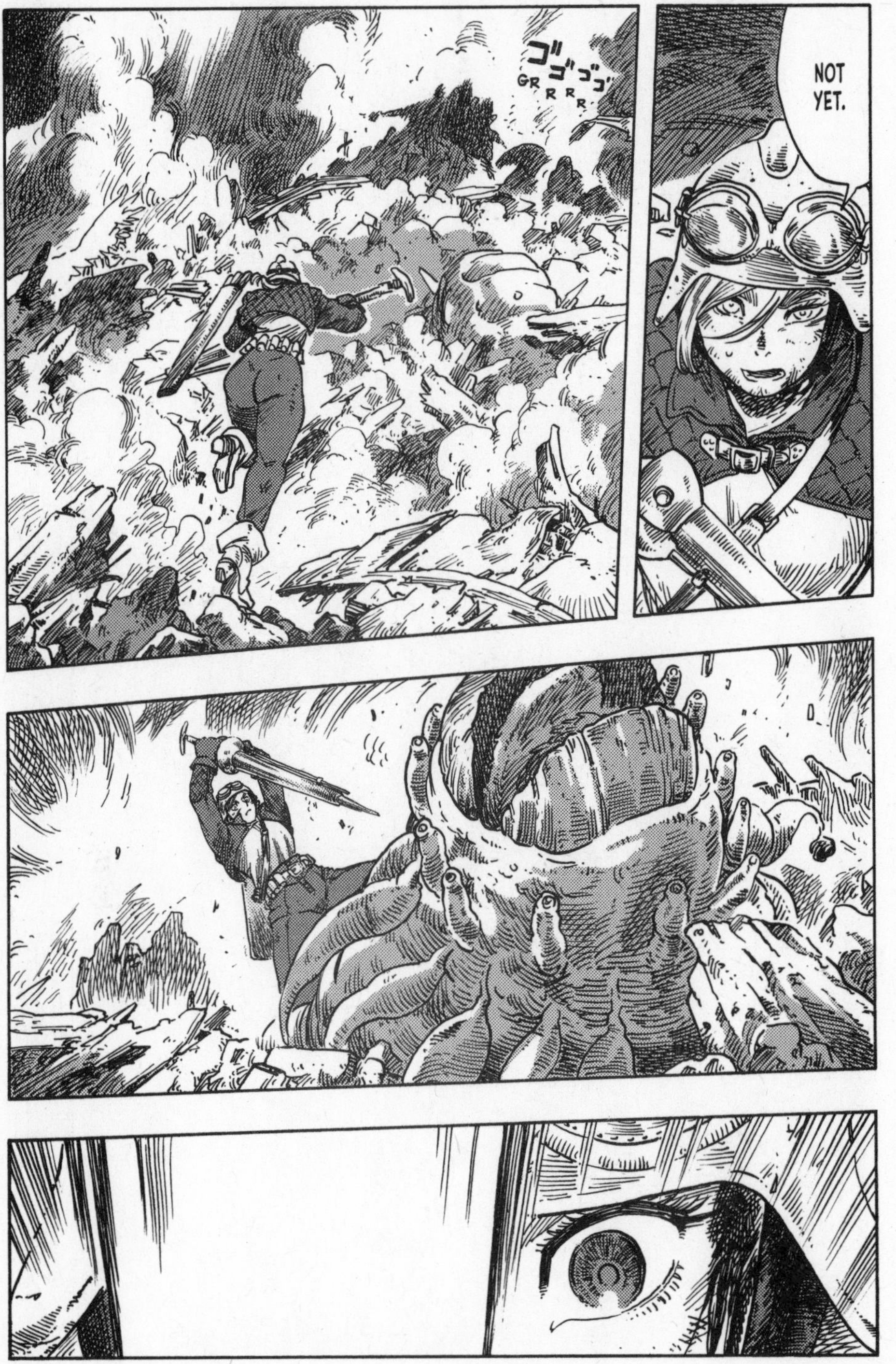
NOT YET.
ゴゴゴゴ
GRRRR

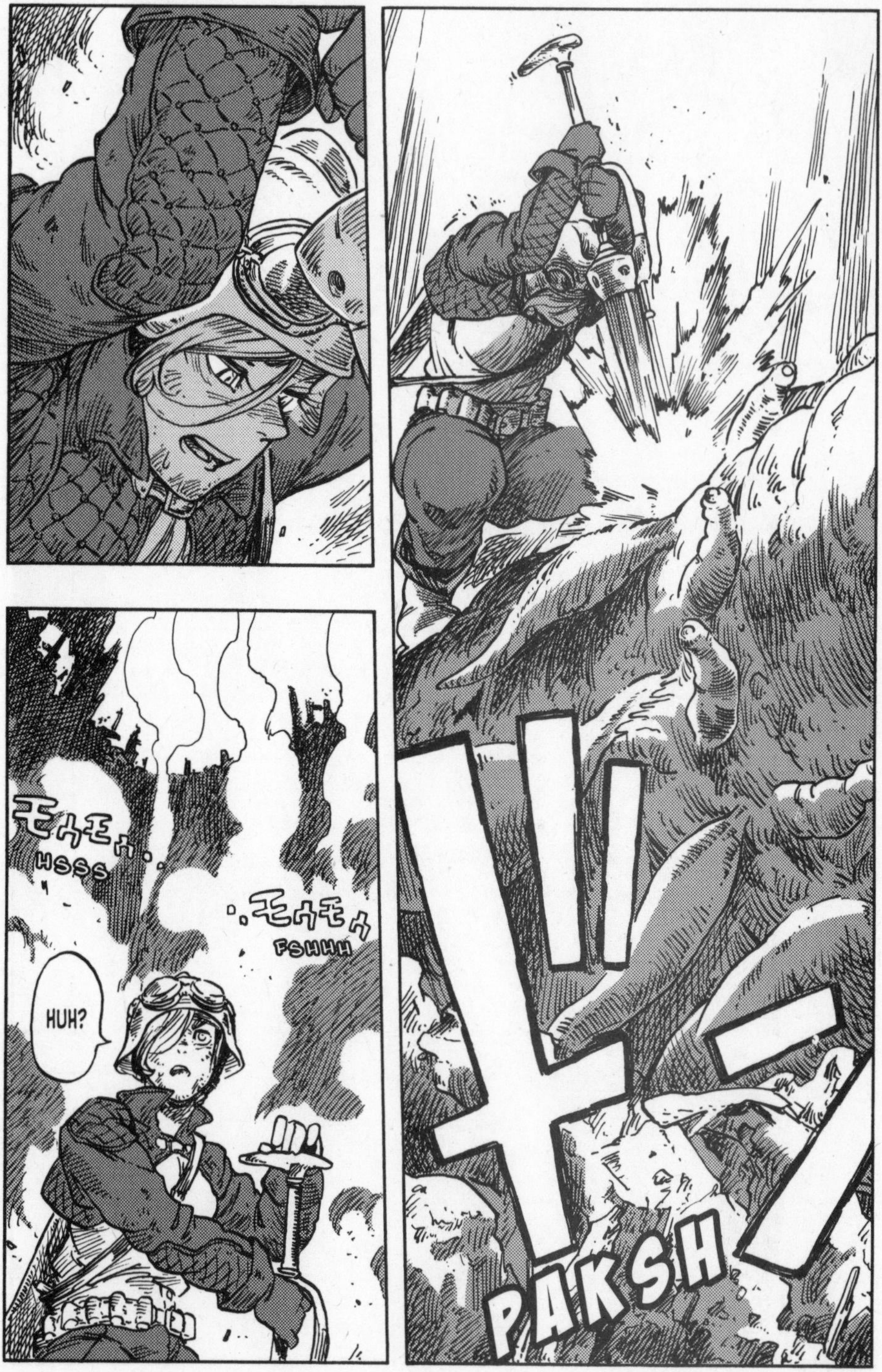
PAKSH
モクモク‥
HSSS
モクモク。
FSHHH
HUH?

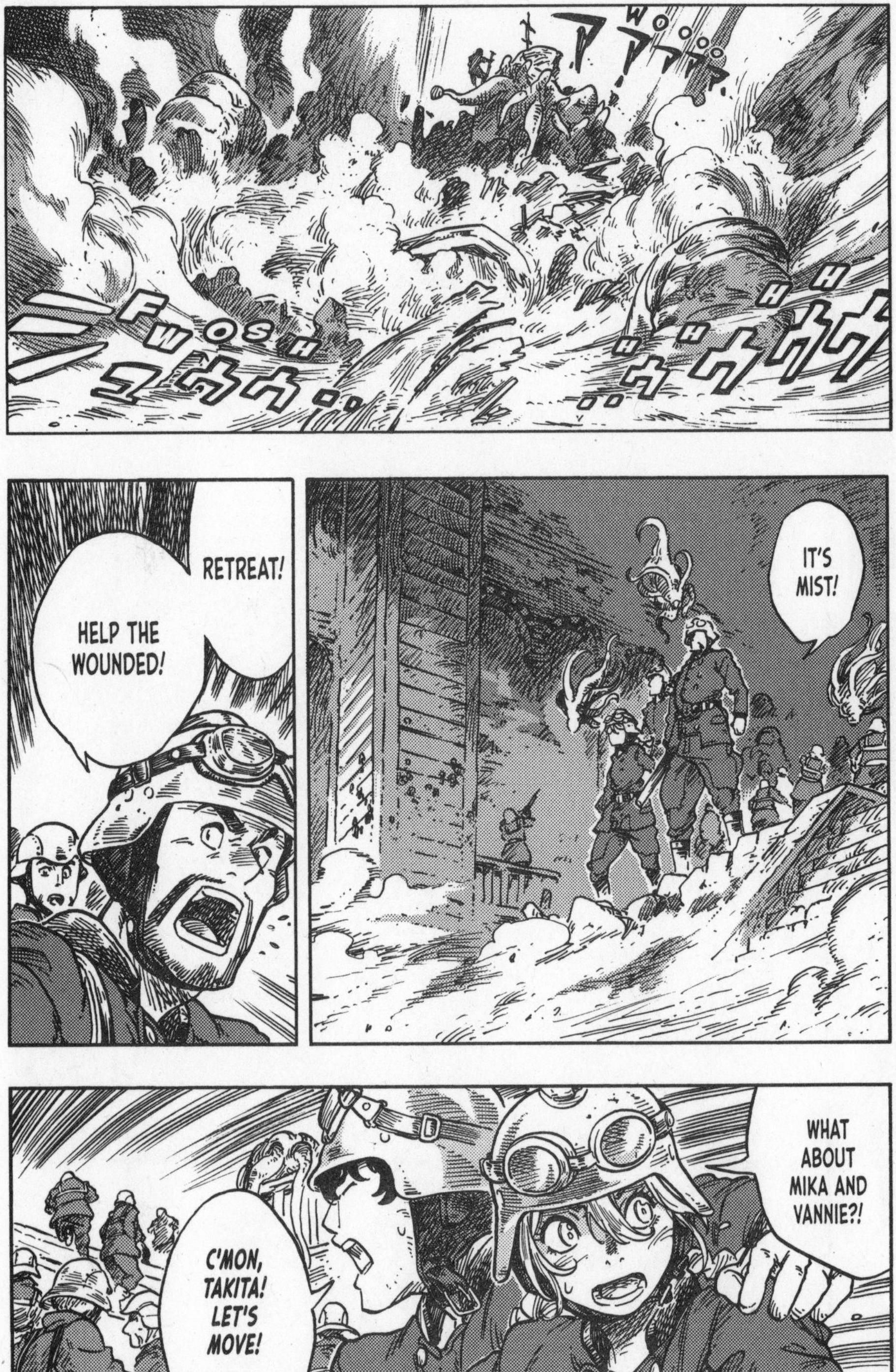
WOOOO
HHHH
FWOSH
IT'S MIST!
RETREAT!
HELP THE WOUNDED!
WHAT ABOUT MIKA AND VANNIE?!
C'MON, TAKITA! LET'S MOVE!

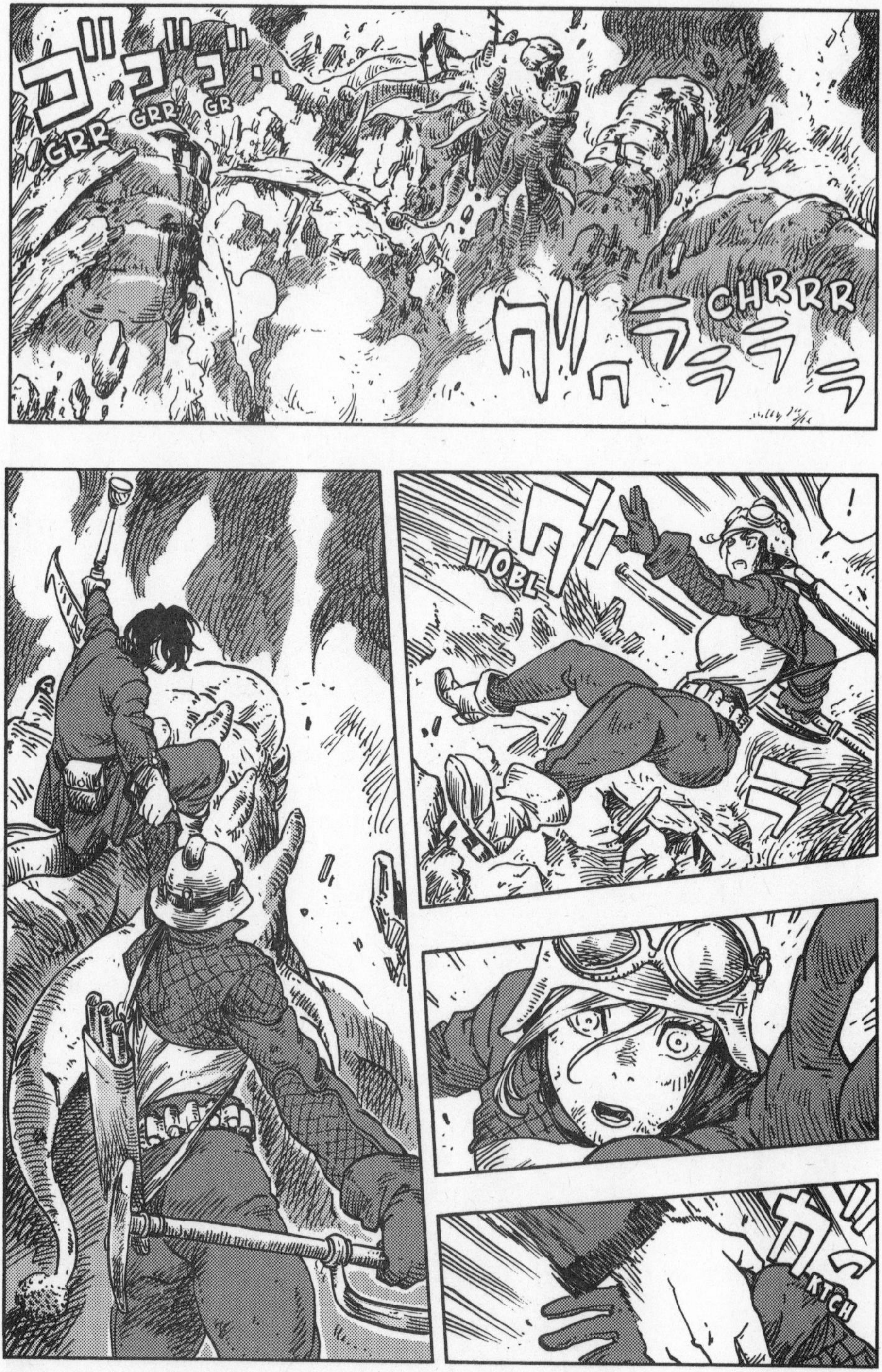
GRR GRR GR
CHRRR
!
WOBL
KTCH

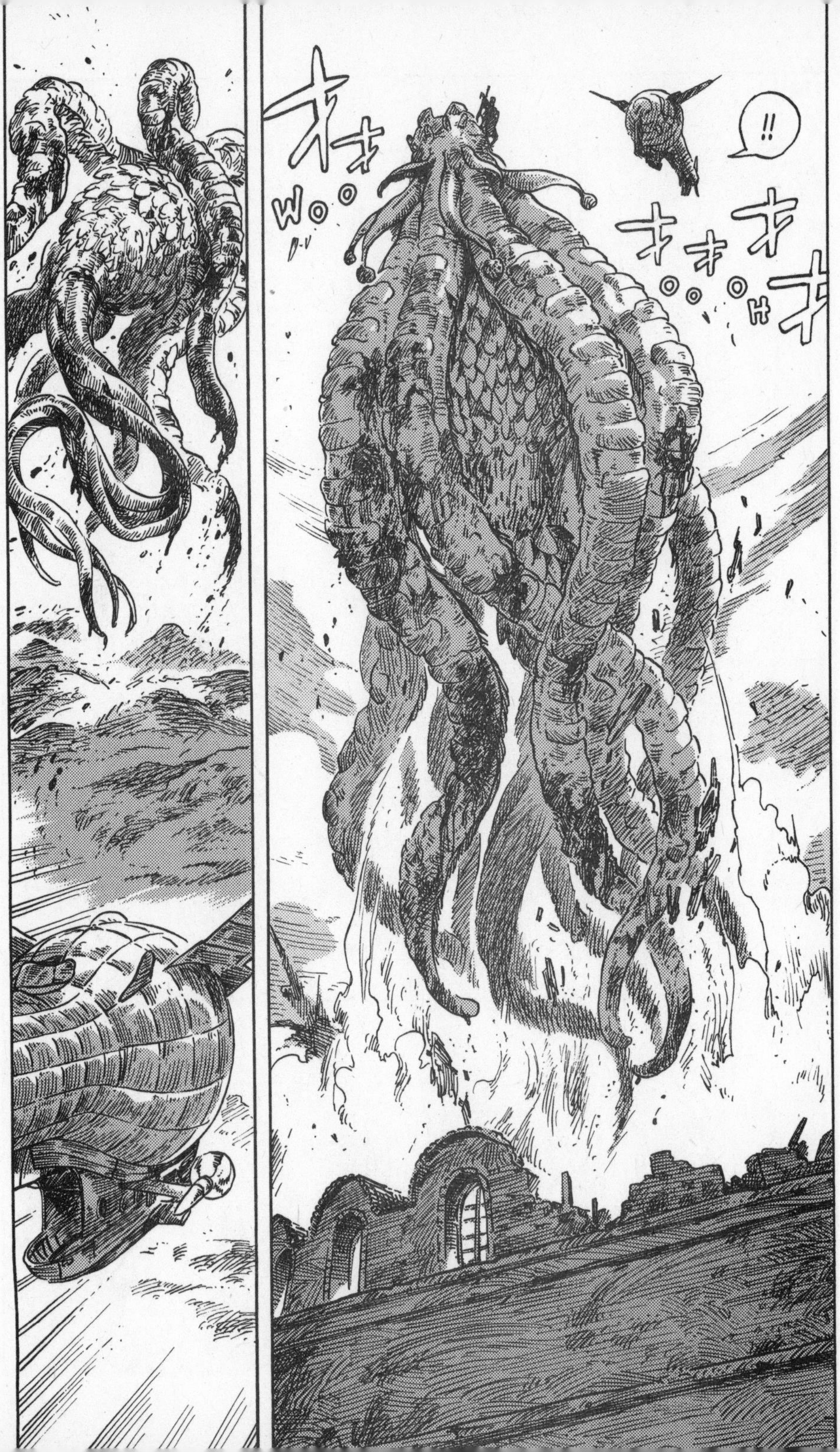
!!
OOOH
WOO

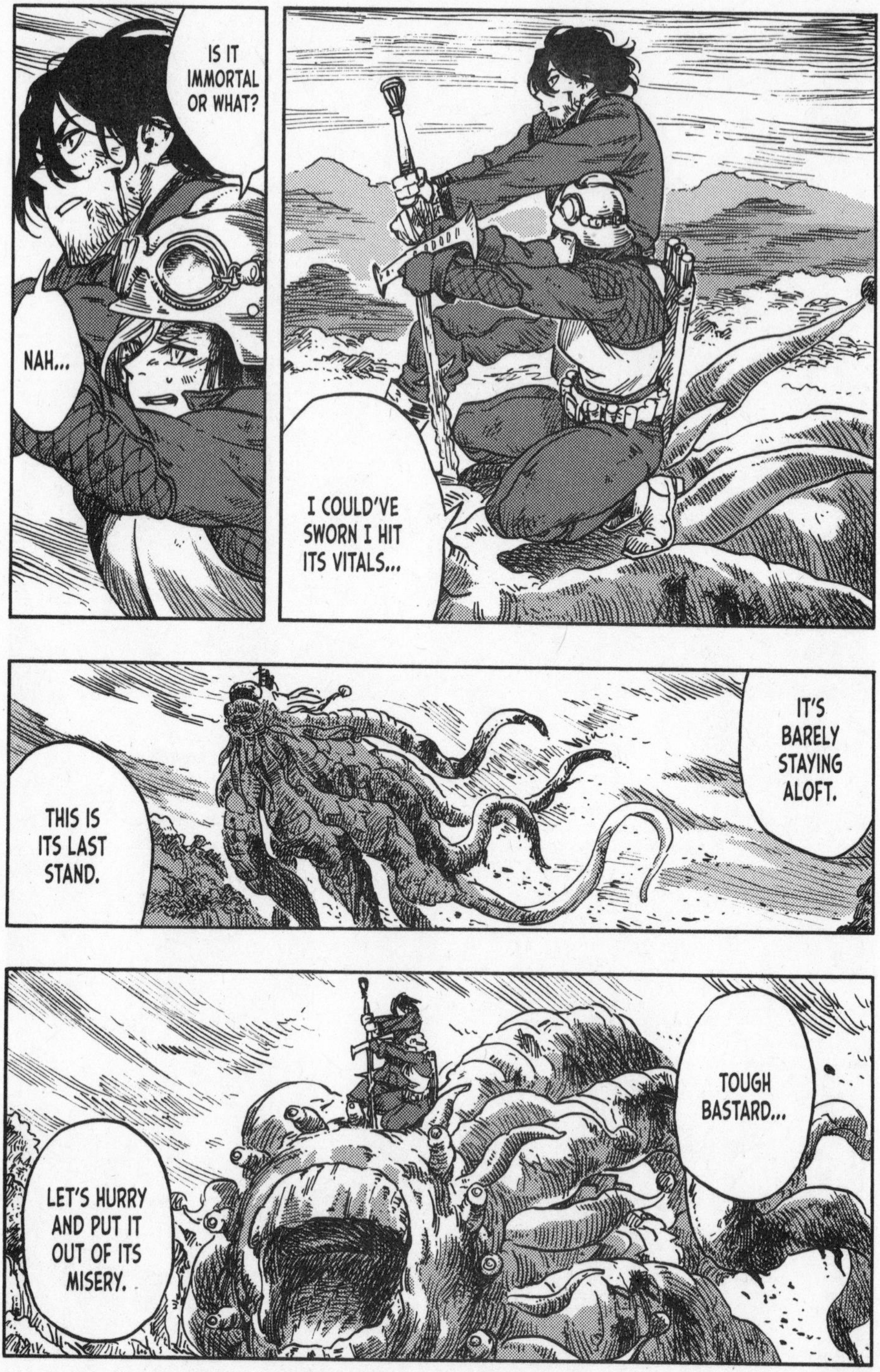
I COULD'VE SWORN I HIT ITS VITALS...
IS IT IMMORTAL OR WHAT?
NAH...
IT'S BARELY STAYING ALOFT.
THIS IS ITS LAST STAND.
TOUGH BASTARD...
LET'S HURRY AND PUT IT OUT OF ITS MISERY.

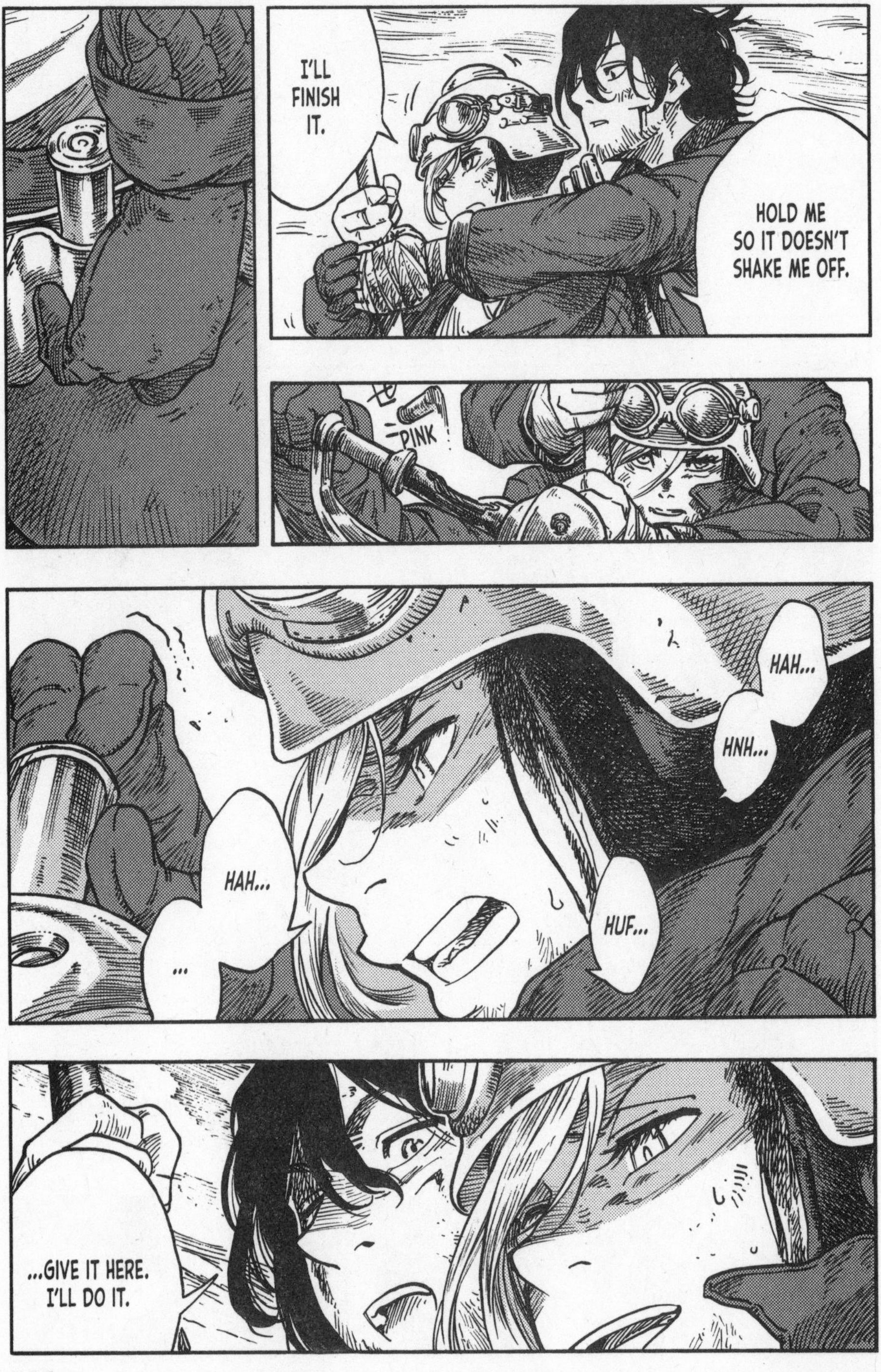
HOLD ME SO IT DOESN'T SHAKE ME OFF.
I'LL FINISH IT.
PINK
HAH...
HNH...
HUF...
HAH...
...
...GIVE IT HERE. I'LL DO IT.

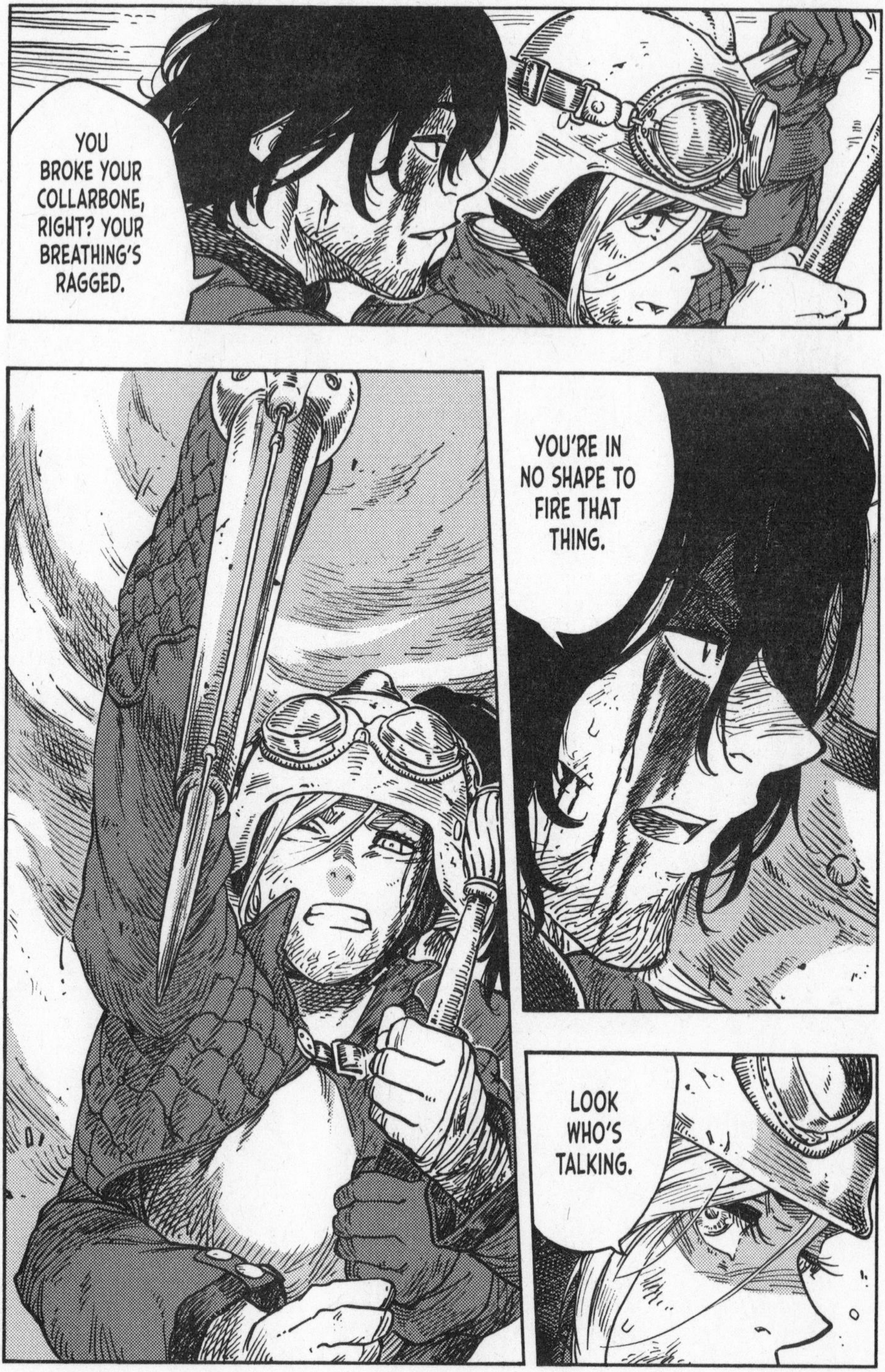
YOU BROKE YOUR COLLARBONE, RIGHT? YOUR BREATHING'S RAGGED.
YOU'RE IN NO SHAPE TO FIRE THAT THING.
LOOK WHO'S TALKING.

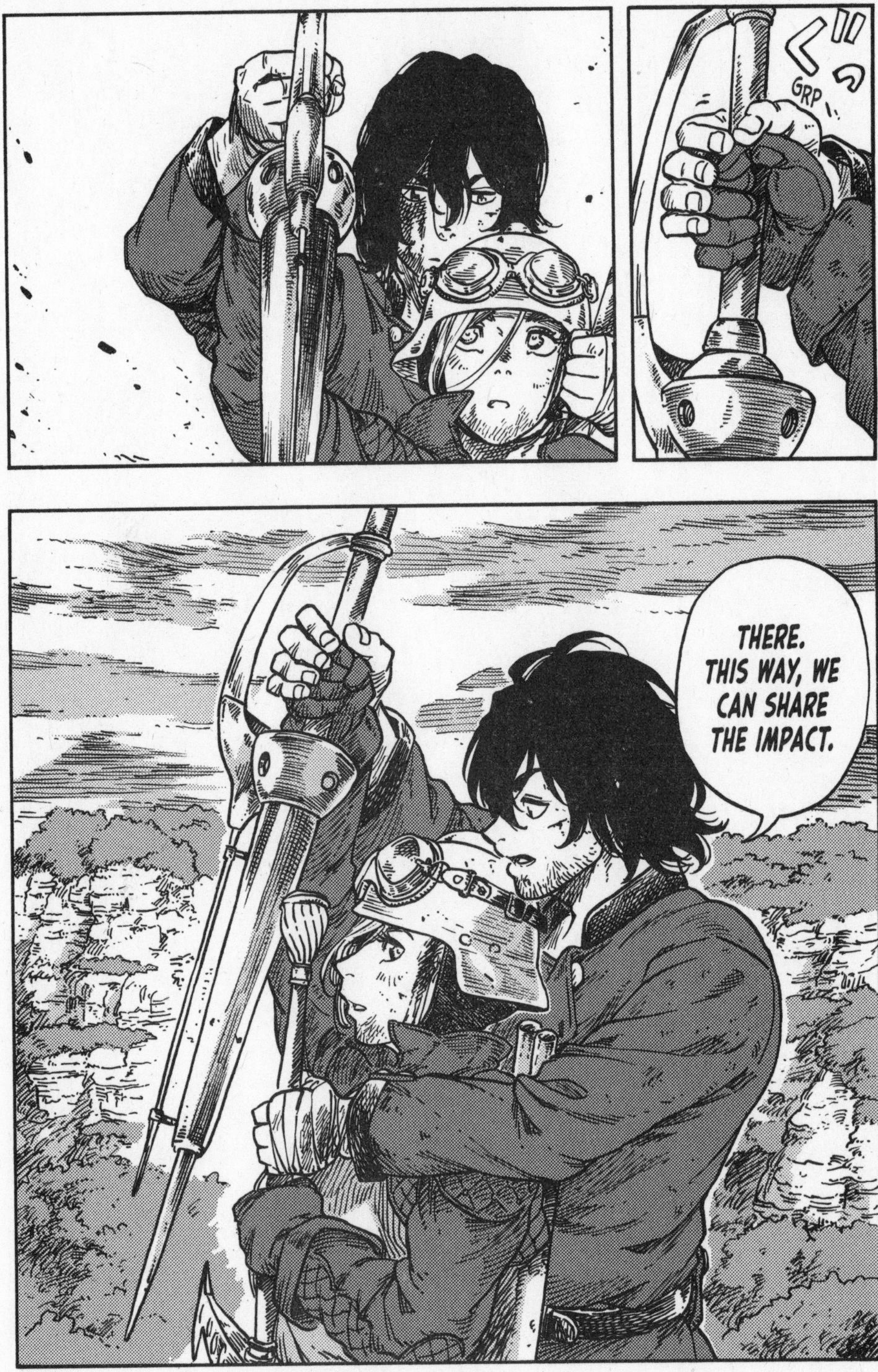
ぐっ
GRP
THERE. THIS WAY, WE CAN SHARE THE IMPACT.

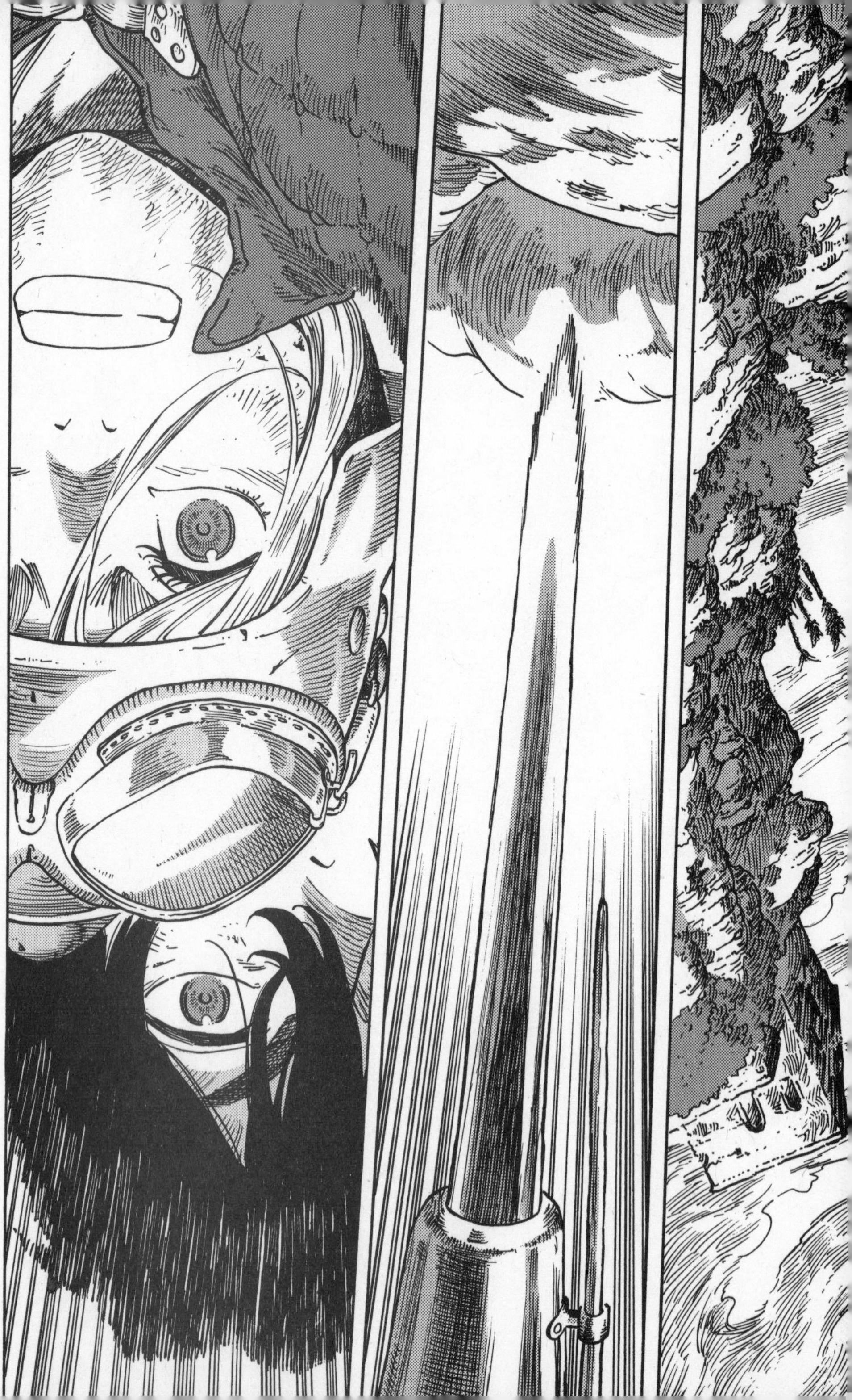

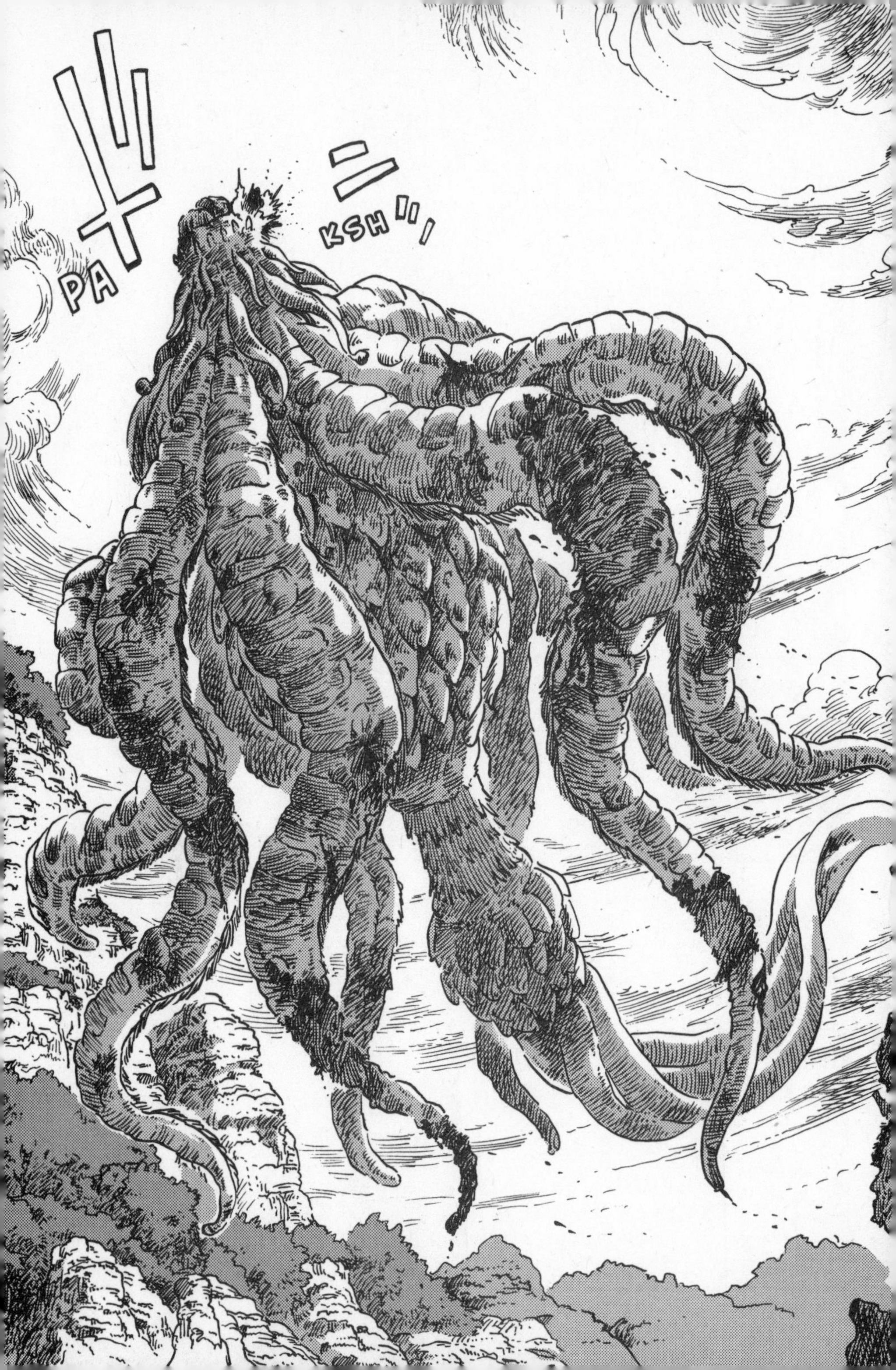
KSH!!!
PA

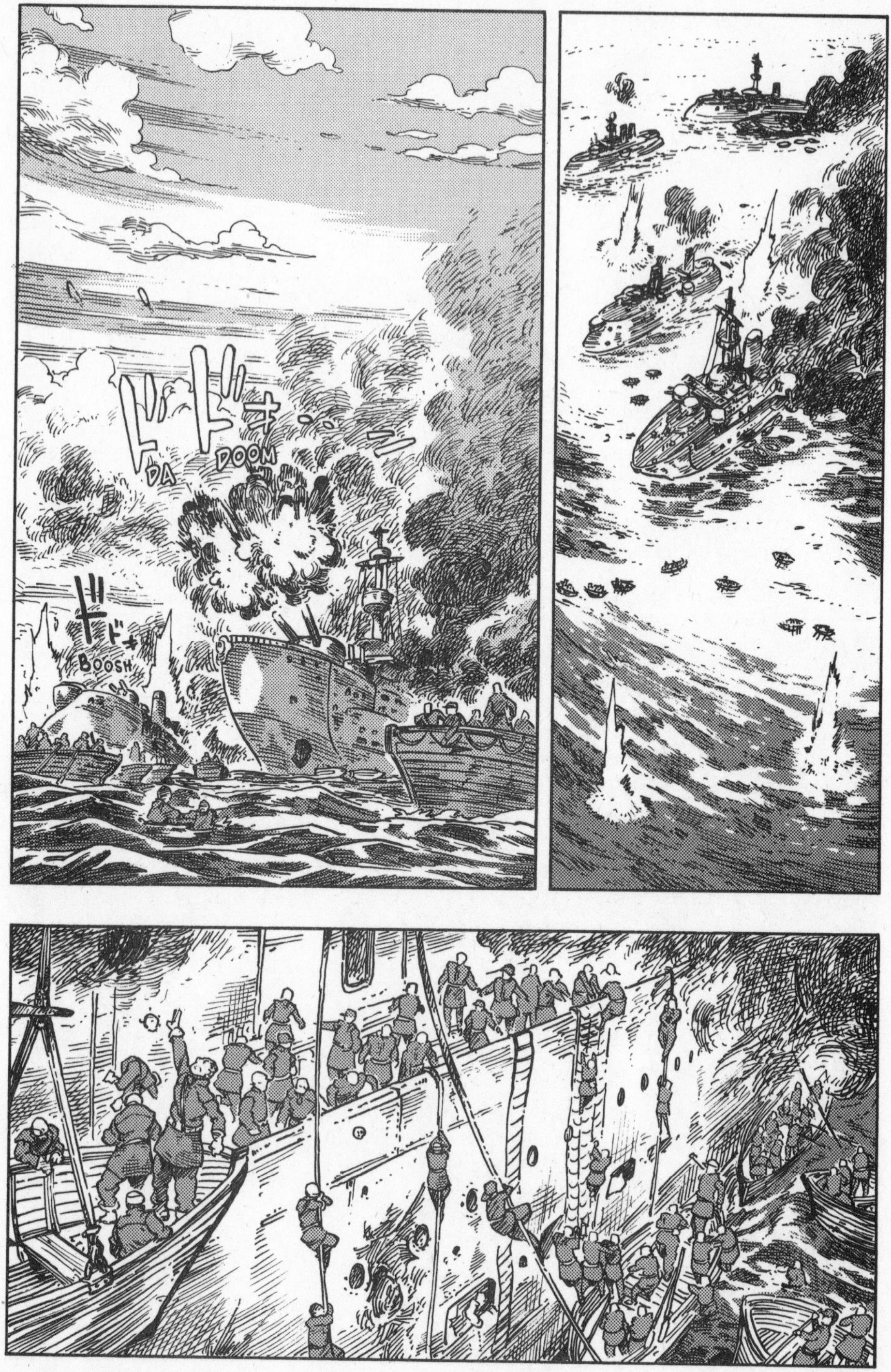
DA
DOOM
BOOSH

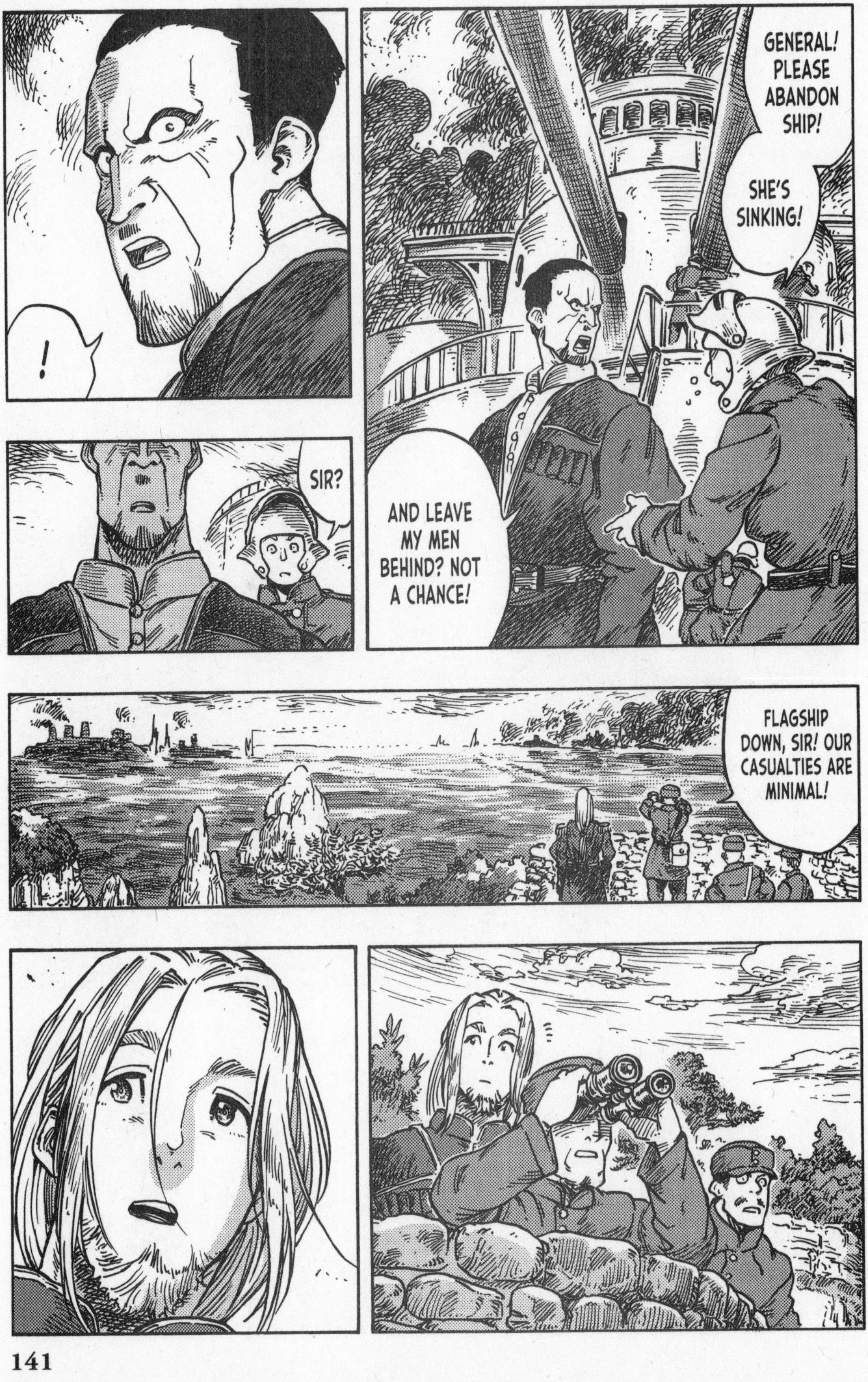
GENERAL! PLEASE ABANDON SHIP!
SHE'S SINKING!
AND LEAVE MY MEN BEHIND? NOT A CHANCE!
!
SIR?
FLAGSHIP DOWN, SIR! OUR CASUALTIES ARE MINIMAL!

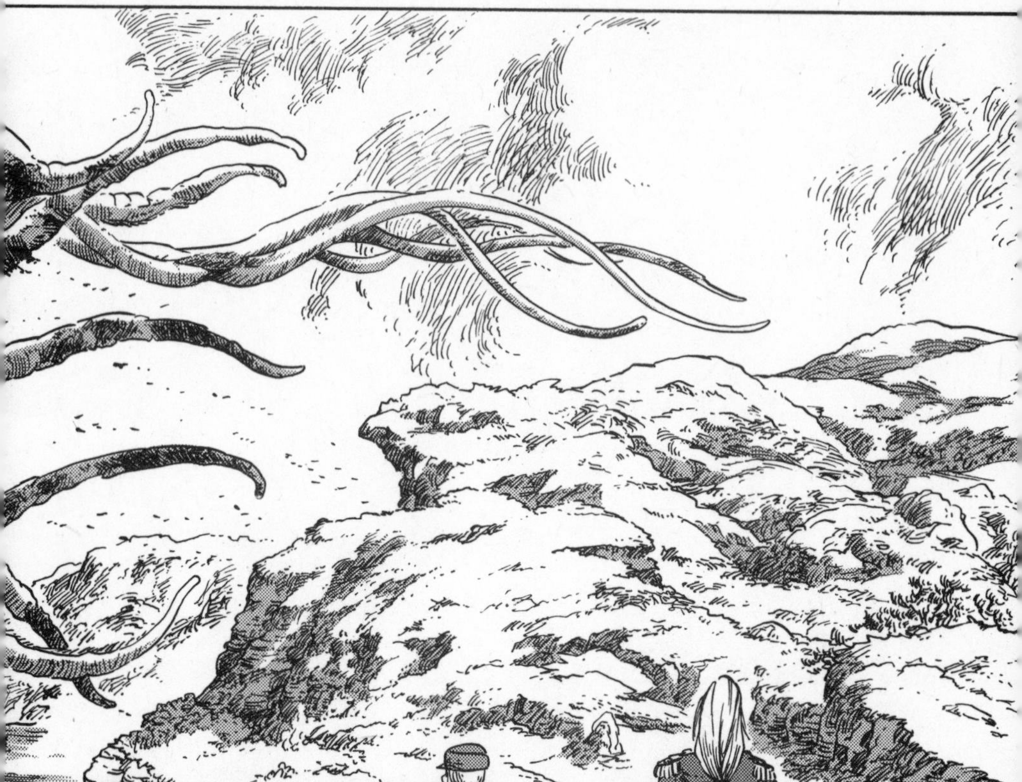
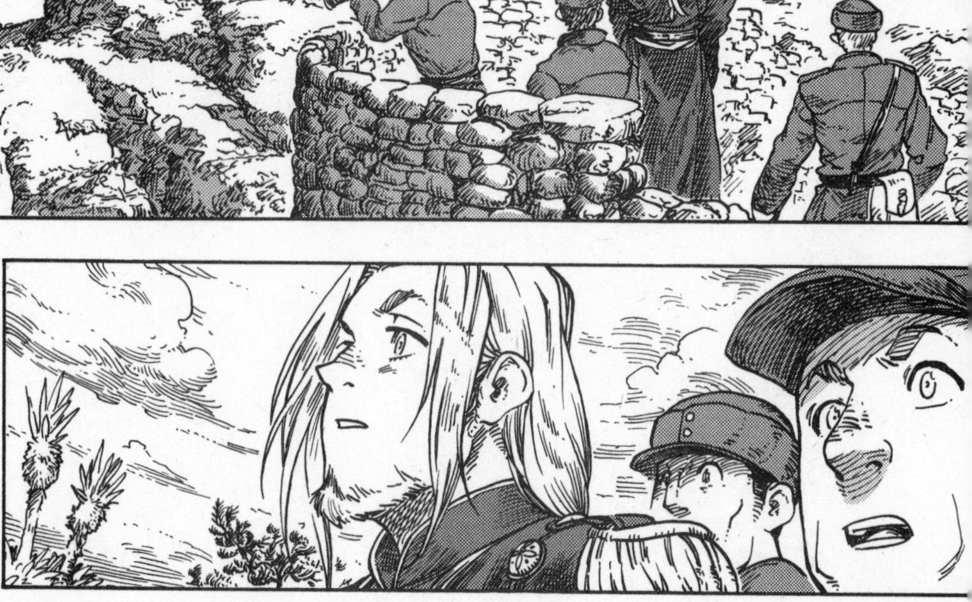

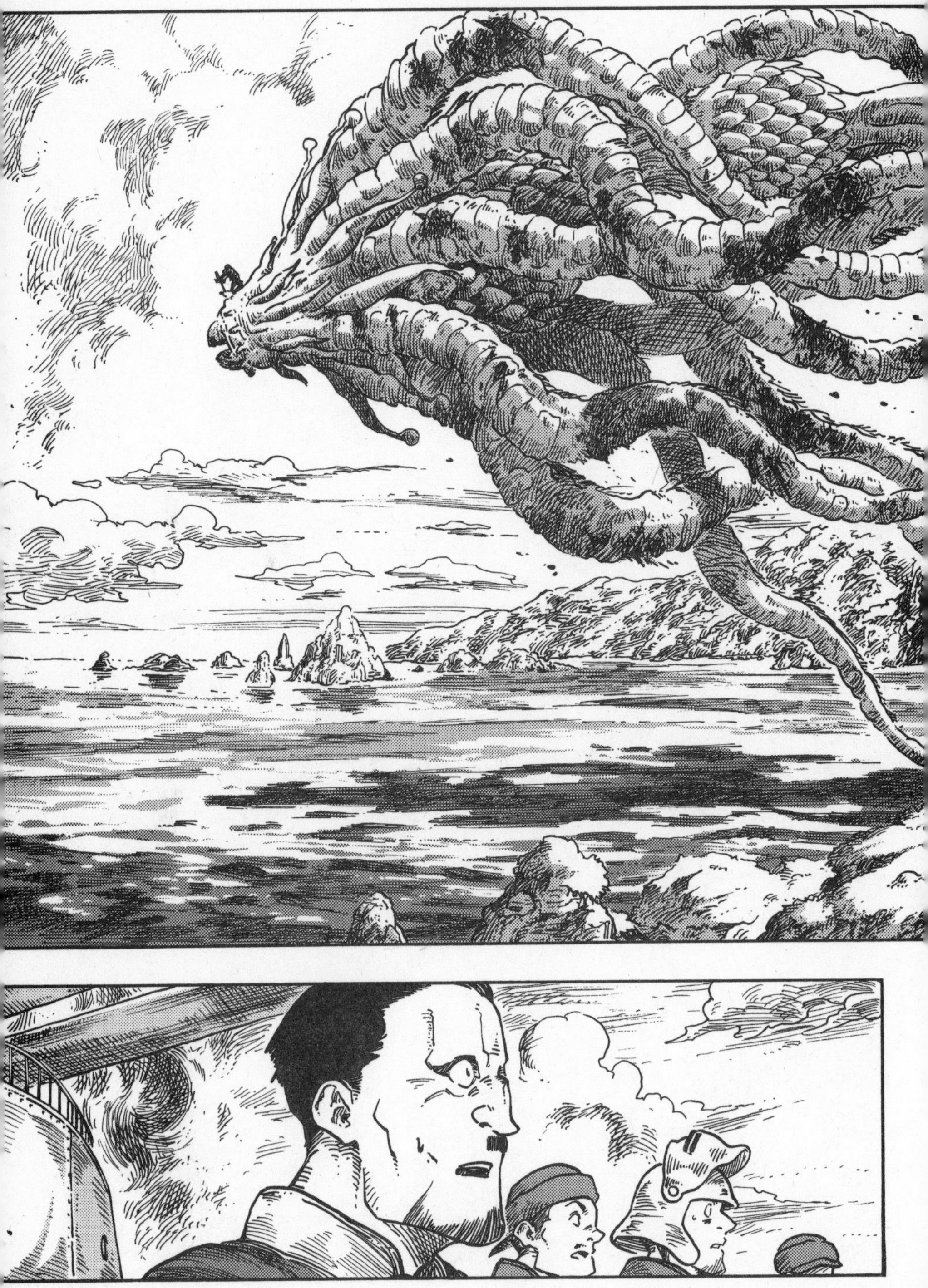

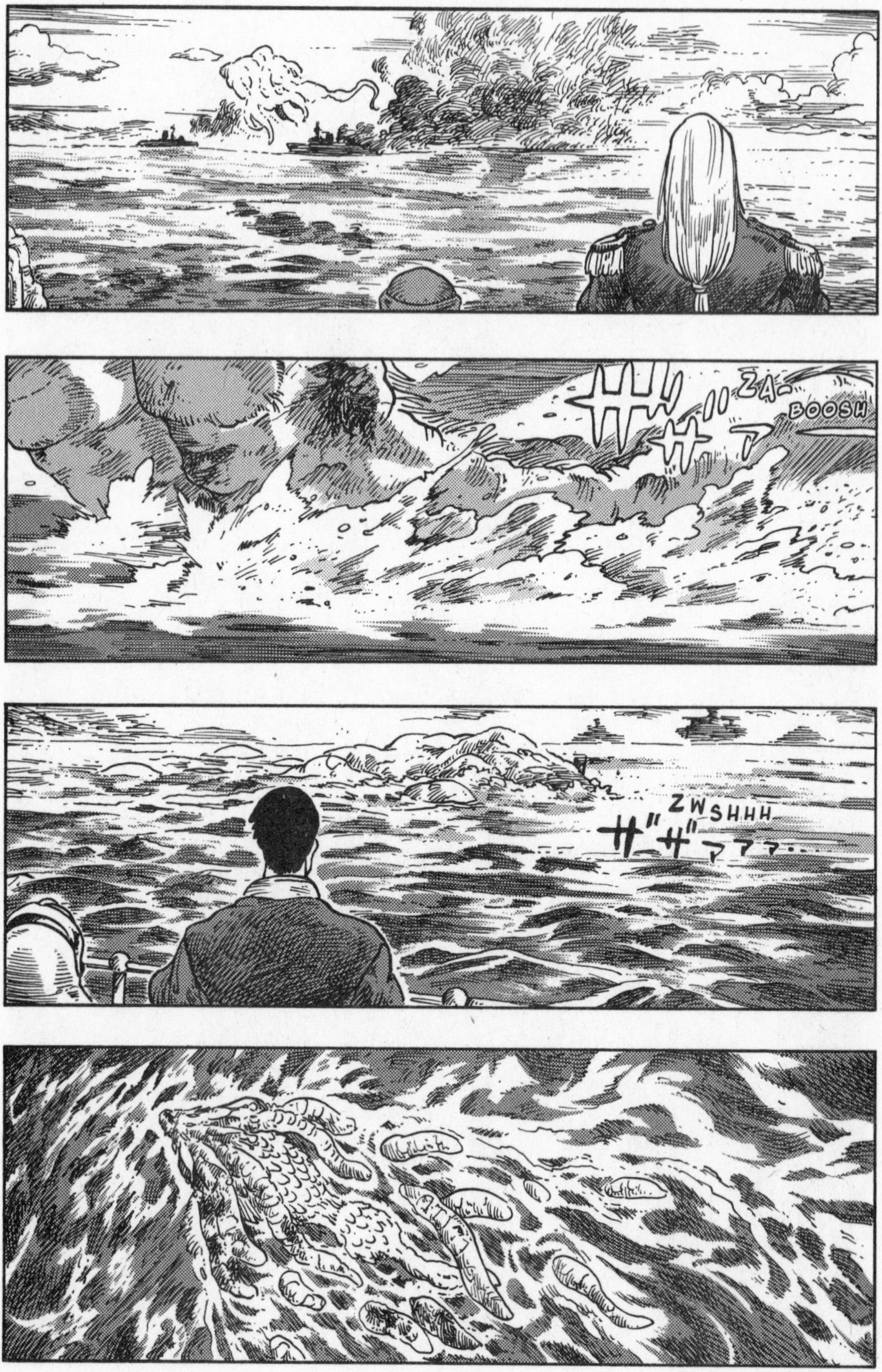
ザザーッ
ZA-BOOSH
ザザァァァ…
ZWSHHH

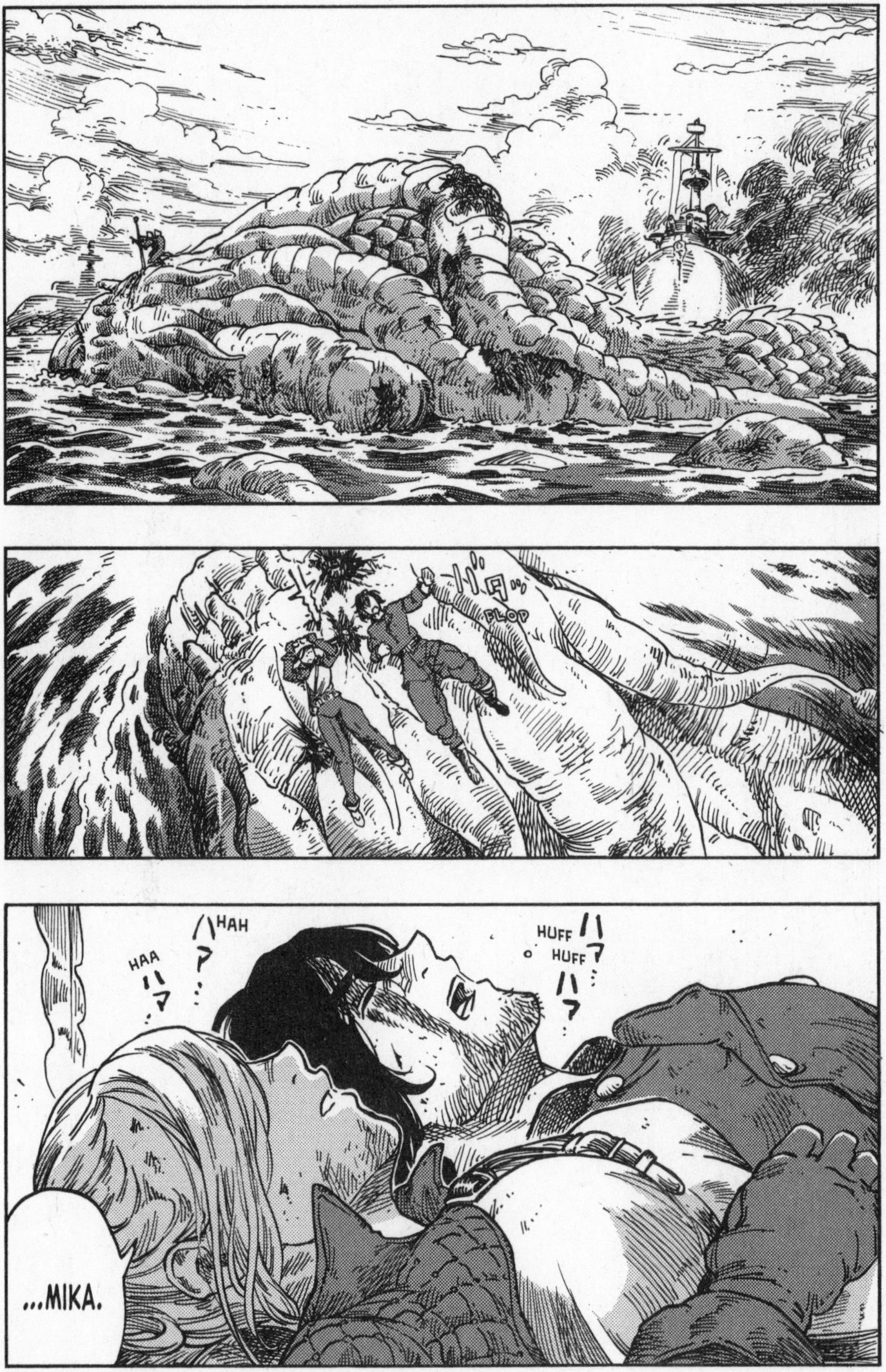

BLOP
HUFF HUFF
HAH
HAA
...MIKA.

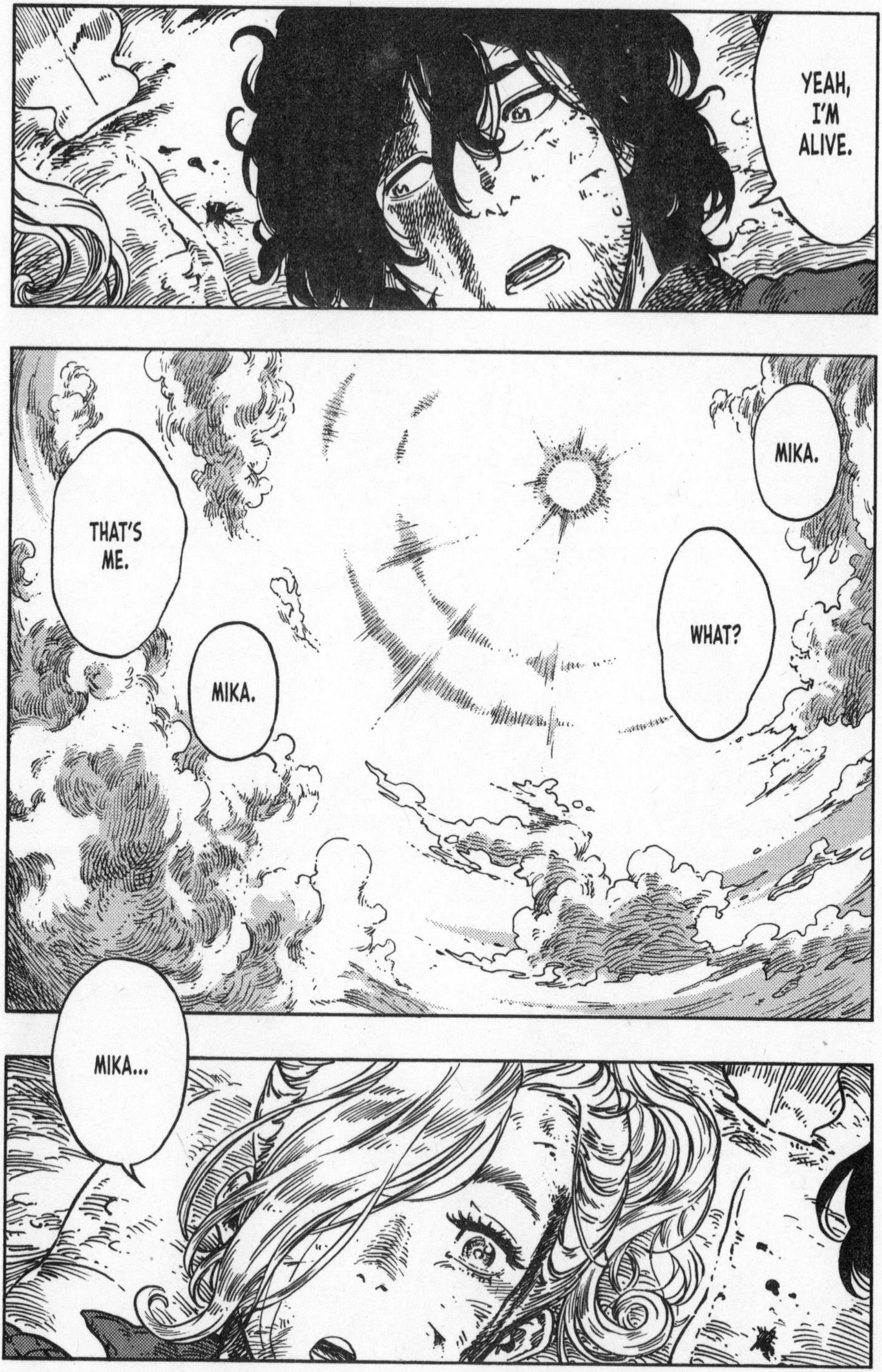
YEAH, I'M ALIVE.
MIKA.
WHAT?
THAT'S ME.
MIKA.
MIKA...

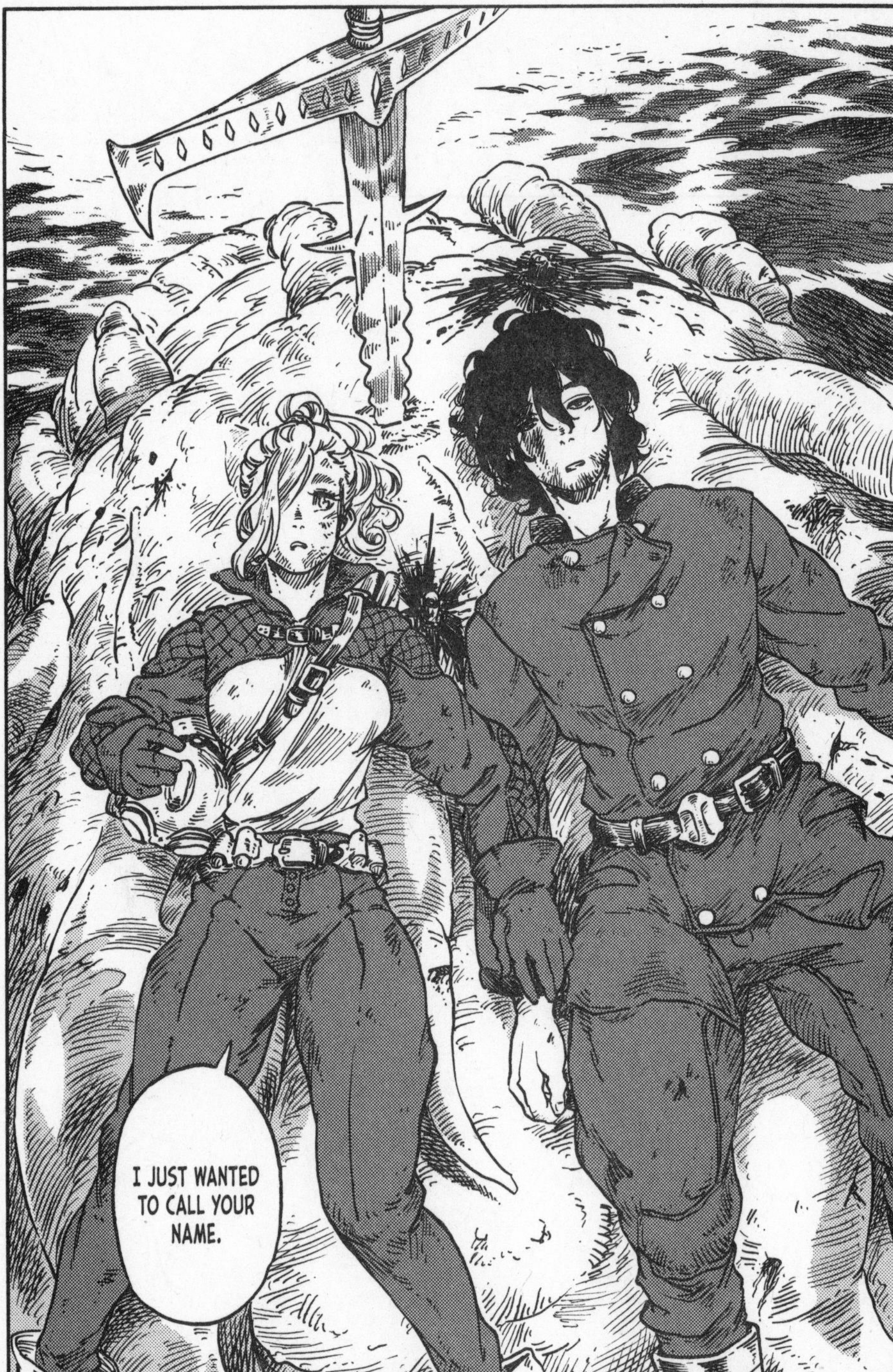
I JUST WANTED TO CALL YOUR NAME.

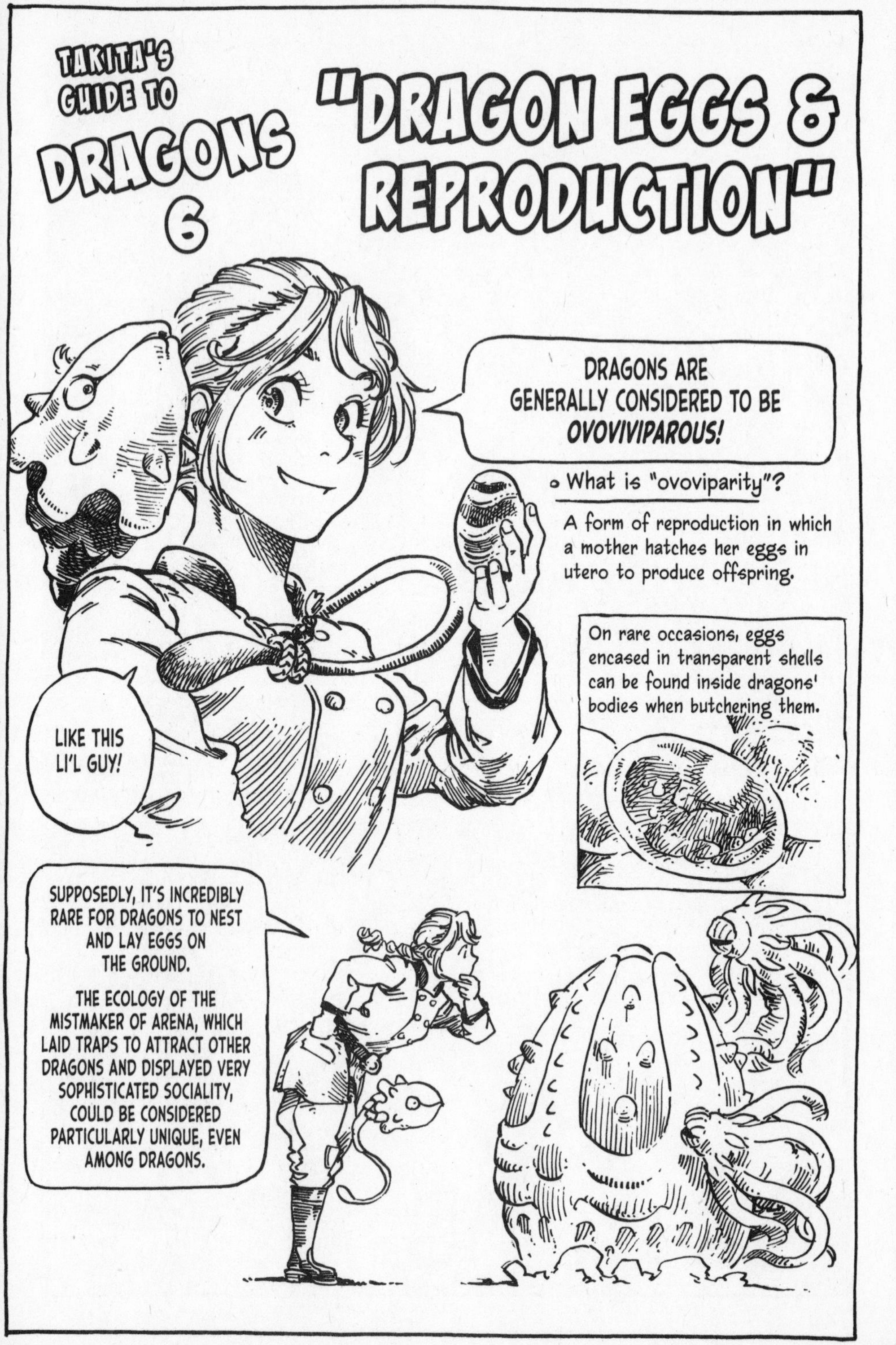
TAKITA'S GUIDE TO DRAGONS 6
"DRAGON EGGS & REPRODUCTION"
DRAGONS ARE GENERALLY CONSIDERED TO BE *OVOVIVIPAROUS!*
What is "ovoviparity"?
A form of reproduction in which a mother hatches her eggs in utero to produce offspring.
LIKE THIS LI'L GUY!
On rare occasions, eggs encased in transparent shells can be found inside dragons' bodies when butchering them.
SUPPOSEDLY, IT'S INCREDIBLY RARE FOR DRAGONS TO NEST AND LAY EGGS ON THE GROUND.
THE ECOLOGY OF THE MISTMAKER OF ARENA, WHICH LAID TRAPS TO ATTRACT OTHER DRAGONS AND DISPLAYED VERY SOPHISTICATED SOCIALITY, COULD BE CONSIDERED PARTICULARLY UNIQUE, EVEN AMONG DRAGONS.

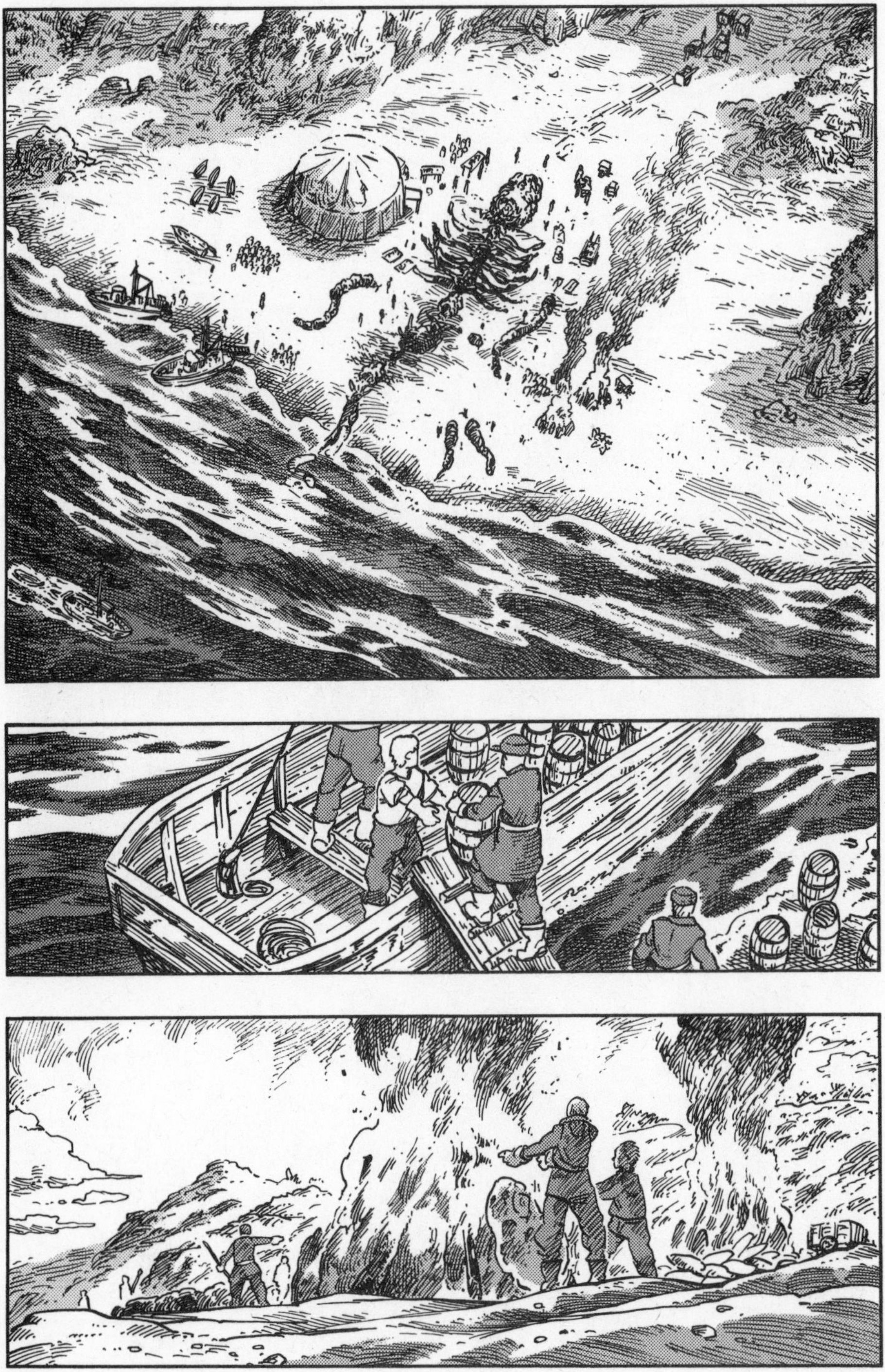

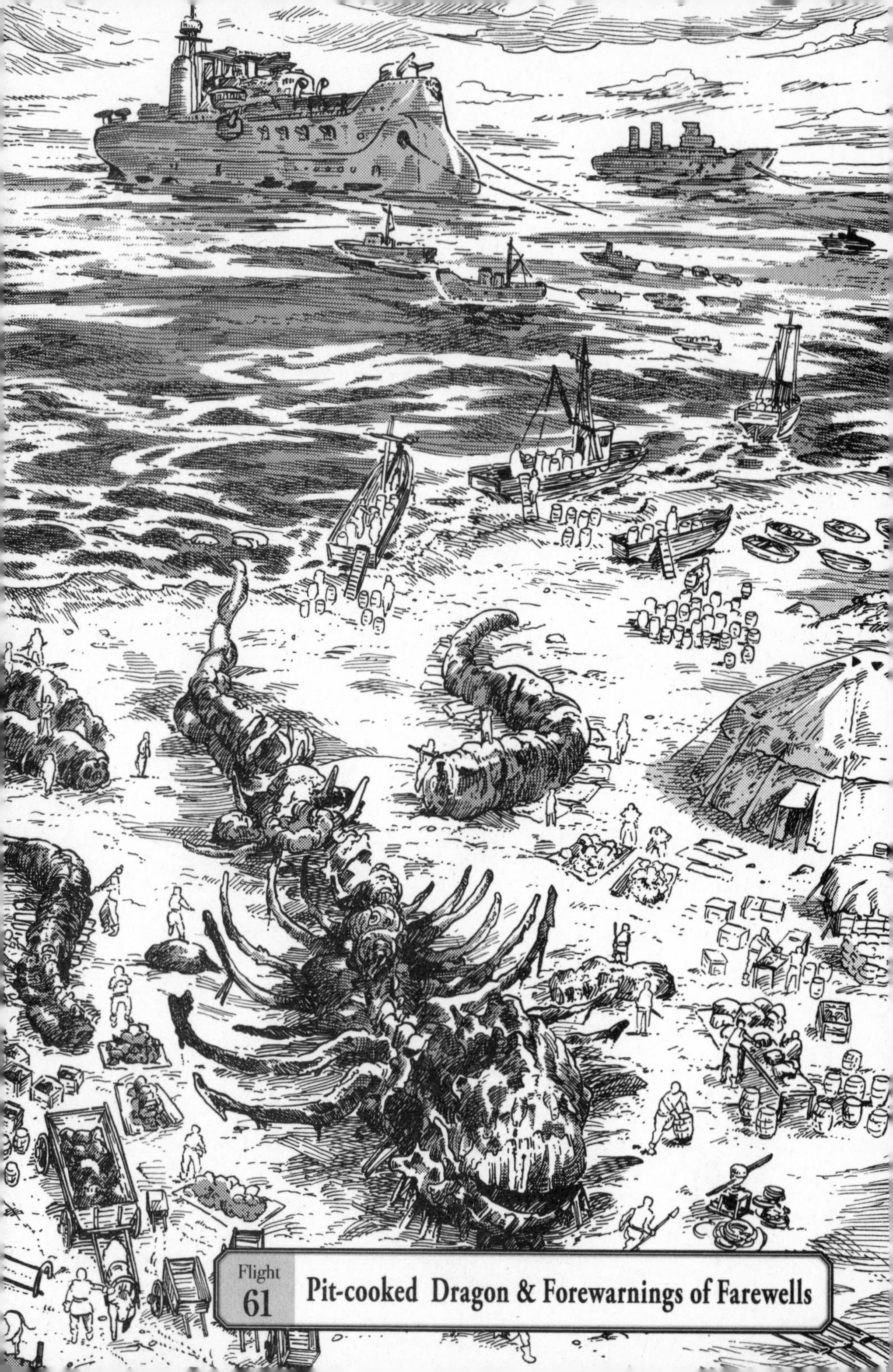

Flight 61 Pit-cooked Dragon & Forewarnings of Farewells

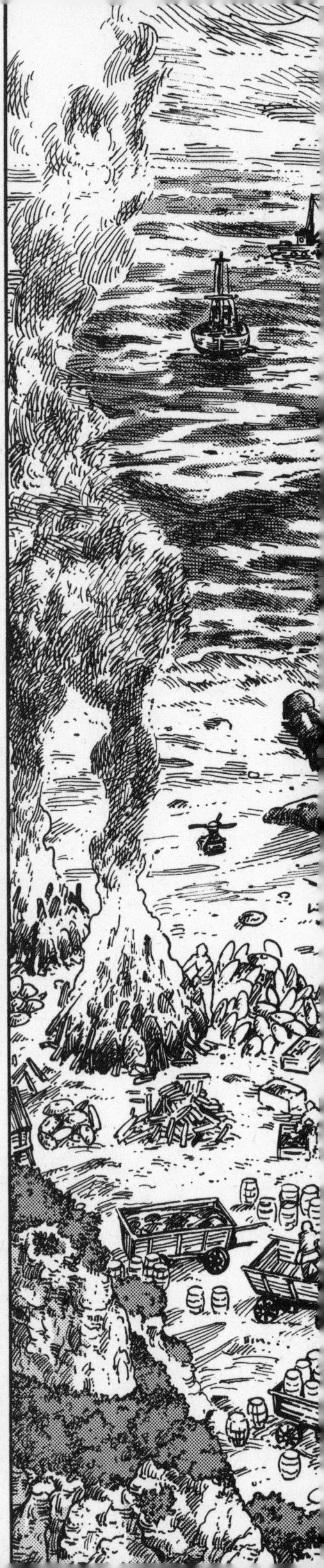

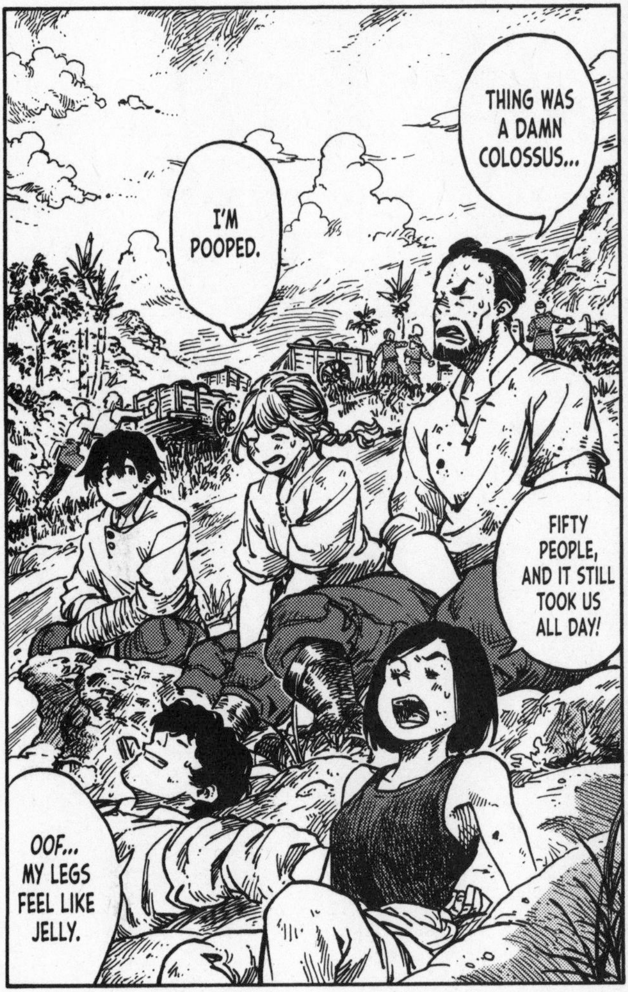
THING WAS A DAMN COLOSSUS...
I'M POOPED.
FIFTY PEOPLE, AND IT STILL TOOK US ALL DAY!
OOF... MY LEGS FEEL LIKE JELLY.

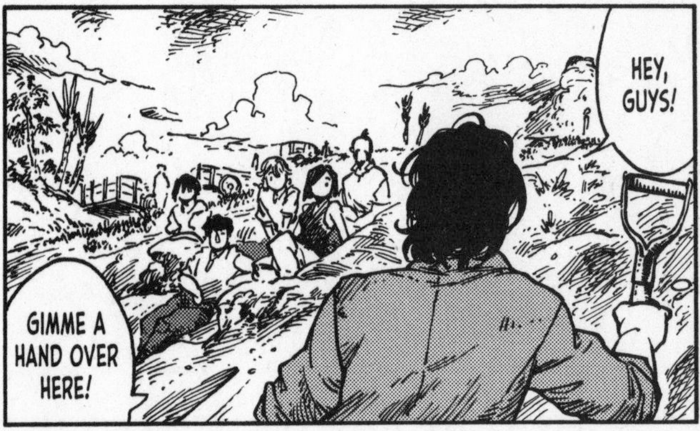
HEY, GUYS!
GIMME A HAND OVER HERE!

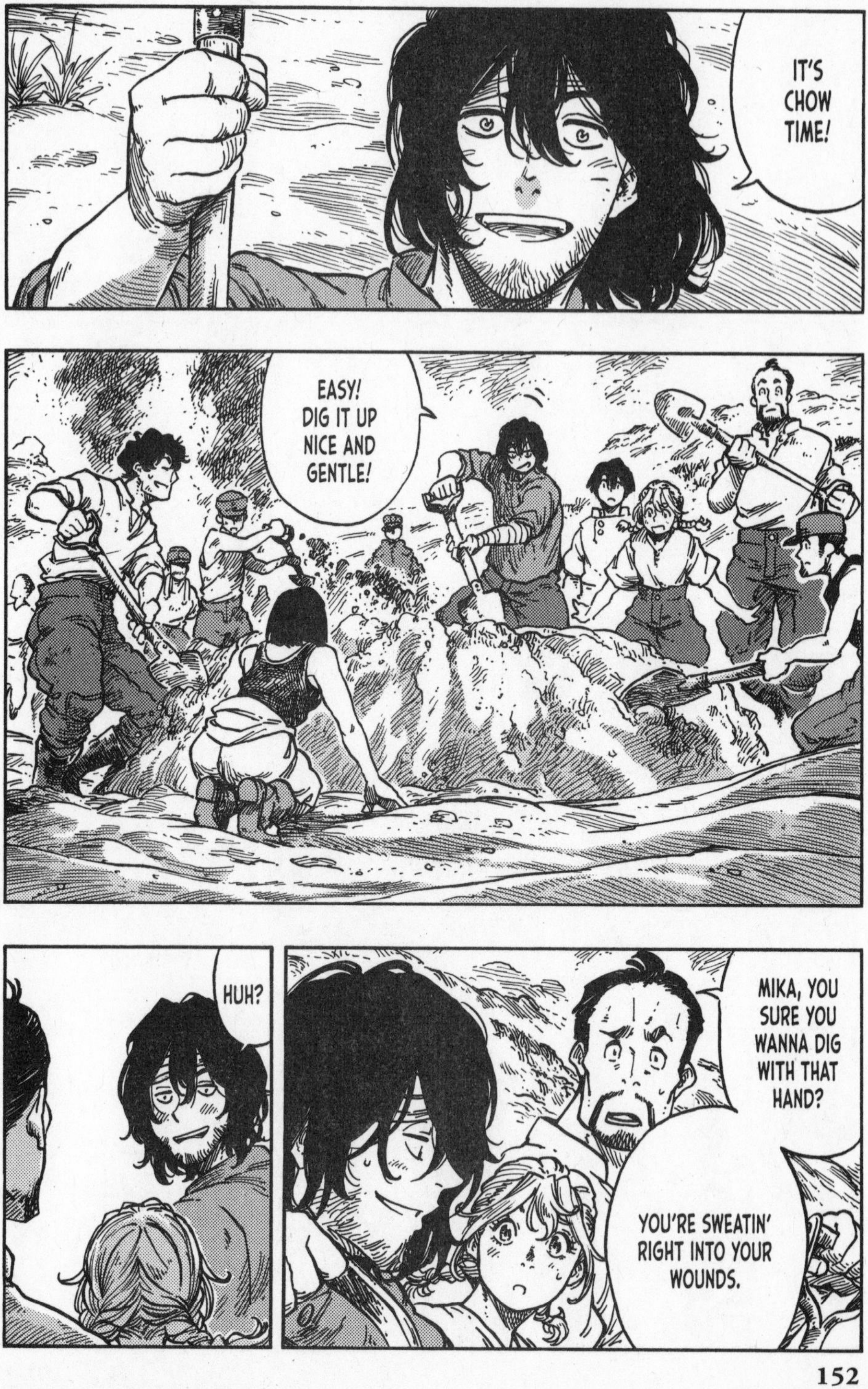
IT'S CHOW TIME!
EASY! DIG IT UP NICE AND GENTLE!
MIKA, YOU SURE YOU WANNA DIG WITH THAT HAND?
YOU'RE SWEATIN' RIGHT INTO YOUR WOUNDS.
HUH?

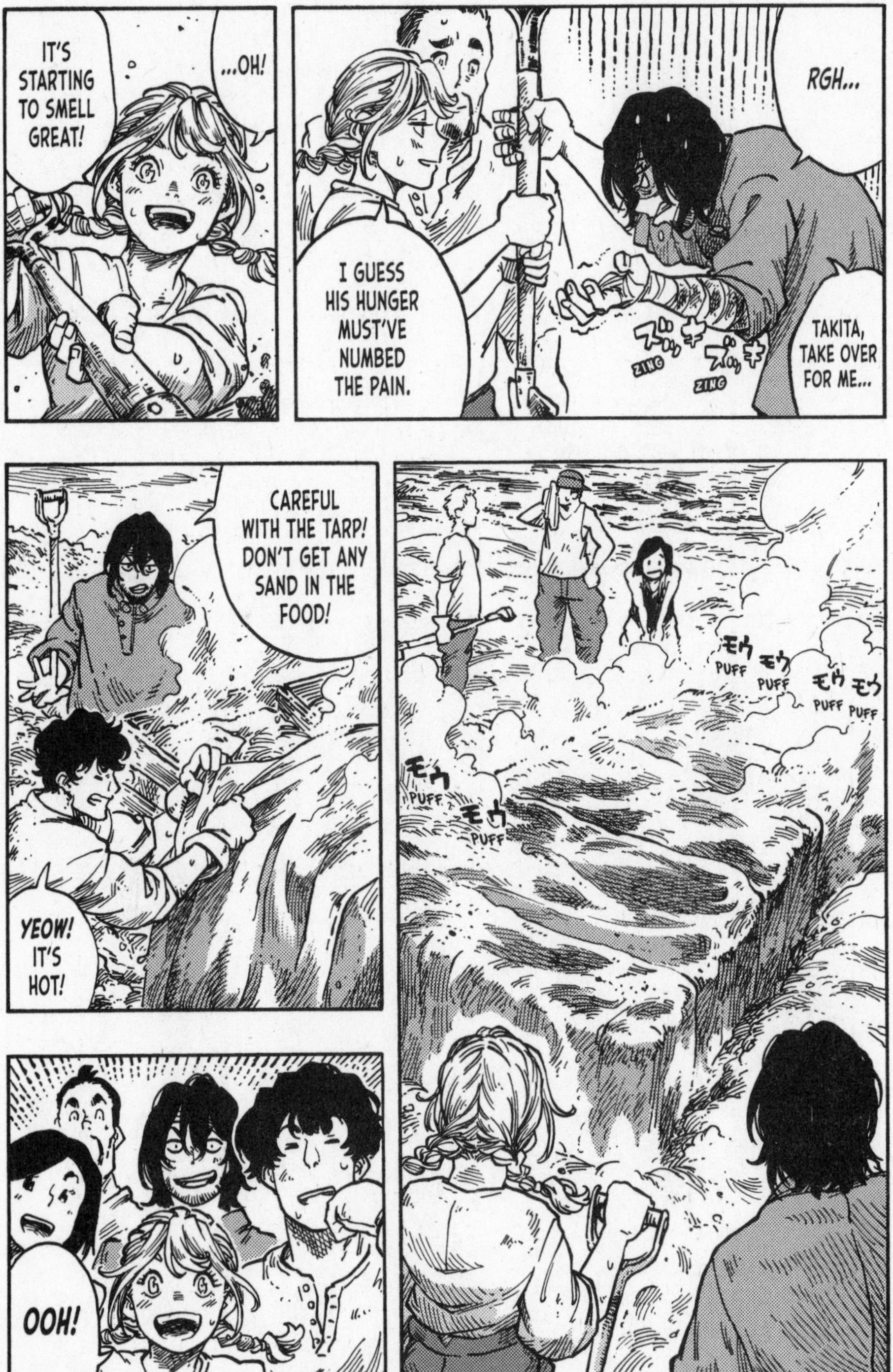
RGH...
ZING
ZING
TAKITA, TAKE OVER FOR ME...
I GUESS HIS HUNGER MUST'VE NUMBED THE PAIN.
...OH!
IT'S STARTING TO SMELL GREAT!
PUFF PUFF PUFF PUFF
PUFF
PUFF
CAREFUL WITH THE TARP! DON'T GET ANY SAND IN THE FOOD!
YEOW! IT'S HOT!
OOH!

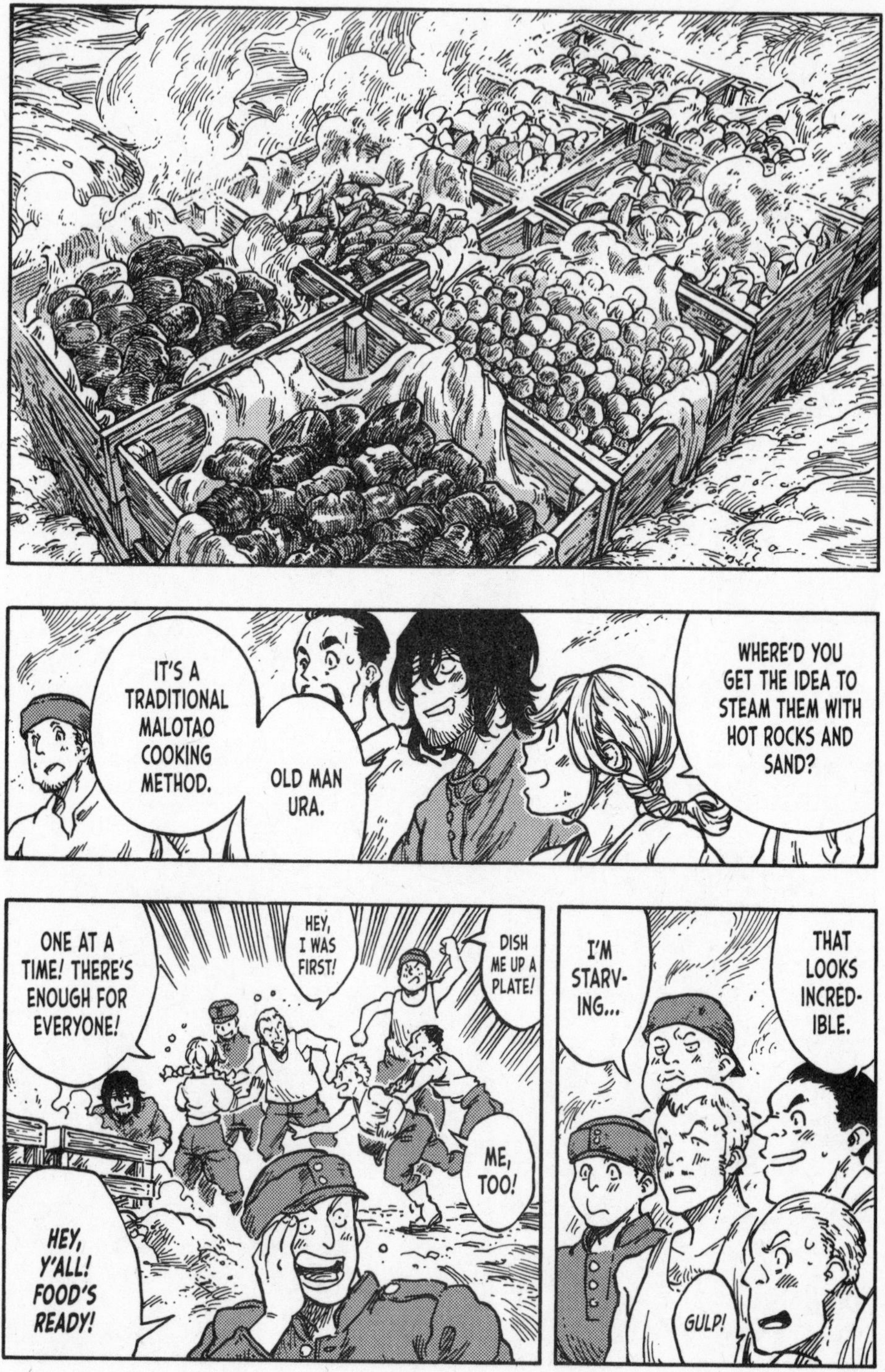
WHERE'D YOU GET THE IDEA TO STEAM THEM WITH HOT ROCKS AND SAND?
OLD MAN URA.
IT'S A TRADITIONAL MALOTAO COOKING METHOD.
THAT LOOKS INCRED-IBLE.
I'M STARV-ING...
GULP!
DISH ME UP A PLATE!
HEY, I WAS FIRST!
ONE AT A TIME! THERE'S ENOUGH FOR EVERYONE!
ME, TOO!
HEY, Y'ALL! FOOD'S READY!

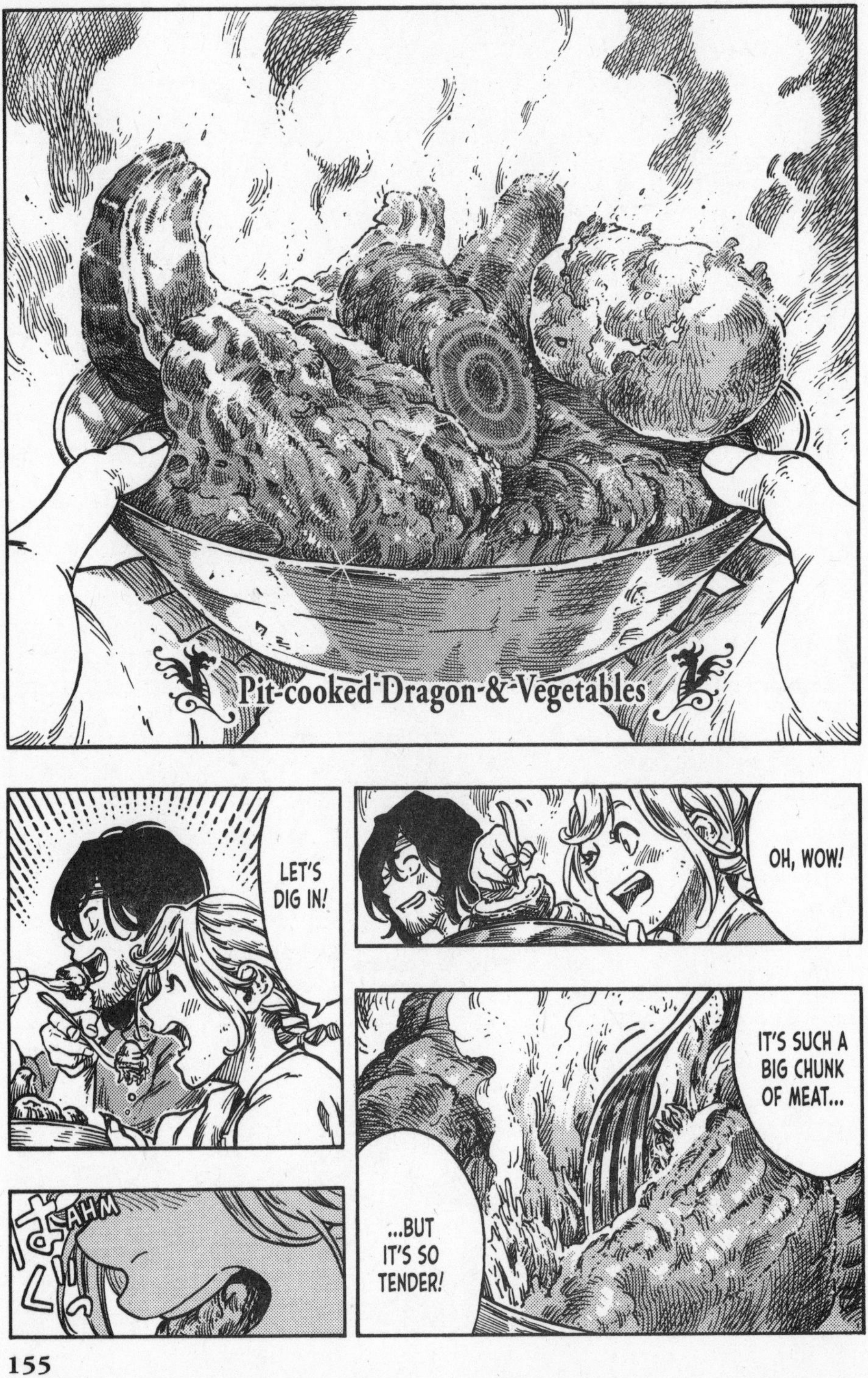
Pit-cooked Dragon & Vegetables
OH, WOW!
LET'S DIG IN!
IT'S SUCH A BIG CHUNK OF MEAT...
...BUT IT'S SO TENDER!
AHM

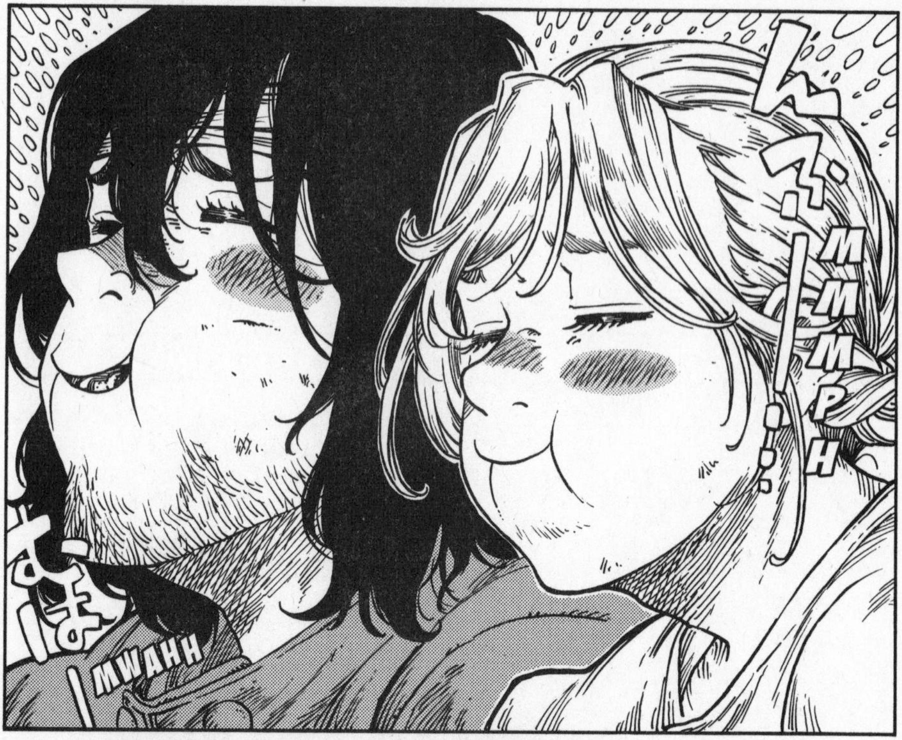
MMMMPH
MWAHH
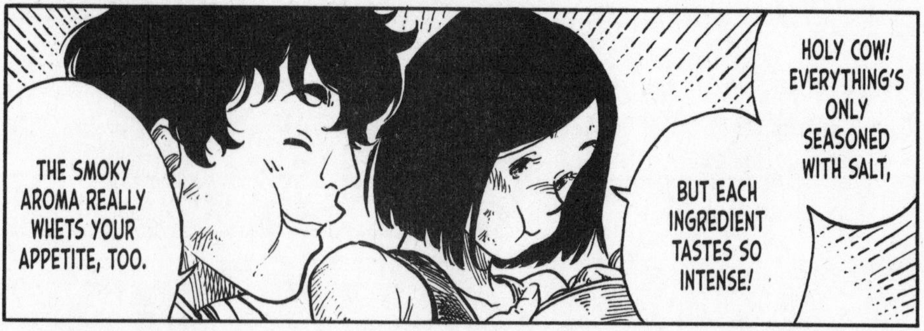
HOLY COW! EVERYTHING'S ONLY SEASONED WITH SALT,
BUT EACH INGREDIENT TASTES SO INTENSE!
THE SMOKY AROMA REALLY WHETS YOUR APPETITE, TOO.
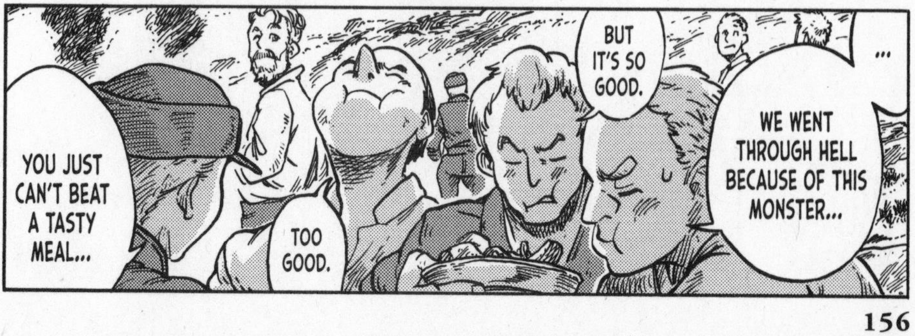
...
WE WENT THROUGH HELL BECAUSE OF THIS MONSTER...
BUT IT'S SO GOOD.
TOO GOOD.
YOU JUST CAN'T BEAT A TASTY MEAL...

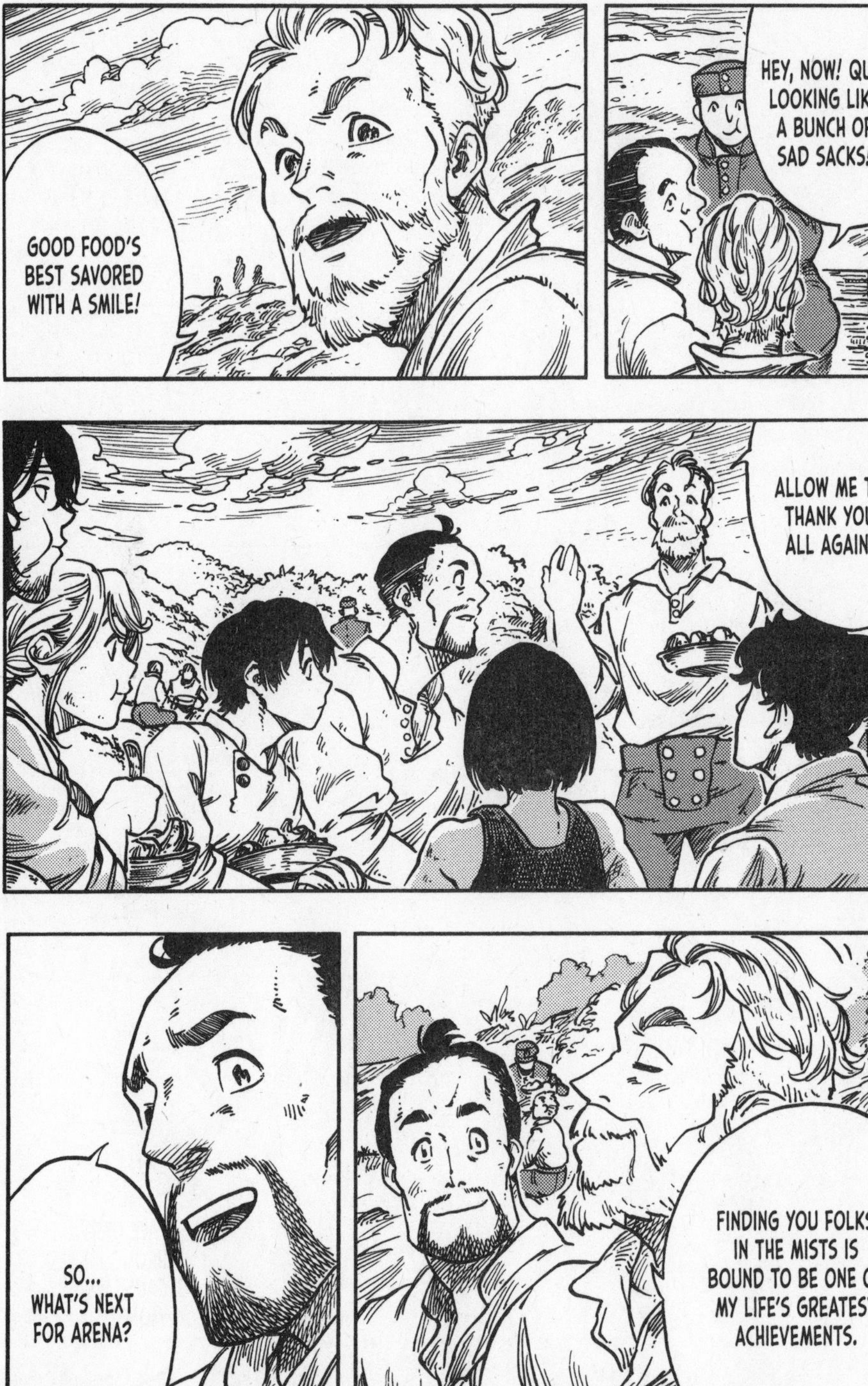
HEY, NOW! QUIT LOOKING LIKE A BUNCH OF SAD SACKS!
GOOD FOOD'S BEST SAVORED WITH A SMILE!
ALLOW ME TO THANK YOU ALL AGAIN.
FINDING YOU FOLKS IN THE MISTS IS BOUND TO BE ONE OF MY LIFE'S GREATEST ACHIEVEMENTS.
SO... WHAT'S NEXT FOR ARENA?

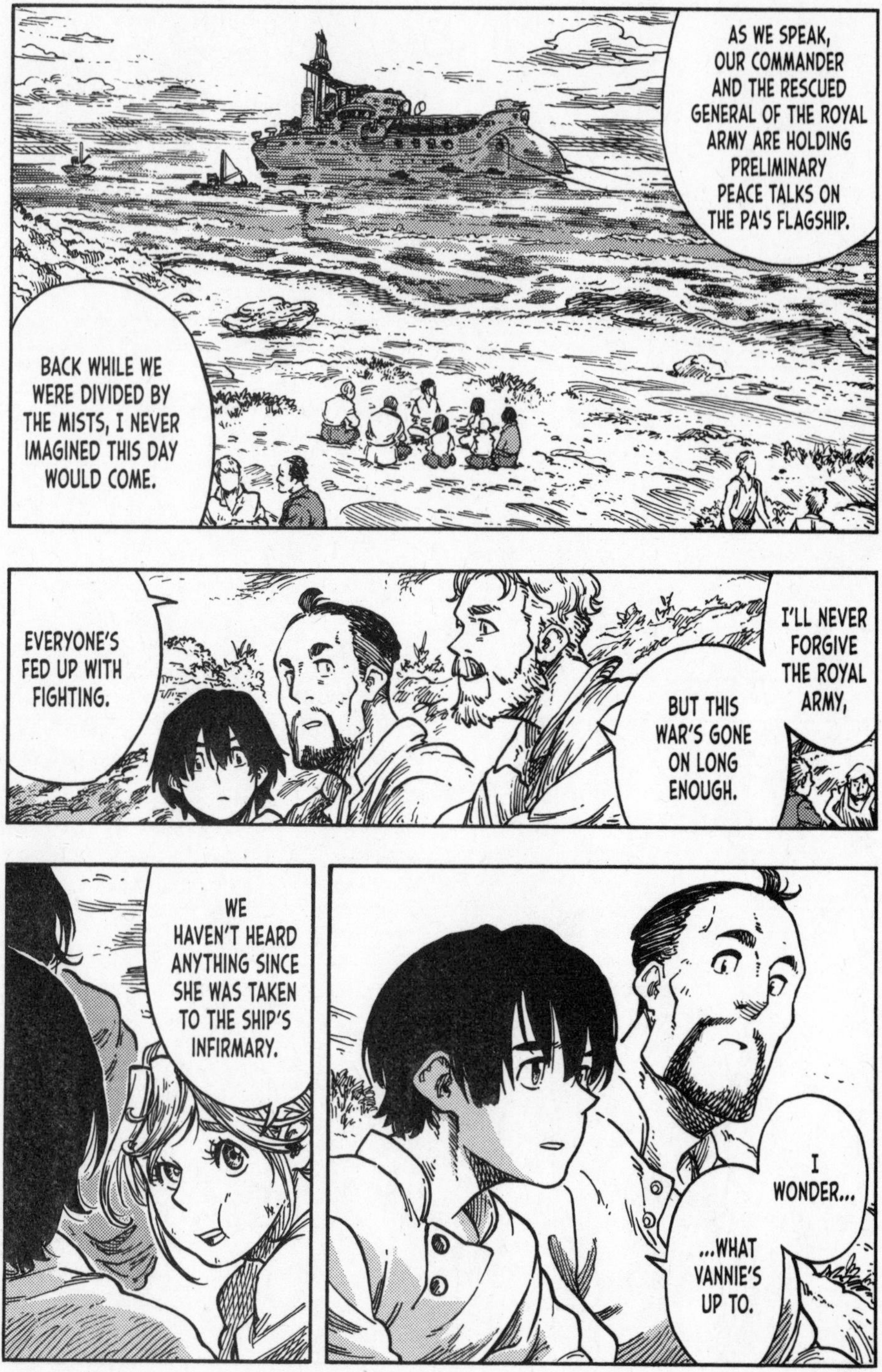
AS WE SPEAK, OUR COMMANDER AND THE RESCUED GENERAL OF THE ROYAL ARMY ARE HOLDING PRELIMINARY PEACE TALKS ON THE PA'S FLAGSHIP.
BACK WHILE WE WERE DIVIDED BY THE MISTS, I NEVER IMAGINED THIS DAY WOULD COME.
I'LL NEVER FORGIVE THE ROYAL ARMY,
BUT THIS WAR'S GONE ON LONG ENOUGH.
EVERYONE'S FED UP WITH FIGHTING.
I WONDER...
...WHAT VANNIE'S UP TO.
WE HAVEN'T HEARD ANYTHING SINCE SHE WAS TAKEN TO THE SHIP'S INFIRMARY.

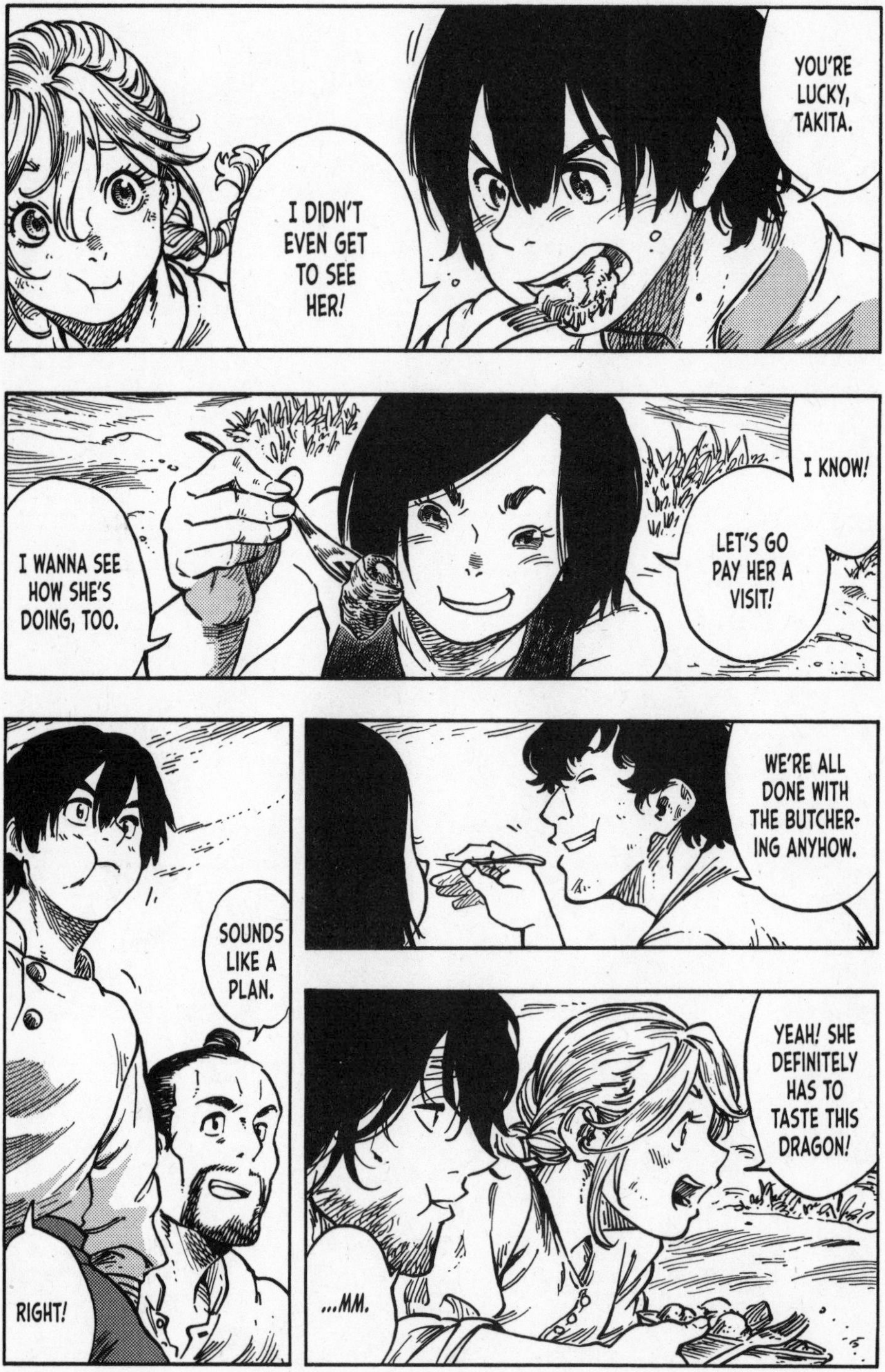
YOU'RE LUCKY, TAKITA.
I DIDN'T EVEN GET TO SEE HER!
I KNOW!
LET'S GO PAY HER A VISIT!
I WANNA SEE HOW SHE'S DOING, TOO.
WE'RE ALL DONE WITH THE BUTCHER-ING ANYHOW.
YEAH! SHE DEFINITELY HAS TO TASTE THIS DRAGON!
...MM.
SOUNDS LIKE A PLAN.
RIGHT!

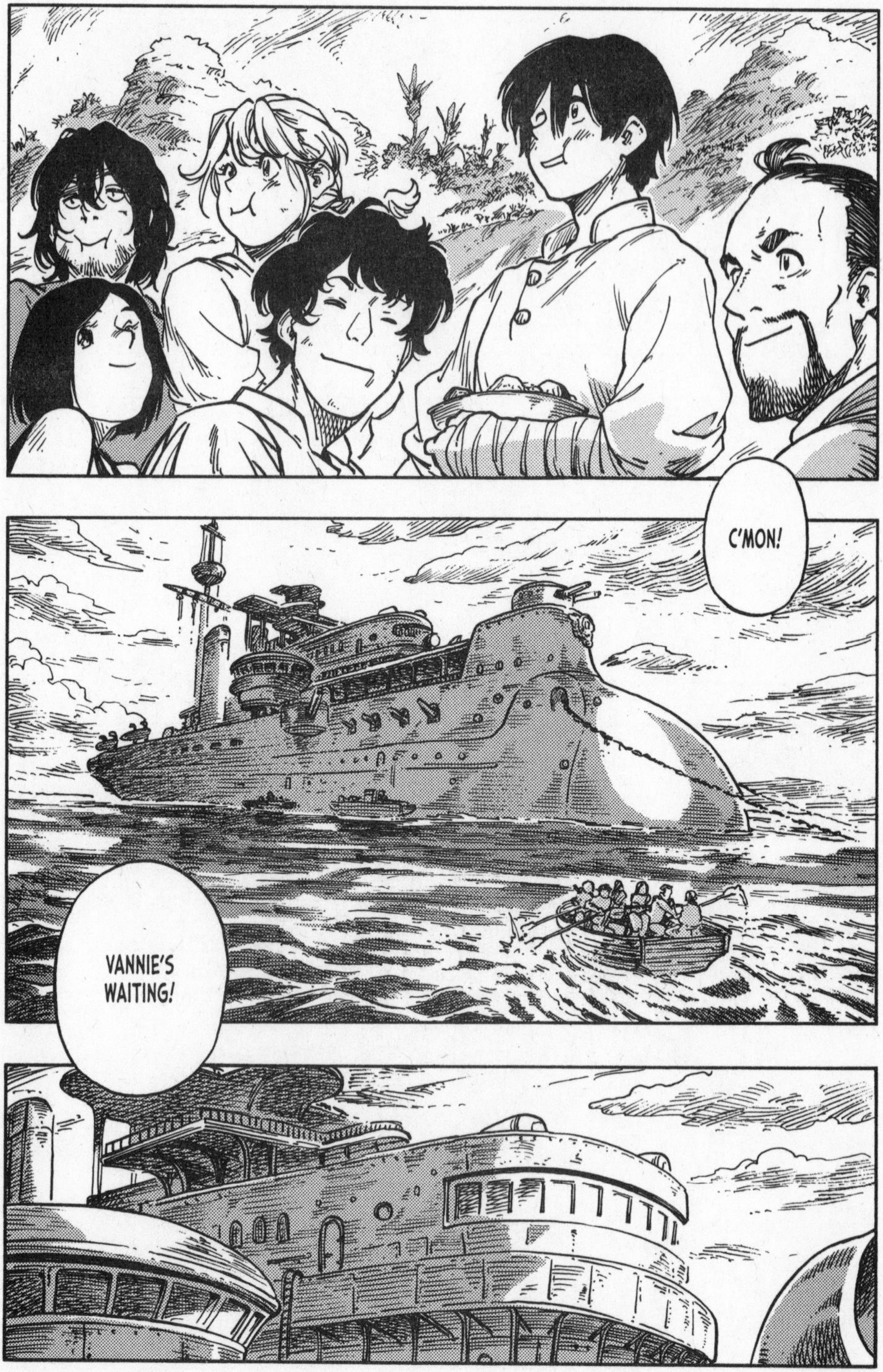
C'MON!
VANNIE'S WAITING!

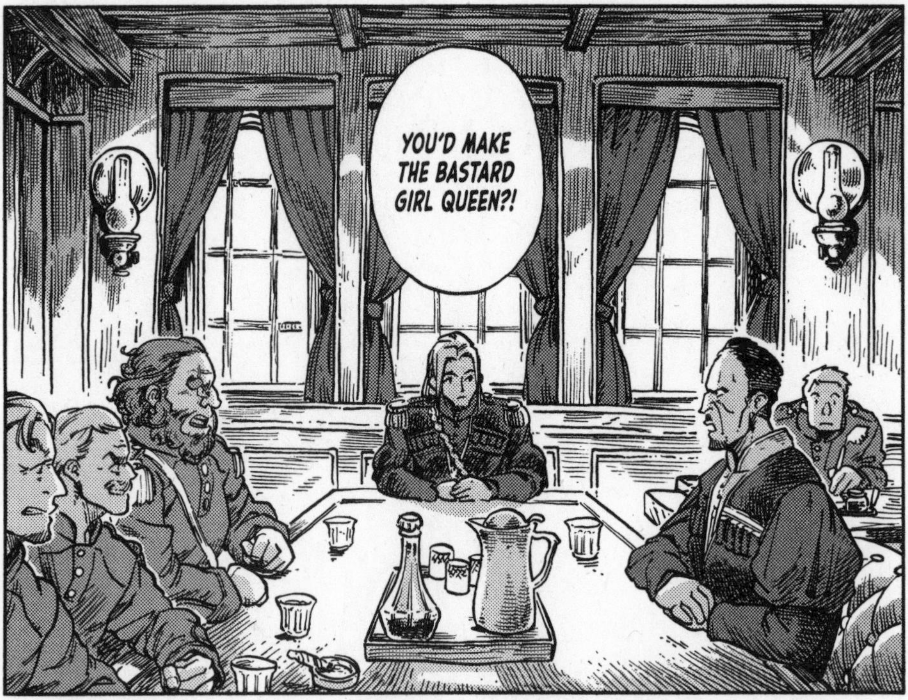
YOU'D MAKE THE BASTARD GIRL QUEEN?!

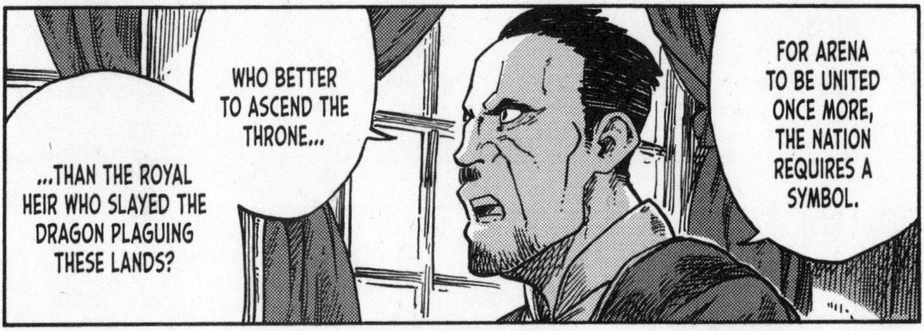
FOR ARENA TO BE UNITED ONCE MORE, THE NATION REQUIRES A SYMBOL.
WHO BETTER TO ASCEND THE THRONE...
...THAN THE ROYAL HEIR WHO SLAYED THE DRAGON PLAGUING THESE LANDS?

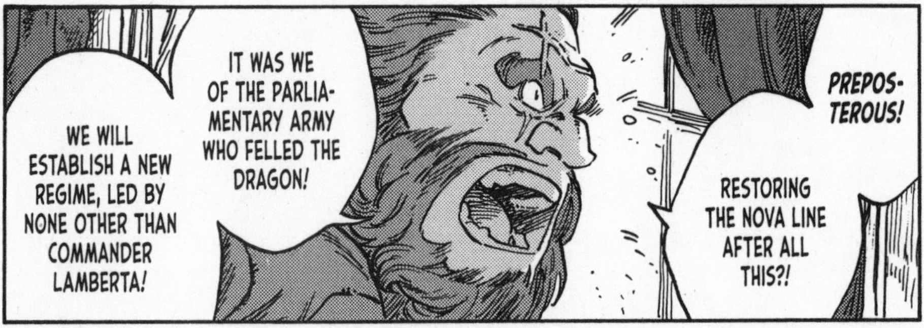
PREPOSTEROUS!
RESTORING THE NOVA LINE AFTER ALL THIS?!
IT WAS WE OF THE PARLIAMENTARY ARMY WHO FELLED THE DRAGON!
WE WILL ESTABLISH A NEW REGIME, LED BY NONE OTHER THAN COMMANDER LAMBERTA!

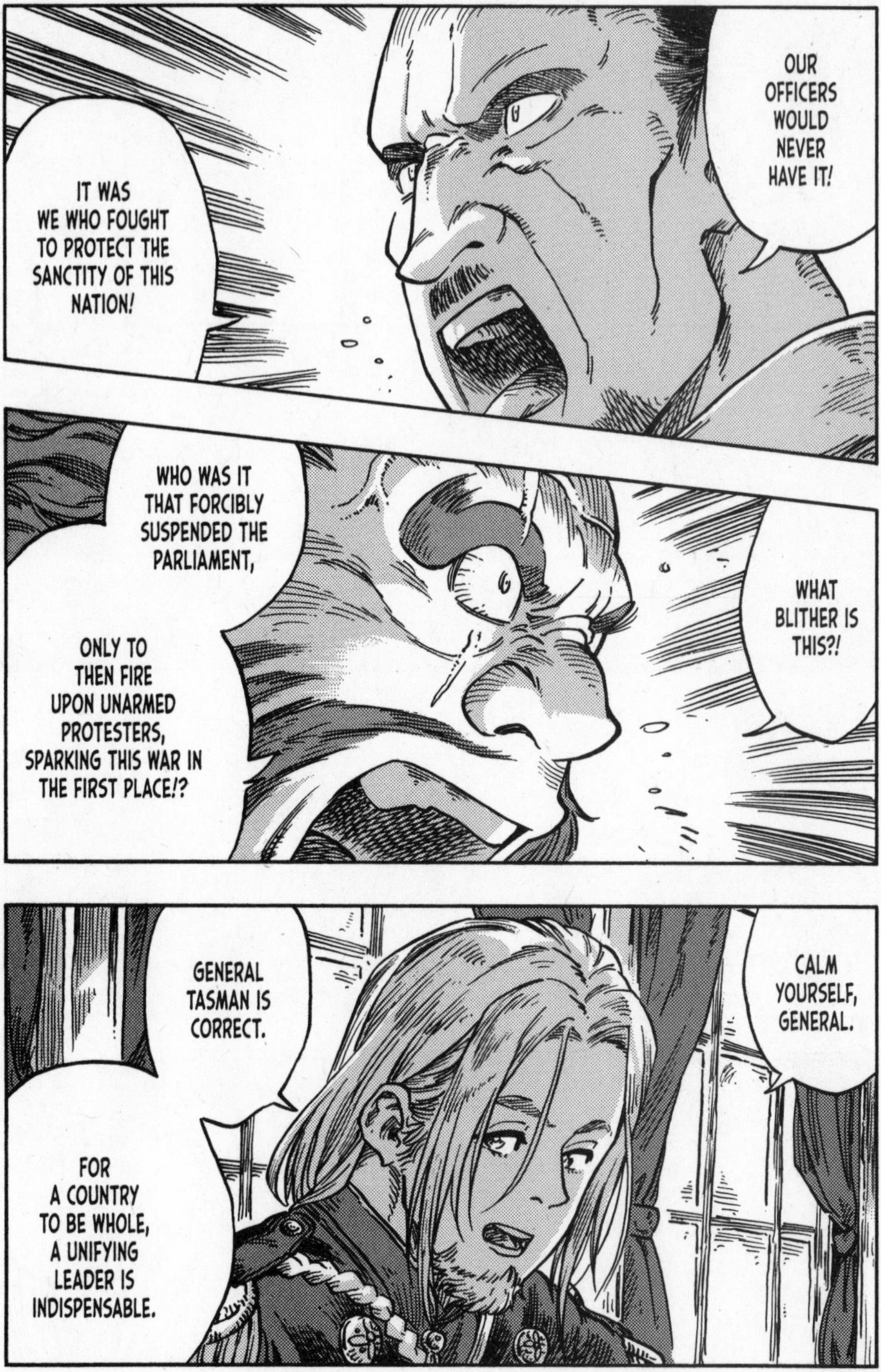
OUR OFFICERS WOULD NEVER HAVE IT!
IT WAS WE WHO FOUGHT TO PROTECT THE SANCTITY OF THIS NATION!
WHAT BLITHER IS THIS?!
WHO WAS IT THAT FORCIBLY SUSPENDED THE PARLIAMENT,
ONLY TO THEN FIRE UPON UNARMED PROTESTERS, SPARKING THIS WAR IN THE FIRST PLACE!?
CALM YOURSELF, GENERAL.
GENERAL TASMAN IS CORRECT.
FOR A COUNTRY TO BE WHOLE, A UNIFYING LEADER IS INDISPENSABLE.

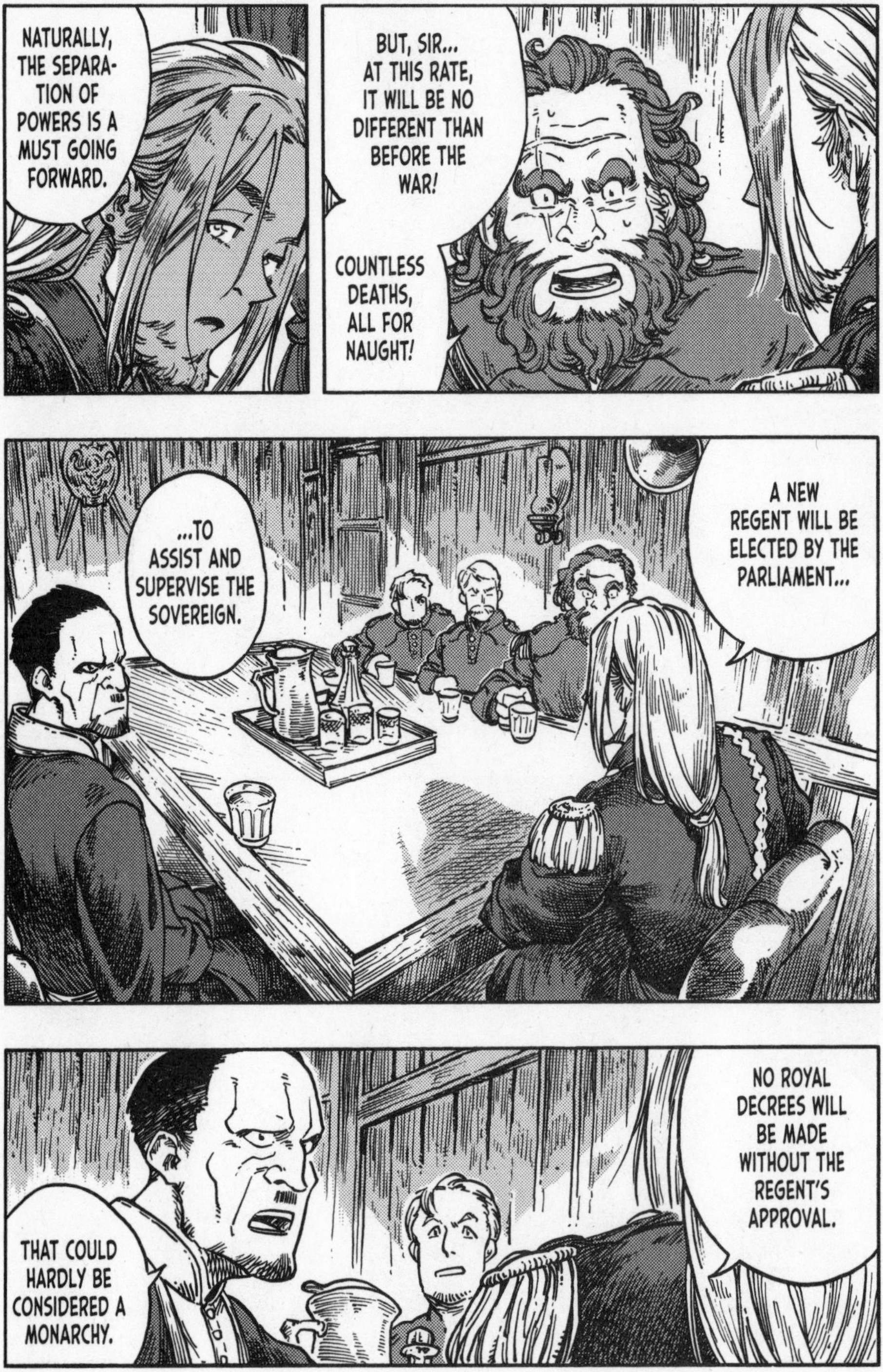
BUT, SIR... AT THIS RATE, IT WILL BE NO DIFFERENT THAN BEFORE THE WAR!
COUNTLESS DEATHS, ALL FOR NAUGHT!
NATURALLY, THE SEPARATION OF POWERS IS A MUST GOING FORWARD.
A NEW REGENT WILL BE ELECTED BY THE PARLIAMENT...
...TO ASSIST AND SUPERVISE THE SOVEREIGN.
NO ROYAL DECREES WILL BE MADE WITHOUT THE REGENT'S APPROVAL.
THAT COULD HARDLY BE CONSIDERED A MONARCHY.

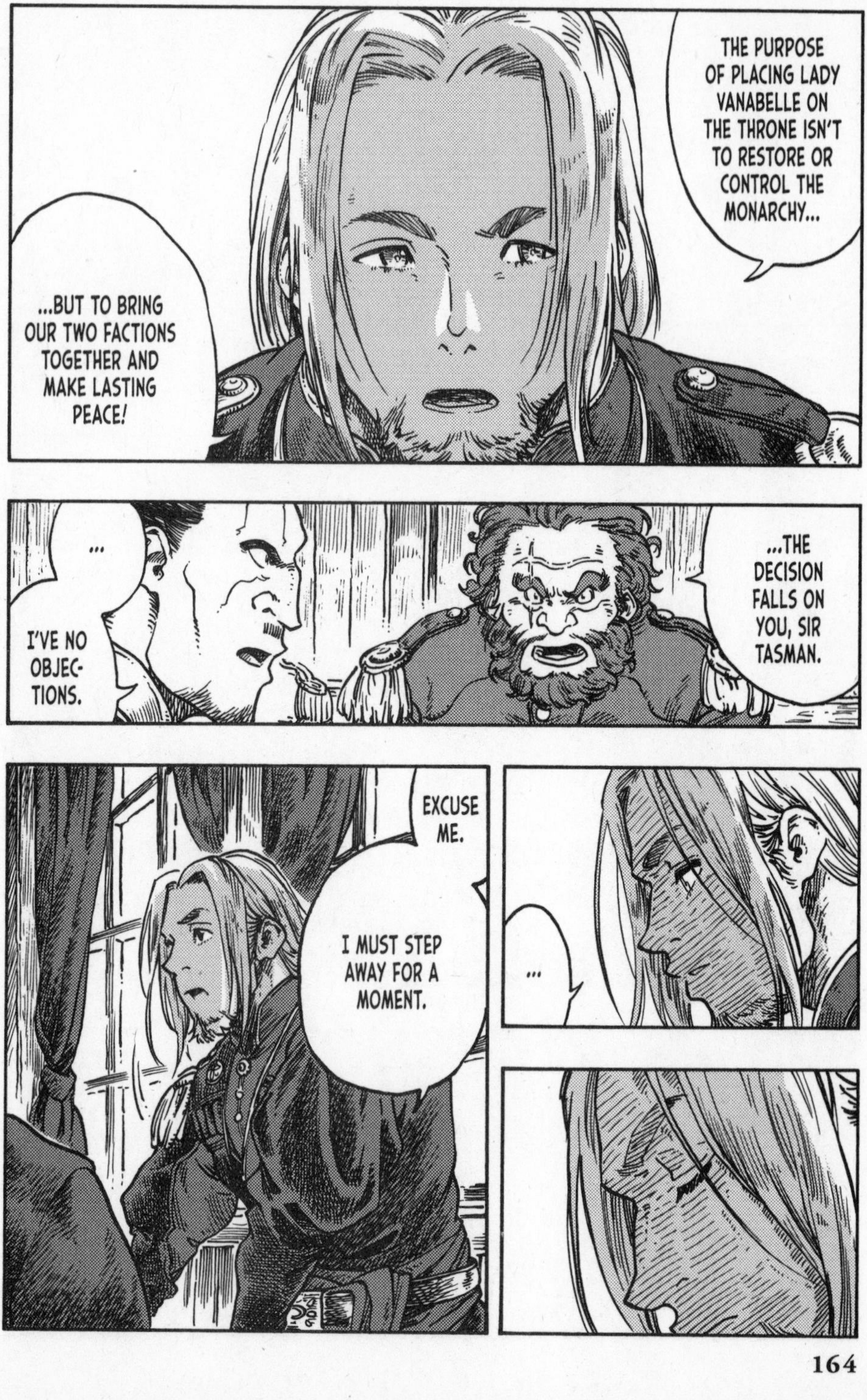
THE PURPOSE OF PLACING LADY VANABELLE ON THE THRONE ISN'T TO RESTORE OR CONTROL THE MONARCHY...
...BUT TO BRING OUR TWO FACTIONS TOGETHER AND MAKE LASTING PEACE!
...THE DECISION FALLS ON YOU, SIR TASMAN.
...
I'VE NO OBJEC-TIONS.
...
EXCUSE ME.
I MUST STEP AWAY FOR A MOMENT.

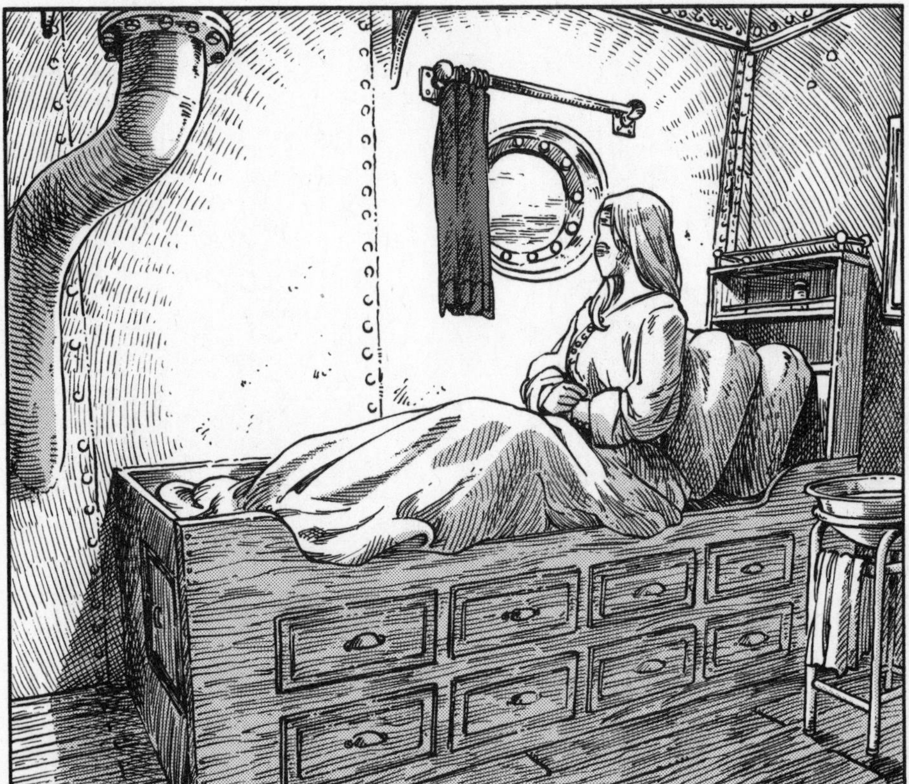
KNOCK
KNOCK

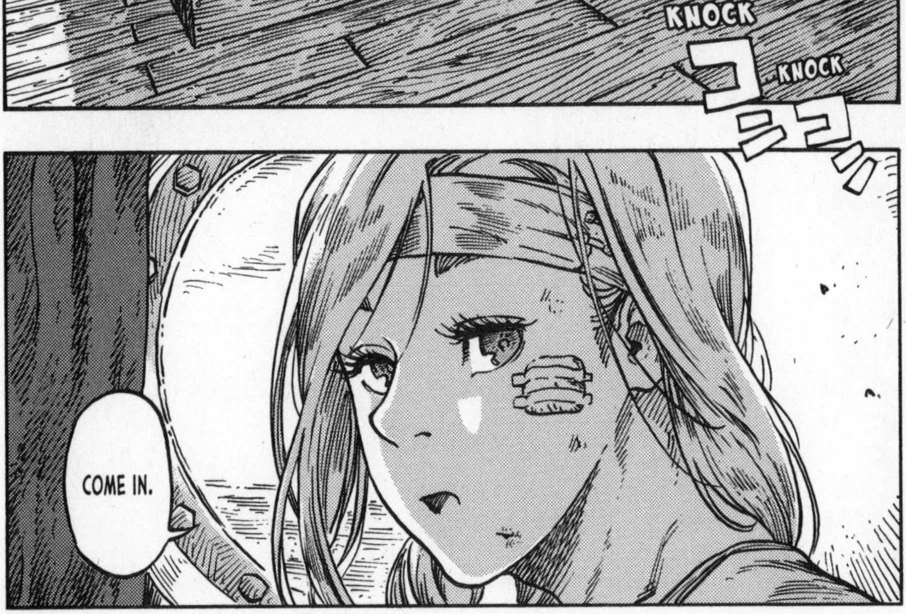
COME IN.

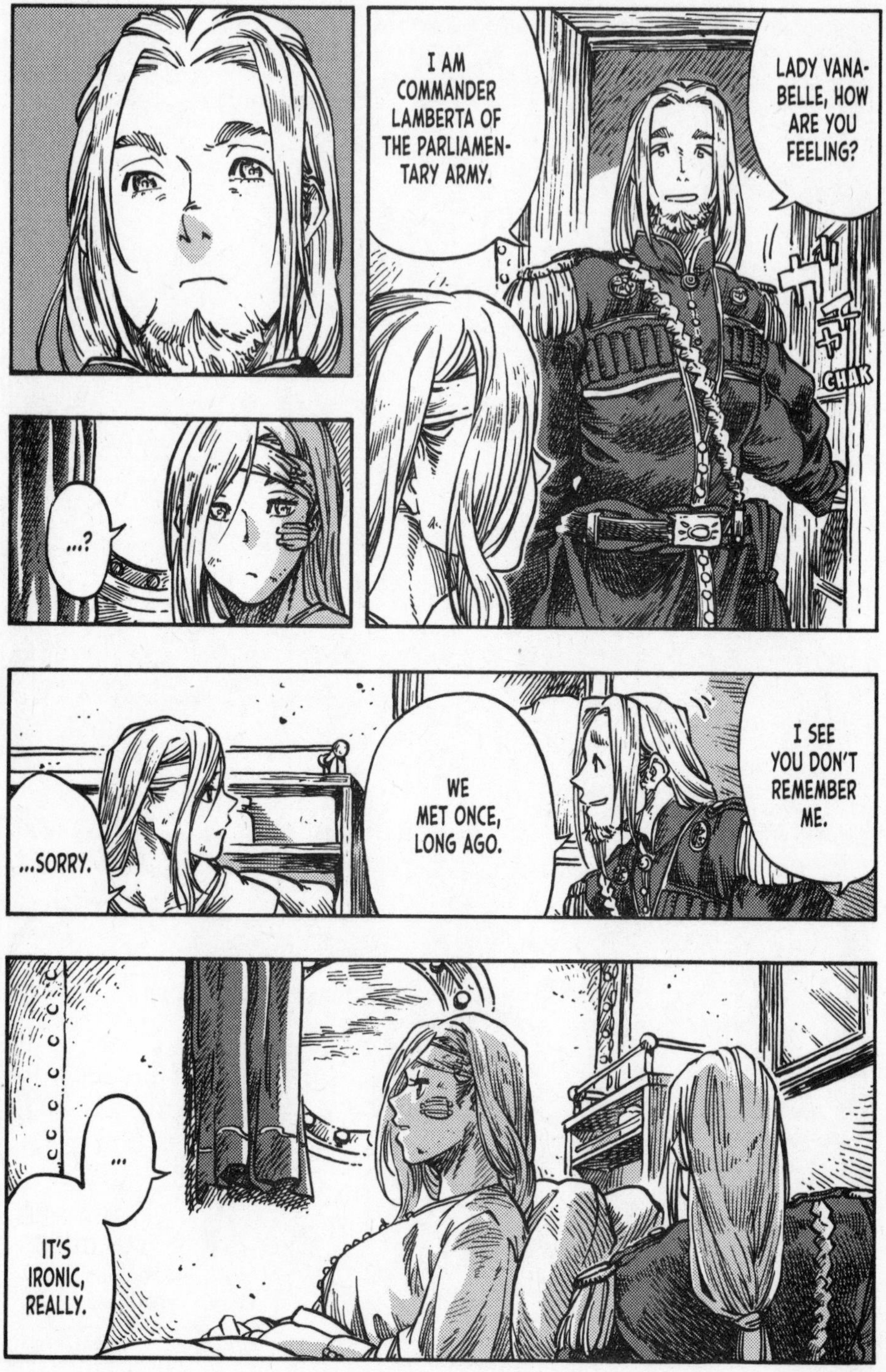
LADY VANABELLE, HOW ARE YOU FEELING?
CHAK
I AM COMMANDER LAMBERTA OF THE PARLIAMENTARY ARMY.
...?
I SEE YOU DON'T REMEMBER ME.
WE MET ONCE, LONG AGO.
...SORRY.
...
IT'S IRONIC, REALLY.

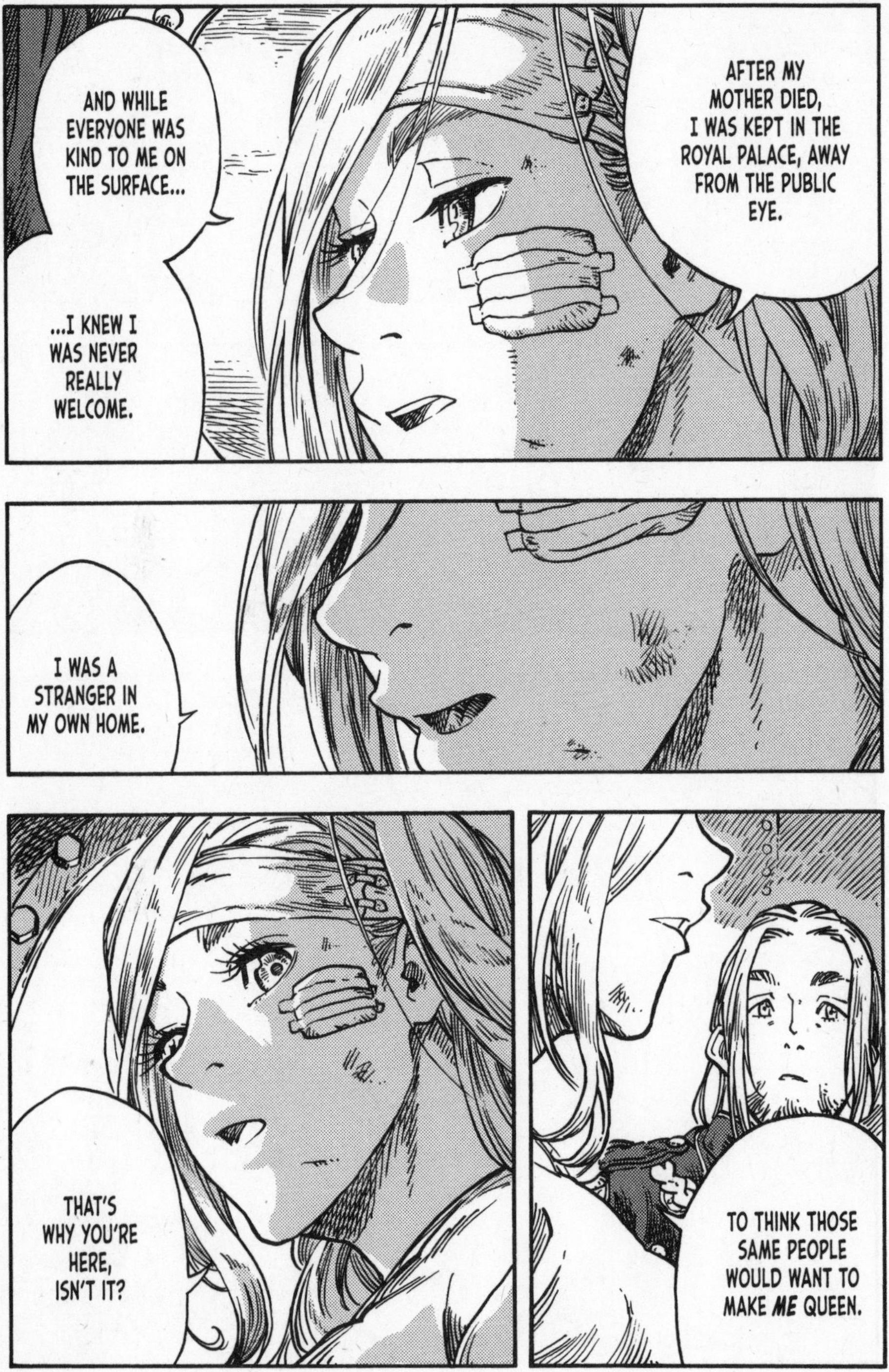
AFTER MY MOTHER DIED, I WAS KEPT IN THE ROYAL PALACE, AWAY FROM THE PUBLIC EYE.
AND WHILE EVERYONE WAS KIND TO ME ON THE SURFACE...
...I KNEW I WAS NEVER REALLY WELCOME.
I WAS A STRANGER IN MY OWN HOME.
TO THINK THOSE SAME PEOPLE WOULD WANT TO MAKE *ME* QUEEN.
THAT'S WHY YOU'RE HERE, ISN'T IT?

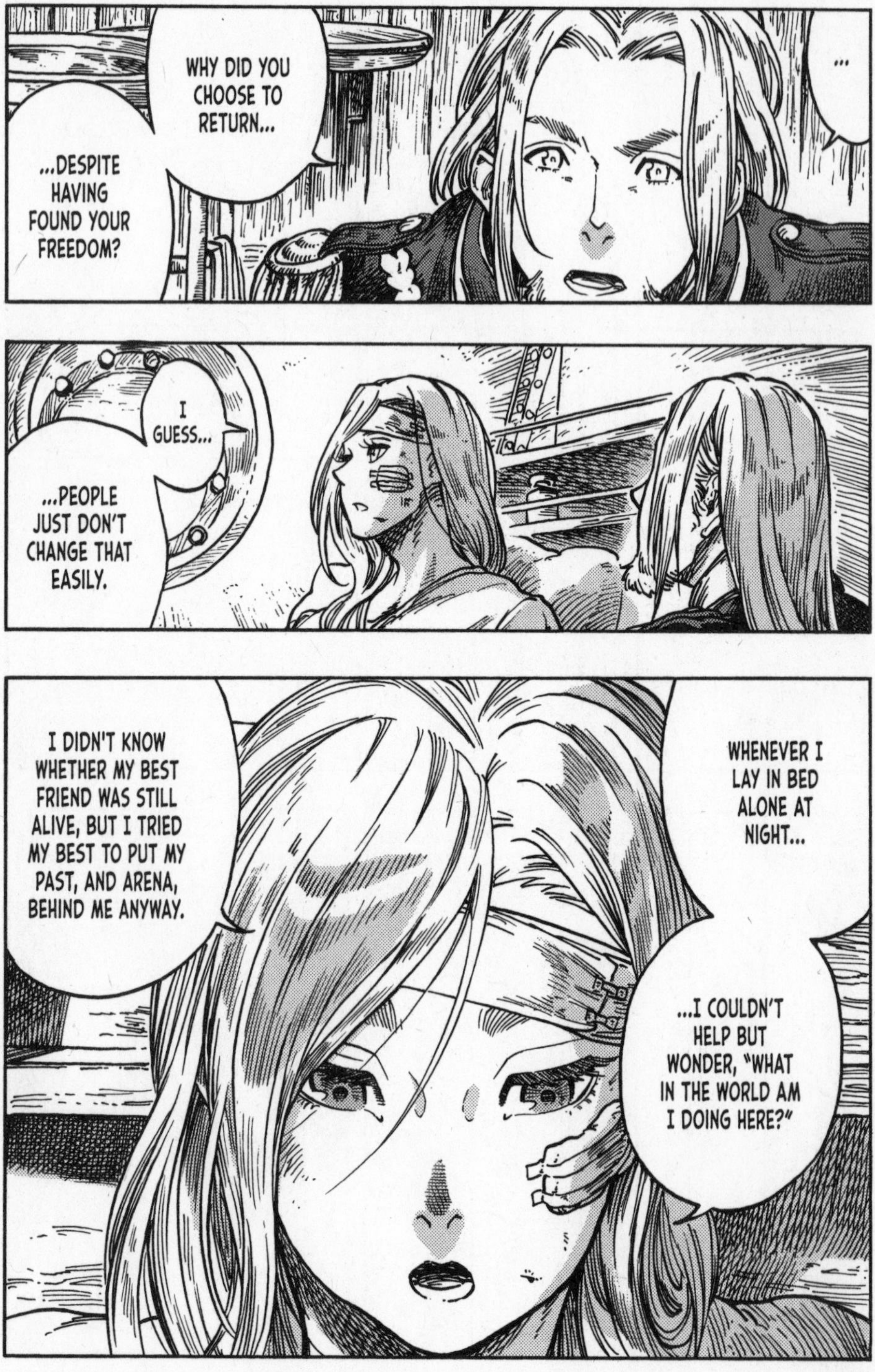
...
WHY DID YOU CHOOSE TO RETURN...
...DESPITE HAVING FOUND YOUR FREEDOM?
I GUESS...
...PEOPLE JUST DON'T CHANGE THAT EASILY.
WHENEVER I LAY IN BED ALONE AT NIGHT...
...I COULDN'T HELP BUT WONDER, "WHAT IN THE WORLD AM I DOING HERE?"
I DIDN'T KNOW WHETHER MY BEST FRIEND WAS STILL ALIVE, BUT I TRIED MY BEST TO PUT MY PAST, AND ARENA, BEHIND ME ANYWAY.

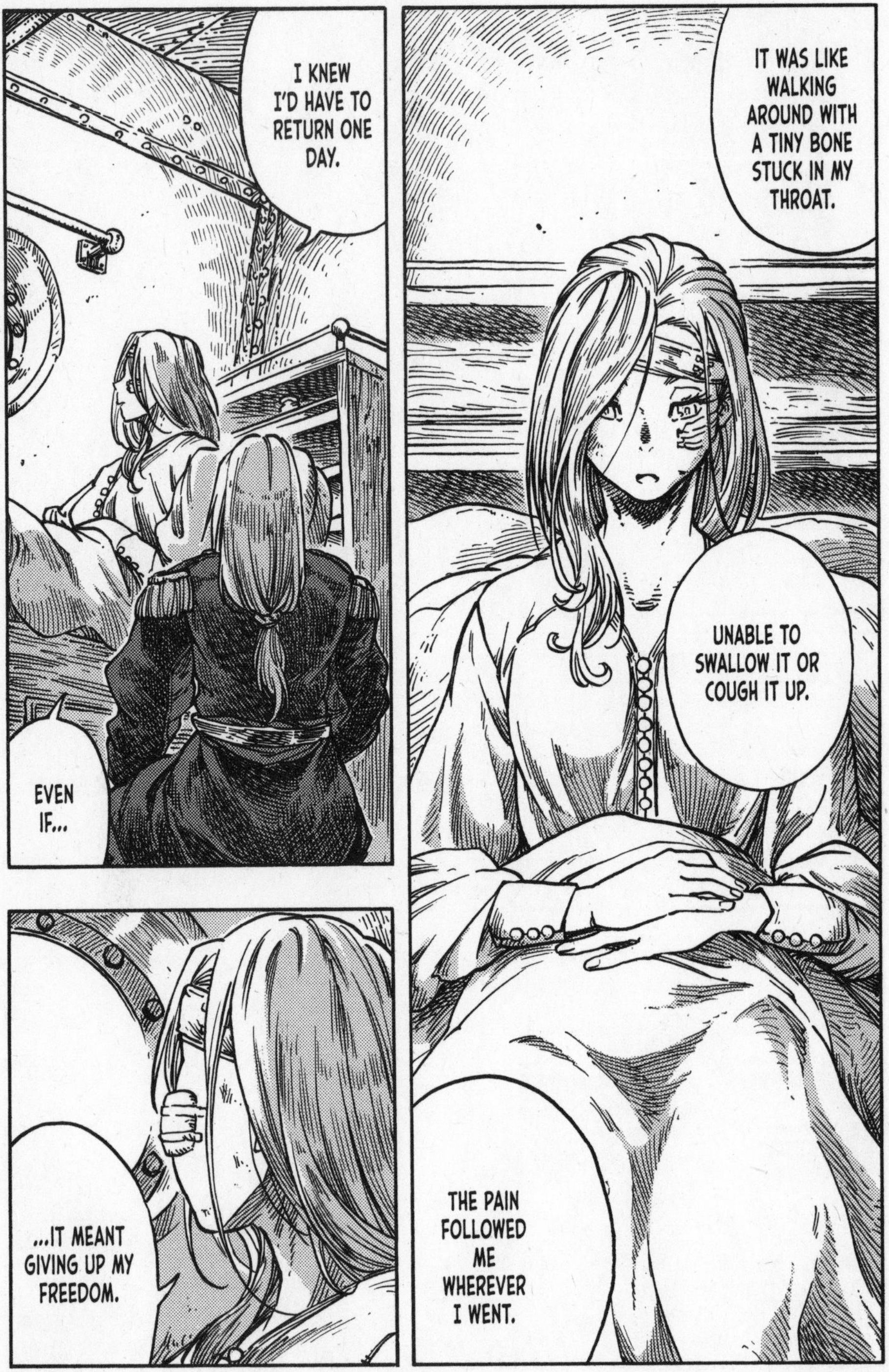
IT WAS LIKE WALKING AROUND WITH A TINY BONE STUCK IN MY THROAT.
UNABLE TO SWALLOW IT OR COUGH IT UP.
THE PAIN FOLLOWED ME WHEREVER I WENT.
I KNEW I'D HAVE TO RETURN ONE DAY.
EVEN IF...
...IT MEANT GIVING UP MY FREEDOM.

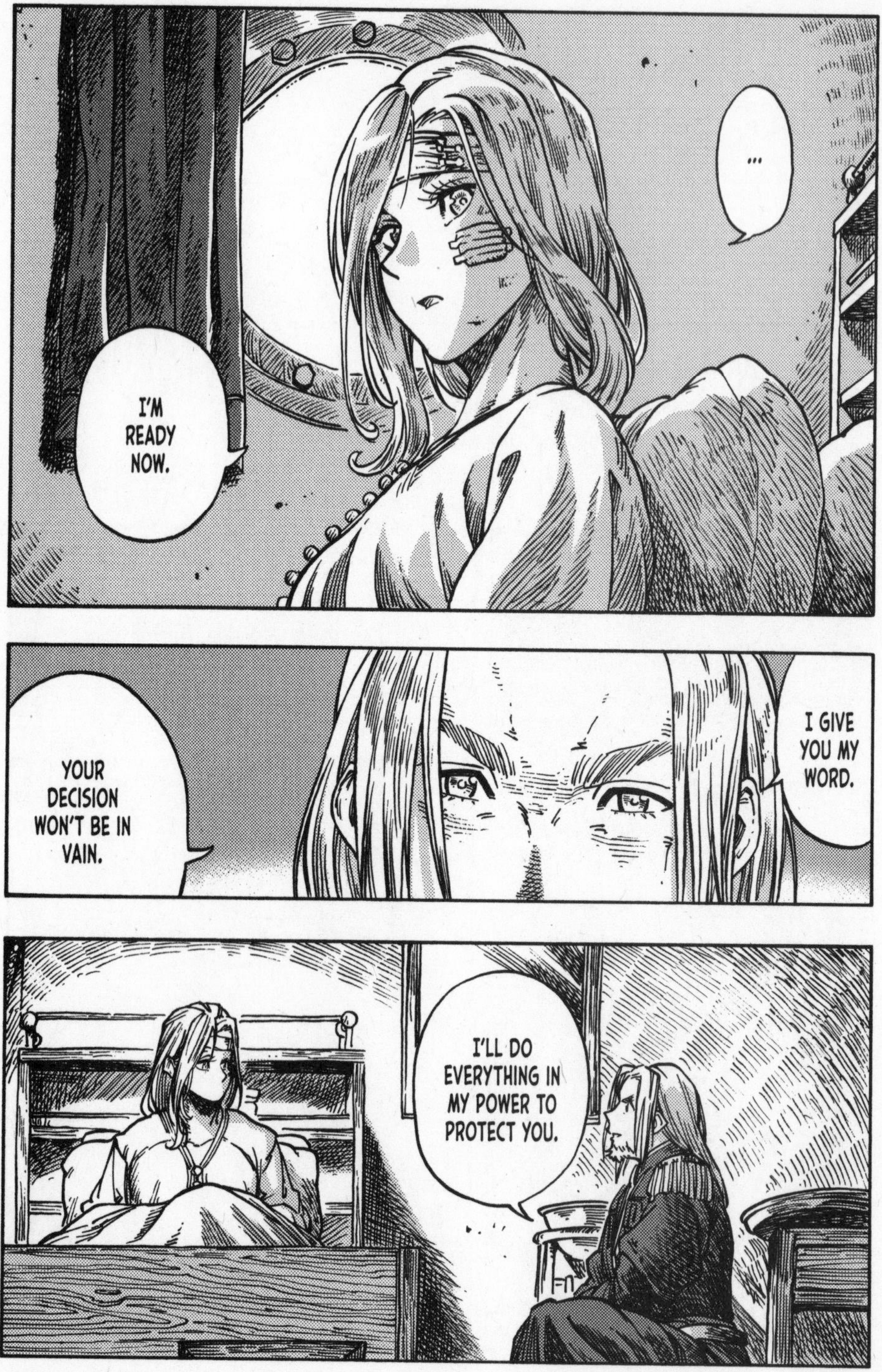
...
I'M READY NOW.
I GIVE YOU MY WORD.
YOUR DECISION WON'T BE IN VAIN.
I'LL DO EVERYTHING IN MY POWER TO PROTECT YOU.

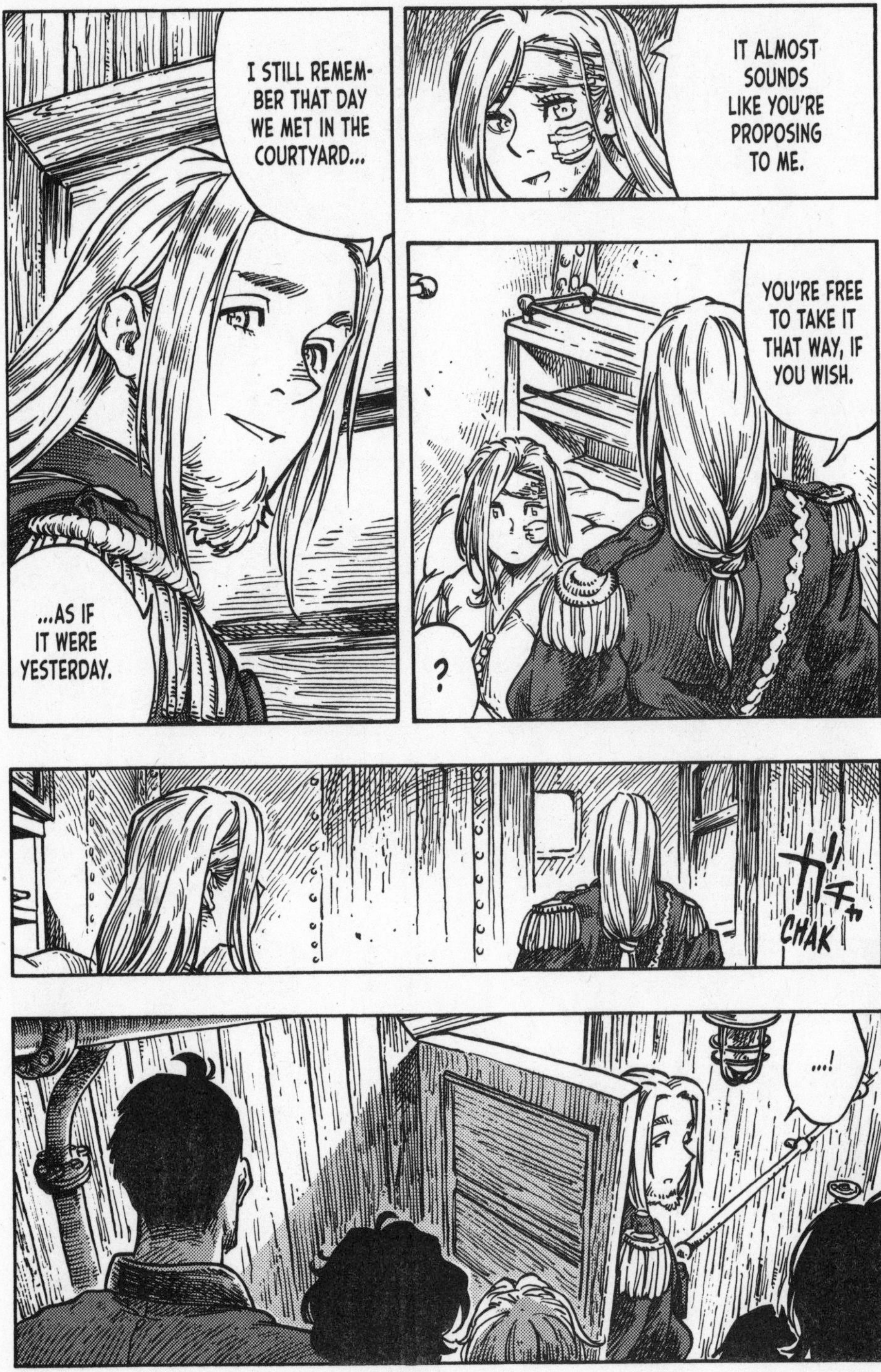

IT ALMOST SOUNDS LIKE YOU'RE PROPOSING TO ME.
YOU'RE FREE TO TAKE IT THAT WAY, IF YOU WISH.
?
I STILL REMEMBER THAT DAY WE MET IN THE COURTYARD...
...AS IF IT WERE YESTERDAY.
ガチャ
CHAK
...!

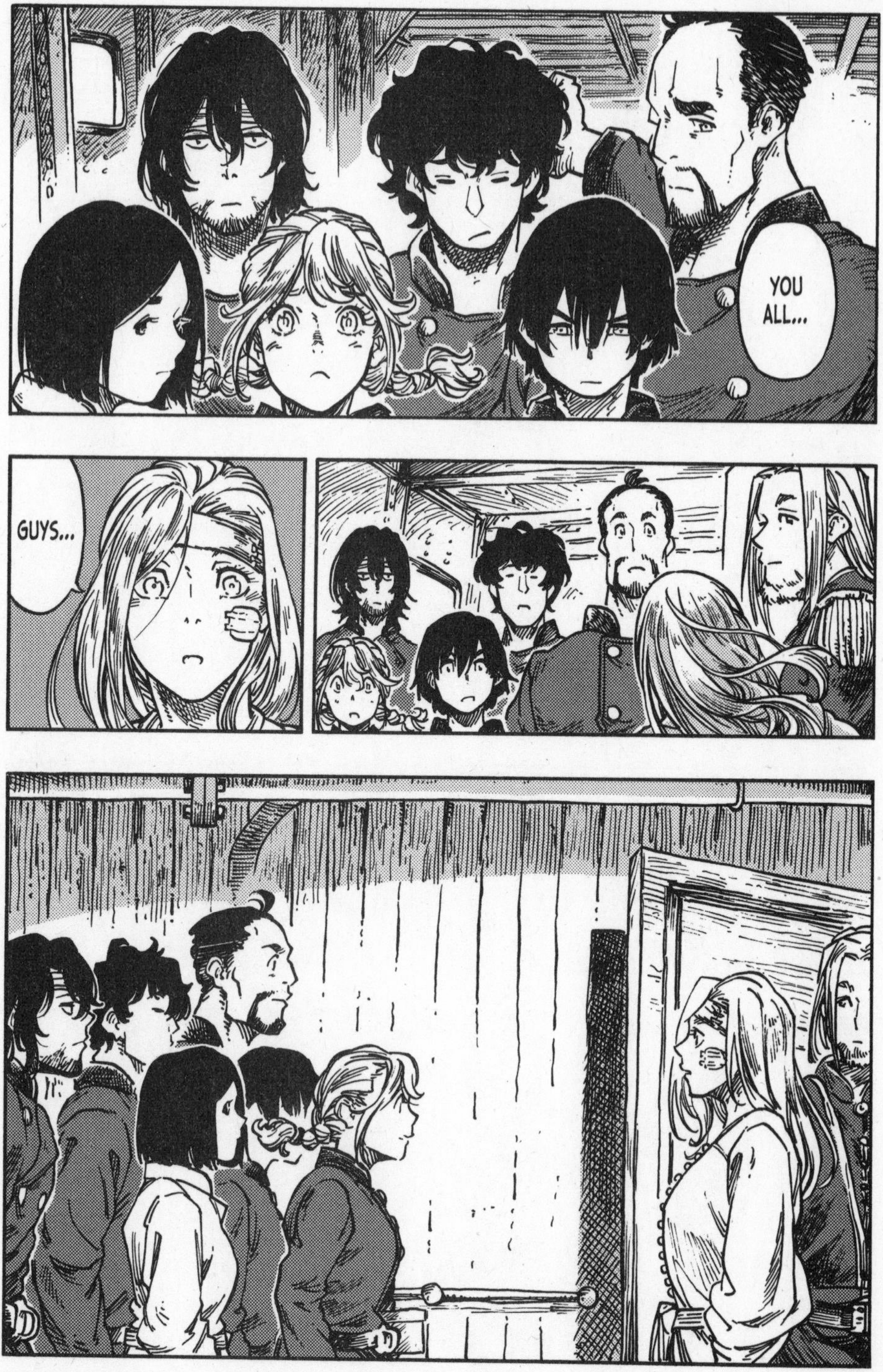
YOU ALL...
GUYS...

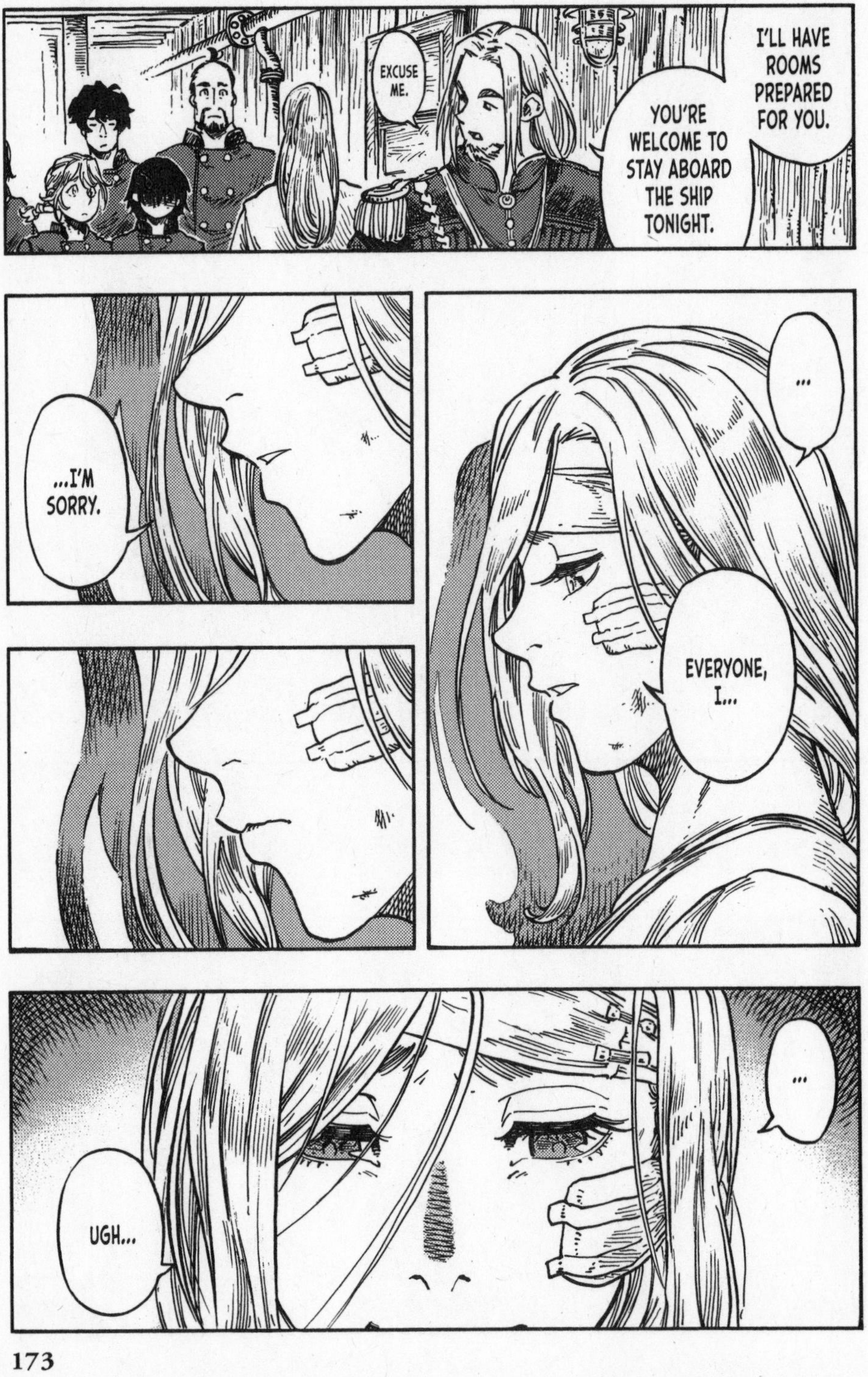
I'LL HAVE ROOMS PREPARED FOR YOU.
YOU'RE WELCOME TO STAY ABOARD THE SHIP TONIGHT.
EXCUSE ME.
...
EVERYONE, I...
...I'M SORRY.
...
UGH...

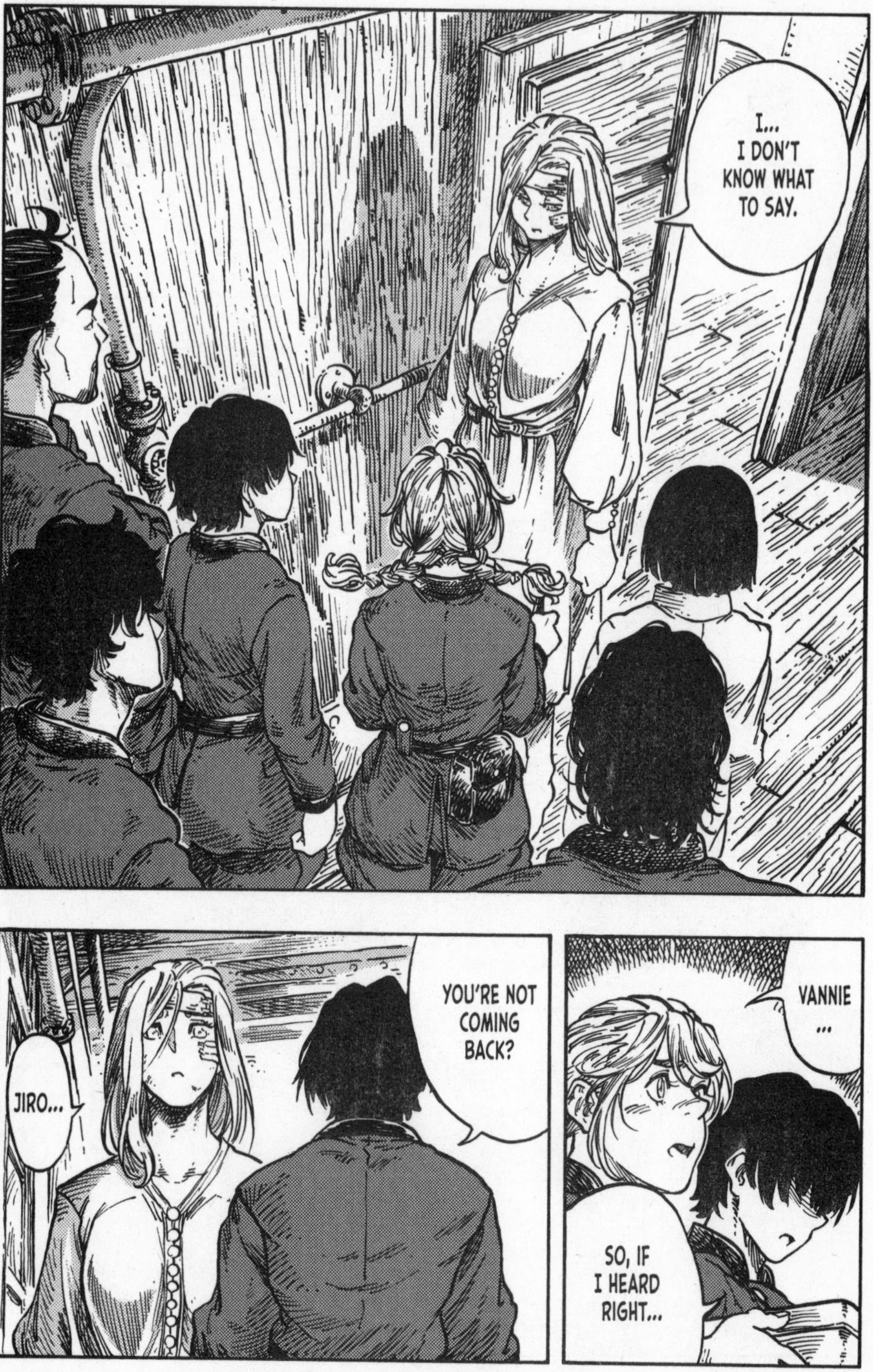
I... I DON'T KNOW WHAT TO SAY.
VANNIE ...
SO, IF I HEARD RIGHT...
YOU'RE NOT COMING BACK?
JIRO...

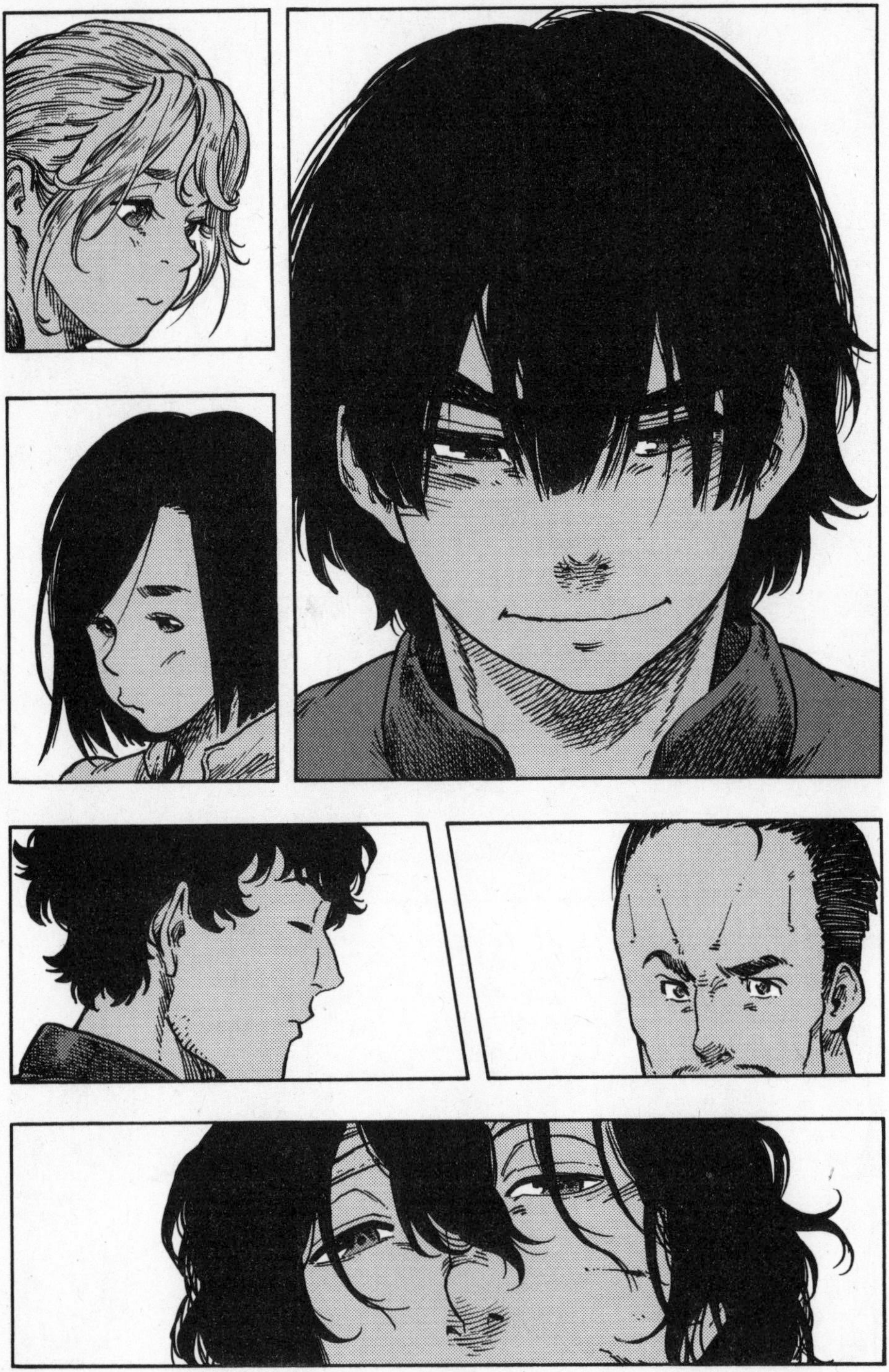

WOBL
WHOA!
EASY THERE, VANNIE!
DON'T WORRY, I'M FINE.
JUST A LITTLE DIZZY FROM THE SEDATIVES.

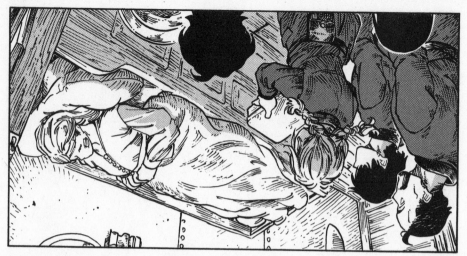

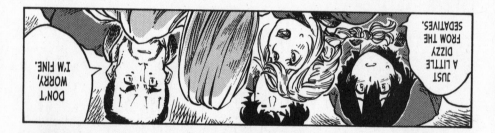

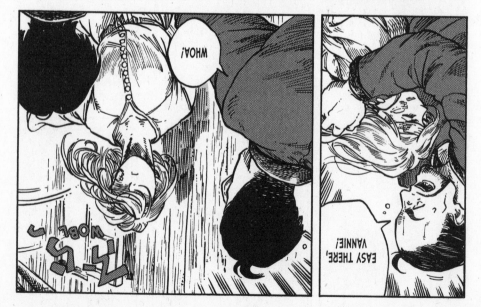

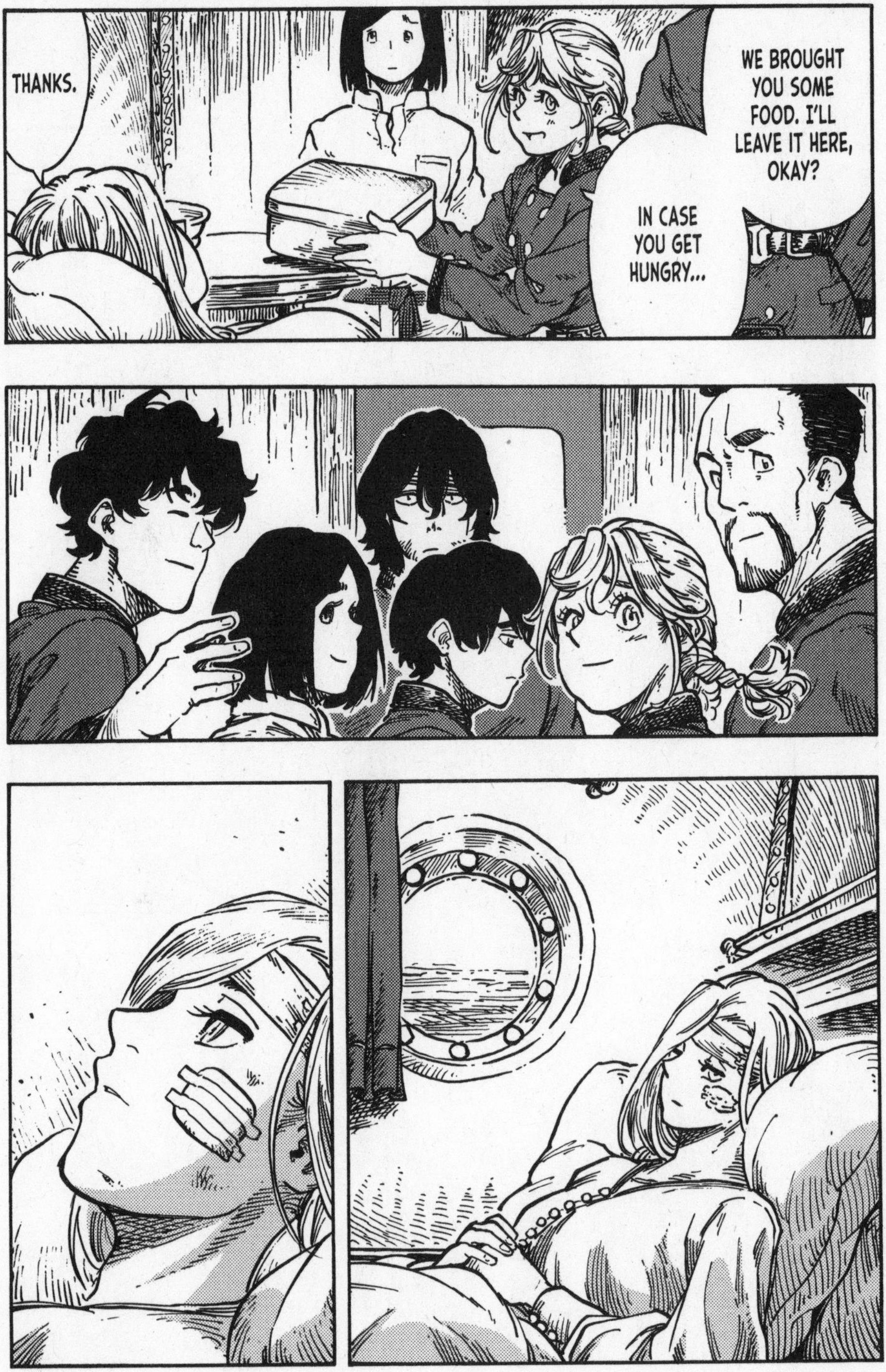
WE BROUGHT YOU SOME FOOD. I'LL LEAVE IT HERE, OKAY?
IN CASE YOU GET HUNGRY...
THANKS.

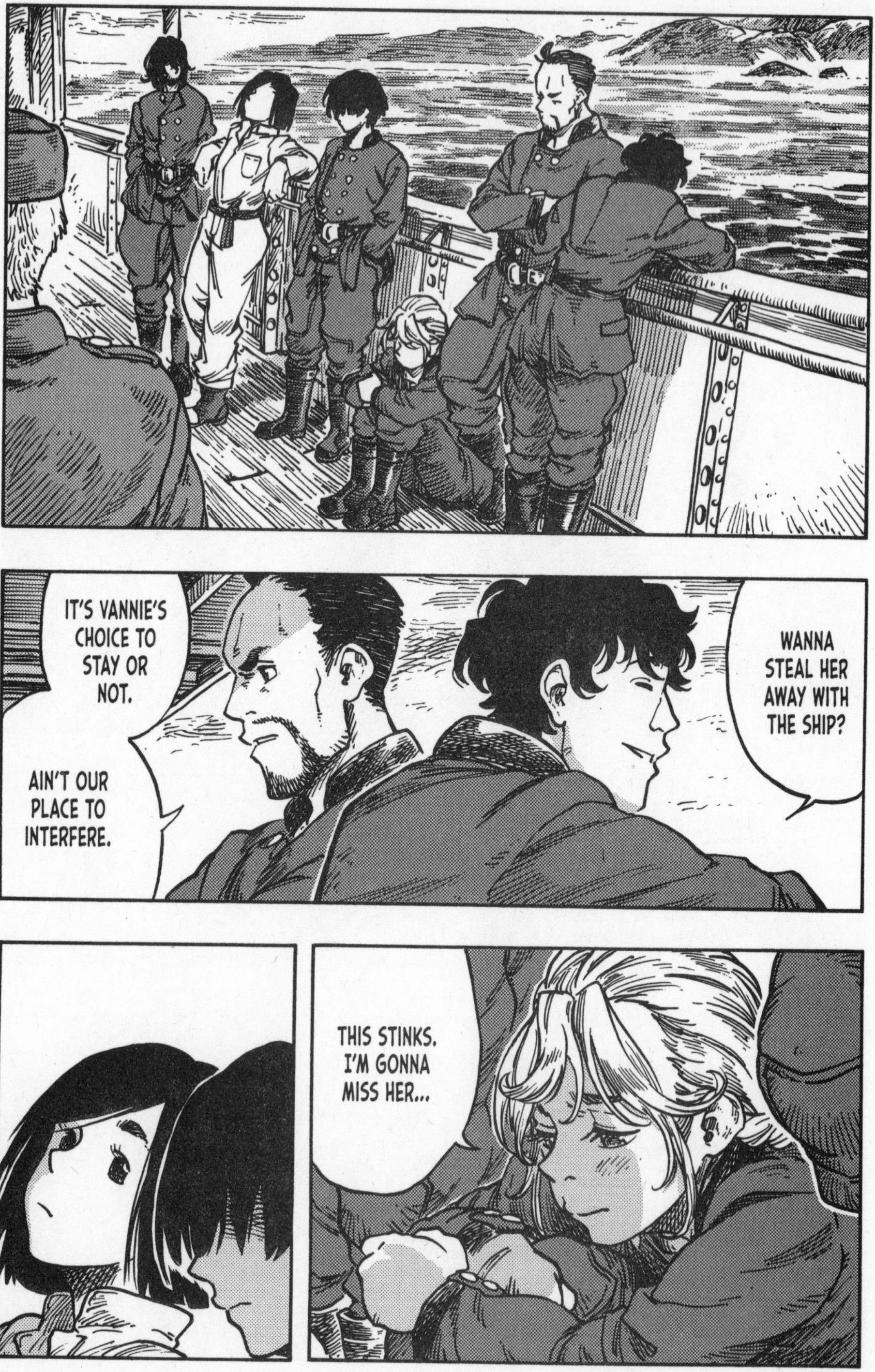
WANNA STEAL HER AWAY WITH THE SHIP?
IT'S VANNIE'S CHOICE TO STAY OR NOT.
AIN'T OUR PLACE TO INTERFERE.
THIS STINKS. I'M GONNA MISS HER...

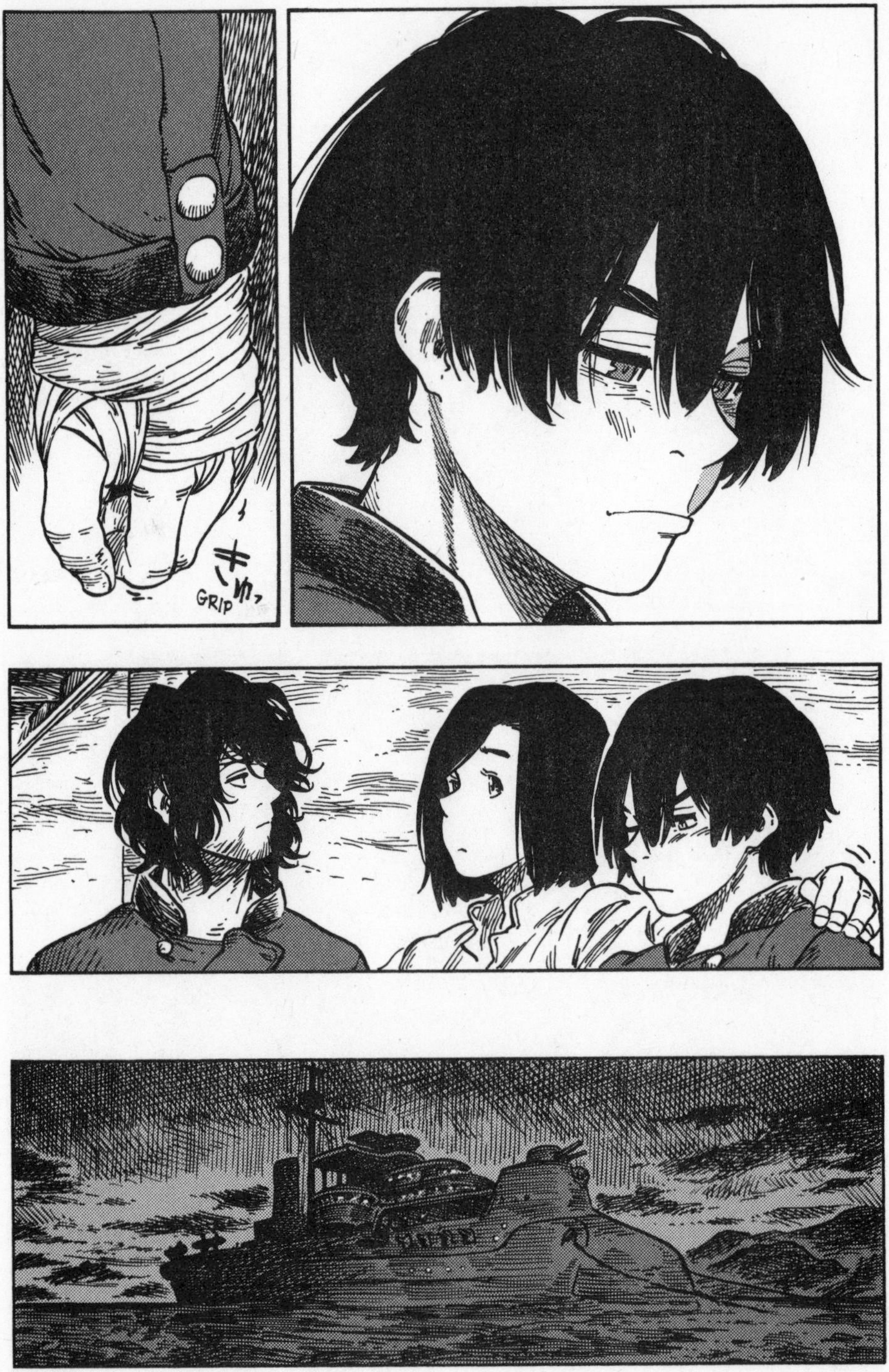
きゅっ
GRIP

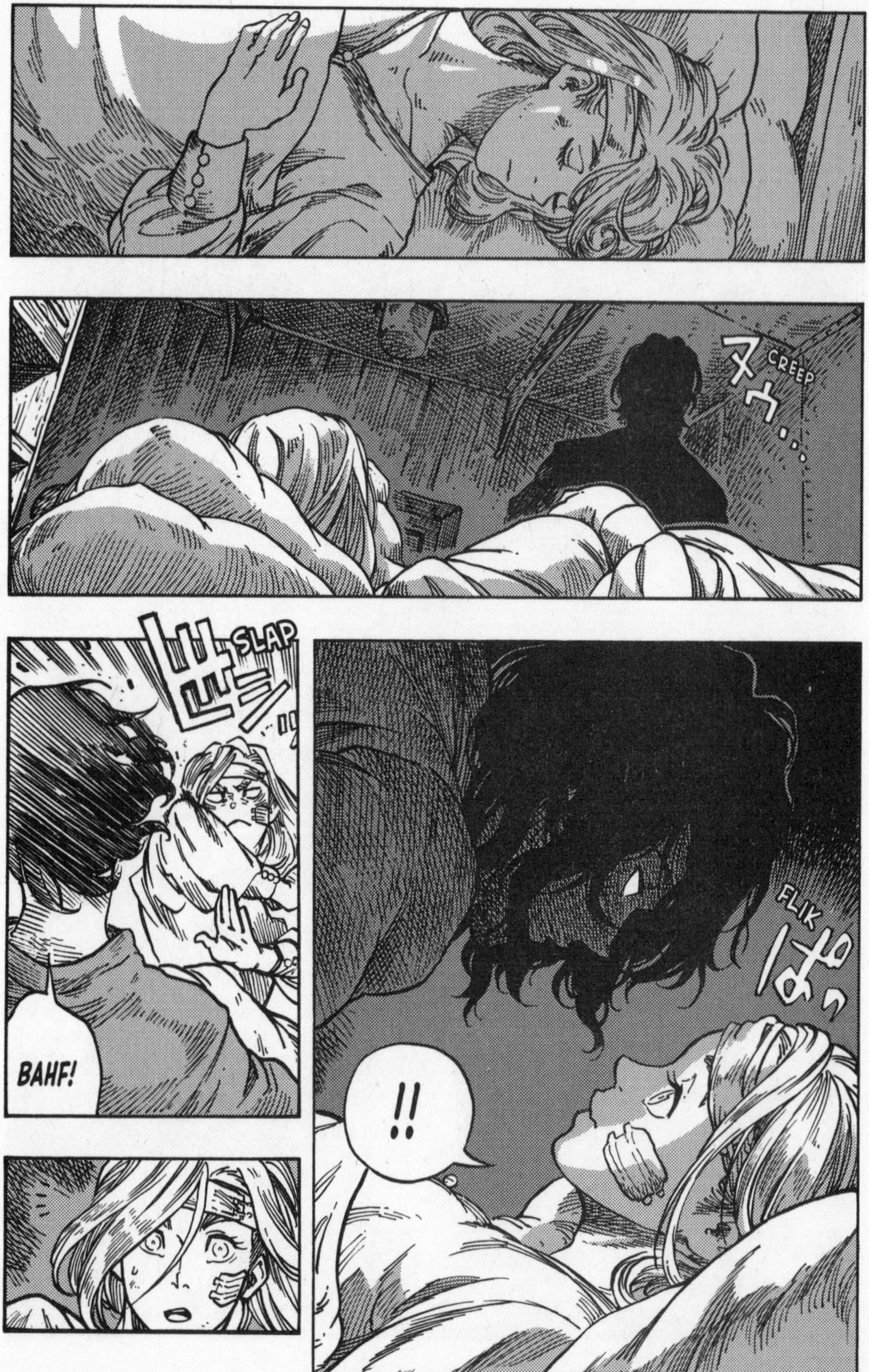
ヌゥ…
CREEP
ぱっ
FLIK
!!
SLAP
BAHF!

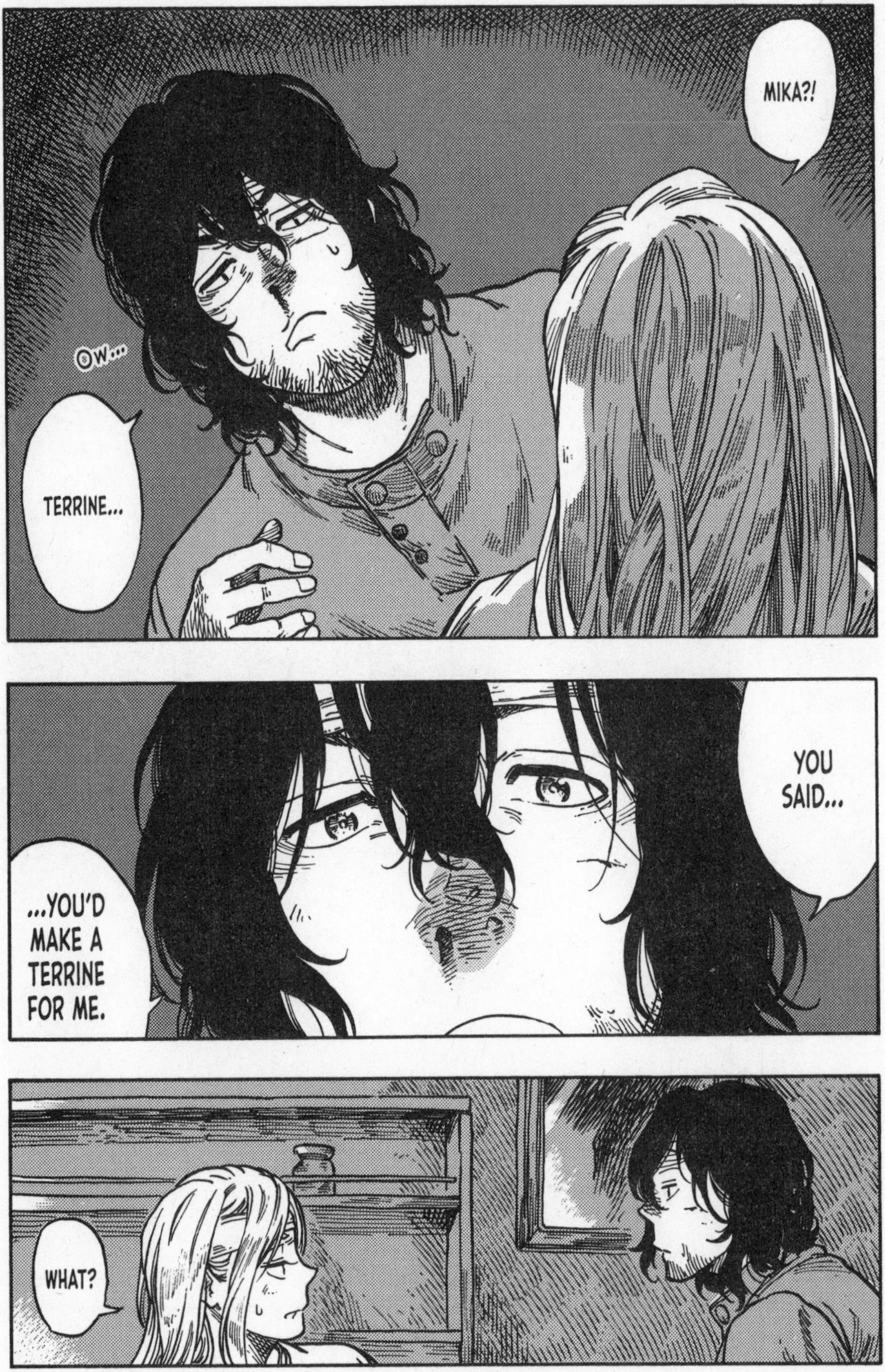
MIKA?!
OW...
TERRINE...
YOU SAID...
...YOU'D MAKE A TERRINE FOR ME.
WHAT?

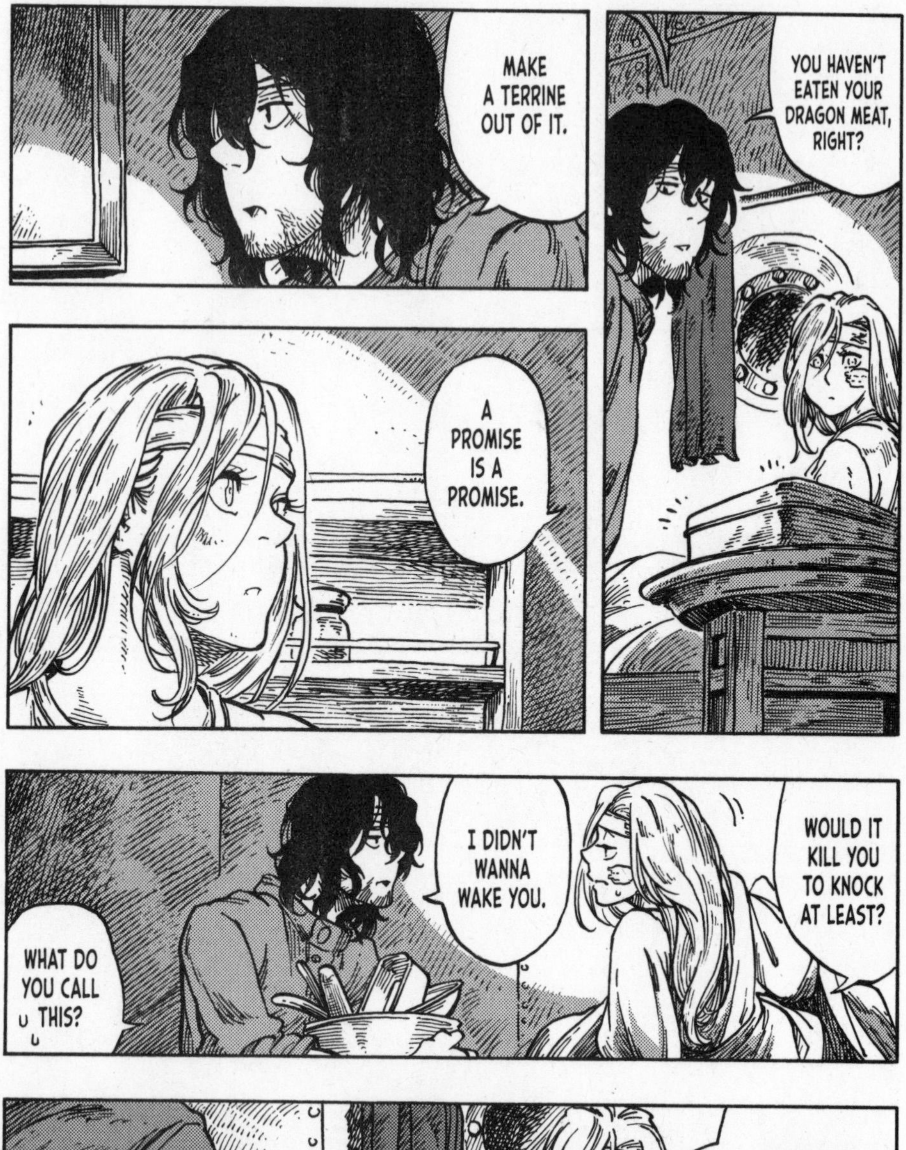
YOU HAVEN'T EATEN YOUR DRAGON MEAT, RIGHT?
MAKE A TERRINE OUT OF IT.
A PROMISE IS A PROMISE.
WOULD IT KILL YOU TO KNOCK AT LEAST?
I DIDN'T WANNA WAKE YOU.
WHAT DO YOU CALL THIS?
WHERE'D YOU GET THOSE ANYWAY?
I BORROWED THEM FROM THE GALLEY.

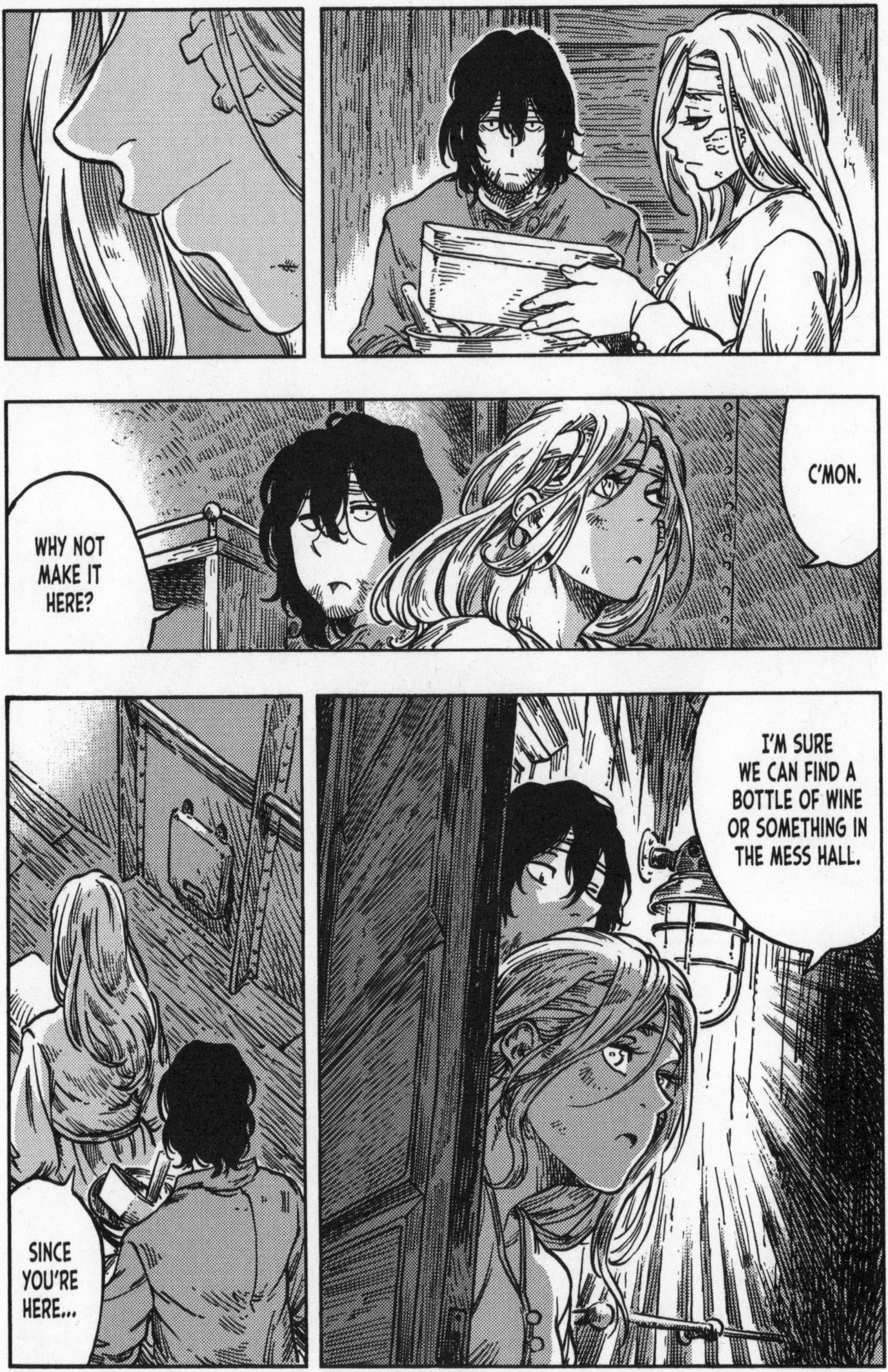
C'MON.
WHY NOT MAKE IT HERE?
I'M SURE WE CAN FIND A BOTTLE OF WINE OR SOMETHING IN THE MESS HALL.
SINCE YOU'RE HERE...

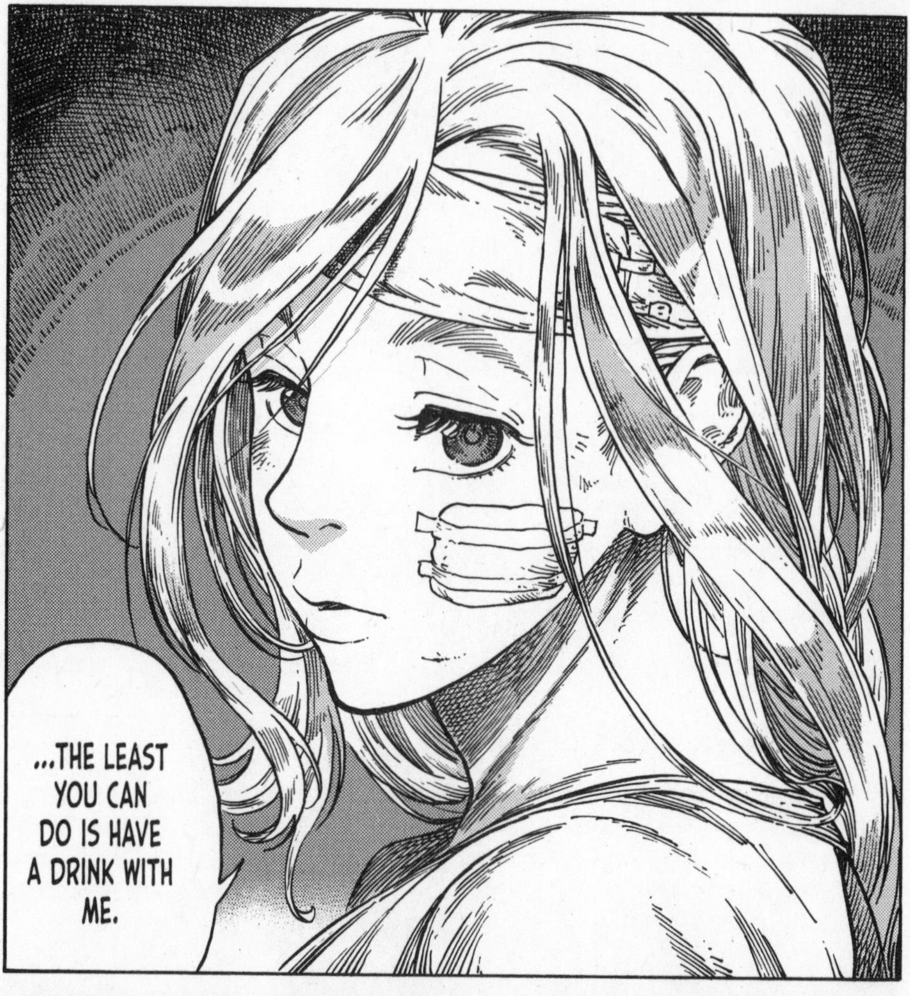
...THE LEAST YOU CAN DO IS HAVE A DRINK WITH ME.

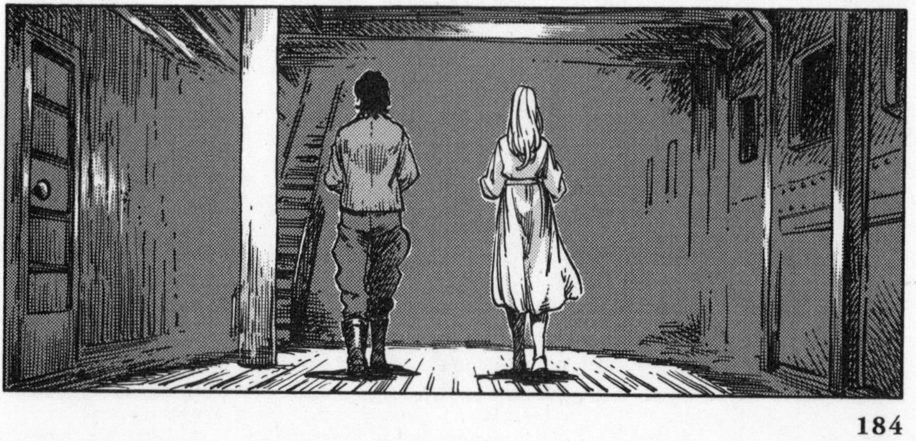

Special Flight

Dragon and Lentil Stew & Cloud Calling

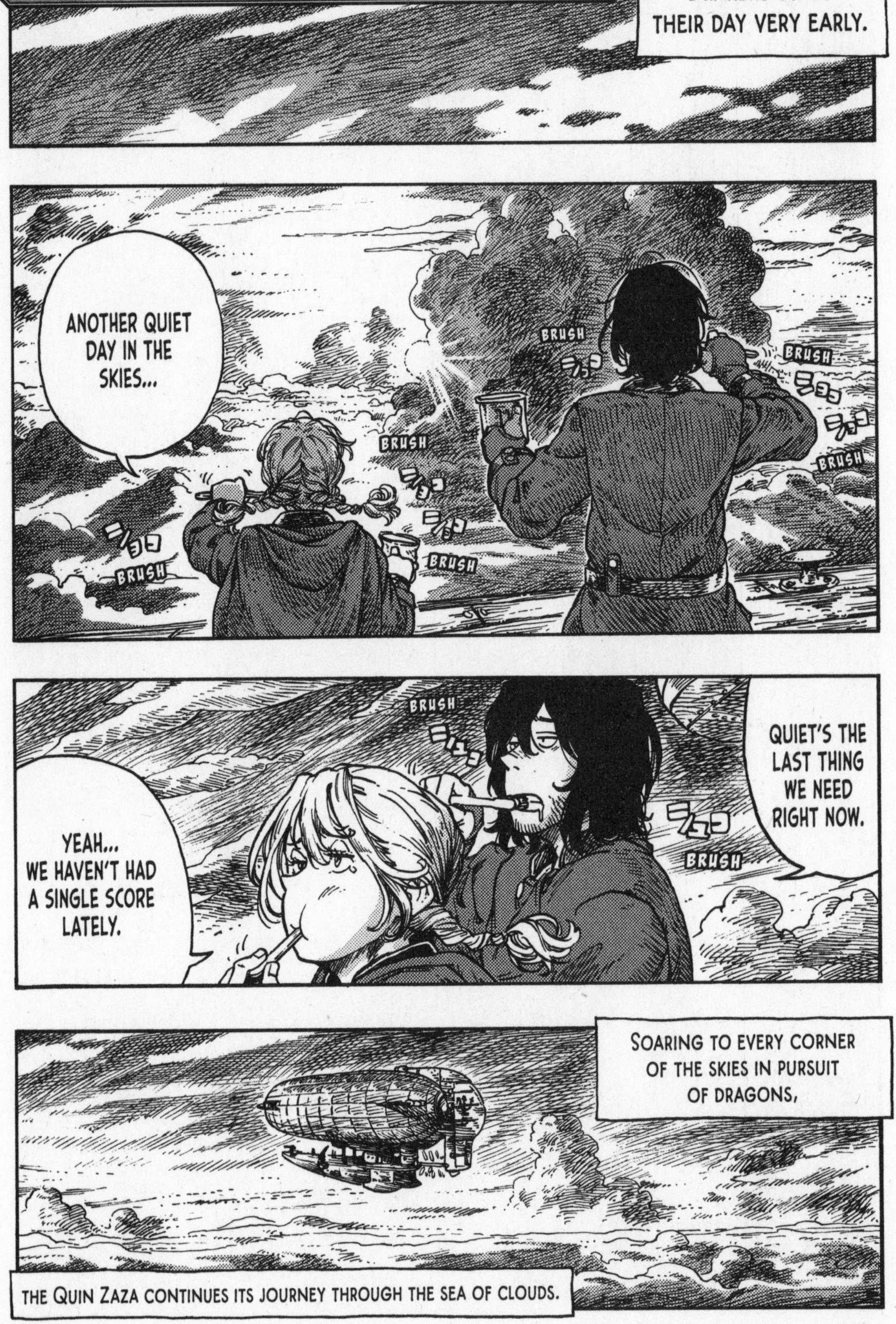

DRAKERS START THEIR DAY VERY EARLY.
BRUSH
BRUSH
BRUSH
ANOTHER QUIET DAY IN THE SKIES...
BRUSH
BRUSH
BRUSH
BRUSH
QUIET'S THE LAST THING WE NEED RIGHT NOW.
BRUSH
BRUSH
YEAH... WE HAVEN'T HAD A SINGLE SCORE LATELY.
SOARING TO EVERY CORNER OF THE SKIES IN PURSUIT OF DRAGONS,
THE QUIN ZAZA CONTINUES ITS JOURNEY THROUGH THE SEA OF CLOUDS.

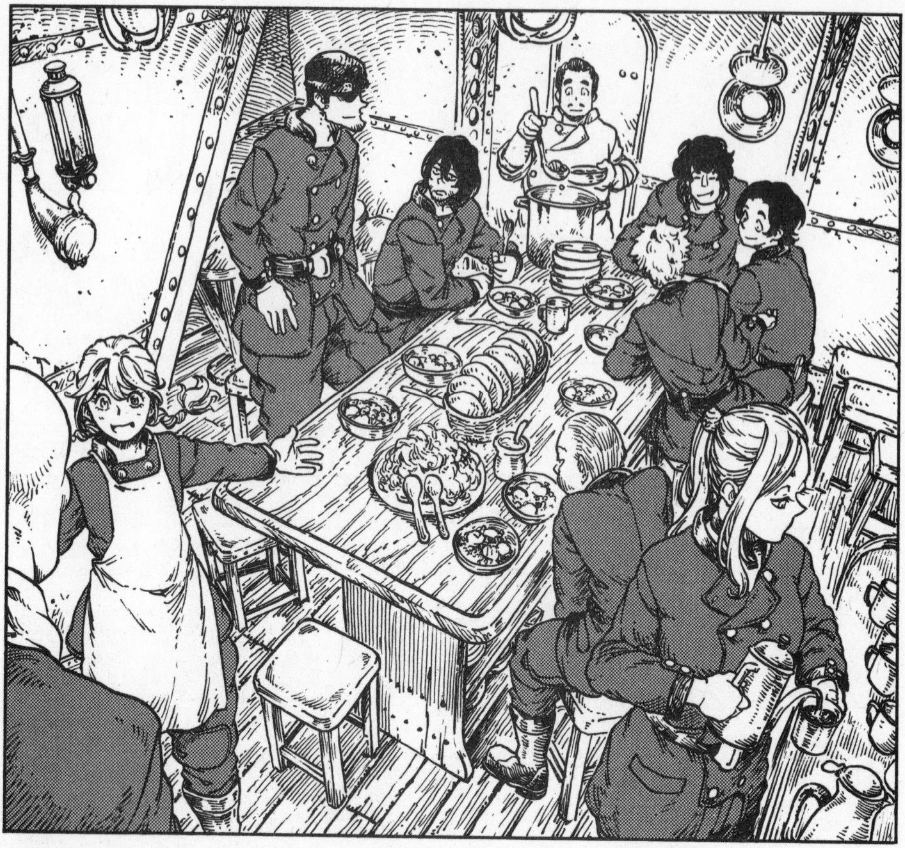

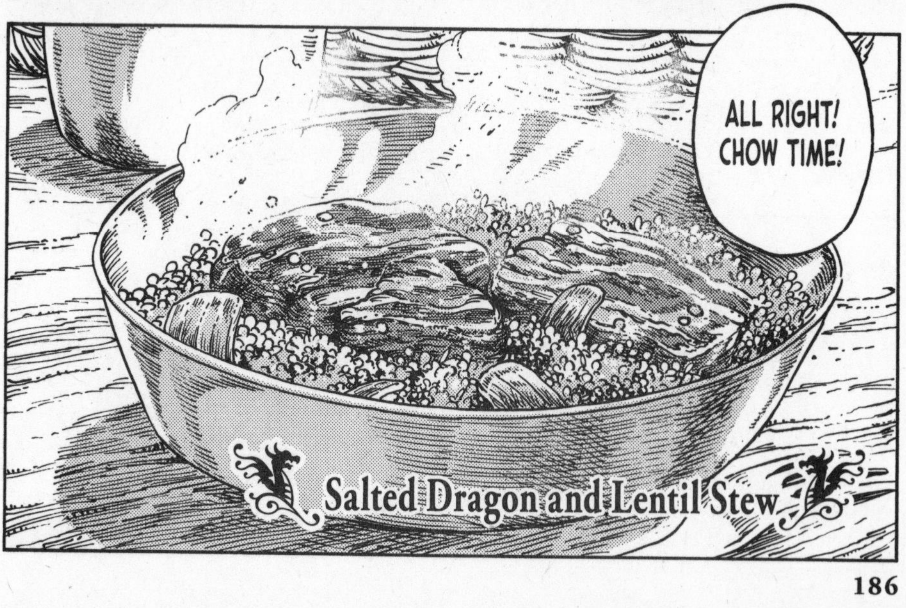
ALL RIGHT! CHOW TIME!
Salted Dragon and Lentil Stew

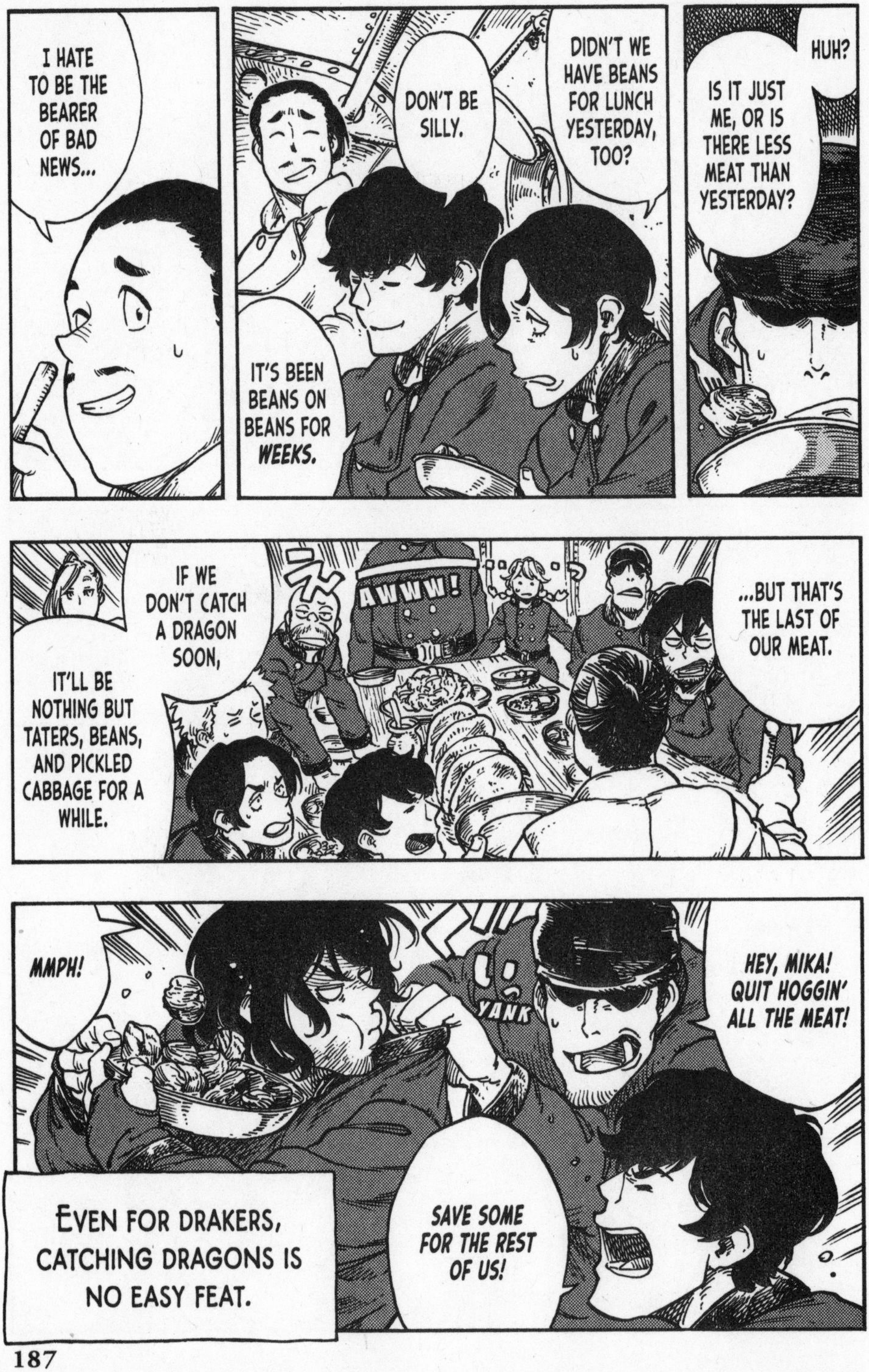
HUH?
IS IT JUST ME, OR IS THERE LESS MEAT THAN YESTERDAY?
DIDN'T WE HAVE BEANS FOR LUNCH YESTERDAY, TOO?
DON'T BE SILLY.
IT'S BEEN BEANS ON BEANS FOR WEEKS.
I HATE TO BE THE BEARER OF BAD NEWS...
...BUT THAT'S THE LAST OF OUR MEAT.
AWWW!
え
IF WE DON'T CATCH A DRAGON SOON,
IT'LL BE NOTHING BUT TATERS, BEANS, AND PICKLED CABBAGE FOR A WHILE.
HEY, MIKA! QUIT HOGGIN' ALL THE MEAT!
YANK
MMPH!
SAVE SOME FOR THE REST OF US!
EVEN FOR DRAKERS, CATCHING DRAGONS IS NO EASY FEAT.

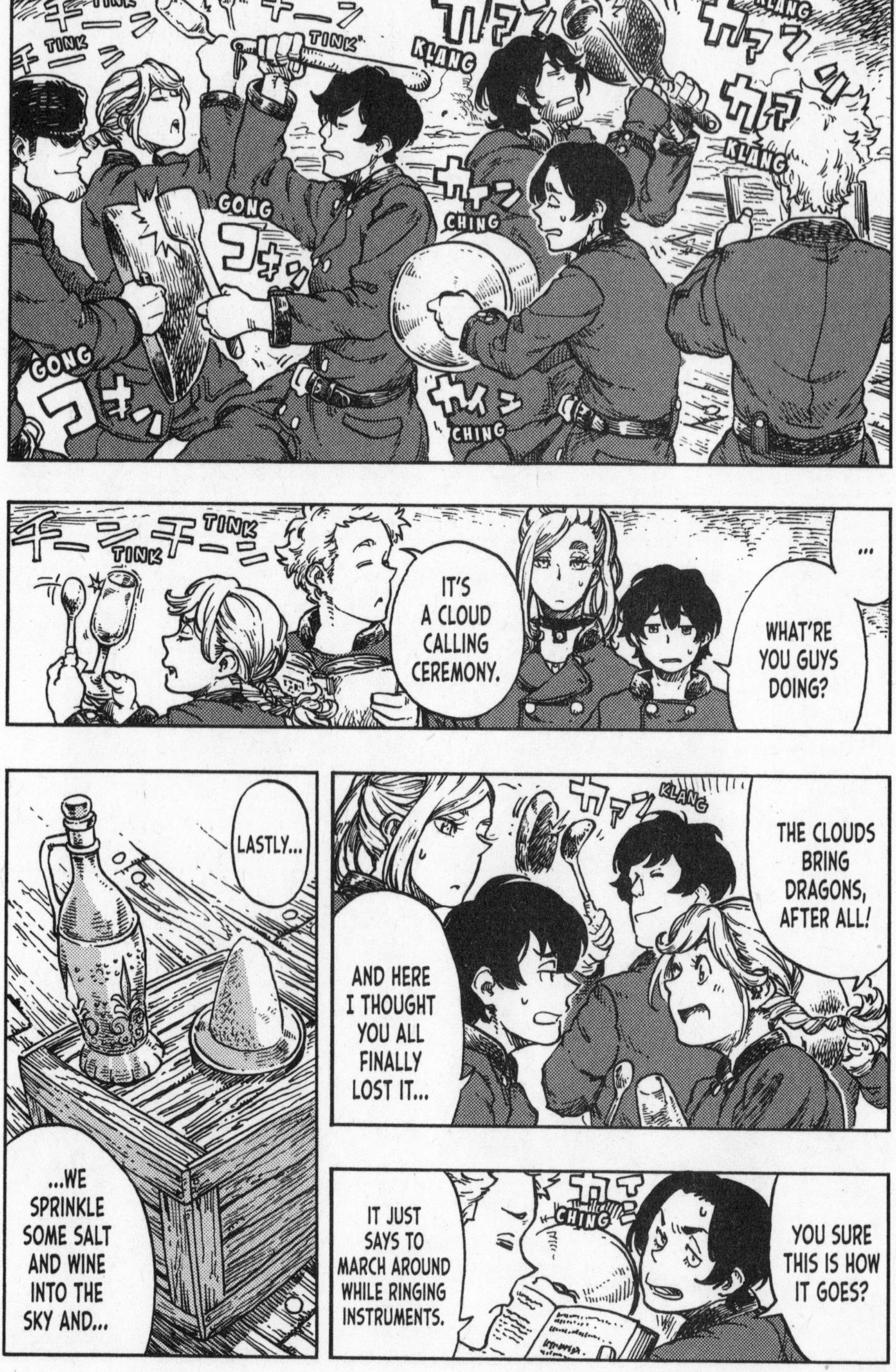
KLANG
KLANG
KLANG
TINK
TINK
TINK
CHING
GONG
GONG
CHING
...
WHAT'RE YOU GUYS DOING?
IT'S A CLOUD CALLING CEREMONY.
TINK
TINK
THE CLOUDS BRING DRAGONS, AFTER ALL!
KLANG
AND HERE I THOUGHT YOU ALL FINALLY LOST IT...
YOU SURE THIS IS HOW IT GOES?
CHING
IT JUST SAYS TO MARCH AROUND WHILE RINGING INSTRUMENTS.
LASTLY...
...WE SPRINKLE SOME SALT AND WINE INTO THE SKY AND...

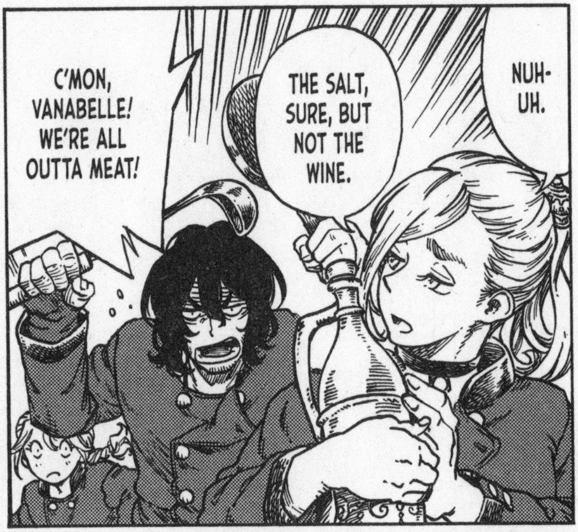
NUH-UH.
THE SALT, SURE, BUT NOT THE WINE.
C'MON, VANABELLE! WE'RE ALL OUTTA MEAT!
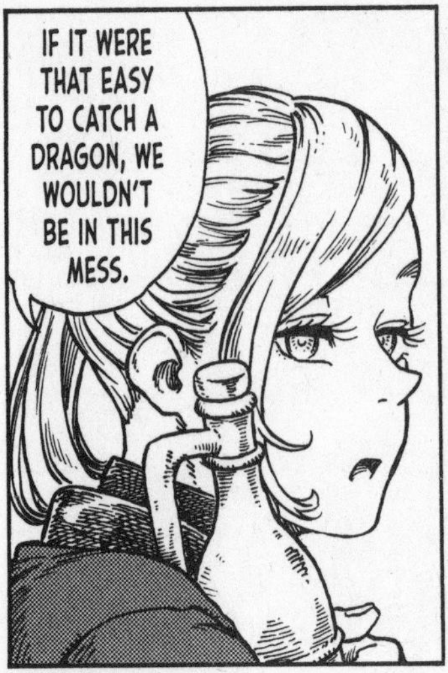
IF IT WERE THAT EASY TO CATCH A DRAGON, WE WOULDN'T BE IN THIS MESS.
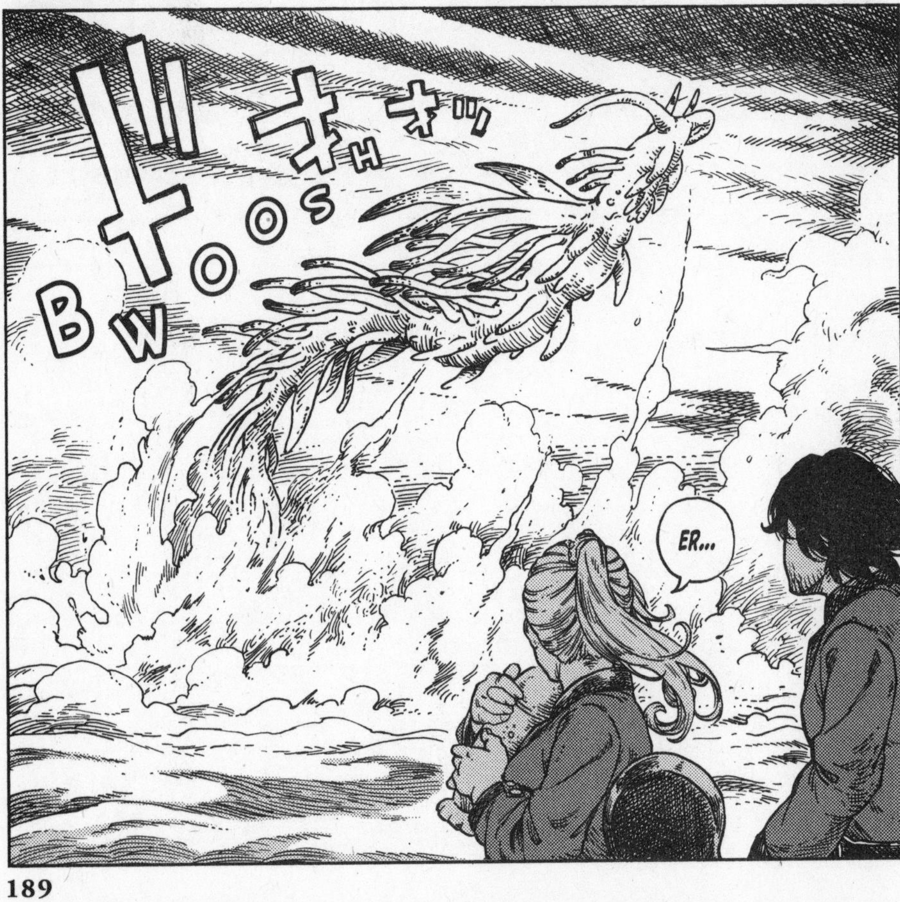
BWOOSH
ER...

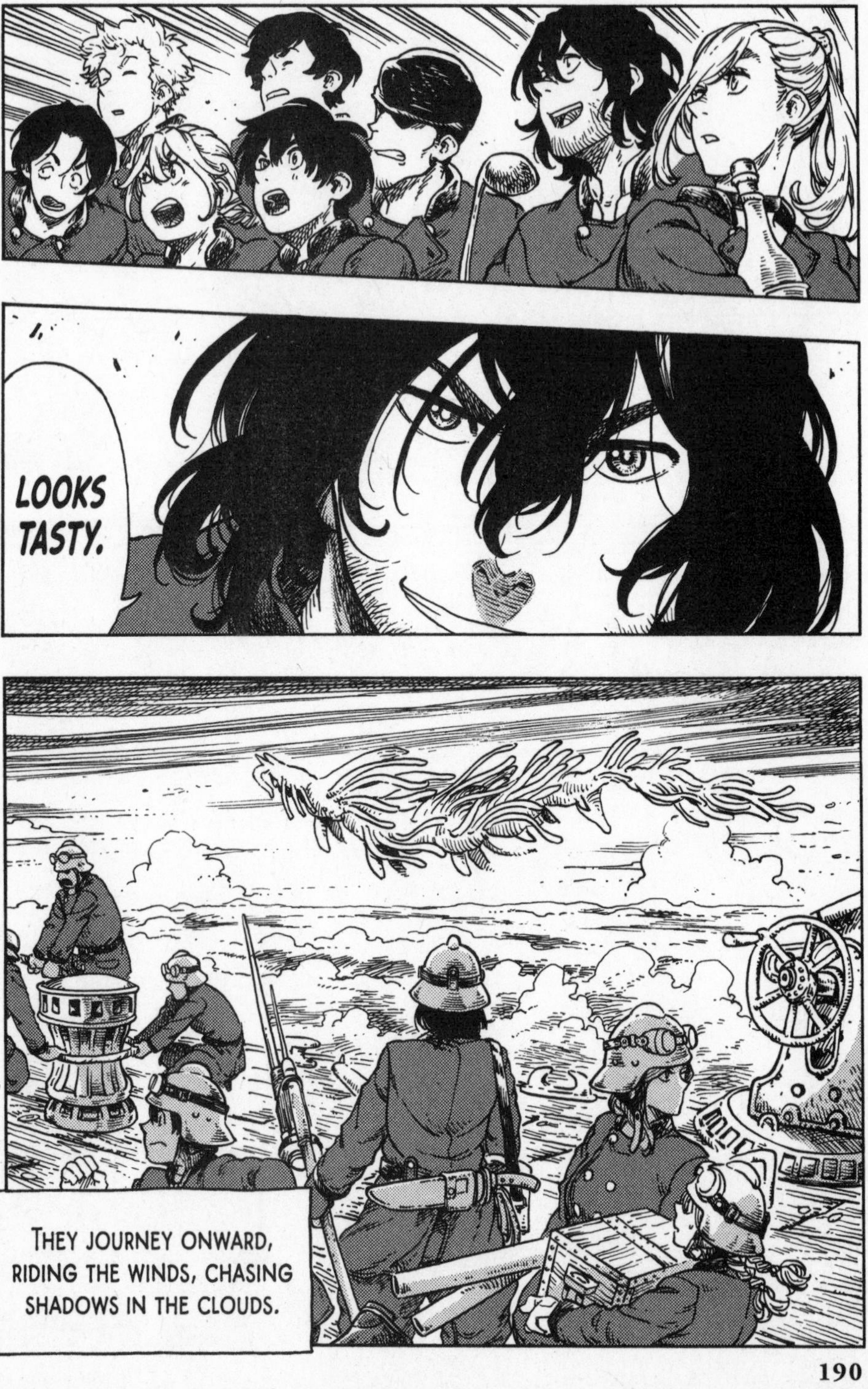
LOOKS TASTY.
THEY JOURNEY ONWARD, RIDING THE WINDS, CHASING SHADOWS IN THE CLOUDS.

Pit-cooked Dragon Hunk & Vegetables

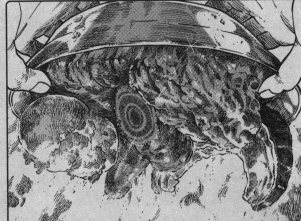

Ingredients (Serves two)

- ✦ Dragon meat: 400g hunk
- ✦ Salt to taste
- ✦ Pepper to taste
- ✦ Rosemary to taste
- ✦ Oregano to taste
- ✦ Pumpkin: ½ gourd
- ✦ Carrots: 2
- ✦ Potatoes: 4

01
Season the dragon meat with salt, pepper, rosemary, and oregano. Roughly chop the pumpkin and carrots. Wash the potatoes with the skin still on.

02
Wrap the ingredients in a clean cloth and place them in a basket or box.

03
Dig a hole about 1m deep in the ground. Pile firewood and kindling at the bottom of the hole and cover it with large stones, leaving some gaps.

04
Light the wood through the gaps and let burn until the rocks turn white.

05
Pour water over the rocks to clear any ashes and place the container of food on the rocks. Cover the container with a large cloth and fill the hole with sand.

06
Let the food cook in the pit for 4-5 hours, dig up, and serve.

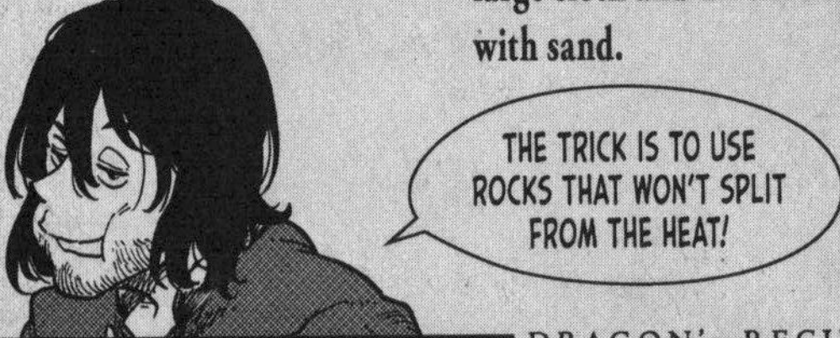

THE TRICK IS TO USE ROCKS THAT WON'T SPLIT FROM THE HEAT!

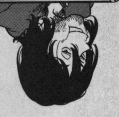

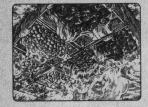

A Kodansha Comics Trade Paperback Original
Drifting Dragons 11 copyright © 2021 Taku Kuwabara
English translation copyright © 2022 Taku Kuwabara

Published in the United States by Kodansha Comics, an imprint of Kodansha USA Publishing, LLC, New York.

Publication rights for this English edition arranged through Kodansha Ltd., Tokyo.

First published in Japan in 2021 by Kodansha Ltd., Tokyo as *Kuutei doragonzu*, volume 11.

ISBN 978-1-64651-434-2

Printed in the United States of America.

www.kodansha.us

1st Printing
Translation: Adam Hirsch
Lettering: Thea Willis
Additional Lettering: Scott O. Brown
Editing: Jordan Blanco
Kodansha Comics edition cover design by Phil Balsman
YKS Services LLC/SKY Japan, INC.

Publisher: Kiichiro Sugawara

Director of publishing services: Ben Applegate
Director of publishing operations: Dave Barrett
Associate director of operations: Stephen Pakula
Publishing services managing editors: Madison Salters, Alanna Ruse, with Grace Chen
Production manager: Jocelyn O'Dowd